MINISTERS-WORKERS TRAINING MANUAL

GODSWORD GODSWILL ONU

Second Edition: 2014

ISBN: 978-1506190013

Many Scriptural quotations or citations were paraphrased, abridged, edited, or summarized, and a combination of the New King James Version and the King James Version of the Holy Bible were used, except where indicated otherwise.

Published by:
Godsword Christian Publications,
Okigwe, Nigeria.

For order, enquiry, seminar, prayer, sponsorship, comments, programmes, etc, contact:
APOSTLE GODSWORD GODSWILL ONU
WHOLE LIFE SPIRIT-WORD MINISTRIES
A.k.a. HOLY GHOST AND GODSWORD CHRISTIAN NETWORK,
OKIGWE, IMO STATE, NIGERIA.

Call or text: +234 8030917546, 8052563967, 8020648283, 8092582282.
E-mail: godswordgodswill@yahoo.com

TABLE OF CONTENTS

DEDICATIONS

I dedicate this work to the Almighty God the Father, Who loves us so dearly; to His Son, the Lord Jesus Christ, Who is my Lord and Saviour; to the Holy Spirit of the Living God, Who is my Great Helper and Comforter; and to all those, who love the Lord Jesus Christ sincerely, and want to know and practice the Truth.

ACKNOWLEDGMENTS/APPRECIATION

I appreciate my Heavenly Father, Who gave me Jesus Christ – my Lord and Saviour. I thank my Lord Jesus Christ, Who gave me the Holy Spirit – the Spirit of Wisdom and of Power. Thank You, Holy Spirit, for making the writing of this book possible; when I consider the strength of the teaching anointing, and when I feel it, I marvel how awesome the Anointing of the Holy Spirit is!

I acknowledge the efforts, prayers, contributions, and encouragements, in one way or the other, of my Christian brothers and sisters, who equip and are being equipped, for the work of the ministry, for the edifying of the Body of Christ, till we all come to the unity of the faith and of the Knowledge of the Son of God, to a perfect man, to the measure of the stature of the Fulness of Christ; that we should no longer be children, tossed to and fro and carried about with every wind of doctrine, by the trickery of men, in the cunning craftiness of deceitful plotting, but, speaking the Truth in love, grow up in all things into Him Who is the Head: Christ.

I appreciate all those who contributed positively, in one way or the other, to my Christian life, my ministry, and the writing and publication of this book. As we look forward to the Rapture of the Saints and Second Coming of our Saviour, Lord, and Master: Jesus Christ the Son of the Living God, don't lose your focus. Look unto Jesus Christ, the Author and Finisher of our faith, Who for the Joy that was set before Him, endured the Cross, despising the Shame, and has sat down at the Right Hand of the Throne of God.

God did not call us to serve Him in vain, but He will reward us abundantly for the labour we have laboured in His Name. He shall also give us the Crown of Life. Remember that there is a Heaven to gain, and there is a Hell Fire to avoid. Live in total obedience to the Word of God; live in righteousness and holiness, without which no eye shall see the Lord. God bless you!

Never Say That God Said What He Did Not Say!
Jesus Christ Is Coming Very Soon: Heaven And Hell Are Real!
Let No One Deceive You: Without Holiness, No One Will See The Lord

This hymn will help keep us focused:

IT PAYS TO SERVE JESUS

1. It pays to serve Jesus; I speak from my heart,
   He'll always be with us, if we do our part,
   There is nothing in this wide-world can pleasure afford,
   There is peace and contentment in serving the Lord.

Chorus:
   I'll love Him far better than in days gone by,
   I'll serve Him more truly than ever before,
   I'll do as He bids me whatever the cost,

I'll be a true soldier; I'll die at my post.

2. And often when I am tempted to turn from the track,
   I think of my Saviour, my mind wanders back,
   To the place where they nailed Him on Calvary's Tree,
   I hear a Voice saying, "I suffered for thee."

3. There is no one like Jesus can share me today,
   His Love and Kindness can never fade away,
   In winter, in summer, in sunshine and rain,
   His Love and Affection is always the same.

APOSTLE GODSWORD

PREFACE

The ministers and church-workers should be trained well so that they can perform well, and do God's Assignments for them faithfully and satisfactorily. Many are in the ministry today without adequate training, and they have either messed things up or performed, by far, below God's Expectation from them. A minister is not supposed to be a novice, and he is to hold the mystery of the faith with a pure conscience. The Word says, "If you instruct the brethren in these things, you will be a good minister of Jesus Christ, nourished in the Words of Faith and of the Good Doctrine which you have carefully followed" (1 Tim. 4:6).

Study to show yourself approved to God, a worker who does not need to be ashamed, righty dividing the Word of Truth. Let the Word of God dwell in you richly in all wisdom, teaching and admonishing one another. Remember that there are training and re-training periods in a minister's life; and learning and experience are for lifetime. That good thing which you received, keep by the Holy Spirit Who dwells in us.

The Word of God shall not depart from your mouth, but you shall meditate in it day and night, that you may observe according to all that is written in it. For then you will make your way prosperous, and then you will have good success − spiritually, mentally, emotionally, physically, and otherwise. Give attention to God's Word; incline your ears to His Sayings. Do not let them depart from your eyes; keep them in the midst of your heart always.

GODSWORD GODSWILL ONU,
2012.

YOU MUST BE BORN AGAIN

Questions for Discussion:

1. What is expected from someone who wants to see the Kingdom of God?
2. What are expected from someone who wants to enter the Kingdom of God?
3. What is the substitute for being born again?
4. Who is exempted from being born again?

You must be born again; you must be born of water and of the Spirit. The Lord told Nicodemus that if a man must see the Kingdom of God, he must be born again.

The Lord emphasized that for a man to enter the Kingdom of Heaven, he must be born of water and of the Spirit. There is a great difference between being born again and being born of water and of the Spirit, even though they are related.

To be born again is compulsory to the one who would see the Kingdom of God, and if the person wants to pass the stage of seeing to the stage of entering, he must be born of water and of the Spirit.

This is 'a must' for anyone and does not depend on whom you are. God is no respecter of persons (Acts 10:34). Whether you are the president of your country, the ambassador, or whatever you may be, makes no difference.

Whether you are a millionaire in any currency, it does not move God. You may be a university-professor or an outstanding scientist or engineer; you must be born again. Whether you are old or young, great or small, rich or poor, male or female, you must be born again.

Whether you have been baptized and confirmed in your church, it makes no difference. As a matter of fact, some have been baptized and made full members of their churches, and yet are not born again.

Do you know that you can be referred to as a pastor and yet not be born again? This reminds me of a story a minister told me of a sectional leader of one Pentecostal church who admitted that he was not born again even though he was referred to as a reverend, after God told a man of God to confront him. He said he entered the ministry to help his family members.

You may be referred to as a deacon, an elder, a bishop, an apostle, a church-leader, and not be born again. To be born again is to be regenerated or made a new creature by the Holy Spirit when you receive the Lord Jesus Christ as your Lord and personal Saviour (though some accept Christ as the Saviour of their souls but not the Lord of their lives).

That is what the Bible means when it says that if any man or woman be in Christ Jesus, he or she is a new creature, old things have passed away and all things have become new (2 Cor. 5:17).

When Adam sinned, he died spiritually and became separated from the Life of God. Man became God's enemy by disobeying God and lost the authority God gave him over all things.

But God sent His Son Jesus Christ to die for the sins of the world, and to pay the Sacrifice for the salvation of men from all bondages of the devil. Jesus Christ shed His Blood for the remission of our sins.

When someone acknowledges that he is a sinner who cannot help himself, and receives the Lord Jesus Christ, he is born again. With the heart, man believes to righteousness, and with the mouth he confesses that he believes on the Lord Jesus Christ to salvation (Rom. 10:10).

As many as received Him, to them gave He power to become children of God, even to them that believe on His Name, Jesus Christ the Son of the Living God (Jn 1:12).

The Lord Jesus Christ has made it known that He will not cast away anyone that comes to Him. No matter how sinful, dirty, immoral, or wicked you may be, once you repent and accept the Lord Jesus Christ, He will cleanse you to the extent that your sins will no longer be remembered (Isa. 43:25).

Consider how wicked Saul, who later became Paul, was: but when he submitted to Jesus Christ, he became one of the most faithful early apostles.

To be born of water is to be changed by the Word of God. The Spirit of God uses the Word of God, which is the Sword of the Spirit to change you. Christ Jesus sanctifies and cleanses the Church with the washing of the water through the Word (Eph. 5:25).

We were born again, not of corruptible seed but incorruptible through the Word of God which lives and abides forever (1 Pet. 1:23). The Gospel that you heard and received is the Word of God, and you believed it, which made it possible for you to be born again by the Action of the Holy Spirit.

The Spirit and the Word agree, and they work together. Since you were born again by means of the Gospel, you will need to continue to live your life according to the Word of God. We must neither resist God nor His Word. You will be fulfilled in life if you obey the Spirit of God and His Word.

God will not force the sinner to receive the Gospel; in the same vein, He will not force you to live according His Word. Some people, after being born again, live lives contrary to God's Word; don't expect to enter the Kingdom of God that way. And you will need to grow in your knowledge of the Word of God.

To be Born of the Spirit is to be led by the Holy Spirit. It is to follow the voice (the conscience) of your recreated human spirit. The Spirit Himself witnesses with our spirit that this or that is right or wrong.

Following God's Spirit will help you overcome evil. The born-again experience, the regeneration of your spirit is the Work of the Holy Spirit. After being born again, you will still have to listen to His Voice if you want to enter the Kingdom of Heaven.

If you are tempted to lie, for instance, the Holy Spirit will speak to you through your spirit, your heart, and make it known to you that lying is sinful; if you go ahead to lie, He will not stop your voice or speech; and you would have sinned against God.

If you live your life contrary to the Spirit of God, you are heading to somewhere else, apart from the Kingdom of Heaven and of God. And it is either you spend eternity with God, or you spend it with the devil; and there is no partiality with God (Acts 10:34).

Whether you speak in tongues and prophesy, it makes no difference. No sinner will inherit the Kingdom of Christ and of God (Eph. 5:5).

Knowing the Terror of God, we persuade men everywhere to change their lifestyles, to change the way they live (2 Cor. 5:11). Because it is a fearful thing to fall into the Hands of the Living God (Heb. 10:31); for our God is a Consuming Fire (Heb. 12:29).

I don't know what they might have told you in the church, ministry, or fellowship that you go; take the Bible and study these things for yourself, and I know you will come to agree with what the Lord has said through me.

Is it not written in the Bible that because iniquity shall abound, the love of many shall wax cold? But those who endure to the end shall be saved (Matt. 24:12). That means that some will not endure to the end.

The Word of God says that Jesus Christ is coming for the Church that has no spot, wrinkle, blemish, or any such thing, but a holy, righteous, and sanctified Church (Eph. 5:27; 1 Thes. 5:23).

Even Apostle Paul, after being in the ministry for many years, and having done many mighty signs, wonders, and miracles, he said that he still brought his body to subjection so that after preaching to others, he himself will not be a castaway (1 Cor. 9:27).

The Lord Jesus Christ asked why some will call Him, Lord, Lord, and not do what He says (Lk. 6:46). Many will say to Him on that Day, "Lord, Lord, have we not done this or that in Your Name?" But He will tell them to depart from Him because He never knew them, as they were workers of iniquity (Matt. 7:20-23).

I believe they had been born again, because they prophesied and did mighty works in the Name of Jesus Christ. However, they will be rejected because they were not born of water and of the Spirit.

You cannot please God if you continue to live in sin, if you continue to live according to the dictates of your flesh, by the lust of the flesh, the lust of the eyes, and the pride of life.

All men shall give account of their lives to God; and all good and evil things shall be brought to light, including all hidden things.

What do you think of God and His Christ? Remember now your God and Creator, and obey what He tells you to do. To believe in the Lord Jesus Christ is to do the Work of God; that is the very first real step to obeying Him.

WITNESSES AND MINISTERS OF THE WORD

To witness is to produce proof or evidence concerning something or somebody. To minister is to take care of somebody. We take care of people and help them using the Word of God. You can give witness to the Word of God by what you say or do.

As witnesses of the Word of God, we speak the Word of God, and God confirms that it's His Word we are declaring by the salvation of men, healing of sick bodies, and other signs and wonders. We minister or preach and teach the Word of God to help men in their different areas of need.

It is the Word of God that has solution to all human problems. If we want people to be met at the points of their needs, we must preach and teach the Word of God. We must preach it as it is, neither adding anything to it nor subtracting anything from it. Never compromise the standard of the Word, no matter what it takes; if it means suffering or persecution, accept it, and God will reward you richly.

There is salvation in the Word; there is healing in the Word; there is the power in the Word to set free from sin. Deliverance, prosperity, success, freedom, protection, and other good things are in the Word. Holiness, consecration, and sanctification are rooted in the Word of God. Whatever it is that you desire from God, check the Word of God to see what God has said about it. Whatever problem your hearers have, God has a solution for it in His Word.

The Word of God is spirit, and it is life. It gives life to any dying or dead situation. The Word is living, powerful, and active. It is sharper than any two-edged sword (Heb. 4:12). There is power in the Word that many of us have not realized. The creation came into being by the Word of God. You can give life to the dying or the dead by speaking the Word of God in faith.

The Word of God, the Bible, came by the Inspiration of God, for holy men of God spoke as they were moved by the Holy Spirit of God (2 Pet. 1:20-21). It is profitable for Doctrine, for correction, for rebuke, and for training in righteousness, that the man of God may be complete, thoroughly equipped for every good work (2 Tim. 3:16-17). The Lord told us to study His Word to show ourselves approved to Him (2 Tim. 2:15). The Word of God should dwell in you richly in all wisdom (Col. 3:16).

What you have is what you give. If you don't have enough Word of God in your spirit, how will you minister effectively to others? All who ever succeeded in ministry succeeded because they soaked themselves in the Word of God.

When a sponge is fully soaked in water, it is so full that any side you touch it, water comes out. When you are full of and soaked in the Word of God, any situation that comes across your way, you are prepared to confront and overcome it. You will be able to answer the many questions in people's minds.

As a witness of the Word of God, the life you live should prove that the Word of God is true. Your life should be exemplary and represent that of Jesus Christ. In character, blessings, and power, the story should be the same. Your character should be the one that is decorated by the Fruit of the Spirit, which is love, joy, peace, goodness, kindness, gentleness, longsuffering, self-control, faithfulness.

Your life should be successful and prosperous. Of course, the cause of the Gospel, persecutions, trials, or tests can make you lack, sometimes. You should not live in sickness, and you should be able to turn your situation around for good by the Power of the Holy Spirit.

The Bible says that the Lord confirmed the words of the apostles with signs and wonders. If your preaching or teaching is not being confirmed by signs and wonders, check whether you are preaching or teaching the Word of God.

Do you know that you can mix the Word of God with unbelief, psychology, and philosophy without even knowing it? Also, check your prayer-life, whether it is stable and whether you spend enough time in prayer. You will need to fast sometimes, even if the duration is short; the Lord looks at the heart.

ACCORDING TO THE PATTERN

Questions for Discussion:
1. Which pattern are we supposed to do God's Work?
2. Who sets the pattern for doing God's Work?
3. Can human pattern be satisfactory in doing God's Work?

When Moses was instructed by God to build the tabernacle, God told him to make it according to all that He showed him, after the pattern of the tabernacle, and the pattern of all the instruments thereof.

God emphasized this when He said, "See to it that you make them after their pattern, which was shown you on the mountain" (Exo. 25:9,40).

Apostle Paul stressed the importance of this when he referred to this interaction between God and Moses in the Book of Hebrews and used it to compare to Jesus Christ's Ministry (Heb. 8:4-6).

God has a pattern for whatever He tells us to do. The Bible speaks of a pattern of good works (Tit. 2:7). We are not to seek the praise of men but that of God. We are ambassadors of Christ, and we should represent Him well.

Even, when we say that this or that person is a man of God, we are saying that the person is sent by God and represents God. Apostle Paul emphasized the importance of doing things the right way when he said that if anyone competes in athletics, he is not crowned unless he competes according to the rules (2 Tim. 2:5).

No wonder he instructed us to run in such a way that we may obtain the prize. Everyone who competes for the prize is temperate in all things. Now they do it to obtain a perishable crown, but we an imperishable crown.

This made him to run thus: not with uncertainty. Thus he fought: not as one who beats the air: but he disciplined his body, and brought it into subjection, lest, when he had preached to others, he himself should become disqualified (1 Cor. 9:24-27).

Paul says, "But what things were gain to me, these I have counted loss for Christ. Yet indeed I also count all things loss for the excellence of the knowledge of Christ Jesus my Lord, for Whom I have suffered the loss of all things, and count them as rubbish, that I may gain Christ,

"And be found in Him, not having my own righteousness which is from the Law, but that which is through faith in Christ, the righteousness which is from God by faith;

"That I may know Him and the power of His Resurrection and the fellowship of His Sufferings, being conformed to His Death, if by any means, I may attain to the Resurrection from the dead.

"Not that I have already attained, or am already perfected; but I press on, that I may lay hold of that for which Christ Jesus has also laid hold on me. Brethren, I do not count myself to have apprehended;

"But one thing I do, forgetting those things which are behind and reaching forward to those things which are ahead, I press towards the goal for the prize of the Upward Call of God in Christ Jesus.

"Therefore, let us as many as are mature, have this in mind, and if in anything you think otherwise, God will reveal even this to you" (Phil. 3:7-15).

God wants faithfulness in whatever He calls you to do. We are pilgrims, sojourners, and strangers in this world, and we must live our lives with that consciousness.

The questions are, "Do you know what He has called you to do? Are you doing it? If so, are you doing it God's Way or Pattern?" God called us to become His children by the acceptance of the Gospel. Have you become born again? If so, are you living the Christian life?

Then how is your Christian life? Also, God calls each of us to do specific thing(s) for Him. Do you know that (those) thing(s)? Are you doing it (them)? How are you doing it (them)?

It is possible to live your whole life on earth without knowing what God has called you to do. This is why many have lived and died without even hearing that there is a Jesus Christ.

Many have heard about Him, but have hardened their hearts to the Gospel; but many have not heard about Him, even now.

We have the responsibility to preach the Gospel and teach the Word of God to the ends of the world. This is what we call 'the Great Commission.' How are you committed to the Great Commission, individually and collectively?

You must preach the Gospel (the Good News of the Kingdom of God). You must preach by yourself because, in a sense, everybody is a preacher and an evangelist. No wonder Apostle Paul told Pastor Timothy, "Do the work of an evangelist" (2 Tim. 4:5).

The Bible tells us that some are called, specifically, as evangelists. But you must preach, starting from your home, office, or school. You can sponsor others financially to help them preach where you may not go.

Then many who have been born again live their Christian lives the way they want to. Many have chosen (consciously or unconsciously) what they will obey and what they will not obey.

People do many different things which are ungodly, unbiblical, and satanic in churches and say, "It does not matter." But what will they do on the Day of Judgment when they find out that they actually matter? But then, it will be too late, and there will be no second chance. God is no respecter of persons, for He created all.

Then they will cry and say, "Had I known, I..." and their cries will not be heard. These will go into everlasting punishment in Hell Fire. They will have their appointment with the hypocrites and compromisers.

The angels told Lot, saying, "Escape for your life, do not look behind you nor stay anywhere in the plain. Escape to the mountains, lest you be destroyed" (Gen. 19:17). My brethren, let us amend our ways while there is still time.

God did not call us to destroy us along the way; but if anyone destroys himself, let him not blame God. Work out your own salvation with fear and trembling. If you live in pleasure, living to gratify your flesh, you are heading to Hell Fire. Live a holy life, and get perfected in holiness.

There is no agreement between light and darkness; do not do evil or exaggerate, thinking you want to help God. Live in righteousness and it will be well with your soul. God's Grace is available to us always.

It is the Will of God that you are sanctified. God wants you to be consecrated to doing His Word and Will, no matter the cost. There are things you must sacrifice for the Cause of Jesus Christ.

You must carry your cross daily and follow Him. We must obey the Commandments of our Lord and Master. We must serve God, our Maker; He is worthy of our service.

Make every effort to make your calling and election sure, because if you do this, you will be with God and the Lord Jesus Christ forever. Take heed to yourself and the doctrine that you preach, teach, and enforce. In doing this, you will save both yourself and the people that hear and follow you.

We are to walk in the light and truth. To walk in the light is to act and do according to the Word of God, which is a lamp to our feet, and a light to our path.

To walk in the truth is to live, act, and speak according to the Word of God, which is truth. Also, to walk in truth is also to be honest, transparent, and truthful.

We are the light and the salt of the world. We are a source of direction to the people of the world; God uses us to show them the right way, and to lead them out of darkness.

As the salt of the world, we are to add flavour and taste to people's lives, and we should cause them to be preserved by the Power of God.

Jesus Christ is our Focus, and the Word of God (the Bible) our standard. Apostle Paul's life and ministry is worthy of emulation, even though he did make some mistakes.

Moreover, brethren, I do not want you to be unaware that all the fathers of Israel were under the cloud, all passed through the sea, all were baptized into Moses in the cloud and in the sea, all ate the same spiritual food, and drank of that spiritual rock that followed them, and that Rock was Christ.

But with most of them God was not well pleased, for their bodies were scattered in the wilderness. Now these things became our examples, to the intent that we should not lust after evil things as they also lusted.

And do not become idolaters as were some of them. As it is written, "The people sat down to eat and drink, and rose up to play." Nor let us commit sexual immorality, as some of them did, and in one day twenty-three thousand fell.

Don't say, "That was in the Old Testament," because God struck Ananias and Sapphira in the New Testament. Let us not tempt Christ, as some of them also tempted, and were destroyed by serpents; nor complain, as some of them also complained, and were destroyed by the destroyer.

Now all these things happened to them as examples, and they were written for our admonition, upon whom the ends of the ages have come. Therefore, let him who thinks he stands take heed lest he fall.

No temptation has overtaken you except such as is common to man, but God is faithful, Who will not allow you to be tempted beyond what you are able, but with the temptation will also make the way of escape, that you may be able to bear it (1 Cor. 10:1-13).

People backslide and fall away from the faith, from Jesus Christ and His Word. Even people who had been used mightily by God have gone away from God and became separated from the Life of God. My brethren, this ought not to be so.

He that has entered God's Rest has himself also ceased from his work as God did from His. Let us, therefore, be diligent to enter that rest, lest anyone fall according to the same example of disobedience.

For the Word of God is living and powerful, and sharper than any two-edged sword, piercing even to the division of soul and spirit, and of joints and marrow, and is a discerner of the thoughts and intents of the heart.

And there is no creature hidden from His Sight, but all things are naked and open to the Eyes of Him to Whom we must give account (Heb. 4:10-13).

The covenant we have in Jesus Christ is a better covenant than the one the Israelites had with God, and it is based on better promises. The punishment for rejecting Jesus Christ and His Word is worse than the punishment the Israelites received for disobeying the Law, though we may not see it now.

Beware of the little leaven that leavens the whole lump; beware of the little foxes that destroy the vine. Beware of the little 'it-doesn't-matter' that spoils things in the House of God. Beware of the false prophets and the false teachers.

Concerning the specific assignment(s) God has for each one of us, let us take time, in prayer, fasting, and waiting on Him, to know what He wants us to do. And whatever the cost and sacrifice, let us not love our lives even to death.

Let us not do what we want to do. Remember that it is to God that you will render account to. Don't love the praise of men.

If God called you to be an evangelist, don't remain a pastor; if He called you to be a pastor, don't remain an evangelist. If God doesn't want you to open a church, don't open one.

Do you know that you can have one of the largest churches in the world, and organize one of the largest crusades in the world, and still not follow God's Plan for your life? God will help you fulfil His Task for you.

God has a pattern for success; follow that pattern to be successful in life. Learn to call what God calls 'success,' 'success,' and what He calls 'failure,' 'failure.' If you follow the pattern of the world, you can't be successful in God's Sight. Remember that life is not in the abundance of what you possess.

Strike the shepherd, and the sheep will be scattered. You have to know that if you don't follow the pattern of Godliness, others will follow you do the same things, as a minister.

BE FULL OF THE WORD OF GOD

Questions for Discussion:

1. What is the Word of God?
2. How should we treat the Word of God?
3. What is our relationship with the Word of God?
4. To what extent should we know the Word of God?
5. Can God compromise His Word?
6. On what basis will God judge the world?

The Word of God is God. The Word of God reveals the Mind of God to us. God works through and by His Word. The Word and the Spirit agree (1 Jn 5:8), for the holy men of God who wrote the Scriptures were moved by the Holy Ghost (2 Pet. 1:21).

All Scripture is God-breathed, is inspired by God; and is profitable for Doctrine, for reproof, for correction, for instruction in righteousness, that the man of God may be complete, thoroughly equipped for every good work (2 Tim. 3:16-17).

We are to fight the good fight of faith. The fight of faith is to contend earnestly for the faith once delivered to the Saints; the fight of faith is to strive to see that the Word and Will of God comes to pass in our lives, and in the lives of others, for faith comes by hearing the Word of God.

We must also grow from faith to faith. The Bible commands us to let the Word of God, of Christ, dwell in us richly in all wisdom (Col. 3:16). That means that we are to get soaked in the Word of God. When a sponge is soaked in water and brought out, any side of the sponge you touch, water sticks on you.

The same thing applies when we are full of the Word of God. Whatever trial, temptation, or situation we may find ourselves in, we have solution in the Word available to us, and we will overcome and succeed.

Search the Scriptures as you would search for hidden treasures, for they are costlier than gold, silver, and diamond. The place we read says that the Word of God should dwell in us, not just in any measure, but in a rich measure, in a full measure, preferably. Also, in the rich measure, it must be in all wisdom.

This is why the Bible speaks of rightly dividing the Word of Truth (2 Tim. 2:15). To divide the Word of God aright is to apply it wisely and to interpret it the right way. This is why you have to compare Scripture with Scripture (you have to compare spiritual things with spiritual things) (1 Cor. 2:13).

You must study the Word of God to show yourself approved to God, a workman who does not need to be ashamed, rightly dividing the Word of Truth. Be diligent to present yourself approved to God (2 Tim. 2:15).

It is the Word of God in your heart and mouth that will help you succeed in life and Godliness, and overcome temptations. Make every effort to hear, read, study, meditate on, believe, and confess the Word of God.

When the devil tempted Jesus Christ, he used the Scripture, by quoting it to Jesus Christ. But he misapplied the Word, and Jesus Christ, being full of the Word of God, quoted the appropriate Word, and the devil was put to shame.

If you don't know the Word of God, the devil will deceive you, misapplying it to you; and you will fall into temptations. The devil has no mercy. If you don't know and apply your rights and authority in Christ, he will keep you miserable.

The Word of God is spirit and life. It will quicken your human spirit and wage your spiritual wars; it will also give life to your body and soul. The Word that you hear is spirit and it is life (Jn 6:63).

The Word of God cleanses you: spirit, soul, and body (Jn 15:3). It will build your spirit and get it to be strong spiritually. The Word is the food of the human spirit that gets him grow and matured. Desire the Word of God (1 Pet. 2:2).

The Word of God is fire that burns all things that are ungodly and satanic; it is the hammer that breaks to pieces all obstacles and hindrances (Jer. 23:29). It is the water that purifies you daily. It is truth, and God's Truth sanctifies you to holiness, blamelessness, and spotlessness (Jn 17:17).

Go for the Word of God, because all things that you ever need in your life are in it. The source of God's Blessings is the Word and the Manifester of the Blessings of God is the Holy Spirit.

When the deacons were to be appointed, the apostles declared that anyone to be appointed must be full of wisdom, and the Wisdom of God is in His Word. That was why Stephen, who was full of faith and the Holy Spirit, was selected (Acts 6:5).

To be full of faith is to be full of the Word, because faith comes by hearing and studying the Word of God (Rom. 10:17). If you have problem with faith, just take enough time to fill yourself with the Word, and you will see faith spring up from within you with great force, frequency, and magnitude.

The Word says that the Word that goes out of the Mouth of God will not go back to Him without accomplishing the purpose for which He sent it (Isa. 55:11). Instead of His Word to fail, heaven and earth shall pass away (Matt. 24:35).

God is not a man to lie, and He cannot change His Mind (Num. 23:19). Except the condition under which He said something is changed by men, He cannot change what He said for that circumstance.

God's Thoughts are higher than our thoughts and His Ways than our ways (Isa. 55:9). Don't be wise in your own eyes, trust in the Lord, and do the right (Prov. 3:7).

If what God told you has not come to pass, don't doubt Him, but be patient in believing, for the vision is yet for an appointment time: it will come to pass and will not tarry (Habk. 2:3).

If God delays His Judgment, it is because He is full of mercy and does not want anyone to perish. However, when He casts His Judgment, He does not respect anybody.

The Word of God says that we are to prove all things, and hold on to that which is true and good (1 Thes. 5:21). Do not believe every spirit, but test the spirits whether they are of God, for many false teachings, ministries, and ministers are in the world today (1 Jn 4:1).

The litmus paper is an indicator that you can easily use to distinguish an acid from an alkali. In the same vein, judging by the Word of God is a good litmus-test for the good and the evil, the Godly and the ungodly. Don't be wise in your own eyes and mind. Even prophecies are to be judged (1 Cor. 14:29).

The people of God perish and suffer because of ignorance or lack of the knowledge of the Word of God (Hos. 4:6). Even though God will want to protect you, know that the devil that is fighting against you has no mercy.

God even said that He will reject some people from being His Original Intention or Plan for them, because they rejected knowledge (Hos. 4:6). If you reject Divine Knowledge, you are heading to disaster.

Don't leave the Word to serve tables (Acts 6:2). The apostles refused to do that. But preach and teach the Word of God, in season and out of season. Convince, rebuke, exhort with all longsuffering and teaching.

For the time has come when they do not endure Sound Doctrine, but according to their own desires, because they have itching ears, they have heaped up for themselves teachers, and they turn their ears away from the truth, and are turned aside to heresies (2 Tim. 4:1-5).

Martha was worried with too much serving when Jesus Christ visited her, but Mary was at the Feet of Jesus Christ listening to Him. When Martha wanted Mary to leave listening to Jesus Christ in order to help in the serving, Jesus Christ told Martha that Mary had taken that one thing which is needful, and it will not be taken away from her.

Receiving the Word of God and keeping it is more important than sacrifices. Also, half-obedience is disobedience in the Sight of God. Don't be hearers only, but be doers of the Word you hear.

BE FULL OF THE HOLY SPIRIT

Questions for Discussion:

1. What does it mean to be baptized with the Holy Spirit?
2. What is the importance of being filled with the Holy Spirit?
3. To what extent should we be filled with the Holy Spirit?
4. What is the alternative to being filled with the Holy Spirit?

When the apostles needed deacons, who were to help them in taking care of the Disciples, they required that the people to be appointed had certain qualifications. They were to be people of good reputation, full of the Holy Spirit, and wisdom.

However, in many churches, many people are appointed deacons and elders, and they do not have these qualifications. Many are appointed to positions of authority in churches based on their fame, financial power, contributions to the church, age, and other human judgments.

Christians have a Wonderful Inheritance Who is the Holy Spirit. The Lord Jesus Christ did not leave us helpless, He sent the Holy Spirit to us (Jn 16:7). The Lord Jesus Christ baptizes with the Holy Spirit and fire.

The Holy Spirit of God is the Manifester of God's Power. In the beginning, when darkness covered the surface of the deep (water), the Spirit of God moved upon the face of the water, and when God declared that anything be on earth, His Spirit brought it to pass.

Some say that the Holy Spirit is the Power of God. That is true and untrue, depending on what you mean. The Holy Spirit is a Personality; He is the Third Person in the Holy Trinity, the Three in One.

Many don't believe in the Trinity, but the Bible teaches so. Jesus Christ told the apostles to baptize the Believers in the Name of the Father and of the Son and of the Holy Spirit (Matt. 28:19).

Apostle Paul prayed that the Grace of the Lord Jesus Christ, the Love of God, and the Communion of the Holy Spirit be with the Corinthian Christians (2 Cor. 13:14). For through Him (Jesus Christ), we both have access by one Spirit (the Holy Spirit) to the Father (Eph. 2:18).

The Lord (Jesus Christ) began the Message of Salvation which God (the Father) bears witness to with signs and wonders, and the Gifts of the Holy Spirit (Heb. 2:3-4).

There are Three that bear witness in Heaven: the Father, the Word (Jesus Christ), and the Holy Spirit; and these Three are One. (1 Jn 5:7). These Scriptures and others speak of the Trinity.

Believers receive power when the Holy Spirit comes upon them, so as to be witnesses to the Lord in their area and to the ends of the earth (Acts 1:8). This is why the Lord Jesus Christ told His apostles not to leave Jerusalem until they are endued with power from on High (Lk. 24:49).

But many try to do the Lord's Work without being filled with the Holy Spirit, and the powerlessness in their lives and ministries is the testimony they may not even be aware of. Will a policeman, who either carries no gun or have a mark 4 gun, put fear to well-armed robbers?

When you are baptized with the Holy Spirit and filled with Him, you have all the potential power that you will ever need, and He will release His Power in your life more and more as you obey Him, control yourself, and please God.

There are levels of anointing, and the Holy Spirit will anoint you with greater anointing as you follow His Leading and increase in your knowledge of the Lord God Almighty. Fasting will be useful.

Baptism in the Holy Spirit will be evidenced by speaking in tongues as in the Early Church. Many, instead of taking up the responsibility, instead of finding out why they have not been baptized and spoken in tongues, settle for a lower Christian life and say that everybody must not speak in tongues.

I could have settled for that also after seeking the baptism for a very long time and not receiving; but thanks to God for His Grace.

You can preach Jesus Christ, but to prove Him with the required signs and wonders, you must be filled with the Holy Spirit.

Note that the apostles and the Disciples had done marvelous things (signs and wonders) when the Lord imparted His Own Anointing on them, and yet, they were to wait for the Promise of the Father (Lk. 10:1-20).

Even though the Name of Jesus Christ in your mouth, as a Believer, can work miracles and wonders, there is a great difference when the anointing is resident on you.

Peter received the revelation of Whom Jesus Christ was when he was not yet filled with the Holy Spirit (Matt. 16:13-20). That you received a revelation, a vision, or that you prayed and God answered the prayer does not mean that you have been filled with the Holy Ghost.

You can only be full of the Power of the Holy Spirit after you must have been filled with the Person of the Holy Spirit (Acts 10:38; 1 Cor. 2:4; 1 Thes. 1:5). There is no other way, your title or position notwithstanding.

Being full of the Holy Spirit is the door to the Spiritual Gifts of the Holy Spirit (1 Cor. 12:1-11). After being baptized with the Holy Spirit, you must maintain the full measure of the Holy Spirit to keep on operating in His Power the way you should.

The Ephesian Christians were told to be filled (literally, be being filled) with the Holy Spirit (Eph. 5:18). The Roman Christians were told to be fervent in spirit (be on fire in the Spirit, maintain the Glow of the Holy Spirit) (Rom. 12:11).

When you are filled with the Holy Spirit, you will speak in tongues and to maintain the fullness of the Spirit, you will continue to speak…. This is a Biblical way, and any other way is not Biblical and cannot work.

This does not mean that God cannot use you if you are not filled with the Holy Spirit. The Disciples were filled with the Holy Spirit on the day of Pentecost and they spoke in other tongues as the Spirit gave them utterance (Acts 2:4).

Apostle Peter said that the Gift of the Holy Spirit is for every Believer (Acts 2:38-39). The Ephesian Believers that Apostle Paul found, even though they were Disciples, had not been filled with the Holy Spirit.

Thanks to God that they were filled with the Holy Spirit when hands were laid on them. Note that they spoke in tongues and prophesied (Acts 19:1-7).

Cornelius and his household only listened and believed Apostle Peter's message, and they were filled with the Holy Spirit and spoke in other tongues (Acts 10:44-48; Acts 11:13-15).

Saul (later known as Paul) was saved when he met Jesus Christ on his way to Damascus. Apostle Paul was filled with the Holy Spirit when Ananias laid hands on him (Acts 9:1-22), and he spoke in tongues (1 Cor. 14:18).

Apostle Paul encouraged Christians to speak with tongues in their individual prayers (1 Cor. 14:4,14; Jude 1:20). Speaking in tongues helps you pray for what you and others may not know about (Rom. 8:26). Speaking in tongues will help you tame the tongue (Jas 3:8).

Don't be afraid of receiving the wrong spirit, if you are born again and God is your Father. If our earthly parents will not give us fake or dangerous things, how much more will the Good, Loving, and Faithful Almighty God give us all good things? (Lk. 11:9-13).

Speaking in tongues is not the evidence of being born again, but of being baptized and filled with the Holy Spirit. The qualification for going to Heaven is being born again, and not speaking in tongues.

When you are born again, you receive a measure of the Holy Spirit to keep you going on in your Christian life, but when you are baptized and filled with the Holy Spirit, you are filled with the Holy Spirit to overflowing and this leads to power for witnessing for Jesus Christ.

The purpose of being filled with the Holy Spirit is to be a witness for Jesus Christ. It is to produce proofs and evidence that Jesus Christ is the Son of God, and He is alive. No wonder the Lord says that Believers will do the works that He did, even greater works than them (Jn 14:12).

The Holy Spirit will lead you into all truth and show you things to come. He will remind you of what you had heard and read (Jn 16:13; Jn 14:26).

There is no substitute for the Holy Spirit. He is in-charge of the world today, and as the Christians co-operate with Him, in obedience and prayer, He will bring the Will of God to pass on the earth.

Personality, learning, certificate, title, position, fame, and money cannot substitute the Holy Spirit, because it is not by power, nor by might, but by the Spirit of the Living God (Zech. 4:6). We must live and walk in the Spirit.

There is a Pentecostal mentality. Some assume that because they go to churches that are called Pentecostal churches, they have more power or gifts in them than others, but that is not the yardstick of measurement of the Power and Gifts of the Spirit.

Some assume that because they speak in tongues, they have arrived in the Things of the Spirit, but there is so much more to the Things of the Spirit. Then some others may assume that if you are not baptized in the Holy Spirit you will not go to Heaven, but this is far from the truth.

When you are full of the Holy Spirit, and you are obedient to Him, you will be full of the Mighty Power of God. Then you will affect your generation in a mighty way and bring much glory and praise to the Almighty God. Amen.

MORE THAN CONQUERORS

Questions for Discussion:

1. Who can separate us from the Love of Christ?
2. Why are we more than conquerors?
3. What weapon that is formed against us will succeed?

We are soldiers of Christ. We are a triumphant people who are to enforce the victory Jesus Christ already got for us. Do not be afraid; do not be dismayed: the Lord God Almighty is our God.

Rejoice in the Lord always; no matter the circumstance or condition you may find yourself in, rejoice in the Lord your God. We are heirs of God and joint-heirs with Christ. The Presence of God goes with us; we have the Power of the Spirit! Great power has been given to us.

Realizing that you are more than conquerors is a step to entering God's Rest. You can do all things through Christ Jesus. All things are possible by the Spirit of God.

It is not by might nor by power, but by the Holy Spirit. Whatever you bind on earth is bound in Heaven, and whatever you loose on earth is loosed in Heaven.

If God is for us, who can be against us? He Who did not spare His Own Son, but delivered Him up for us all, how shall He not with Him also freely give us all things? Who shall bring a charge against God's Elect? It is God Who justifies.

Who is He who condemns? It is Christ Who died, and further more has also risen, Who is even at the Right Hand of God, Who also makes intercession for us.

Who shall separate us from the Love of Christ? Shall tribulation, or distress, or persecution, or famine, or nakedness, or peril, or sword? Yet in all these things we are more than conquerors through Him Who loved us.

For I am persuaded that neither death nor life, nor angels nor principalities nor powers, nor things present nor things to come, nor height nor depth, nor any other created thing, shall be able to separate us from the Love of God which is in Christ Jesus our Lord (Rom. 8:31-39).

In righteousness you shall be established, you shall be far from oppression, for you shall not fear; and from terror, for it shall not come near you.

Indeed they shall surely assemble, but not because of God. Whoever assembles against you shall fall for your sake. Behold, God created the blacksmith who blows the coals in the fire, who brings forth an instrument for his work; and He created the spoiler to destroy.

No weapon formed against you shall prosper, and every tongue which rises against you in judgment you shall condemn. This is the heritage of the Servants of the Lord, and their righteousness is from Him (Isa. 54:14-17).

We are in the New Testament which is established upon better promises than the Old Testament. In the Old Testament, the Lord demonstrated His Power to show that His people are more than conquerors.

When Jacob laboured for Laban, Laban cheated him; but the Lord intervened supernaturally, so that Jacob outsmarted Laban and God restored to him the years that the enemy had cheated him (Gen. 30)

In God's Plan, God told Abraham that his descendants will be slaves in a foreign land for four hundred years, and after that, they will come out. This came to pass in the land of Egypt where Israelites were held in bondage for hundreds of years.

When God sent Moses to Pharaoh to tell him to let the Israelites go, Pharaoh said, "Who is the Lord that I should obey Him?" As God brought different plagues to the Egyptians, Pharaoh was frightened, even though his heart was still hardened, and he gave conditions upon which they could go.

But when God slew all the firstborns of the Egyptians, they themselves had to beg the Israelites to go and the people of Israel plundered them. The enemy who stands by your way to stop you from having the inheritance that the Lord has provided for you will fall for your sake.

When the Lord told Joshua that He has given him and the people of Israel Jericho, many of the Israelites doubted the possibility of it, because they thought that they were not their match. The ten spies confessed that they saw giants in Jericho.

But thanks to God for Joshua and Caleb who believed God, and shunned the other ten spies, telling the people that they were well able to take Jericho. Can you speak differently, according to the Word of God, even when the surrounding circumstances say otherwise?

When Jericho had been circled seven times and the trumpets were blown, according to the Instruction of the Lord, the walls of Jericho crumbled, and the people captured it.

Even when the less powerful Ai defeated Israel because there was sin in their midst (make sure there is no sin in your life, for God is of Purer Eyes than to behold iniquity, and He is no respecter of persons), when they repented and removed sin from their midst, Ai fell to them.

It is only sin, disobedience, and unbelief that will hinder you from taking your inheritance in Christ Jesus. Therefore, strive to be holy, obedient, righteous, and full of faith.

Gideon had planned to go with several thousands to battle, but God told him that all he needed were three hundred men. When he went to the battle with only three hundred men, they won the battle, because the battle is the Lord's.

No wonder Sampson was a one-man army who could defeat the Philistines alone. The man's anointing functioned greatly that he could pull out the doors of the gate to the city with bare hands and carry them up a hill. One will chase a thousand, and two will chase ten thousand.

Even though Goliath had been a man of war for many years and was well armoured with offensive weapons of sword, spear, and javelin, David who had the Anointing of the Spirit of God (who had killed both a bear and a lion by that anointing), and did not have experience in warfare, used only stones and a sling to attack the mighty Goliath of Gath.

A single stone, empowered by the anointing, sank into his forehead, and the man fell flat. The Anointing of the Spirit of the Living God breaks every yoke of the devil and destroys his burdens (Isa. 10:27).

If you study the deeds and exploits of David's mighty men in 2 Sam. 23:1-39, you will come to understand that if God is for us, no man can be against us. How much more shall our exploits be when we live in the New Testament which is established upon better promises?

In the New Testament, God is for us, with us, in us, and upon us; what a great reinforcement! The hosts of Heaven are on our side.

No wonder Prophet Elisha prayed that the eyes of his servant be opened that he might know that they which were with them were more than they which were against them. The servant had only been looking at the situation from the physical point of view; but Elisha saw beyond the physical.

We are of God (we were Born of God and we belong to Him) and greater is He that is in us than he that is in the world (1 Jn 4:4). Have you been afraid before? Don't be again. Had you been doubting before? Remove doubt now, and grab your strong faith.

Faith, as little as the mustard seed, will remove mountains. Remove sin and disobedience, for they block the door to the supernatural; grab holiness and righteousness, for they open the door-way of Heaven!

Be anxious for nothing; but in everything, by prayer and supplication, with thanksgiving, let your requests be made known to God. And the Peace of God which passes knowledge, will guard your hearts and minds through Christ Jesus.

When the storm and the sea raged and roared so much that the Disciples of Jesus Christ thought they were going to get drowned, they cried for help from Jesus Christ. The Lord rebuked their unbelief and fear.

Just as the Lord commanded and the storm ceased, you too can speak peace and calmness to your circumstances in the Name of Jesus Christ, and there will be peace and tranquility. Stand still and see the Salvation of the Lord your God, for the battle is not yours but the Lord's.

All you need to do is to speak the Word in faith, and see God turn your circumstances around for your good. Peace, be still!

If you consider the life of Elijah who stopped rainfall for three and half years, and after that brought it back; who brought down fire from Heaven on three occasions: to consume his prepared sacrifice and consume the captains the king sent to fetch him with their fifties, you will know that we are more than conquerors.

Prophet Elisha healed the water of a land and healed Naaman of his leprosy. Fire couldn't even set the dresses of Shadrach, Meshach, and Abed-Nego ablaze. Lions refused the meat of Daniel. God is powerful and miraculous!

God has sent, provided, and commissioned His angels to protect us. Angels are ministering spirits sent to minister for the heirs of salvation: us. You have got to learn how to put your angels to work.

Of course, there are duties of angels you don't have anything to do with. Your relationship with Jesus Christ, your life of obedience and holiness, your prayer-life and faith-life have a lot to do with how angels attend to your cause.

Considering the Life and Ministry of Jesus Christ, you will come to know that our God is too much, and we, His people, are a people of signs, wonders, and miracles!

Jesus Christ walked on water, raised the dead, cast out demons, brought calmness to a raging storm on the sea, opened the eyes of the blind, and did many other mighty works. Before He left, He told His Followers that He who believes on Him shall do the same works, and even greater works (Jn 14:12).

No wonder the lives of the apostles, prophets, and Disciples of the Early New Testament time were filled with signs and wonders. The early apostles and Disciples walked with God so much that their opponents became afraid of them, because they could not deny the miracles which they performed.

Apostle Peter healed a lame man so that he walked. It even got to the level whereby Peter's shadows could heal the sick and diseased. Apostle Paul's handkerchiefs could heal the sick and drive out demons (Acts 5:15; Acts 19:11-12).

Apostle Paul commanded an opposer of the Gospel and he did not see again for a period of time. Even when the people thought that he would swell from a viper's attack, nothing happened to him so that they changed their mind and said that he was a god. They were right because we are gods (Pas. 82:1,6; Jn 10:34-35).

We have been given the Name of Jesus Christ, the Name above every other name, and at the Name Jesus Christ, every knee should bow, of those, beings, or things in heaven, on earth, and under the earth, and that every tongue should confess that Jesus Christ is Lord, to the Glory of God the Father.

Use that Name, and you will see wonderful changes in your circumstances. The Name of Jesus Christ is stronger than your strength, and you can accomplished more in a minute by using the Name of Jesus Christ than you can accomplish in a year by using your human strength.

No witch or wizard has any power over you, except you give them an opportunity by sin, disobedience, and faithlessness. Jesus Christ says, "Behold, I give you power to tread on serpents and scorpions, and over all the power of the enemy, and nothing shall by any means hurt you" (Lk. 10:19).

He says that the purpose the Holy Spirit came upon you is to empower you to be a witness for Him. As His witness, you will have to give evidence and proof that He is alive by signs and miracles.

In this dispensation, the Lord God Almighty is for us, with us, in us, and upon us. We cannot fail because greater is the Holy Ghost that is in us than the satan that is in the world. Confront anything that confronts you, and it will certainly bow to the Name of Jesus Christ and the Anointing of the Holy Ghost.

Resist the devil yourself, and he will flee from you (Jas 4:7). Don't wait for God to do it, because God has appointed that assignment for you. Take it up! No weapon fashioned against you shall prevail over you, for the Lord is with you.

We have Jesus Christ, Who is our Great Intercessor. Jesus Christ intercedes for us at the Right Hand of the Father, and His Intercession keeps us safe, protected, and free.

We must have the rugged mentality. The Kingdom of God suffers violence, and the violent take it by force. The Church is marching on and the gates of Hades shall not prevail.

We must advance by force, and take what belongs to us in Christ Jesus. We must advance into the kingdom of the devil and take souls from there for the Lord our God.

CONFRONTING YOUR CONFRONTATIONS

Questions for Discussion:

1. How should we handle the things that confront us?
2. What should we be afraid of?
3. What is it that will overcome us?

All things are possible to the Believer. Christians are Offsprings of God Himself. Since the days of John the Baptist, the Kingdom of God suffers violence, and the violent take it by force (Matt. 11:12).

Turn your conditions around for good, and obtain your rights, privileges, and inheritances in Christ by confronting your confrontations. The righteousness which is of faith speaks in this way, "Do not say in your heart, 'Who will ascend into Heaven?' (that is, to bring Christ down from Above) or, 'Who will descend into the deep?' (that is, to bring Christ up from the dead)."

But what does it say? "The Word is near you, in your mouth and in your heart" (that is the Word of Faith which we preach). That if you shall confess with your mouth…and shall believe in your heart…you shall be saved.

For with the heart man believes…and with the mouth confession is made…. Whoever believes on Him shall not be put to shame (Rom. 10:6-11).

We, having the same spirit of faith, according as it is written, "I believed, and therefore have I spoken"; we also believe, and therefore speak (2 Cor. 4:13). You have to confront your confrontations to receive your victory.

It is not God that will do the confrontation for us. If we wait for God, we may die waiting for Him. This is why the Scripture tells us to resist the devil so that he will flee from us (Jas 4:7).

You have to resist him steadfastly in faith (1 Pet. 5:9). Don't give any place to the devil (Eph. 4:27). The devil will have the place you give him, he will occupy that place.

But the mistake many people make is to sit back and wait for God to remove the obstacles the devil has brought along their ways. Your word of faith can break that barrier. This is why God gave us the responsibility to pray.

The Word of God is the Sword of the Spirit; use the Word actively, and see the Spirit of God change your circumstances for good, better, and best. Contend, earnestly, for the faith and the Word; the Promises of God are 'Yes', and 'Amen.'

No matter how long you might have been oppressed and confronted, you can still confront your confrontations and get free. Even generational curses and covenants will crumble if you confront them.

Believe the Word of God more than any person's story or idea. The Anointing of the Holy Spirit of the Living God destroys the yokes and lifts the burdens the enemy puts on people. Jesus Christ gives peace, abundant peace.

The Philistines gathered their armies together to battle with Israel. And a champion went out from the camp of the Philistines, named Goliath, from Gath, whose height was six cubits and a span (that is, 13 feet, 4 inches).

He had a bronze helmet on his head, and he was armed with a coat of mail, and the weight of the coat was five thousand shekels of bronze (about $194\frac{1}{2}$ ibs in weight). And he had bronze armour on his legs and bronze javelin between his shoulders.

Now the staff of his spear was like a weaver's beam, and his iron spearhead weighed six hundred shekels (about $23^1/_2$ ibs, counting 224 grains to the shekel); and a shield-bearer went before him.

Can you imagine this type of a devil? He was armoured very well. He had offensive weapons of javelin and spear. Bronze is an alloy metal which is very hard. Brass is a mixture of zinc and copper, while bronze is a mixture of zinc, copper, and tin. He had both well-made defensive and offensive weapons.

Added to that is that a shield-bearer went before him. If you were to fight with Goliath naturally, his shield-bearer (who could be taller than you: Goliath himself was a giant) would stop your arrow, spear, and sword, while Goliath will thrust you through with his spear or javelin.

But I don't care about the barrier, opposition, stronghold, or attack the enemy and his demons have brought along your way, to stop you from enjoying the full benefit of the inheritance you have in Jesus Christ; if you will withstand him, he will flee.

It may not take a minute, an hour, a day or a week to break that barrier and stop the attack, but if you withstand him steadfastly in faith and pray, he will bow.

There are cases and situations that you will have to add fasting to prayer for the devil's handiwork to be destroyed. The Word says that some demonic works will be broken only by prayer and fasting (Matt. 17:21).

This does not mean that you can't cast out a demon unless you are fasting, but if the anointing in your life (gained by former prayer and fasting) is not strong enough for confronting that demonic attack, then you must fast until you have a breakthrough.

However, demons bow to the Name of Jesus Christ. Sometimes, the fasting may have to take a long time of about three, seven or more days. Imagine what would have happened if Prophet Daniel had stopped praying and fasting the twentieth day.

The answer to his prayers, which was released the first day, might have not reached him. An angel who was not a high-ranking warring angel was sent to deliver the answer, but a stronger satanic spiritual wickedness in high places withstood him.

But thanks to God that Daniel did not give up, and on the twenty-first day, another angel was sent to help the other angel. This made it possible for him to deliver the answer to Daniel (Dan. 10).

Some say that fasting is not that important; well, can you explain what you mean? Jesus Christ fasted; Apostle Paul fasted; and (I don't want to go the Old Testament now) the early Disciples and Believers fasted.

The truth is that there is a level of anointing the Holy Spirit will not anoint you with if you don't fast. Whether partial fasting, fruit-fasting, juice-fasting, the fasted life, water-fasting, or dry fasting, you will fast. Of course, dry fasting or water-fasting may, sometimes, not take as long as partial fasting.

Goliath of Gath, the Philistine, intimidated Israel many days, and said, "I defy the armies of Israel this day, give me a man that we may fight together." When King Saul and all Israel heard these words of the Philistine, they were dismayed and greatly afraid. By this time, God had rejected Saul as a king, and the anointing that was upon him had lifted.

Maybe, it was the same anointing that lifted from Saul that came upon David, because Saul was rejected by God in chapter fifteen, David was anointed king in chapter sixteen, and here comes Goliath in chapter seventeen.

But one thing we know is that the anointing had lifted from Saul, and God had anointed David as king, even though, physically, he had not become one. But what has been settled in the spiritual realm will certainly come to pass physically, because the spiritual realm is very real.

After Goliath had terrorized Israel for forty days, the youngest son of Jesse, who had been anointed with the Power and Boldness of the Spirit of God, came to the camp of Israel and heard that thrash from the mouth of Goliath. All the men of Israel, when they saw the man, fled from him, and were dreadfully afraid.

And David said, "Who is this uncircumcised Philistine, that he should defy the armies of the Living God?" Eliab, his oldest brother, heard him and was very annoyed with him. He would have thought in his mind, saying, "What can this proud small boy do?"

Do you know that people can judge you, and take you to be proud when you say what you can do by the Power of God through the Name of Jesus Christ? Apostle Peter said, "I give you what I have, and in the Name of Jesus Christ, rise up and walk" (Acts 3:1-11).

David told Saul that their hearts should not fail because of Goliath, and that he will go and fight him. Saul said, "You are not able to go against this Philistine to fight with him; for you are a youth, and he a man of war from his youth." David told Saul that he had killed a lion and a bear, and he will kill Goliath also.

You see why you shouldn't be afraid. The anointing that removed malaria can also open the eyes of the blind. Just be dedicated to making God's Anointing stronger and stronger in your life. All you need are the anointing and the real faith.

David declared that the Lord will deliver him. The anointing emboldened him and moved him. Saul armoured David with his armour and gave him a sword, but David could not use them. Some think that it must be done the same old way, but this is not true.

Find out the direction and the strategy God has for you, and you will conquer when you obey God. David used stones and a sling. The Philistine looked at David and disdained him. He cursed David by his gods. But David was not moved; he knew the outcome.

David said, "You come to me with a sword, with a spear, and with a javelin. But I come to you in the Name of the Lord of Hosts…the Lord will deliver you into my hand, and I will strike you and take your head from you….

"That all the earth may know that there is a God in Israel…the Lord does not save with sword and spear; for the battle is the Lord's…."

David hurried, took out a stone, and slung it and struck the Philistine in his forehead. The Philistine died and the others fled. David and Israel overcame by their God (1 Sam. 17).

The spiritual controls the physical. Stand upon the Word of God without doubting, and act: you will overcome always! No devil, demon, witch, or thing should stop you, as a Christian and a minister. Don't make yourself stoppable.

If you are confronting your confrontations and it seems that you are not achieving your purpose, you may have to change your strategy or battle plan. That God worked a certain way to solve a problem does not mean He will always work that way. Find out from God always how you have to approach your difficult situations.

EVANGELISM BY POWER

Questions for Discussion:

1. What is the Great Commission that our Lord gave to us?
2. How should we evangelize?
3. Where should we evangelize?
4. Who should we win to Christ?
5. Why should evangelism go along with the demonstration of power?

Before the Lord Jesus Christ left, He told the apostles and the Disciples that they will receive power, after that the Holy Ghost has come upon them; and they shall be witnesses to Him from their place to the ends of the world (Acts 1:8).

This Statement is applicable to us also for we are in the same dispensation. Even though the world needed to be evangelized quickly, He told them to tarry in Jerusalem until they are endued with power from on High (Lk. 24:49).

When the power came upon them, they went out and preached everywhere, the Lord working with them and confirming the Word through signs and wonders (Mk 16:20).

We are called as fishers of men, and we must occupy till the Lord Jesus Christ comes. We are labourers together with God.

We cannot expect to preach the Gospel any other way, for Apostle Paul declares that the Kingdom of God is not in word but in power (1 Cor. 4:20).

No wonder when he preached to the Corinthians, he did not go with excellence of speech or of wisdom, declaring to them the Testimony of God.

He was with them in weakness, in fear, and in much trembling, having decided to know nothing among them except Jesus Christ and Him crucified.

And his speech and his preaching were not with persuasive words of human wisdom, but in demonstration of the Spirit and of power, that their faith should not be in the wisdom of men but in the Power of God (1 Cor. 2:1-5).

This happened wherever he went, for, concerning the Thessalonians, he said, "For our Gospel did not come to you in Word only, but also in power, and in the Holy Spirit, and in much assurance, as you know what kind of men we were among you for your sake" (1 Thes. 1:5).

Jesus Christ drew people's attention more by the miracles He performed than by His Teachings and Preachings. I am not saying that miracles are greater than the Word of God.

As a matter of fact, the Word of God is greater than signs, wonders, and miracles; but it is the signs, wonders, and miracles that will draw people to you so that they can receive the Word.

After Jesus Christ was filled with the Holy Spirit, the Spirit led Him into the wilderness, being tempted for forty days by the devil. And in those days He ate nothing, and afterward, when they had ended, He was hungry. Now when the devil had ended every temptation, he departed from Him until an opportune time.

Then Jesus Christ returned in the Power of the Spirit to Galilee, and News of Him went out through the entire surrounding region. And He taught in their synagogues, being glorified by all (Lk. 4).

The miracles and healings He performed attracted the attention of the people so that they themselves advertised for Him (they advertised His Ministry) throughout the entire surrounding region. When He went down to Capernaum, they were astonished at His Teaching, for His Word was with authority.

When you are full of the Holy Spirit and the Word of God, when you are filled with power, people will notice a recognizable difference and authority in your preaching and teaching.

As He was in their synagogue, a man with an unclean spirit cried out with a loud voice. But Jesus Christ rebuked the demon, saying, "Be quiet, and come out of him!" The demon came out immediately. That is power and authority.

He did not spend hours or days trying to cast out the same devils. He did not even want to know from the people whether it was a generational or an ancestral spirit. The anointing, the liquid-fire anointing, knows of no yoke that cannot be broken.

The people there were all amazed and spoke among themselves, saying, "What a Word is this! For with authority and power He commands the unclean spirits and they come out." I like that! The problem is that many move out without the power.

However, this is not to say that you have to wait for your whole life for the power. Some pray and wait too long. It took Jesus Christ forty days. Your own may last for only three days, because the Lord has conquered the devil for us. We operate in His Name!

Once you are filled with the Holy Spirit, and you are obedient to God and prayerful, devils and their works will yield to your commands.

Of course, there are levels of the anointing, but start with the one you have, and as you are faithful in the little you have, the Lord will increase the anointing in your life. You wouldn't have all at the same time.

The Report about Him went out into every place in the surrounding region. As He stood over Simon's wife's mother and rebuked the high fever she had, it left her. And immediately she arose and served them.

When the sun was setting, all those who had any that were sick with various diseases brought them to Him; and He laid His Hands on every one of them and healed them (verse 40). Many demons also left.

The people tried to keep Him there, but He told them that He must preach the Kingdom of God to other cities also. He did not settle down to establish a church and pastor it against God's Will for Him!

The story was the same throughout His Ministry. He operated supernaturally. After using Peter's boat to preach to the multitude, He told Peter to launch out for a catch. When Peter did, they caught a great number of fish, and their net was breaking.

Peter had said, "Master, we have toiled all night and caught nothing; nevertheless at Your Word I will let down the net." What you have toiled for the past twenty years, God can give it to you in an hour.

He healed the leper. He healed the paralyzed. He restored the withered hand of a man. He raised the dead. He did all manner of healings.

He fed five thousand people with five loaves of bread and two small fish. The people were so much amazed that had it been that Jesus Christ did not leave them, they would have taken Him by force to make Him king. The people kept on looking for Him, and even used boat, seeking for Him.

Don't say, "That was Jesus Christ the Son of the Living God." Yes, He was, but Jesus Christ Himself said, "Most assuredly, I say to you, he who believes in Me, the works that I do he will do also, and greater works than these he will do, because I go to My Father (Jn 14:12).

What happened after Apostle Peter had healed the lame man at the gate of the Temple called Beautiful? As the man held on to Peter and John, all the people ran together to them, greatly amazed. Peter used that opportunity to preach to them, and they listened to him attentively.

Even though their opponents came upon them and arrested them, many of those who heard the Word believed; and the number of the men came to be about five thousand. God has not changed. It is the Believers that doubt God (Acts 3).

The eight chapter of the Book of Acts gives us a story that will convince the 'doubting Thomas' of the need for the demonstration of the Power of the Holy Spirit through the Believers.

This story will convince you that even witches and wizards will leave their witchcraft practices and come after your Jesus Christ when the power in your life is strong enough. Philip, who was not even one of the apostles, went down to Samaria and preached Christ to them.

The Bible says, "And the multitudes with one accord heeded the things spoken by Philip, hearing and seeing the miracles which he did.

"For unclean spirits, crying with a loud voice, came out of many who were possessed; and many who were paralyzed and lame were healed. And there was great joy in the city.

"But there was a certain man called Simon, who previously practiced sorcery in the city and astonished the people of Samaria, claiming that he was someone great, to whom they all gave heed, from the least to the greatest, saying, 'This man is the Great Power of God?'

"And they heeded him because he had astonished them with his sorceries for a long time. But when they believed Philip as he preached the things concerning the Kingdom of God and the Name of Jesus Christ, both men and women were baptized.

"Then Simon himself also believed; and when he was baptized he continued with Philip, and was amazed, seeing the miracles and signs which were done." Even the sorcerer, Simon, wanted that power and authority, because he had seen something that was greater than his sorcery.

When power jam power, the lesser power will bow! I know there are people whose hearts have been hardened to the extent that even when they know the truth, they would rather die than serve Christ. But God can deliver them from that hardened state.

Jesus Christ is the same yesterday, today, and forever (Heb. 13:8). He has not changed and He still works with His people to expand the Kingdom of God on earth. The Lord God Almighty does not change (Mal. 3:6).

God cannot lie and He cannot disappoint His people. It is not possible for God to fail to fulfill His Word. Jesus Christ came to destroy the works of satan and save men.

In preaching the Gospel of our Lord Jesus Christ, you must remove shame, fear, and timidity. If you are ashamed of the Lord before sinners, He will be ashamed of you before His Father and the holy angels.

Do not be afraid of him who only has power to kill the body; rather fear God, Who has power to destroy both the body and the soul in Hell. Only Jesus Christ is the Light of the world, and He has made us the light of the world, as His representatives and brethren.

We have been given the ministry of reconciliation, and we must not fail in this task. Jesus Christ came to reconcile men to God and we are labourers together with Him. Jesus Christ came to seek those who were lost in order to save them. We must seek the lost and get them saved.

THE SPIRITUAL CHRISTIAN

Questions for Discussion:

1. What does it mean to be spiritual?
2. What should we set our mind on?
3. What is the result of being carnally minded?
4. What is the importance of being spiritually minded?

There is therefore now no condemnation to those who are in Christ Jesus, who do not walk according to the flesh, but according to the Spirit. For the Law of the Spirit of Life in Christ Jesus has made me free from the law of sin and death.

For what the Law could not do in that it was weak through the flesh, God did by sending His Own Son in the likeness of sinful flesh, on account of sin.

He condemned sin in the flesh, that the righteous requirement of the Law might be fulfilled in us who do not walk according to the flesh but according to the Spirit.

For those who live according to the flesh set their minds on the things of the flesh, but those who live according to the Spirit, the Things of the Spirit. For to be carnally minded is death, but to be spiritually minded is life and peace.

Because the carnal mind is enmity against God; for it is not subject to the Law of God, nor indeed can be. So then those who are in the flesh cannot please God. But you are not in the flesh but in the Spirit, if indeed the Spirit of God dwells in you.

Now if anyone does not have the Spirit of Christ, he is not His. And if Christ is in you, the body is dead because of sin, but the Spirit is Life because of righteousness.

But if the Spirit of Him Who raised Jesus Christ from the dead dwells in you, He Who raised Christ from the dead will also give life to your mortal bodies through His Spirit Who dwells in you.

Therefore, brethren, we are debtors – not to the flesh, to live according to the flesh. For if you live according to the flesh, you will die; but if by the Spirit you put to death the deeds of the body, you will live.

For as many as are led by the Spirit of God, these are the sons of God. The Spirit Himself bears witness with our spirit that we are children of God, and if children then heirs   heirs of God and joint-heirs with Christ, if indeed we suffer with Him, that we may also be glorified together.

For I consider that the sufferings of this present time are not worthy to be compared with the glory which shall be revealed in us. For the earnest expectation of the creation eagerly waits for the revealing of the sons of God.

The creation itself also will be delivered from the bondage of corruption into the glorious liberty of the children of God. For we know that the whole creation groans and labours with birth pangs together until now.

Not only that, but we also, even we ourselves groan within ourselves, eagerly waiting for the adoption, the redemption of our body.

The Spirit also helps in our weakness. For we do not know what we should pray for as we ought, but the Spirit Himself makes intercession for us with groanings which cannot be uttered.

Now He Who searches the hearts knows what the Mind of the Spirit is, because He makes intercession for the Saints according to the Will of God.

And we know that all things work together for good to those who love God, to those who are the called according to His Purpose.

For whom He foreknew, He also predestined to be conformed to the Image of His Son, that He might be the Firstborn among many brethren.

Moreover whom He predestined, these He also called; whom He called, these He also justified; and whom He justified, these He also glorified (Rom. 8:1-30).

If God has called you, make every effort to be chosen by Him also. As a chosen vessel of His, be faithful so that you will be commended, rewarded, and glorified at last, because the end of a matter is better than the beginning.

Walk in the Spirit, and you shall not fulfill the lust of the flesh. For the flesh lusts against the Spirit, and the Spirit against the flesh, and these are contrary to one another, so that you do not do the things that you wish. But if you are led by the Spirit, you are not under the Law.

The Fruit of the Spirit is love, joy, peace, longsuffering, kindness, goodness, faithfulness, gentleness, self-control. Against such there is no Law. And those who are Christ's have crucified the flesh with its passions and desires.

If we live in the Spirit, let us also walk in the Spirit. Let us not become conceited, provoking one another, envying one another. Bear one another's burdens and so fulfill the Law of Christ.

Do not be deceived, God is not mocked; whatever a man sows, that he will also reap. For he who sows to his flesh will also of the flesh reap corruption, but he who sows to the Spirit will of the Spirit reap Everlasting Life.

And let us not grow weary while doing good, for in due season, we shall reap if we do not lose heart. Therefore, as we have opportunity, let us do good to all, especially to those who are of the Household of Faith (Gal. 5 and 6).

God tells us that we should seek those things which are Above, where Christ is, sitting at the Right Hand of God. Set your mind on things Above, not on things on the earth. For you died, when you received Christ; and your life has been hidden with Christ in God.

When Christ Who is our Life appears, then we also will appear with Him in glory. Therefore put to death your members which are on the earth: fornication, uncleanness, passion, evil desire, and covetousness, which is idolatry. Put off all these: anger, wrath, malice, blasphemy, filthy language out of your mouth.

As the Elect of God, holy and beloved, put on tender mercies, kindness, humility, meekness, longsuffering; bearing with one another, and forgiving one another; if anyone has a complaint against another, even as Christ forgave you, so you also must do.

But above all these things put on love, which is the bond of perfection. And let the Peace of God rule in your hearts, and be thankful.

Let the Word of Christ dwell in you richly in all wisdom, teaching and admonishing one another in psalms and hymns and spiritual songs, singing with grace in your hearts to the Lord.

And whatever you do, in word or in deed, do all in the Name of the Lord Jesus, giving thanks to God the Father through Him. Continue earnestly in prayer, being vigilant in it with thanksgiving.

Walk in wisdom toward those who are outside, redeeming the time. Let your speech always be with grace, seasoned with salt, that you may know how you ought to answer each one (Col. 3 & 4).

Walk worthy of the calling with which you were called, with all lowliness and gentleness, with longsuffering, bearing with one another in love, endeavouring to keep the Unity of the Spirit in the bond of peace.

Put off, concerning your former conduct, the old man which grows corrupt according to the deceitful lusts, and be renewed in the spirit of your mind. Put on the new man who was created according to God, in true righteousness and holiness.

And do not grieve the Holy Spirit of God, by Whom you were sealed for the Day of Redemption. Be imitators of God as dear people of God. And walk in love, as Christ also has loved us and given Himself for us, an Offering and a Sacrifice to God for a sweet-smelling aroma.

See then that you walk circumspectly, not as fools but as wise, redeeming the time, because the days are evil. Therefore, do not be unwise, but understand what the Will of the Lord is. And do not be drunk with wine, in which is dissipation, but be filled with the Spirit.

Submit to one another in the fear of God. Be strong in the Lord and in the power of His Might. Put on the whole Armour of God that you may be able to stand against the wiles of the devil.

For we do not wrestle against flesh and blood; but we wrestle against principalities, against powers, and against the rulers of the darkness of this age, against spiritual hosts of wickedness in the heavenly places.

Therefore, take up the whole Armour of God that you may be able to withstand in the evil day, and having done all to stand.

Stand therefore, having girded your waist with truth, having put on the breastplate of righteousness, and having shod your feet with the preparation of the Gospel of Peace; above all, taking the shield of faith with which you will be able to quench all the fiery darts of the wicked one.

And take the helmet of salvation, and the Sword of the Spirit, which is the Word of God: praying always with all prayer and supplication in the Spirit, being watchful to this end with all perseverance and supplication for all the Saints (Eph. 4, 5, & 6).

Work out your salvation with fear and trembling: for it is God Who works in you both to will and to do for His Good Pleasure.

Do all things without complaining and disputing, that you may become blameless and harmless, children of God without fault in the midst of a crooked and perverse generation among whom you shine as lights in the world, holding fast the Word of Life, so that your salvation will not be in vain (Phil. 2:12-16).

Learn to build up yourself spiritually; be diligent to energize your spirit. Remember that weight hinders your Christian walk, while sin entangles you to the devil and the world. The Will of God for you in Jesus Christ is that you go and sin no more.

Also, you can't serve two masters at the same time. You can't serve God and money; you can't serve God and men. Live in all good conscience toward God and men.

Remember that your body is the Temple of God; therefore don't defile it. The Saints are to be perfected; they are to get matured and established in the Lord.

THE UNTOUCHABLE CHRISTIAN

Questions for Discussion:

1. What does it mean to be untouchable?
2. Do we have enemies as Christians?
3. What will make you to be untouchable?

We know that whoever is Born of God does not sin; but he who has been Born of God keeps himself, and the wicked one does not touch him. We know that we are of God, and the whole world lies under the sway of the wicked one (1 Jn 5:18-19).

Sin and disobedience is the basis through which the devil and his agents touch people. Without sin in your life, no devil nor demon, no witch nor wizard, no principal agent of the kingdom of darkness can touch you. Don't be ignorant of the devices of the devil.

It was when Adam disobeyed God that the devil touched him. The devil stole what God had given to Adam from him. And we know that the devil does not come except to steal, and to kill, and to destroy. Jesus Christ came that we may have life, and that we may have it more abundantly (Jn 10:10).

The purpose the Son of God was manifested is that He might destroy the works of the devil. Whoever has been Born of God does not sin, for His Seed remains in him, and he cannot sin because he has been Born of God (1 Jn. 3:1-10).

Children of God purify themselves as Jesus Christ is pure. Whoever commits sin also commits lawlessness, and sin is lawlessness. And you know that He was manifested to take away our sins, and in Him there is no sin. Whoever abides in Him does not sin. Whoever sins has neither seen Him nor known Him.

Let no one deceive you. He who practices righteousness is righteous, just as He is righteous. He who sins is of the devil. Whoever does not practice righteousness is not of God, nor is he who does not love his brother.

Other things that can give the devil an opportunity in your life are unbelief and doubt. When you don't believe the Word of God, doubt sets in. Doubt prevents the manifestation of the Word of God in your life.

The Word of God says that he who doubts is like the wave of the sea, tossed to and fro, and that person should not expect to get anything from God. But God can neither lie nor fail to perform His Promises.

As Christians, we are untouchable beings, when we abide in Christ and in His Word. But the problem is that many Christians open a hole for the devil in their lives, and when you give him a loophole or place in your life, he will come in. He who breaks the hedge will be beaten by the serpent.

Be sober; be vigilant; because your adversary the devil walks about like a roaring lion, seeking whom he may devour. Resist him, steadfast in the faith (1 Pet. 5:8-9).

Therefore submit to God. Resist the devil and he will flee from you. Draw near to God and He will draw near to you. Cleanse your hands, you sinners; and purify your hearts, you double-minded.

Lament and mourn and weep! Let your laughter be turned to mourning and your joy to gloom. Humble yourselves in the Sight of the Lord, and He will lift you up. God resists the proud, but gives grace to the humble (Jas 4:6-10).

The devil will bring different things across your path, but whatever he throws at you, resist him and he will flee. To flee is to run away with fear.

In righteousness you shall be established; you shall be far from oppression, for you shall not fear; and from terror, for it shall not come near you. Indeed they shall surely gather, but not by God.

Whoever gathers against you shall fall for your sake. Behold the Lord created the blacksmith who blows the coal in the fire, who brings forth an instrument for his work; and He created the spoiler to destroy.

No weapon formed against you shall prosper, and every tongue which rises against you in judgment you shall condemn. This is the heritage of the Servants of the Lord, and their righteousness is from Him (Isa. 54:14-17).

Do not fear, for the Lord is with you; be not dismayed, for His is your God. He will strengthen you, yes, He will help you, and He will uphold you with His Righteous Right Hand.

Behold, all those who were increased against you shall be ashamed and disgraced, they shall be as nothing, and those who strive with you shall perish. You shall seek them and not find them; those who contend with you shall be as nothing, as a non-existent thing (Isa. 41:10-12).

Fear not, for the Lord has redeemed you, He has called you by your name; you are His. When you pass through the waters, He will be with you; and through the rivers, they shall not overflow you. When you walk through the fire, you shall not be burned, nor shall the flame scorch you.

For the Lord is your God, the Holy One of Israel, your Saviour; He gave Egypt for Israel's ransom. Since you are precious in God's Sight, He will honour you, for He loves you. Therefore He will give men for you, and people for your life. Fear not (Isa. 43:1-5).

The ninety-first chapter of the Book of Psalms tells us what it means to be untouchable. He who dwells in the Secret Place of the Most High shall abide under the Shadow of the Almighty. I will say of the Lord, "He is my Refuge and my Fortress; my God, in Him I will trust."

Surely He shall deliver you from the snare of the fowler and from the perilous pestilence. He shall cover you with His Feathers, and under His Wings you shall find refuge; His Truth shall be your shield and buckler.

You shall not be afraid of the terror by night, nor of the arrow that flies by the day, nor of the pestilence that walks in darkness, nor of the destruction that lays waste at noonday. A thousand may fall at your side, and ten thousand at your right hand; but it shall not come near you.

Only with your eyes shall you look, and see the reward of the wicked. Because you have made the Lord Who is my Refuge, even the Most High, your Dwelling Place, no evil shall befall you nor shall any plaque come near your dwelling.

He shall give His angels Charge over you, to keep you in all your ways. In their hands they shall bear you up, lest you dash your foot against a stone. You shall tread upon the lion and the cobra, the young lion and the serpent you shall trample underfoot.

Because you have set your love upon God, therefore He will deliver you, He will set you on high, because you have known His Name.

You shall call upon Him, and He will answer you. He will be with you in trouble: He will deliver you and honour you. With long life He will satisfy you, and show you His Salvation.

The Lord delivered Shadrach, Meshach and Abed-Nego from the fiery furnace of King Nebuchadnezzar. The fire had been heated seven times more as commanded by the king in his rage. The king also gave them a second opportunity to bow to the image so that they will not be burnt.

However, they maintained their steadfastness in the Lord their God and the Lord God delivered them (Dan. 3).

Don't compromise your faith and stand because of threats, persecutions, and trials. Even if it involves your losing your life, do not love your life to death and you will have it back at the Appearing of the Lord Jesus Christ.

The Lord delivered Daniel from lions when he was put into the den of lions. The Lord closed the mouths of the lions so that they could not eat him up; when Daniel was brought out, it was found out that not only did the lions not touch him, there was also no wound on him (Dan. 6).

When the Jews wanted to push Jesus Christ down the cliff, the Lord turned and walked through them and passed, and they could not touch Him. An angel of the Lord came into the prison where Peter was being held and delivered him.

Paul and Silas were also delivered when they prayed and sang praises to the Lord their God. God delivered Paul from shipwreck so that he did not die through it.

Even now, the Christian who is obedient to God, who is holy, prayerful, full of the Holy Spirit, full of faith, and who is sensitive to the Leading of the Holy Spirit, is untouchable.

Neither the devil nor man can destroy him. He is above destruction; it is only by persecution, for the Sake of Jesus Christ, that he himself can decide to lay down his life for the Cause of Christ.

Witches and wizards are so afraid of that Christian that they tremble because of him. The Precious Blood of Jesus Christ protects us and speaks good things that work for our good. Dare to be untouchable!

Don't keep the things that belong to the devil with you, so that they will not attract the devil and his works to you. Don't live his life, so that you will not attract his presence into your life or suffer the same thing(s) God has apportioned for him!

Using contaminated things will invite the devil into your life. If you bring an accursed thing to your house, God will count your house as accursed and you will not stand before your enemies (Josh. 7:10-13). That God might have had mercy on you this far does not mean that it will always be like that. Remove the accursed thing before the devil destroys you.

That is the danger the people that carry chaplets and moulded things they call Jesus' and Mary's structures have fallen into. God said that you must not make for yourself a carved image of anything or anybody, and you shall not bow down to them (Exo. 20:4-5). That is idolatry!

Using things dedicated to the devil will contaminate you and bring heavy loss into your life. You girls and ladies that use another person's dress, powder, shoe, etc can get initiated into secret societies, especially the mermaid kingdom, by that simple act. Many of the people you see are not what they pose to be, even inside the church.

The devil walks around the clock. Many focus their minds on 12:00 a.m., 3:00 a.m., etc as when the devil will attack them; and they prepare to backfire at those times.

Well, inasmuch as there are times of concentrated demonic works, know that the devil does not sleep.

Many times, just spending enough time with God will neutralize demonic works programmed against you, even without having prayed specifically against them. Yes, you will need to destroy the works of the devil, but don't give the devil three hours while you give God ten minutes.

As a matter of fact, devil's power is nothing before God's Power. If you spend two or three hours with God, only five minutes' declaration after that can neutralize all the works of the devil against you. But many fear satan, demons, and witches more than they fear God. Sorry!

SECRETS TO SUCCESSFUL MINISTRY

Questions for Discussion:

1. What does ministry mean?
2. How should we see or take our ministries?
3. What does it mean to be successful in the ministry?
4. How can we be successful in ministry?

We are surrounded by a great cloud of witnesses, those who had run this race before us. They succeeded and made God happy. We cannot fail God, because that will not be good at all.

If the people that went before us succeeded, we also can succeed; the God that enabled them is our God, and He cannot fail. He is all-powerful, and the host of Heaven is on our side.

The secret of successful ministry is obedience. You can't obey God fully and not be successful in ministry. But obedience presupposes foreknowledge of what to do. We know what to do in our Christian walk, in ministry, and in our present life by the Word of God and the Leading or Prompting of the Spirit of God.

Therefore, the secret of successful ministry is the Word of God and the Spirit of God. Actually, the Spirit of God inspired the writing of the Word of God, the Bible, and He also explains the Word to us, and brings it to our remembrance when we need it.

If you want to be successful (in God's Sight) in ministry, then you must make up your mind to obey God absolutely, no matter the cost or sacrifice. Whatever you may sacrifice for God and His Work, He is able to give it back to you many folds.

God did not call us to serve Him in vain. He will reward us very abundantly, both in this life, and in the life which is to come. Don't allow the devil deceive you with the temporal things of this world.

The Word of God tells us the Mind of God. The Word of God is forever settled in Heaven (Psa. 119:89). As a minister, the Word admonishes that you study the Bible to show yourself approved to God a workman that needs not to be ashamed, rightly dividing the Word of Truth.

To divide the Word of Truth the right way is to put every Word where it is supposed to be, and to compare Scripture with Scripture. It is to understand the Word of God clearly.

The devil misapplied the Scripture when he quoted ninety-first chapter of Psalm to Jesus Christ. Doing what the devil quoted would have amounted to testing God; but he quoted the Bible you carry.

In these days when occult men and agents of darkness carry Bible and call Jesus, you require a clear understanding of the Scripture so that you will not be led astray by fellow preachers. If you are led astray, you will also lead the people following you astray. If you lead them astray, God will hold you responsible.

Take heed to yourself and the Doctrine (the correct Doctrine); continue in them, for in doing this you will save both yourself and them that hear you (1 Tim. 4:16).

A demon may even speak to you audibly in the Name of (as if it is) the Holy Spirit, but with the Word, you can distinguish the Voice of the Holy Spirit from the voices of devils and manipulators. Let the Word of God dwell in you richly in all wisdom (Col. 3:16).

When you are full of the Word of God, no trial, scandal, or persecution will weigh you down; for the Word will give you strength and direction.

As said earlier, you need the Holy Spirit to function effectively in the ministry. Without the Holy Spirit you are a failure. It is not by power, nor by might, but by the Holy Spirit of the Living God (Zech. 4:6).

Jesus Christ never intended to leave us comfortless and helpless in life and ministry. That is why He sent the Holy Spirit to us after He left for Heaven. The Holy Spirit is our Comforter, Helper, Counselor, Intercessor, Advocate, Strengthener, and Standby. He is the Manifester of God's Power.

The Holy Spirit reveals Jesus Christ to us. He teaches us the Word and Will of God. He reminds us of what we had known before. The Holy Spirit reveals what is to come to us.

He helps our weaknesses; in prayer, the Spirit makes intercession for us with groanings that cannot be uttered (or uttered in an articulate speech), of which speaking in tongues is among.

Jesus Christ, after He was filled with the Holy Spirit, was led by the Spirit into the wilderness, and after being tempted by the devil (He ate nothing in those days), He returned in the Power of the Holy Ghost.

The Holy Spirit had anointed Him with the power He required to be fruitful and productive in His Ministry. You can't function any other way, except you want people to either neglect you or clap hands for you when God is not clapping for you.

Without the anointing, people will neglect your ministry, except you are keeping them with something else like traditions of men or demonic powers. I know some go to church to hear the Word of God for them, but you need the anointing to preach or teach effectively or more effectively.

If you are not prayerful, you can't be as effective in ministry as God wants you to be. Some ministers were very prayerful in the early years of their ministries, but when their ministries expanded and grew, they became too busy that they don't spend enough time with God in prayer again.

To maintain a strong anointing, you must be prayerful. No wonder the Word tells us to continue earnestly in prayer (Col. 4:2). Pray without ceasing. Men ought always to pray and not faint (Lk. 18:1).

Another booster to the ministry is fasting. As a matter of fact, there are levels of the anointing and empowerment by the Spirit of God that you will never reach in your life without fasting.

Of course, I am not saying that you can't be in the ministry without fasting, but why will it take someone a week or two to cast out a demon, while another can cast out same demon in few seconds?

The difference is the anointing. The difference is faith. I am not necessarily saying that someone who doesn't fast to a great extent can't have a larger church or ministry than another who fasts to a great extent.

First, there are other issues a minister should address, both in his life and in the lives of those who follow him, apart from fasting. If you fast long, but live in sin and disobedience, they will hinder your ministry.

Also, if you don't study the Word to increase your knowledge of God and His Word, it will also hinder your ministry, because there are levels of anointing God will not give you if you are a novice. Second, what you may judge as being large or big by human standard may be judged differently by God.

There are different ministries: an intercessor can sustain the ministry of a traveling evangelist, though the intercessor himself may not be well-known.

Holiness will also boost your ministry. All other things being equal, the holier you are, the more God will manifest His Power and Glory through you. There is perfecting or perfection in holiness. To perfect in holiness is to mature in holiness; it is to make your life of holiness steady.

Also, sin can stop the anointing from flowing through you. This is why many started as good ministers, but when they started living in sexual immorality, pride, and covetousness, they lost the anointing, and later went after demonic powers.

Obedience and righteousness will boost your ministry as well. By obedience, I mean doing what God tells you to do. By righteousness, I mean doing the right things at the right time.

If, for instance, you make up your mind to fast for seven days in order to minister to someone, and on the third day God tells you to go and minister to the person, obey God instead of obeying yourself.

He has the power, and the anointing is not your own. As a matter of fact, when you are filled with the Holy Ghost, you have all the potential power you need for life, Godliness, and the ministry.

But even though the potential is there, the Holy Spirit anoints people with different levels of the anointing. Why? There is a level of anointing God can give you at a certain state and that anointing will lead to your destruction: first of all, it can lead to pride, and you know that God hates pride, and will not share His Glory with another.

Secondly, there are levels of the anointing that will make satan mad, and if God gives it to you and you don't live the life of commitment and discipline required for it, satan will kill you. At any time and place, do what God tells you to do, and it will be well with you.

A minister ought to be able to tame his tongue and his emotions. Don't say anything that comes to your mind. Also, don't get depressed so that you will not get discouraged; and don't get too excited that you can't control your conduct.

You should be an example to your followers because they are watching you. Strike the shepherd and the sheep will scatter. There is something you will do and their trust for you will die. You are not a church-member but a leader or an overseer, as a pastor. There are things you can do and the church will scatter in a week.

Also, relate with other good ministers. Don't relate with someone your spirit feels uncomfortable with, except for casual relationships. Don't allow the devil pull you down through your wife or your children.

Show love, compassion, and kindness to those you minister to. Don't only receive: give also, as you are led. If you sow a little to your followers, they will be happy, and when God leads them to give you, they will be more sensitive to the Voice of God.

Avoid pride, for it destroys the minister. Be humble, patient, and diligent. Persevere, no matter what. The Christian life and the ministry require steadfastness and persistence. Operating in unity will boost your productivity and fruitfulness in the ministry.

Walk worthy of your Christian life and the calling that the Lord has called you! Run the race that the Lord has set before you with determination and commitment. Abstain from all appearances of evil.

Don't be lazy in the work that the Lord has committed to your trust. Avoid idleness, but commit your time to the Lord's Service and be dedicated to seeing that the Lord's Work does not suffer in your hand.

Don't sleep, don't slumber in the ministry that the Lord has committed to your trust. Be zealous for the work or task the Lord has committed into your hand. Expect persecutions and sufferings in the course of the ministerial work.

Beware of covetousness and love of money. Also, beware of women: avoid lust, fornication, and adultery. Always remember your reward in Heaven, for that will give you the zeal, passion, and endurance you require for this work. Don't be earthly minded but heavenly minded.

THE FRUIT OF THE SPIRIT

Questions for Discussion:

1. What is the Fruit of the Spirit?
2. Who brings forth or manifests the Fruit of the Spirit?
3. To what extent should we manifest the Fruit of the Spirit?

The Fruit of the Spirit is in all goodness, righteousness, and truth. What the spirit of man produces by the Holy Spirit's Indwelling is in all that have to do with goodness, righteousness, and truth (Eph. 5:9).

When a sinner repents and gives his heart to the Lord Jesus Christ, confessing Him as his Saviour, the Holy Spirit of the Living God regenerates, recreates, and makes new that person's spirit. If any man is in Christ, he is a new creature (new creation); old things have passed away, and all things have become new (2 Cor. 5:17).

It is the spirit of man that is born again or recreated. Man is a tripartite being who is a spirit, has a soul, and lives in a body. Your soul which is the seat of your thinking, reasoning, and emotions, is not born again but is saved or restored by the renewing of your mind with the Word of God so that you begin to think God's Way.

Then you need to present your body and its members a living sacrifice to God, holy and acceptable to Him. Present your body and its members as instruments of obedience to holiness and righteousness (Rom. 12:1-2; Rom. 6:13,19).

The human spirit of a Christian wants to please God, but his body may still desire some things that displease God. Your mind is the point of decision where you decide whether to obey your spirit or your flesh.

If your mind has been renewed by the Word of God, it will agree with your spirit to please God. Apostle Paul said he beat his body and brought it to subjection.

It was his spirit, his inward man that controlled his body, because his mind took side with his spirit. To be spiritually minded is life, but to be carnally or fleshly minded is death. The carnal mind is enmity with God, for it is not subject to God's Commandments, and can never be subject to them.

This is why those that are in the flesh cannot please God. But you are not in the flesh (Rom. 8:6-9). Get rid of the works of the flesh out of your life. As Christians, we are good trees; and good trees are supposed to bear good fruits.

The Presence of the Holy Spirit in the human spirit enables the human spirit to produce, among other things: love, joy, peace, longsuffering, kindness, goodness, faithfulness, gentleness, self-control. Against such there is no Law (Gal. 5:22-23).

Love makes you obey God, no matter the cost, and gets you to do to others as you would have them do to you (as it will please you that they do to you, not as they will do to you). Joy makes you happy and to take pleasure in the Lord your God. No matter what may be surrounding you, you have joy in the Holy Spirit.

Peace will make you calm, removing worry and fear from you, no matter how harsh the external situations or circumstances may be. Longsuffering will make you patient in your Christian race, and to wait patiently for God's Time and Intervention. He that endures to the end will receive the promise; the same will be saved.

Kindness will make you say or do things that show you care about other people and want to help them or make them happy; you will have a compassionate feeling for people.

Goodness is the quality of being good. Being good will make you profitable and of advantage to others. Goodness has to do with actions or behaviours that are morally right or that follow the Christian Principles. Do not be weary in doing good, for in due time, you will reap your reward if you do not give up (Gal. 6:9).

Faithfulness will make you loyal and trustworthy. Integrity and honesty must be part of you. Gentleness will make you kind and careful in your character or behaviour and not at all violent or unpleasant. Self-control is the ability to behave calmly and sensibly, even when you feel very excited, angry, sad, etc.

Do not walk as the rest of the unbelievers walk, in the futility of their mind, having their understanding darkened, being alienated from the Life of God, because of the ignorance that is in them, because of blindness of their heart; who being past feeling, have given themselves over to lewdness, to work all uncleanness with greediness.

But you have not so learned Christ, if indeed you have heard Him and have been taught by Him, as the truth is in Jesus Christ.

Put off, concerning your former conduct, the old man which grows corrupt according to the deceitful lusts, and be renewed in the spirit of your mind; and put on the new man which was created according to God, in true righteousness and holiness.

Let no corrupt word proceed out of your mouth, but what is good for necessary edification, that it may impart grace to the hearers. Let all bitterness, wrath, anger, clamour, and evil-speaking be put away from you, with all malice. Be tenderhearted and forgive others as God forgave you.

Be imitators of God, as Christians: and walk in love, as Christ also has loved us and gave Himself for us. But fornication and all uncleanness or covetousness, let it not even be named among you, as is fitting for Saints; neither filthiness, nor foolish talking, nor coarse jesting, which are not fitting, but rather giving of thanks.

For this you know, that no fornicator, unclean person, nor covetous man, who is an idolater, has any inheritance in the Kingdom of Christ and of God.

Walk as children of light, finding out what is acceptable to the Lord. And have no fellowship with the unfruitful works of darkness, but rather expose them.

See then that you walk circumspectly, not as fools but as wise, redeeming the time because the days are evil. Submit to one another in the fear of God (Eph. 4 & 5). Walk in the Spirit, and you shall not fulfil the lust of the flesh.

If you are led by the Spirit, you are not under the Law. Those who are Christ's have crucified the flesh with its passions and desires. Let us not become conceited, provoking one another, envying one another.

Let your love abound more and more in knowledge and all discernment; approve the things that are excellent, and be sincere and without offence till the Day of Christ, and be filled with the fruits of righteousness which are by Jesus Christ (Phil. 1:9-11).

Be like-minded with the true brethren, having the same love, being of one accord, of one mind. Let nothing be done through selfish ambition or conceit, but in lowliness of mind, let each esteem others better than himself. Let each of you look out not only for his own interest, but also for the interest of others (Phil. 2:2-16).

Work out your own salvation with fear and trembling; for it is God Who works in you both to will and to do for His Good Pleasure.

Do all things without complaining and disputing, that you may become blameless and harmless, children of God without fault in the midst of a crooked and perverse generation, among whom you shine as lights in the world, holding fast the Word of Life.

Be anxious for nothing. Rejoice in the Lord always. Let your gentleness be known to all men. The Lord is at hand.

Whatever things are true, whatever things are noble, whatever things are just, whatever things are pure, whatever things are lovely, whatever things are of good report, if there is any virtue, and if there is anything praiseworthy, meditate on those things (Phil. 4:4-8).

The Foundation of God stands, having this seal: "The Lord knows those who are His," and "Let everyone who names the Name of Christ depart from iniquity." Flee youthful lusts; but pursue righteousness, faith, love, and peace with those who call on the Lord out of a pure heart.

In a great house there are not only vessels of gold and silver, but also of wood and clay, some for honour and some for dishonour. Therefore, if anyone cleanses himself from the later, he will be a vessel for honour, sanctified and useful for the Master, prepared for every good work.

Avoid foolish and ignorant disputes, knowing that they generate strife. And a Servant of the Lord must not quarrel, but be gentle to all, able to teach, patient (2 Tim. 2:19-24).

Whoever commits sin also commits lawlessness, and sin is lawlessness. Whoever abides in Him does not sin. Whoever sins has neither seen Him nor known Him. Let no one deceive you. He who practices righteousness is righteous, just as He is righteous.

He who sins is of the devil. Whoever has been Born of God does not sin, for His Seed remains in him, and he cannot sin, because he is Born of God. In this the children of God and the children of the devil are manifest: whoever does not practice righteousness is not of God, nor is he who does not love his brother (1 Jn 3:3-10).

Produce the Fruit of the Spirit in abundance! You have the ability, by the Holy Spirit to do so. Believers are to be like Christ (Christian); they are to be like God (Godly). Ask yourself, in every situation, what Jesus Christ would have done or what God would have you do in that same situation.

THE CHRISTIAN MARRIAGE AND HOME

Questions for Discussion:

1. What is the Christian home?
2. How should the members of the home relate with one another?
3. Who is the head of the Christian family?
4. What are the duties of the husband?
5. What are the responsibilities of the wife?
6. What are obligations of the children?

The Christian marriage and home ought to be different from the marriages and homes of non-Christians. The Christian marriage and home should serve as a pattern and a model to show the people of the world what marriage and home should be.

A good marriage will lead to a good home, and a good home is a product of following the Word of God and His Spirit. Marriage is based on love, faith, and obedience, and when these virtues are abundant in any home, joy and peace will abound.

Marriage is honourable among all, and the bed undefiled; but fornicators and adulterers God will judge (Heb. 13:4). God has a pattern for the Christian home, and He has shown us how each member of the family should relate with one another.

However, a look into many Christian homes (I mean homes of born-again Believers) shows that they lag behind what God expects from them; this displeases God and makes the devil happy.

The devil fights to thwart God's Purpose on earth, but Christians have been delivered from his power and authority. Even though we have the right and power of children of God, yet the devil will have a place in our lives if we let him.

And the Word has said that we should give no place to the devil (Eph. 4:27). Therefore, submit to God. Resist the devil and he will flee from you. Draw near to God and He will draw near to you.

Cleanse your hands, you sinners; and purify your hearts, you double-minded. Lament and mourn and weep! Let your laughter be turned to mourning and your joy to gloom. Humble yourselves in the Sight of God and He will lift you up (Jas 4:7-10).

Be sober; be vigilant; because your adversary the devil walks about like a roaring lion, seeking whom he may devour. Resist him, steadfast in the faith, knowing that the same sufferings are experienced by your Brotherhood in the world.

Cast all your cares upon Him, for He cares for you (1 Pet. 5:7-9). Don't carry your burdens, but give them to the Lord. And when you have given them to Him, don't take them back from Him.

The Lord Jesus Christ tells us to watch and pray so that we will not enter into temptation, because even though the spirit is willing, yet the flesh is weak. If you pray and don't watch, you will still fall into temptation; and if you watch and don't pray, the same thing will apply.

Many of the problems we see in Christian homes are as a result of the members not being watchful and prayerful. The spirit-realm controls the physical realm, and some don't even know it.

Many of the misbehaviours you notice in your husband, wife, or children are not just a product of the flesh, but a direct attack against you by the devil and his forces. Therefore, if you don't know the source of the problem, you may live your life fighting physically and you will achieve no true success.

Of course, there is a room for physical discipline, and there is no need for laws and commandments if there are no punishments and rewards.

Let every soul be subject to the governing authorities. For there is no authority except from God, and the authorities that exist are appointed by God.

Therefore whoever resists the authority resists the Ordinance of God, and those who resist will bring judgment on themselves. For rulers are not a terror to good work, but to evil. Do you want to be unafraid of the authority? Do what is good, and you will have praise from the same. He is God's minister to you for good.

But if you do evil, be afraid; for he does not bear the sword in vain; for he is God's minister, an avenger to execute wrath on him who practices evil. Therefore you must be subject, not only because of wrath but also for conscience sake (Rom. 13:1-5).

For because of this you also pay taxes, for they are God's ministers attending continually to this very thing. Render therefore to all their due: taxes to whom taxes are due, customs to whom customs, fear to whom fear, honour to whom honour.

Owe no one anything except to love another; for he who loves another has fulfilled the Law (Rom. 13:6-8).

Therefore submit yourself to every ordinance of man (not to talk of Ordinances of God) for the Lord's Sake, whether to the king as supreme, or to governors, as to those who are sent by him for the punishment of evildoers and for the praise of those who do good.

As free, yet, not using your liberty as a cloak for vice, but as Bondservants of God. Honour all people: love the Brotherhood. Fear God. Honour the king. Servants, be submissive to your masters with all fear, not only to the good and gentle, but also to the harsh (1 Pet. 2:13-20).

For this is commendable: if because of conscience toward God, one endures grief, suffering wrongfully. For what credit is it if when you are beaten for your faults you take it patiently?

But when you do well and suffer, if you take it patiently, this is commendable before God. But let none of you suffer as a murderer (or as the disobedient); a thief, an evildoer, or as a busybody in other people's matters.

Yet if anyone suffers as a Christian, let him (or her) not be ashamed, but let him glorify God in this matter (1 Pet. 4:15-16).

Those who are sinning, rebuke in the presence of all, that the rest also may fear (1 Tim. 5:20). Apostle Paul told Pastor Timothy this as a way to govern his church or churches.

Brother and sister, do not despise the Chastening of the Lord (or of anyone that the Lord has given authority over you), nor be discouraged when you are rebuked by Him: for whom the Lord loves He chastens, and scourges (punishes or disciplines) every son whom He receives.

If you endure chastening, God deals with you as with sons; for what son is there whom a father does not chasten? But if you are without chastening, of which all have become partakers, then you are illegitimate and not sons.

Be in subjection to the Father of spirits and live. God chastens us for our profit, that we may be partakers of His Holiness.

Now, no chastening seems to be joyful for the present but painful; nevertheless, afterward it yields the peaceable fruit of righteousness to those who have been trained by it (Heb. 12:5-11).

Those things are applicable to husbands, pastors, and rulers. Those things are applicable to wives, children, church-members, and the country citizens.

But there are much more to this: whatever you do to your subjects or those you have authority over, should be out of love and maintenance of order, and never out of bitterness, hatred, or unforgiveness.

The Bible tells us not to lord it over the Lord's Heritage (or those entrusted to you) (1 Pet. 5:3). But you must learn to take your stand and do the right things.

Many husbands refuse to exercise authority over their homes. The result is disorder in the home. Sometimes, you will see pastor's children living ungodly lives because of lack of discipline in the home.

Train up the child in the way he should go, and when he is old, he will not depart from it (Prov. 22:6). He who spares his rod hates his son, but he who loves him disciplines him promptly (Prov. 13:24).

Husbands must love their wives as their own bodies. Wives on the other hand, must not become stumbling blocks to their husbands, by insulting and offensive words, because, even though many of them will not slap you, yet you make them die on the inside and get weak inwardly to do God's Assignments for them.

Children, obey your parents in the Lord, for this is right. Honour your father and mother. Fathers, do not provoke your children to wrath, but bring them up in the Training and Admonition of the Lord (Eph. 6:1-4).

Let each husband so love his own wife as himself, and let the wife see that she respects her husband (Eph. 5:33). Wives, submit to your own husbands as is fitting in the Lord. Husbands, love your wives and do not be bitter towards them.

Children, obey your parents in all things, for this is well-pleasing to the Lord (Col. 3:18-20).

Wives are to submit to their husbands, contrary to their own wills. Many wives pray and fast concerning their husbands, when their problem is inadequate submission. Obedience is better than sacrifice.

Wives, be submissive to your own husbands and let them observe your chaste conduct accompanied by fear (1 Pet. 3:1-7). Husbands, dwell with them in knowledge and understanding, giving honour to the wife as to the weaker vessel.

Husbands, learn to say, "I am sorry" to your wives; if you don't kneel down for your wife, who will you kneel down for? Many wives fear their bosses at office more than their husbands: they will not disobey their bosses, but they disobey their husbands easily and talk to them anyhow.

I am talking about Believers here. As a husband, pray well and depend on God to direct you on how to manage your family. Before you accept any man or lady for a husband or a wife, take time to pray and wait on God. Don't rush because all that glitters is not gold. There are agents of satan, even in churches.

What about divorce and remarriage? God hates divorce. What God has joined together, let no man or woman put asunder. Forgive your husband or wife of whatever he or she might have done against you, as Christ also forgave you (Eph. 4:32). Divorce has many negative adverse effects both on the husband and on the wife.

Divorce makes the children suffer what they are not supposed to suffer. If you put away your wife or husband, you are enabling the devil trap him or her in adultery, and you will answer to the Lord on the Day of Judgment (Matt. 5:32).

Even when the Bible says that "if she departs, let her remain unmarried or be joined to her husband," we are not to live by alternatives, but by God's Perfect Will. You know that Moses permitted the Israelites to write a certificate of divorce because of the hardness of their hearts (Matt. 19:8-9). Is your heart hardened?

PLEASING GOD

Questions for Discussion:
1. What does it mean to please God?
2. How can we please God?
3. In what areas should our lives be pleasing to God?

The Heartbeat of God is that all men may come to the knowledge of His Son Jesus Christ, and that they obey and fear Him always. This is why we must evangelize to the ends of the world.

To please God should be your goal in life; it should be your highest priority. Why? Because this is the Whole Duty of man, and that is why man was made.

To fear God and keep His Commandments is the Whole Duty of man (Eccl. 12:13-14). To please God is to do those things that make Him happy and proud of you. If you do those things that please God always, He will never leave you, as He never left Jesus Christ (Jn 8:29).

But without faith, it is impossible to please Him, for he who comes to God must believe that He is, and that He is a Rewarder of those that diligently seek Him (Heb. 11:6).

This is to say that if you know that you will gain a lot from pleasing God, it will make you please Him so that, among other things, you will receive the reward. Of course, we have to please God because we love him, and not just because of what we can get from Him.

Jesus Christ had this attitude when the Bible says that Jesus Christ, for the Joy that was set before Him, endured the Cross, despising the shame, and has sat down at the Right Hand of the Throne of God (Heb. 12:2).

Because Jesus Christ humbled Himself and became obedient to the point of death, God also has highly exalted Him and given Him the Name which is above every other name, that at the Name of Jesus Christ every knee should bow, and every tongue confess that Jesus Christ is Lord, to the Glory of God the Father (Phil. 2:8-11).

Can you say, like Apostle Paul, "For me to live is Christ, and to die is gain?" To live for Christ is to surrender your will to His, so that, no matter how difficult His Will may seem to you, you will do it.

When you say that to die is gain, you are saying that you have lived for Christ, and if you die now, you will be ushered into Heaven by the angels of God. My brother, no one who died and went to Hell, or is cast out into the Outer Darkness, gained.

God has not called us to serve Him in vain; there are so many good things we gain by serving God and doing His Will, both in this life and in the life which is to come.

Being conscious of this will make you to do anything, and sacrifice anything (even your life) for the Name of the Lord. Christians do not love their lives to death as Christ also surrendered His (Rev. 12:11).

Another thing that you should be conscious of is that there are punishments associated with disobeying God and displeasing Him, both in this life and in the life which is to come.

Hence, Apostle Paul said that knowing the Terror of God, we persuade men everywhere to repent, for He has appointed one day when He will judge all men by Jesus Christ (2 Cor. 5:11).

It is a fearful thing to fall into the Hands of the Living God Who is a Consuming Fire (Heb. 10:31; Heb. 12:29).

Many don't care about God and His Christ because they don't know what lies ahead of them. If their eyes are opened to see 10% of what they will suffer for ignoring God and His Word, they will run for their lives to save themselves from Him Who can destroy both body and soul in Hell Fire.

Whether you know of it or not, great punishment is coming on you for despising God, for he that dishonours God, God will dishonour him also (1 Sam. 2:30).

If you love the Lord, then keep His Commandments: as a proof that you love Him (Jn 14:15). Love is the Great Commandment: loving God and your fellow human beings.

To please God, you must bear fruits in your life. You must bear the Fruit of the Spirit which is in all goodness, righteousness, and truth (Eph. 5:9-10). The Fruit of the Spirit finds out what pleases the Lord.

The Fruit is love, joy, peace, longsuffering, kindness, goodness, faithfulness, gentleness, self-control. Against such there is no Law (Gal. 5:22-23). You must live the life of holiness and obedience to God.

Another area you must bear fruit is in the area of soulwinning. He who wins souls is wise and shall shine like stars forever. God had only One Son and He made Him a Soulwinner; but many parents will rather have it that their children are doctors, lawyers, engineers, accountants, business directors, and university-professors.

Well, in your own life, you must win souls for the Lord Jesus Christ, for that is why He died. Build your spirit up by the Word, by training, and by prayer, even praying in the Holy Spirit.

Walking by faith pleases God, for the righteous shall live by faith. We walk by faith and not by sight (2 Cor. 5:7). God called Abraham out of his father's place, and he obeyed God and went, not knowing where he was going to, because he believed God and walked by faith.

Thomas told the other apostles that he will never believe that Jesus Christ has risen until he sees Him by himself. That is not faith and it displeases God. Renew your mind with God's Word and live according to the Word.

To please God, you must not love your life to death. The Saints overcame the devil by the Blood of the Lamb and by the Word of their Testimony, and they did not love their lives to the death (Rev. 12:11).

You have not yet resisted to bloodshed striving against sin (Heb. 12:4). If you love any person or your own life more than Jesus Christ, you are not worthy of Him. You must take up your cross daily and follow Him (Lk. 9:23). Find out the Will of God for your life and follow it; don't compete with others.

To please God and make Him proud of you as He was proud of Job, you must not love the world or anything in the world. He who loves the world does not have the Love of the Father in him.

The things that are in the world are: the lust of flesh, the lust of the eyes, and the pride of life. The world will pass away with its entire works, but he who does the Will of God abides forever (1 Jn 2:15-17). What is there in the world that a Christian should envy?

Brethren, you have been called to liberty; only do not use your liberty as an opportunity for the flesh, but through love serve one another. Walk in the Spirit and you shall not fulfill the lust of the flesh.

For the flesh lusts against the Spirit, and the Spirit against the flesh; and these are contrary to one another, so that you do not do the things that you wish. But if you are led by the Spirit, you are not under the Law.

Now, the works of the flesh are evident, which are: adultery, fornication, uncleanness, lewdness, idolatry, sorcery, hatred, contentions, jealousies, outbursts of wrath, selfish ambitions, dissensions, and heresies.

The list continues with: envy, murders, drunkenness, revelries, and the like; of which the Bible declares that those who practice such things will not inherit the Kingdom of God (Gal. 5:13-21).

Let no corrupt word proceed out of your mouth, but what is good for necessary edification, that it may impart grace to the hearers. And do not grieve the Holy Spirit of God, by Whom you were sealed for the Day of Redemption.

Let all bitterness, wrath, anger, clamour, and evil speaking be put away from you, with all malice (Eph. 4:29-32). Crucify your flesh and its desires.

Be kind to one another, tenderhearted, forgiving one another, even as God in Christ forgave you. Therefore be imitators of God as dear children; walk in love.

But fornication and all uncleanness or covetousness, let it not even be named among you, as is fitting for Saints; neither filthiness, nor foolish talking nor coarse jesting, which are not fitting, but rather giving of thanks.

For this you know, that no fornicator, unclean person, nor covetous man, who is an idolater, has any inheritance in the Kingdom of Christ and of God.

Let no one deceive you with empty words, for because of these things the Wrath of God comes upon the sons of disobedience. Therefore do not be partakers with them (Eph. 5:1-7). Set your mind on things Above, not on things on the earth. When Christ Who is our Life appears, then you also will appear with Him in Glory.

Therefore, put to death your members which are on the earth: fornication, uncleanness, passion, evil desire, and covetousness. Put off all these things: anger, wrath, blasphemy, filthy language out of your mouth.

Do not lie to one another, since you have put off the old man with his deeds, and have put on the new man. Put on tender mercies, kindness, humility, meekness, longsuffering, bearing with one another, and forgiving one another.

To please God, you must remove pride, because pride goes before destruction. Be humble always, because God resists the proud, but gives grace to the humble. Learn to praise God always; worship and thank God, for He is worthy of our praise.

The Will of God in Christ Jesus for us is that we bring glory to Him. No matter how bad the surrounding circumstances may look like, praise and worship Him. God seeks those who will worship Him in spirit and in truth.

Renew your mind so that you can think and judge the Way God thinks and judges. If Enoch, Noah, Abraham, Elijah, Elisha, Samuel, Moses, Joshua, Caleb, Jeremiah, Daniel, Jesus Christ, Peter, John, Paul, and others could please God, you too can.

Can the Lord describe you as a burning and shining light as He described John the Baptist? John was described thus because he did what God called him to do effectively; he did not love the world, but lived a separated life.

The period you spent not pleasing God is a wasted period, and the years you spent not pleasing God are wasted years. Remember that there is a Crown of Righteousness to be given to those who please God at the Coming of the Lord.

The Word of God is our reference point to know what pleases Him. Prove all things. Don't walk and live according to your senses and reasoning!

As you please God, you are laying up treasures in Heaven, and nothing can happen to any treasure you store in Heaven. However, strive to endure to the end, so that no one takes your crown and reward.

It is the Lord Who works in you, both to will and to do according to His Will and Good Pleasure. It is not of him who runs, nor of him who wills; however, it is of the Lord who shows mercy. Therefore, be careful to give Him all the glory. You could become nothing without Jesus Christ. Life outside Jesus Christ is a mess.

One may plant, while another may water. But it is the Lord that makes His Work to grow. Therefore, both he who plants and he who waters are nothing; the One that should receive the glory is the Lord that makes His Work (the seed) to grow. And it is Him Who also gives seed to the planter, strength to the one who waters, and life to both of them.

Do not walk, sit, or stand among sinners. This is not to say that you will avoid them completely, for then, you will have to leave this world. Don't be unequally yoked together with unbelievers.

Remember that evil company corrupts good manners. Of course, you must have to preach to them so that they may be saved. Don't be an accomplice to their evil deeds.

Your number one enemy to pleasing God is your flesh, and not the devil, the world, or anything else. Therefore, if you can subdue your flesh and its passions, you will do well in every area. If you do that and discipline yourself, then you are already a champion, because you cannot fail!

The devil has used films to corrupt the world so much. Even some so-called Christian films are not directed by the Word of God and the Spirit of God. You see a lot of nudity in many of those films, and they corrupt your mind. You may call them home-movies, but it makes no difference.

Have you not observed that even when people want to do advertisement of their products, they use seductive pictures to attract people's attention? Some of them don't know what they are doing, but many of them are conscious of what they are doing, because agents of the kingdom of darkness are out to corrupt people's minds as they pass the roads.

Many spend their time in pornographic sites in the internet. Some websites will bring those seductive and destructive pictures to you by 'force' once you log in there. Many spend many hours watching films, but how long do they spend reading their Bibles and praying? Satan has destroyed many children and adults through films and movies.

BEING FRUITFUL AND PRODUCTIVE

Questions for Discussion:

1. What does it mean to be fruitful?
2. What does it mean to be productive?
3. In what areas are we to be fruitful?
4. To what extent should we be fruitful?
5. What is the gain of being fruitful and productive?

God wants us to be fruitful, and to produce the expected results. One area we should be fruitful in is in winning of souls. Jesus Christ is the True Vine and we are the branches. The Father, Who is the Vine-dresser, takes away every branch that does not bear fruit.

However, He prunes the branches that bear fruit, that they may bear more fruit. We are in Jesus Christ, and just as Jesus Christ bore Fruit by getting Followers and pleasing the Father, we too ought to win souls and please God.

Abide in Jesus Christ, and let Him abide in you. As the branch cannot bear fruit of itself, unless it abides in the vine, neither can you, unless you abide in the Lord. He who abides in Him, and He in him, bears much fruit; for without Him, you can do nothing.

Anyone who does not abide in Him is cast out as a branch and is withered and burnt. The Father is glorified when we bear much fruit, so as to confirm that we are Jesus Christ's Disciples.

If we abide in Him and His Words abide in us, we will ask what we desire, and it shall be done for us. If we keep His Commandment, we will abide and remain in His Love, just as He kept His Father's Commandments and abides in His Love.

We are His Friends if we do whatever He commands us. We did not choose Him, but He chose us and appointed us that we should go and bear fruit, and that our fruit should remain, that whatever we ask the Father in His Name He may give us (Jn 15).

For us to be fruitful and productive requires that we have patience, endurance, and longsuffering. Just as different crops and trees take different periods to mature and produce fruits, so is the Christian life and the ministry.

Therefore be patient, brethren, until the Coming of the Lord. See how the farmer waits for the precious fruit of the earth, waiting patiently for it until it receives the early and the latter rain (Jas 5:7).

Jesus Christ says that if we are ashamed of Him and His Word, especially before this sinful and adulterous generation, He Himself will be ashamed of us before His Father (Mk 8:38). If we confess Him before men, He will also confess us before His Heavenly Father and before the holy angels (Matt. 10:32-33).

Those who are wise shall shine like the brightness of the firmament, and those who turn many to righteousness like the stars forever and ever (Dan. 12:3). We must strive to win souls for the Lord no matter the cost.

Giving all diligence, add to your faith virtue, to virtue knowledge, to knowledge self-control, to self-control perseverance, to perseverance Godliness, to Godliness brotherly kindness, and to brotherly kindness love.

For if these things are in you and abound, you will be neither barren nor unfruitful in the knowledge of our Lord Jesus Christ. For he who lacks these things is short-sighted, even to blindness, and has forgotten that he was cleansed from his old sins.

Therefore, brethren, be even more diligent to make your call and election sure; for if you do these things, you will never stumble; for so you will be abundantly allowed to enter the Kingdom of Christ (2 Pet. 1:5-11).

Apostle Paul, writing to the Galatians, spoke of what Apostle Peter said in another way. The Book of Galatians speaks of what the Bible translators translated as the Fruit of the Spirit (Gal. 5:22), even though it is actually 'the fruit of the spirit (the human spirit).'

It is talking about what the recreated human spirit (by the Help of the Holy Spirit) produces. The fruit of the human spirit by the Holy Spirit is love, joy, peace, longsuffering, kindness, goodness, faithfulness, gentleness, self-control. Against such there is no Law (Gal. 5:22-23).

As you were once darkness, but now you are light in the Lord, walk as children of light (for the Fruit of the Spirit is in all goodness, righteousness, and truth), finding out what is acceptable to the Lord.

And have no fellowship with the unfruitful works of darkness, but rather expose them (Eph. 5:8-11). And those who are Christ's have crucified the flesh with its passions and desires. If we live in the Spirit, let us also walk in the Spirit (Gal. 5:24-25).

Father Abraham started as one person; God called him and as he believed God and obeyed Him, God multiplied him into a multitude as innumerable as the stars and as uncountable as the sand by the sea-shore (Heb. 11:12).

And today we are part of the offspring of Abraham through Jesus Christ. God will make great things out of anyone who trusts Him and does His Will.

Jesus Christ came alone, He followed God's Plan for His Life, and before He left for Heaven, He had got the twelve apostles and many other strong Disciples. Today, we are part of the Believers in Him; we are part of His Body (the Church) and the number of the sons brought to glory increases day by day.

This was made possible because He laid down His Life for the salvation of many. When you sacrifice for the Lord, and deny your body of its pleasures (as the Spirit leads), you can't be an ordinary person.

The early apostles and Disciples multiplied greatly, and that was God's Will for them. Apostle Peter's first preaching brought about three thousand souls to the Lord Jesus Christ. Another preaching brought more souls (in thousands) to repentance (Acts 2:41; Acts 4:4).

The story became the same as the days went by and the number of the Disciples multiplied greatly in Jerusalem and many of the priests were obedient to the faith (Acts 6: 7). Even when serious persecutions came, the Disciples preached wherever they went.

You must preach the Word (the Gospel), in season and out of season; reprove, rebuke, exhort with all longsuffering and Doctrine (2 Tim. 4:2). If you are ashamed of Jesus Christ and His Gospel, He will also be ashamed of you.

If you confess Him before men, He also will confess you before His Father and before the holy angels (Lk. 9:26). God will reward you abundantly if you win souls, because Jesus Christ gave up His Life for that purpose.

In every area of your life, be fruitful and productive. Be fruitful and productive: spirit, soul, and body. God told Adam to be fruitful and multiply and replenish the earth.

That is still His Will for today: in finance, in health, in academics, in job, in ministry. Once you have found out God's Perfect Will for your life, work towards it and show God that He has not invested in you in vain, and He will be glad.

Fight the good fight of faith, lay hold on Eternal Life. Flee evil things and pursue righteousness, Godliness, faith, love, patience, gentleness (1 Tim. 6:11-12).

Let no one despise you, but be an example to the Believers in word, in conduct, in love, in spirit, in faith, in purity. Do not neglect the gift that is in you. Meditate on these things; give yourself entirely to them, that your progress may be evident to all.

Take heed to yourself and to the Doctrine. Continue in them, for in doing this, you will save both yourself and those who hear you (1 Tim. 4:12-16).

You must discipline your body and bring it to subjection in order to obey God and fulfil His Purpose for your life. Run so as to obtain: if people who take part in games train hard to excel, how much more you whose engagement and investment is eternal?

Love not the world or anything in the world. Without holiness, no eye shall see the Lord (Heb. 12:14). God is of a Purer Eyes than to behold iniquity (Habk. 1:13); and only the pure in heart shall see Him.

If God turned His Face away from Jesus Christ, as He hung on the Cross carrying the sins of the whole world, who are you that God will compromise His Standards? Be holy for the Lord is holy.

And if you call on the Father, Who without partiality judges according to each one's work, conduct yourselves throughout the time of your stay here in fear (1 Pet. 1:16-17). Work out your salvation with fear and trembling, for God is no respecter of persons.

Daniel and his friends feared God and God promoted them and delivered them. The Eyes of the Lord run to and fro the face of the earth to show Himself strong on behalf of anyone, who will believe Him, obey Him and cooperate with Him. With God, nothing shall be impossible.

The Church is marching on and the gates of Hades shall not prevail against it. The Letters that the Lord wrote to the seven Churches tell us what He expects from us, how some of us are, and the reward He has for us.

Break up your fallow ground, and do not sow among thorns. Stop procrastination and do what you are supposed to do now. Don't wait for tomorrow, for you don't know what tomorrow will bring forth.

THE POWER OF FAITH

Questions for Discussion:

1. What is faith?
2. Can you please God without faith?
3. How does faith come?
4. To what level should we increase our faith to?

Faith makes it possible for someone to please God. Why? Because whoever comes to God must believe that He is and that He rewards those who diligently seek Him (Heb. 11:6). Faith comes by hearing, and hearing by the Word of God (Rom. 10:17).

Faith is: believing that God can neither lie nor disappoint you. God cannot fail to fulfill His Word. Instead of His Word not to come to pass, heaven and earth shall pass away (Matt. 24:35).

Faith is: "I will do this because God said I should do it." It is: "I will not do this because God said that I should avoid it." As a matter of fact, faith is comprehensive and embraces many things.

The study of the eleventh chapter of the Book of the Hebrews will confirm this to you. Faith is not just about receiving healings, prosperity, breakthroughs, miracles, and such things. In fact, faith is obedience to the Word of God.

Faith will make you offer a more excellent sacrifice. Your work of faith gives you certified righteousness. Faith will make you please God against all odds. Pleasing God will make you rapturable.

Believing that God exists and that He rewards diligence and faithfulness will make you please Him. Faith will make you give heed to Godly fear and Godly fear leads to righteous living.

Faith will make you obey God no matter how difficult. God can tell you to do a difficult thing, but not an impossible thing. Faith will make you not to hold on to the things of this world.

Faith will make you have confidence in God, and you will wait patiently for the fulfillment of God's Promises. Faith will make you ride above natural laws; faith will give you a tangible miracle. Faith is judging God faithful; it is believing that God cannot lie and He is able to fulfil His Word without fail.

Believing God's Word will expand and multiply you beyond your imagination and expectation. Faith is being sure of God's Promises, even though you see it afar off. It is better to die believing God than to die a sinner and an unbeliever.

Faith is comprehensive and touches all aspects of the Word of God. No part of the Word of God can be separated from faith, for faith comes by the Word of God.

Faith involves believing the Word of God, embracing it, and confessing the Word of God. When you go for the Word of God and give enough time to it, your faith will grow exceedingly. Now faith is the substance of things hoped for, the evidence of things not seen.

Having faith in God makes you see yourself as a pilgrim and a stranger in this world. Faith seeks a Homeland for it is not foolish. The end of faith (real faith) is Heaven. You cannot separate faith from repentance and holiness.

Being mindful of your past and the things of this world can make you go back (withdraw from the faith-life). The things you may be proud of may be the devil offering you an opportunity to go back from God.

Heavenly Country is a better country and cannot be comparable to anything in this life, anything in this world. God is not ashamed to be called your God as you live by faith. He has prepared very good things for you.

Faith will make you offer up your most treasured asset, even your life, for God's Sake. Whatever you may give up for God, God will give it back to you many folds and in better ways.

Faith will make you bless yourself and declare good things ahead of time. Faith will make you declare to others the things that God has spoken, and you will plan and work towards them.

Faith will make you not to fear men. You will fear and honour God, risking even your life for Him instead of following men. Faith will make you refuse to be regarded higher, against God's Plan for your life.

You will give up fame for the Cause of Jesus Christ. Faith will make you choose to suffer affliction with God's people and for God's Sake.

Faith will open your eyes to the temporal and temporary nature of the things of this world. Unbelief and faithlessness will blind your eyes to everlasting and eternal realities.

Faith will open and sharpen your understanding and make you put first things first. Walking by faith will remove the authority of men from you, and no matter what, you will do the Bidding of God, for your faith will give you protection; and protection is in obedience.

You will do what men cannot do and you will live supernaturally. Faith will give you victory over your enemies, and you will see breakthroughs in tough matters. Your work of faith will save you, even when you don't deserve it.

There is so much to faith that time and space will not permit to expose all about it and to declare what the heroes of faith have done. For by faith the elders obtained a good testimony.

By faith we understand that the worlds were framed by the Word of God, so that the things which are seen were not made of things which are visible. The spirit-realm controls the physical realm; the things which happen in the physical realm have been settled in the spirit-realm, directly or indirectly.

Instead of quarreling with or fighting someone, you may just have to deal with the spirit behind him or her, which uses him or her to carry out its wishes. The enemy is behind the scene.

Faith subdues kingdoms. Faith works righteousness; it obtains God's Promises. Faith stops the mouth of lions and the devourers. Faith quenches the violence of fire, trials, and persecutions.

It will cause you to escape the edge of the sword and other weapons, even atomic, hydrogen, and cobalt bombs. Faith will make you valiant in battle and turn to flight the armies of the enemies. Faith will cause the dead to come back to life.

Faith will make you pass through persecutions, even death because you have hope for the Resurrection and the reward. Faith will make you live a separated and an abnormal life for the Sake of Jesus Christ.

Faith will make you not to regard this world and its pleasures. You can receive a good report or testimony and still not obtain a particular promise, even your desire. Faith leads to perfection.

There are great faith and small faith (Matt. 8:10); feigned faith and unfeigned faith (1 Tim. 1:5, 2 Tim. 1:5); weak faith and strong faith (Rom. 4:17-20; Rom. 14:1); Abrahamic faith and Thomas' faith (Jn 20:19-29); wrecked faith and unwrecked faith (1 Tim. 1:19).

But, however small your faith may be, if there is no doubt in your heart, you can remove mountains (Matt. 17:20). Feigned faith is a pretending faith, while unfeigned faith is a sincere faith.

Abraham was not weak in faith but strong in faith, and did not consider his own body, already dead by human standards. He did not waver at the Promise of God through unbelief, but was strengthened in faith, giving glory to God, being fully convinced that what He had promised He was also able to perform.

He believed in hope contrary to hope, in the Presence of Him Whom he believed God, Who gives life to the dead and calls those things which do not exist as though they did.

Abrahamic faith does not see and yet believes, while the Thomas' type sees before believing. Believe that the Lord shall supply all your needs, according to His Riches in Glory in Christ Jesus, our Lord.

And no matter how the surrounding circumstances may look like, believe that the Lord will supply whatever you need: spiritually, mentally, physically, financially, materially, ministerially, maritally, etc.

Wrecked faith is as a result of backsliding. Faith works by love, and without love, your great and strong faith is nothing (1 Cor. 13:2). Also, faith must be accompanied by works, for without works, faith is dead, as the body without the spirit is dead (Jas. 2:26).

Have faith in God, or rather, have the Faith of God; have the God-kind of faith: the God-kind of faith works by speaking forth into existence those things that do not exist. God calls invisible things by names as though they did exist.

Faith works by speaking and believing; you can speak with your spirit, and you can speak with your mouth. Therefore, be very careful how you speak, and what you speak. Ask, seek, and knock. He who asks receives; he who seeks finds; and to him who knocks the door will be opened to.

Jesus Christ is the Solid Rock. All other grounds are sinking sand. If you have Jesus Christ, your faith should be very strong because He can neither lie, fail, nor disappoint. He is the same yesterday, today, and forever.

POWER OVER ALL DEVILS AND EVIL

Questions for Discussion:

1. Who are satan, fallen angels, demons, and their human agents?
2. Do they have power over us?
3. Do we have power over them?
4. How can we give them access into our lives?

When the Lord Jesus Christ rose up from the dead, He declared that all power in Heaven and on earth has been given to Him. Now, Jesus Christ is God, and has never lost power as God (though He emptied Himself of His Divine Power before coming to the earth).

God is Lord over the entire universe, including the earth, whether it is physical, spiritual, or any other realm. Even the devil is nothing before God, and cannot do anything without God's Permission.

When God was to send satan out of Heaven, He did not need to fight with the devil because that would have amounted to giving much credit to the devil: He only sent Archangel Michael to do the job.

All the things that the devil is doing today and all his plans, boastings, and pride are because God allowed him (God permitted him, even though He never commissioned him). When his time is up, God will put him into the Lake of Fire which burns with brimstone.

However when you (as a landlord) leases your house to somebody for a period of time, within that period of time, you don't intrude anyhow into the house, except with your tenant's permission.

This is what happened when God created man and gave him dominion over the earth and the things in it. The devil came and tempted Adam (the first man), and because Adam disobeyed God, Adam lost the dominion God gave him to the devil.

It is that dominion, and for the restoration of mankind that the Lord Jesus Christ came. You know, when man sinned, demons, pain, sicknesses, diseases, poverty, and things like them started to have effects on men.

But Jesus Christ triumphed over principalities and powers, and made a public show of them. He said, "Go therefore…." He meant that the restored man, the Church, should go in the power and authority that He collected from the devil (which was originally man's).

However, the devil will continue to operate and rule over people (except the Christians) until Adam's time is over, that is, at the Second Coming of Jesus Christ. This is why the devil is called the god of this world (2 Cor. 4:4).

It is only Christians that have power and authority over the devil. Christ delivered us from the power of darkness and translated us to His Kingdom, and the devil doesn't have power and authority over us.

Therefore, none of us should get entangled in sin and disobedience, so that the devil will not lord it over us. It is not a matter of who has power but who has the legal ground to use the power, because the devil's power is powerless before the Holy Spirit's Power (the Spirit that lives in us).

You will punish every act of disobedience when your obedience is complete (2 Cor. 10:6). A word is enough for the wise.

Some Believers wonder why the devil prevails over them, why they still suffer under him, contrary to the Will of God. I said, 'contrary to the Will of God,' because we will pass through persecutions, trials, tests, and temptations, and the devil is responsible for the persecutions, trials, and temptations.

However, many suffer what they shouldn't have suffered because they broke the hedge around them, and gave the devil and his demons openings.

"Behold I give to you power to tread on serpents and scorpions and over all the power of the enemy, and nothing shall by any means hurt you" (Lk. 10:19).

This is the Word of Jesus Christ the Son of the Living God, Who can neither lie nor fail to perform what He has said. Instead of His Word not to come to pass, heaven and earth shall pass away.

But why do the devil, his demons, and his human agents hurt and harm those who believe in Christ? It is a matter of breaking the defence.

You can let the devil have a place in you by carelessness, disobedience, compromise, unbelief, and sin. And the Word of God tells us to give the devil no place in our lives, even in the lives of our family members (Eph. 4:27).

That is why the Word says, "Believe in the Lord Jesus Christ, and you will be saved, you and your family" (Acts 16:31). You have authority over your family and you can command the devil, in the Name of Jesus Christ, to remove his hands from your family members.

The devil oppresses, obsesses, and possesses people through his demons. Demonic oppression involves afflicting your body with sicknesses, diseases, pains, etc. Demonic obsession involves influencing your mind so that you are pressed to feel or think a particular way. Demonic possession involves their taking over your spirit, soul, and body completely.

We have power over the devil and his works and the weapons of our warfare are not carnal but mighty in God for pulling down of strongholds, casting down arguments and every high thing that exalts itself against the knowledge of God, bringing every thought into captivity to the obedience of Christ (2 Cor. 10:4-5).

We have the power and authority to subdue things and beings that are not subject to God. God anointed Jesus Christ with the Holy Spirit and with power, and He went about doing good and healing all who were oppressed by the devil, for God was with Him (Acts 10:38).

And the Lord tells us that we will do the works that He did; we will do greater works than those He did. The Holy Spirit was sent to us when He went back to Heaven, and the Lord sits at the Right Hand of God, where He lives to make intercession for us. We are not alone!

The Holy Spirit of the Living God, Who lives in us, is our Helper, Advocate, Intercessor, Standby, Comforter, Strengthener, and Counselor. You have overcome because greater is He that is in you than he that is in the world.

The Believers will cast out demons in the Name of Jesus Christ; they will take up serpents and won't be harmed by them; if they drink deadly poison (witchcraft or chemical), it will not hurt them; and they will lay hands on the sick, and they will recover.

When the Lord sent out the twelve, they were empowered to preach the Gospel, heal the sick, cleanse the lepers, raise the dead, and cast out demons (Matt. 10:7-8). We are to do the same.

The Spirit of God that came upon you is not just for speaking in tongues. It is to preach the Good News of the Kingdom of God, to heal the broken-hearted, to proclaim liberty to the captives, and recovery of sight to the blind.

He came upon you to set at liberty those who are oppressed, and to proclaim the Acceptable Year of the Lord (Lk. 4:18-19). You carry the very Power of God!

Christians receive power when the Holy Spirit comes upon them, and they are made witnesses, who by signs and wonders, prove that Jesus Christ is the same yesterday, today, and forever. The anointing breaks every yoke and lifts every burden. The Kingdom of God is not in word but in power.

We ought to be so anointed that we can no more be yoked. We should give ourselves to consistent prayer-life, with self-discipline and self-denial, so that we will move well with the Holy Ghost.

Indeed they shall surely assemble, but not because of God. Whoever assembles against us shall fall for our sake. No weapon that is formed against us shall prosper, and every tongue which rises against us in judgment, we shall condemn.

This is the heritage of the Servants of the Lord, and their righteousness is from Him (Isa. 54:15,17). Live a holy and a righteous life, and no devil nor their works will hurt you! In Christ Jesus, you are secure and protected.

Surely the Lord shall deliver you from the snare of the fowler and from the perilous pestilence. He shall cover you with His Feathers, and under His Wings you shall take refuge; His Truth shall be your shield and buckler.

You shall not be afraid of the terror by night nor of the arrow that flies by day, nor of the pestilence that walks in darkness, nor of the destruction that lays waste at noonday.

A thousand may fall at your side and ten thousand at your right hand, but it shall not come near you. Because you have made the Lord your Refuge, no evil shall befall you, nor shall any plague come near your dwelling; for He shall give His angels Charge over you to keep you in all your ways.

In their hands they shall bear you up, lest you dash your foot against a stone. You shall tread upon the lion and the cobra. He will deliver you and set you on high. When you call on Him, He will answer you. He will be with you in trouble, deliver you, and honour you.

With long life He will satisfy you and show you His Salvation (Psa. 91). You need not fear death, for you cannot die except the Lord permits it.

The Lord has called us to contend with the forces of darkness, and pull down the strongholds of the enemy, the devil.

No matter what you may be going through, there is power to set you free, and that power and authority is available in Jesus Christ and His Holy Spirit. The Lord has sent us to preach deliverance to the captives. These days, seducing spirits and doctrines of devils abound.

The Anointing of God's Spirit on you breaks every yoke of the devil and lifts the burdens of the enemy. Therefore, learn to wait on the Lord to renew your strength and increase the anointing in your life so that you can accomplish what God wants to be accomplished through you.

When the anointing in your life is strong enough, witches and wizards will run away from you. You should walk in the mountain-moving faith.

When you walk that way, no arrow the devil throws at you will succeed. Faith is the shield which protects you from the fiery darts of the enemy. Just as Daniel stayed with the lions without being hurt, you too can stay where the power of the devil is concentrated, and yet nothing will harm you.

Learn to praise God always. Praise puts the enemy to the flight. Prayer is like throwing bomb to the camp of the enemy; they will run for their lives, and many will be destroyed thereby. However, praise brings down God's Presence, and they cannot escape God's Intention; God is fearful in praises.

The walls of Jericho fell down when God's people praised Him. In prayer, God sends angels; but in praises, God comes down to do the work by Himself. When God comes down, which devil will stand?

God will remove sicknesses and diseases from you, so that none of the diseases or sicknesses the enemy may throw at you will get you. But you must be obedient to God; you must keep a close and intimate relationship with God to be covered by Him always.

Don't be afraid while doing what the Lord has called you to do. God calls people and commissions them without leaving them helpless; rather, the Lord commissions us with power. It is the Power and Anointing of the Holy Spirit that will break every shackle, destroy every yoke, and lift every burden.

A HEAVEN TO GAIN AND A HELL TO AVOID

Questions for Discussion:

1. What is Heaven?
2. What is Hell?
3. Which people is Heaven meant for?
4. Which people is Hell meant for?
5. How can we enter Heaven?
6. Is it possible for a Believer to end up in Hell Fire?

Heaven and Hell are real. I know many people don't believe in them. Some believe in literal Heaven but not in literal Hell. Some believe that Heaven and Hell are in this world; what a pity! Many think that a Loving God Who is full of mercy cannot throw someone into Hell Fire.

However, they might have not considered the fact that He is not only a Consuming Fire (Heb. 12:29), but it is also a fearful thing to fall into the Hands of the Living God (Heb. 10:31). God is no respecter of persons. Even though He is full of mercy, He is also the God of Justice. God is a Loving God, Who also is a Consuming Fire.

If God's Word says that there are Heaven and Hell, then they exist. God cannot lie and does not have the ability to deceive. It is the devil that lies and deceives people.

Jesus Christ told His apostles that if there were not many mansions in His Father's House, He would have told them (Jn 14:2). He went to prepare a Place for us and when He is through, He will come back to take us with Him, so that where He is, there we may be also.

Hell was not made for mankind. Hell was made for satan and his fallen angels and demons. Hell was made for them because they rebelled against God. When man disobeyed God and rebelled against Him, he put himself into the same position as them and so was destined for Hell.

It is only Jesus Christ that can save man from Hell. If you want to avoid Hell, then you must accept Jesus Christ and live to please God.

Heaven is a very good place. It is the Abode of God. Everything in Heaven is perfect. There is neither evil, sin, nor pain in Heaven. Our tears will be wiped out in Heaven. No human word can describe the beauty of Heaven.

You must do all you can to be there. It will profit you nothing if you gain the whole world and lose your own soul (Matt. 16:26). There is no devil or demon in Heaven.

Hell, on the other hand, is a very bad place. No human word can express the horror and suffering of Hell. The suffering of Hell cannot be equated to that of this world, except you are going to use an infinite relationship.

The fire of Hell does not quench and the worms of Hell do not die (Mk 9:43-48). In Hell, there is gnashing of teeth; if you enter there, you will thirst and thirst and thirst, and there will be no water to quench your thirst.

The Kingdom Of Heaven is eternal and forever, just as Hell Fire is eternal and forever. Once you enter any of them, there is no turning back. If you enter Heaven, you will spend eternity with God, and if you enter Hell Fire, you will spend eternity with satan.

Actually, God will neither put you into Heaven nor Hell; you are the one who chooses where you will go. Your life on earth and your relationship with Jesus Christ, the Word of God, and the Spirit of God, will determine where you will spend eternity.

The Word of God declares that He will make a New Heaven and a New Earth (Isa. 65:17). The Heaven it is talking about here is not the Third Heaven where God lives and where we will be. There is a first heaven (the sky), and there is the second heaven (the planetary bodies).

The Word says that when the Lord shall come again, the heavens shall pass away with a great noise and the element shall melt with fervent heat; the earth also and the works that are there shall be burned up (2 Pet. 3:10).

Seeing that these things shall be dissolved, what manner of persons ought you to be in all holy conversation and Godliness, looking for and hastening the coming of the Day of the Lord?

We, according to His Promise, look for New Heavens and a New Earth wherein righteousness dwells. Seeing that you look for such things, be diligent that you may be found by Him in peace without spot, and blameless (2 Pet. 3:11-14).

One day is with the Lord as a thousand years, and a thousand years as one day. The Lord is not slack concerning His Promise, as some men count slackness, but is longsuffering towards us, not willing that any should perish but that all should come to repentance.

But the Day of the Lord will come as a thief in the night (2 Pet. 3:8-10). Don't reason within you that the Lord will not come again since He has not come all these while.

Follow peace with all men, and holiness without which no man shall see the Lord (Heb. 12:14). It is only the pure in heart that shall see the Lord (Matt. 5:8). Make up your mind and make every effort to be holy, righteous, obedient, spotless, and blameless.

No impure thing will enter either the Kingdom of Heaven or the New Earth. Sin leads you to Hell Fire. Don't live in sin; you have no reason to serve satan.

Many have been taken to Heaven and to Hell, and they have told us what they saw. We know that their testimonies are true because the Bible says so. Apostle Paul was taken to Heaven, the Third Heaven (2 Cor. 12:2).

Apostle John was taken to both Heaven and Hell (Rev. 19 to 22). It is because of God's Love for us that He shows us things ahead of time, and warns us to labour for Heaven and to avoid Hell. Don't be foolish but understand God's Plans. Apostle John also spoke of a New Heaven and a New Earth (Rev. 21:1).

Do not lay up for yourselves treasures upon the earth, where moth and rust do destroy, and where thieves break through and steal.

But lay up for yourselves treasures in Heaven, where neither moth nor rust do destroy, and where thieves do not break through and steal: for where your treasure is, there will your heart be also (Matt. 6:19-21).

And if either your right eye or your right hand will cause you to sin, pluck it out and cut it off, and cast them off: for it is profitable for thee that one of your members should perish than that your whole body be cast into Hell (Matt. 5:29-30).

Not everyone that calls on the Lord Jesus Christ shall enter the Kingdom of Heaven, but he that does the Will of our Heavenly Father. Many will say to the Lord in that Day, "Lord, Lord, have we not prophesied in Your Name? And in Your Name have cast out devils? And in Your Name done many wonderful works?"

And then will He say to them, "I never knew you: depart from Me, you that work iniquity" (Matt. 7:21-23). Why do you call Him, Lord, Lord, and do not do what He tells you to do? (Lk. 6:46).

The wicked shall be turned into Hell (Psa. 9:17). The way of the adulteress leads to Hell (Prov. 7:27). Because the sinners have increased themselves, Hell has enlarged itself to accommodate them (Isa. 5:14).

Do not fear them who can kill the body but are not able to kill the soul: but rather fear Him Who is able to destroy both soul and body in Hell (Matt. 10:28).

The story (not a parable, because Jesus Christ said, "There was a certain rich man…") of the rich man and Lazarus gives us an insight into the suffering of Hell (Lk. 16:19-31).

God took Enoch and Elijah to Heaven so that they did not see death because they pleased God. God's Presence fills the Heaven and the earth. If your name is written in the Book of Life, in Heaven, rejoice.

Heaven cannot be compared to anything on this earth. If all the gold, the silver, the oil, and whatever there is, are combined together and given to one person, they will not compare to the bliss of Heaven. The gold of Heaven is pure gold.

It is not the Will of God that any soul should perish but that all should come to repentance (2 Pet. 3:9). He would have all men to be saved. However, God will not force anyone: He has set before men good and bad, life and death, Heaven and Hell.

Men choose what they want and God implement them. You cannot run away from God; you cannot hide yourself from Him. Today is the acceptable time, the day of salvation (2 Cor. 6:2).

Don't say that you will change your ways tomorrow, because tomorrow may be too late. Your life is like a vapour that vanishes and a flower that withers easily (Jas 1:11; Jas 4:14). The Mill of God grinds so slowly, but it grinds so small.

Keep on doing good, and don't faint; God will surely reward you at last. He who is unjust, let him be unjust still; he who is filthy, let him be filthy still; he who is righteous, let him be righteous still; he who is holy, let him be holy still.

Behold, the Lord is coming quickly, and His Reward is with Him, to give to everyone according to his work. Are you ready for the Lord's Coming?

Be faithful till death and you can never lose anything. Whatever you may lose in this life, the Lord will replace for you many folds. He who finds his life will lose it, but he who loses his life for the Lord will save it. God knows everything about you, including your works of faith: the things you do for His Name.

THE GOD-APPROVED MINISTER

Questions for Discussion:
1. Who is a minister?
2. What does it mean by a minister being approved by God?
3. How can a minister be approved by God?

The Bible says that it is not he that approves himself that is approved but whom the Lord approves (2 Cor. 10:18). It is not him that men approve that is approved, but whom the Lord approves. Do you know that a group of Christians may approve you, and yet God will not approve you?

This is why you should not seek the praise of men, but the Praise of God. To seek the approval of men is death, but to seek the Approval of God is life. Of course, if you do the right thing, good people will approve you and that is good.

When you please God, He will approve you. Enoch walked with God and pleased Him, and God approved him and took him away that he did not see death (Gen. 5:24; Heb. 11:5). Moses pleased God and received the testimony that he was faithful in all his house (Heb. 3:2).

Joshua and Caleb pleased God, and while the other adults that left Egypt with them died, two of them entered the land of Canaan. Daniel, Shadrach, Meshach and Abed-Nego pleased God when they refused to defile themselves, and God blessed them exceedingly in the land of Babylon.

The Word of God says that we should be diligent (King James Bible says, 'study') to show ourselves approved to God, workmen that need not be ashamed, rightly dividing (that is, correctly handling) the Word of God, the Word of Truth (2 Tim. 2:15).

This means that to be approved, you must be diligent, having made the decision. Approval by God requires sacrifice and self-discipline.

Ask yourself if you know what God wants you to be doing or to do. If you know, are you doing it? Have you done it? If you are doing it, are you doing it (did you do it) the Lord's Way?

Doing what God wants you to do the Lord's Way is what gets you His Total Approval. Don't settle for God's Permissive Will; go for His Perfect Will.

The minister that God will approve must be prayerful. It is said that prayer is the master-key. Jesus Christ prayed well during His Earthly Ministry and that was why He could fulfil God's Assignment for Him. Through prayer, He was able to know God's Will for His Life and was able to do it.

Jesus Christ prayed daily and His ministers must pray daily too. Don't pray well some days, and be prayerless the others. Maintain a consistent prayer-life. I think every minister should spend a minimum of two hours in prayer everyday.

The minister that God will approve should be full of the Word of God. No wonder the Word of God tells us to study to show ourselves approved to God, a workman that needs not be ashamed, rightly dividing the Word of Truth (2 Tim. 2:15).

Let the Word of Christ dwell in you richly in all wisdom (Col. 3:16). It has to dwell in you richly, and not just by manageable measure. Also, it must be in all wisdom: the Word of God says that we should rightly divide the Word of God and compare Scripture with Scripture (1 Cor. 2:13).

Apostle Paul told Timothy to preach the Word, to be instant in season and out of season. Timothy was to reprove, rebuke, exhort with all longsuffering and Doctrine (2 Tim. 4:2).

Timothy was to put the brethren in remembrance of good teaching to be a good minister of Jesus Christ, nourished up in the Words of Faith and of Good Doctrine, which he had attained (1 Tim. 4:6). He was to give attention to reading, to exhortation, to Doctrine (1 Tim. 4:13).

It is the Word that saves, sanctifies, and builds up. To be approved by God, you are to preach the message that works: you are to preach Jesus Christ, and not yourself. The message that works is the preaching and teaching of the Word of God, and not philosophy, psychology, and things of unbelief, doubt, and human wisdom.

If the Lord is going to approve you, you must do what you preach and teach. Don't be like the Pharisees who would say one thing and do the contradictory thing. God hates hypocrisy. Whatever may be hidden now will be brought to light at the Coming of the Lord Jesus Christ.

Ask God to give you the grace to practice what you preach. You have to be an example to the Believers and to your followers (1 Tim. 4:12). Let not God's Name be blasphemed for your sake (Rom. 2:24).

The Lord Jesus Christ tells us that we are to be doing the works that He did, even greater works (Jn 14:12). The Works of Jesus Christ include: preaching, teaching, healing, casting out devils, miracles, signs, and wonders.

Don't be afraid of the devil and his works because you are sitting with Christ at the Right Hand of God (Eph. 2:6). You have the power and authority to trample on serpents, scorpions, and all the power of the enemy, and nothing shall by any means hurt you (Lk. 10:19).

You must be holy, for the Lord is holy (1 Pet. 1:15). Be perfect as your Father in Heaven is perfect (Matt. 5:48). Be dedicated to God in absolute obedience and consecration. Jesus Christ came to save us from the power of sin and the effects of sin.

God may tell you to do a difficult thing, but never an impossible thing. His Commands are not grievous and burdensome (1 Jn 5:3). God's Yoke is easy and His Burden is light (Matt. 11:30). God will bless you abundantly if you are obedient to Him.

The minister that God is going to approve must be led by the Spirit of God. As many as are led by the Spirit of God, these are the sons of God (Rom. 8:14). Don't be like the horse that will run faster than is necessary; and don't be like the mule that will need to be pulled to move as needed (Psa. 32:9).

Be sensitive to the Holy Spirit's Promptings and Witness. He will teach you all things and show you things to come (Jn 14:26; Jn 16:13). He will remind you of what you had learned and known (Jn 14:26). It is not by power nor by might, but by the Spirit of God (Zech. 4:6).

The Word of God says that we are to prove all things, and hold on to the good (1 Thes. 5:21). Believe not all spirits, but test the spirits whether they are God's, for many false prophets have gone into the world (1 Jn 4:1).

Beware of the ministers you relate with, because evil company corrupts good manners (1 Cor. 15:33). Don't try to help God, and never try to get a substitute to God's Power and Blessings.

Patiently, wait on God for His Appointed Time. Don't be associated with demons, for whatever they offer is worthless.

If you want God to approve you, then you must be blameless, a husband of one wife, temperate, sober-minded, of good behaviour, hospitable, apt to preach and teach, not given to wine, not violent, not greedy for money, but gentle, not quarrelsome, not covetous.

You should rule your own house well, having your children in submission with all reverence. You must not be a novice, and you should have a good testimony among those who are outside (1 Tim. 3:2-7).

For God to approve you, you must be reverent, not double-tongued. You must hold the mystery of the faith with a pure conscience. Even, your wife ought to be reverent, not slanderer, temperate, faithful in all things (1 Tim. 3:8).

I used 'ought to' instead of 'must' for the minister's wife because the devil is fighting many ministers through their wives and trying to suppress their Christian lives and ministries through them. The wives of many of them are the ways they are, because many of them don't know how to handle them.

Of course, many ministers married before they were born again and their wives have refused to be born again also. But even believing wives are not exempted.

Of course, the King James Version italicized the word 'must,' showing that it is not in the original text, but was added for a better understanding. Take authority over your wife and break the power of the enemy over her life in the Name of Jesus Christ and you will see a change.

This is why a minister should not depend on physical appearance to marry someone. Pray well and depend on the Holy Spirit. That is not to say that your God-given wife may not give you headache.

As a matter of fact, God can allow your wife to trouble you (though the trouble was induced by the devil) to train you the way He wants to. But He will be there always to help you overcome.

The Christians and the ministers are responsible for many of the things we accuse satan and the unbelievers of. The work of the devil is to kill, steal, and destroy, while our work is to stop and destroy the works of the devil; if we don't do our part, the devil will succeed, and God will hold us responsible.

An unbeliever who dies in sin will be punished, but the Christian who refused to preach to him will be held responsible.

There is nothing like being approved by God. When God approves you, you can be sure of Heaven; and you will inherit the Kingdom of Heaven with great rewards.

Don't seek the praise of men, but do every thing you can to please God. If you are sure that God is moving you this way, then go the very way and it will be well with your soul.

From the Life of Jesus Christ, we learn that we should make prayer our priority; we also learn that we should submit ourselves to the Will of God, no matter the cost. From the life of Apostle Paul, we learn that if you sell yourself out to God to do His Will, you will go through severe trials and persecutions.

From the life of Moses, we learn that how you end is more important than how you started. The Old Testament heroes and heroines of faith, and the early New Testament Disciples and ministers left us a rich inheritance of examples to emulate.

Being approved by God is not in titles or names. You can be famous among Believers and yet not be approved by God. You can go by such titles as, 'pope,' 'archbishop,' 'bishop,' 'reverend,' 'apostle,' 'prophet,' 'evangelist,' 'pastor,' 'senior apostle,' 'prophetic evangelist,' 'reverend (doctor),' and the rest, and still not be approved by God.

Actually, some people assume someone took a particular title because of pride, but it is not always like that. By the way, ministry is not in names, but titles can help define your ministry and keep you focused.

Someone may use a big title and not be proud, while someone with a seemingly lesser title may be proud. Do you know that someone can even be proud to be humble without people's knowledge?

God is interested in our continuance with what He has called us to do. Many times, we obey God, but we don't continue with it. Sometimes, we may stop doing the right thing because we do not see the results we expect immediately. But be courageous because God's Word can never fail, though it may tarry.

Never leave your first love, and never stop doing your first works. Continue in them because, it is by forbearance that you inherit the promise.

It is him that endures to the end that will be saved. God is not a man and does not judge as men judge. You may be rich and holy in people's eyes, while before God, you are poor and corrupt.

If a sinner forsakes his sins and does righteousness, none of his sins will be remembered; rather, he will be remembered for his present righteousness.

Likewise, if a righteous man forsakes his righteousness and does evil and wickedness, none of his righteousness will be remembered; rather, he will die and suffer for his present sins and wickedness.

Whenever God calls you, follow Him. Whatever He tells you to do, do it. However the Lord tells you to do what He wants you to do, do it that way.

God knows better than any man, and He is more dependable than any other. Do not be wise in your own eyes, but trust in the Lord and do the right things.

As a leader, there are steps you must take. Remember that many are looking up to you, and if you fall and fail, they may fall and fail too. Follow the pathway to leadership to lead effectively. When you lead effectively, God will approve you and reward you abundantly.

Speak whatever the Lord has commanded you to speak, and don't be afraid. You have been called for rooting out and planting, pulling down and building up. None shall prevail against you. Neither devil nor man can stop you from doing what the Lord has commissioned you to do for Him, if you keep in pace with God.

Remember Lot's wife. She turned to a pillar of salt because she disobeyed the Commandment given to them. Who knows whether she looked back because she called to remembrance the much wealth they left behind! But life is more important than riches.

No one who puts his hand to the plough and looks back is fit for service in the Kingdom of God. Sit down and count the cost of being a Christian; consider the reward for obedience and the punishment for disobedience.

BEING STRONG IN THE LORD

Questions for Discussion:

1. What does it mean to be strong in the Lord?
2. How can we be strong in the Lord?
3. Who do we wrestle and fight against?
4. Is it possible for us to win against our enemies?
5. How can we be free from their plans, tricks, and devices?

The Church is marching on, and the gates of Hades shall not prevail! Be strong in the Lord and in the power of His Might (Eph. 6:10). This is a Command which the Lord has given to us. If the Lord has commanded us to be strong in Him, then we must obey Him and do just that.

How do we get strong in the Lord? There are many ways to get strong in the Lord, but we will start with the way that is given to us in the same chapter, and that is by putting on the whole Armour of God.

Armour is a defensive weapon; this is why we talk of armoured cars or vehicles in warfare. But looking at the armour we are given, we notice that one of them is an offensive weapon, and that is the Word of God, which the Bible calls 'the Sword of the Spirit' (Eph. 6:17).

There are many more offensive weapons we use and can use in our spiritual warfare. You know that we do not war against flesh and blood but against spiritual entities. The weapons we fight with are not carnal but mighty through God to the pulling down of strongholds (2 Cor. 10:4).

Other weapons (defensive and offensive) that we will consider include: the Name of Jesus Christ, the Blood of Jesus Christ, the Fire of the Holy Spirit, the anointing, speaking in tongues, praises, fasting, etc.

God showed me, by revelation, that certain situations require certain weapons; therefore, don't expect to use only particular ones and say that others are not necessary. I might have thought the same way, but God showed me otherwise.

One mighty weapon to use in our Christian life and spiritual warfare is the weapon of obedience. We will be able to punish every act of disobedience when our own obedience is complete (2 Cor. 10:6).

Absolute obedience to God is holiness. Obedience is better than sacrifice and self-denial (1 Sam. 15:22).

According to the sixth chapter of the Book of Ephesians, we should be strong in the Lord and in the power of His Might. We should put on the whole Armour of God that we may be able to stand against the wiles of the devil.

For we wrestle not against flesh and blood, but against principalities, against powers, against the rulers of the darkness of this age, against spiritual hosts of wickedness in the heavenly places.

Therefore, take up the whole Armour of God, that you may be able to withstand in the evil day, and having done all, to stand.

We are to gird our waist with the belt of truth. It is the belt that holds your armour or wears together. The Word of God is the Word of Truth. The Word speaks of sanctification by the Word which is truth (Jn 17:17).

The Word of God cleanses us as we hear it (Jn 15:3). We are to rightly divide the Word of God (2 Tim. 2:15). To rightly divide the Word of Truth is to interpret the Word aright. It is to put Scripture where it belongs; and the Bible speaks of comparing Scripture with Scripture (1 Cor. 2:13).

Let the Word dwell in you richly in all wisdom (Col. 3:16). The belt of truth is a clear understanding of the Word of God.

Then, we should put on the breastplate of righteousness. The breastplate of righteousness protects your heart, your spirit, for your heart is located around your breast or chest. When we believed on the Lord Jesus Christ, we received the gift of righteousness from Him, which gave us a right-standing with God.

But the Bible says that he who does righteousness is righteous as Jesus Christ is righteous. If you commit sin, if you live in sin, you are of the devil (1 Jn 3:8). Righteousness is doing right; it is doing the good that you ought to do (Jas 4:17).

Then comes the shoeing of our feet with the preparation of the Gospel of Peace. It is the Gospel, the Good News of the Kingdom that brings peace to men; therefore, preach the Gospel, the Word of God, in season and out of season (2 Tim. 4:2).

Follow peace with all men (Heb. 12:14). Inasmuch as it lies with you, live peaceably with all (Rom. 12:18). Don't allow strife, envy, quarrels, and contentions into your life.

You must take the shield of faith with which you will be able to quench all the fiery darts of the wicked one. The devil throws many wicked arrows at us, and it is only faith that can protect us.

Faith is the assurance of things hoped for, the evidence of things not seen (Heb. 11:1). Faith comes by hearing and hearing by the Word of God (Rom. 10:17). Therefore, faith is being convinced of, being sure of the Word of God.

When you have faith, you are confident that your Almighty God will do for you what He says He will do for you.

Also, take the helmet of salvation. The Word speaks of the hope of salvation which shall be revealed in the Last Day (1 Thes. 5:8). It is the helmet that will protect your head; if your head is not protected, you may as soon become a dead man.

Many are walking around as Christians while they are already dead. In this age where evil abounds, it is your salvation, which is the hope of the Glory that shall be revealed when Christ comes, that will protect you.

Without such hope, your love will grow cold and you will backslide. But it is only those who endure to the end that shall be saved (Matt. 24:13).

Take the Sword of the Spirit which is the Word of God. The Sword of the Spirit is the offensive declaration and confession of the Word of God with your mouth.

As you speak the right Scriptures, in the spiritual realm, the Word you speak come out of your mouth as sword, piercing the devil. The Word of God comes out of your mouth as fire and as hammer (Jer. 23:29).

Then you are to pray always with all prayer and supplication in the Spirit, being watchful in prayer with all perseverance and supplication for all the Saints (Eph. 6:18).

Watch and pray that you may not fall into temptation. The spirit indeed is willing, but the flesh is weak (Matt. 26:41). Have you known that prayer is one of the things that Christians find very hard to do, even though it is indispensable and should be part of our lives?

Maintain a consistent prayer-life. Add fasting to your prayer, for fasting multiplies the power of prayer many times. If you say you can't fast, even till 12:00 p.m. or 4:00

p.m. because you are pregnant or sick, the day you may have miscarriage or die, you will judge for yourself whether you are wiser than God.

Other weapons include the Name of Jesus Christ. At the Name of Jesus Christ, every knee should bow, of things (beings) in heaven, and of things (beings) on earth, and of things (beings) under the earth, and every tongue should confess that Jesus Christ is Lord, to the Glory of God the Father (Phil. 2:9-11).

The Blood of Jesus Christ protects us from the attacks of the enemy. The Blood speaks better things than the blood of Abel (Heb. 12:24). Learn to plead the Blood of Jesus Christ; it is a good attitude. However, don't plead the Blood in fear, for the hosts of Heaven are for you and with you.

The Holy Ghost's Fire is a mighty weapon that is at our disposal. Many don't believe in it. However, inasmuch as there are ways people pray which I don't like, the Lord showed me the effectiveness of the Fire of the Holy Ghost in spiritual warfare (Matt. 3:11).

The anointing is another mighty weapon of spiritual warfare, and there are different kinds and levels of the anointing. The Anointing and Power of the Holy Spirit breaks every yoke (Isa. 10:27).

Speaking in tongues is another mighty weapon. When you speak in tongues, you speak mysteries (hidden things) to God, you confuse the devil, and you pray for what you don't know of, the right way (1 Cor. 14:2; Rom. 8:26).

Praise is a weapon that scatters devils and sets confusion into the kingdom of darkness. Use it always. The last weapon we will discuss is spiritual gifts. The Manifestation of the Spirit (spiritual gift) is given to everyone for the good of all (1 Cor. 12:7). Use your own spiritual gift(s) effectively.

But to put on any armour, you must be spiritually alive and strong. First, you must be born again. Then you should be filled with the Holy Spirit, for you are endued with God's Power when you are filled. Be sensitive to the Holy Spirit and let Him lead you.

Let the fruit of the recreated human spirit (or the Fruit of the Spirit, according to the King James Version and some other versions) be abundant in you (Gal. 5:22-23). Make every effort to stand so that you will not fall.

As Christians, we are supposed to be mighty in words and deeds. When people see us, they are supposed to see Jesus Christ. God does not expect us to remain as spiritual babies, but we are to grow and mature to the fulness of the Stature of Christ Jesus. Seek to know the Lord more than before; seek God more than anything else.

Learn to praise and worship God always. The angels in Heaven worship God always. They sing, "Holy, holy, holy, Lord God Almighty…" and they fear and bow down before the Lord. Worship the Lord in the beauty of holiness. The more you praise and worship God, the more satan will run away from you.

They that know their God shall be strong, and they shall do exploits. To know your God, you have to know His Word and also know Him personally and intimately in prayer.

Knowing God will lead to your doing exploits, in signs, wonders, and miracles. You shall do the works that Jesus Christ did, even greater works than them.

Don't live the normal life that everybody lives. Dare to live extra-ordinarily. That is God's Will for you: living the extra-ordinary life. That extra-ordinary life is the supernatural life, and it transcends natural laws. It is the life by the Spirit of God; it is living by faith, and not by sight.

SIGNS OF BELIEVERS

Questions for Discussion:
1. Who are the Believers?
2. Is it possible to recognize the Believers?
3. How can we recognize the Believers?

Believers are those that believe on the Lord Jesus Christ. Disciples are those who follow the Way of the Lord Jesus Christ. Christians are those who are like Christ Jesus.

Believers, Disciples, Christians, or whatever we may be called, they mean the same thing; and they also mean different things. This is why someone can say there is a difference between a child of God and a son of God.

The difference or the similarity depends on what you have in mind, and on your interpreting them Biblically by the Spirit of God.

The Lord Jesus Christ tells us that Believers can be recognized. There are many ways to recognize a Believer. Of course, someone can put up a sign or character of a Believer to be taken as one, when in reality, the same is an unbeliever and a sinner.

One reason that policemen, sometimes, check and search cars with stickers having such inscriptions as 'clergy,' 'man of God,' 'evangelist,' etc, is because many had camouflaged as preachers and got away with crimes.

Therefore, all that glitters is not gold. This is one reason why you should follow the Leading of the Holy Ghost. You should follow the Witness of the Holy Spirit of the Living God in your heart.

Be sensitive to the stop signals and the go-ahead signals He gives you. He will guide you always. There are many wolves in sheep's clothing (Matt. 7:15). Beware of men.

But there are many signs that can help you recognize a Believer. Because that lady sang wonderfully in the church does not make her a Believer.

Do you know that there are many agents of the kingdom of darkness who sing in choirs? Many church-workers are satanic agents. Some even pastor, preach, and teach the Bible. They can call Jesus Christ in pretence.

I am not saying this for you to become afraid or suspicious, but for you to be careful and be sensitive to the Leading of the Holy Spirit. This is one reason why you should know the Bible very well.

Did you notice that satan tried to deceive Jesus Christ using the Scriptures? But the Word of God says that we should rightly divide the Word of God. To divide it aright is to put it the right way, to interpret it well (2 Tim. 2:15).

We are instructed to compare Scripture with Scripture, to compare spiritual things with spiritual things (1 Cor. 2:13).

One of the signs of Believers is that they do the works that Jesus Christ did (Jn 14:12). The works include: the preaching, the teaching, the miracles, the healings, etc.

Of course, simply because God used or is using someone to perform miracles, signs, and wonders doesn't mean that everything in his life or everything that he preaches or teaches is right. Remember that God used a donkey to speak to Balaam (Num. 22:30).

The Holy Spirit that we received when we were baptized in the Holy Ghost and filled with Him is the Spirit of Power. God created the whole universe by the Power of His Spirit.

It is not by power (human strength), nor by might (military power), but by the Spirit of God (Zech. 4:6). We receive power after that we are filled with God's Spirit, after He comes upon us, and that Power of the Holy Spirit makes us witnesses (proof-providers) for Jesus Christ (Acts 1:8). We are partakers of the Divine Nature.

But we need to be anointed with the Anointing and Power of the Holy Spirit. The more we are led by Him, the more we obey God, and the more we discipline and deny our flesh, the more the Holy Spirit anoints us with His Power.

The Anointing and Power of the Holy Ghost breaks every yoke of the enemy (Isa. 10:27). The walls of Jericho crumbled under this power.

Therefore, the next time you are confronted with challenges, it is an opportunity to prove to the world and the devil that you carry the Power of the Living God. Don't shake the next time you see a blind man.

Apostle Peter commanded the lame man at the Beautiful Gate to rise up in the Name of the Lord Jesus Christ, and, fearlessly, held the man and lifted him up (Acts 3:6-8). That deaf and dumb man that will come your way will be set free! Amen.

Jesus Christ was anointed by God with the Holy Spirit and power, and He went about doing good and healing all that were oppressed by the devil, for God was with Him (Acts 10:38).

When the Disciples went everywhere, preaching Jesus Christ, God worked with them, and confirmed their words with signs following (Mk 16:20). That power and anointing is available for us today, for we are in the same dispensation.

The signs that follow Believers are that they cast out devils or demons in the Name of Jesus Christ; they speak in new tongues; they are not harmed by serpents; if they drink poison or any deadly thing, it will not hurt them; and they lay hands on the sick and the sick recover (Mk 16:17-18).

Believers are given power to tread upon or trample on serpents (demons) and scorpions (their agents) and over all the power of the enemy, and nothing shall by any means hurt or harm them (Lk. 10:19).

You are supposed to be casting out demons. Don't be afraid of them; it is the Holy Spirit, not you that expels them. Your responsibility is to give the command in the Name of the Lord Jesus Christ, and the Finger of God (the Holy Ghost) will accomplish it.

This is why you need to build yourself up by the study of God's Word, by prayer and fasting, and by obedience to God's Word so that the devil will find nothing in you (Lk. 11:20; Jn 14:30).

God has made us kings and priests, and we must operate in that power, authority, and realm! As kings, we should reign with the Lord. We should make commands and decrees that carry power and come to fulfilment. As priests, we should offer praises to God; we should stand in the gap and make intercession for people and places.

You are supposed to speak and to be speaking in new, other, or unknown tongues. There are the tongues of men and of angels (1 Cor. 13:1). When you are baptized and filled with the Holy Ghost, it will be evidenced by speaking in new tongues (Acts 2:4; Acts 19:1-7; Acts 10:44-46).

Don't stop there, but continue to speak in tongues because, by speaking in tongues, you speak mysteries to God (1 Cor. 14:2), you build yourself up spiritually (1 Cor. 14:4), and you allow the Holy Spirit to help you pray for the right things in the right way (Rom. 8:26-27).

If you come across snakes, they should not harm you. Apostle Paul was expected to drop dead by the heathen, when he was attacked by a viper, but nothing happened to him (Acts 28:3-6).

This is not to say that you should tempt God by running around for snakes to show them that you have God's Power. Don't be like the man that was eaten up by a lion in a zoo, in an attempt to show that he possessed God's Power.

Neither chemical nor witchcraft poison should hurt you. Acid will not burn you because when power jam power, the lesser power will bow. When you visit someone, control your appetite for food and drinks. However, if you want to eat or drink, it is good.

Don't be afraid, but rather pray over the food and drink, and bless them by the Word of God and by prayer, and nothing will harm you (1 Tim. 4:4,5).

According to the place we are discussing, the Believer will lay his hand on the sick, and the sick shall recover. Notice that this place says that they will recover. Not all healings are instant; therefore, the next time you pray for the sick in faith, don't be discouraged if the healing is not instant.

Of course, there are the gifts of healings (1 Cor. 12:9), but the prayer of faith shall save the sick (Jas 5:15). There are many other signs of the Believers in Jesus Christ.

Believers are a chosen generation, a royal priesthood, a holy nation, a peculiar people, and we are to proclaim the Praises of Him Who called us out of darkness into His Marvelous Light.

There are certain qualities that should be seen in you as a Christian. The presence and degree of those qualities in your life determine how important you are to God.

The sons of God are to manifest as His sons. Don't die as a mere man when you are a son of God and a god. The Lord predestined us to be conformed to the Image of His Son Jesus Christ, that He might be the Firstborn among many brethren.

Also, have it in mind that many times, the sons of the devil associate with or exist among the sons of God, pretending to be sons of God. They may put on some of the characters of the Believer in pretence. Be sensitive to the Holy Spirit and He will not allow you to be deceived.

God blesses Believers and makes them blessings. Believers are blessed by the Lord, and when He blesses, empowers, and anoints Believers, it is so that they may be sources of blessings to others. A Believer you may consider as a poor man can speak forth a word of faith to you and you will see a surprising result in your life.

We must learn to walk in the Anointing and Power of the Holy Spirit that is upon us. Renew and increase the anointing upon your life by prayer, fasting, and waiting on God. Elijah said, "If I am a man of God, let fire fall down," and fire fell down. What proves you are empowered, as a Believer?

OBEDIENCE, HOLINESS, AND RIGHTEOUSNESS

Questions for Discussion:
1. What is obedience?
2. What is holiness?
3. What is righteousness?
4. What do you gain by being obedient, holy, and righteous?

God created the universe and everything in it. God created all men for His Good Pleasure. When the Lord God made man, He gave him all good things that he needed.

God gave Commandments to Adam on how he should live. However, when the devil tempted Eve, she ate of the forbidden fruit and gave to her husband, Adam, and Adam did eat. Due to that disobedience to God, man was separated from God and became God's enemy, even though God still loved him.

God demands our obedience to His Commandments. To disobey God's Commandments is to displease God. Disobedience is sin. Sin is the transgression of the Law; sin is lawlessness (1 Jn 3:4).

Sin is: knowing what to do and refusing to do it (Jas 4:7). Sin is anything done out of faith (Rom. 14:23). Faith comes by hearing and hearing by the Word of God (Rom. 10:17). Therefore, to do something out of faith is to do something contrary to the Word of God.

If God tells you to do something, do it. If He tells you to avoid something, avoid it: that is what obedience is. If you go to many Christian families, you will come to know that many don't understand what obedience is.

Will it surprise you to see a born-again wife whose husband tells to do something (something that is not contrary to God's Word) and she will not do it? Some will not only disobey their husbands that God has told them to submit to, but they will even abuse their husbands.

Now, those same women, if they are working in offices, will neither disobey nor abuse their bosses in the offices. Apart from the fact that the devil is using them to fight their husbands, that is demonic obsession.

Demonic obsession is a situation where, though someone is not demon-possessed, yet the person's mind is influenced by demons to dance to their tone. Even ministers' wives are not left out.

Do you know that many ministries and ministers are suffering and pressed down spiritually, because the devil is using the ministers' wives to torment, irritate, and discourage the ministers?

The same thing is seen in churches. Many people don't obey their pastors whom the Lord has set over them. Many talk to their pastors as if they are talking to church-members. However rich you may be in the church, the Lord has set the pastor over you and commanded you to obey your pastor.

Of course, I am not telling you to obey your pastor if your pastor tells you to do evil. If you make your pastor's work burdensome for him, you will give account of it to God on the Judgment Day (Rom. 14:12; Heb. 13:17).

Think of how a student will go out immediately to run an errand for his teacher or lecturer, even when the time is contrary to his schedule. Learn to respect and honour your pastor more than your boss at office or your lecturer at school.

You may have money more than them, but they represent God; and I tell you, they are higher than you spiritually. Even if you pray more than your pastor, there is a place of authority he has over you that you don't have.

In the military, people understand obedience and ranks. However, the devil fights in homes, churches and ministries to frustrate the leaders so that the leaders will not fulfill the God-given Assignments for them, and possibly offend God and perish in Hell.

But woe to him that will put a stumbling block to a Christian or to a minister of the Gospel (Matt. 18:6-7). If you can't obey your husband or your pastor, how will you obey God? Stop deceiving yourself before it will be too late for you. Of course, the husband must love his wife, and the pastor must take care of his members in love.

The Bible says that the Whole Duty of man is to fear God and keep His Commandments (Eccl. 12:13-14). You can't keep God's Commandments if you don't fear Him. If you don't have fear for your husband or your pastor, you can't obey him, and you wouldn't even know when you start insulting and abusing him.

The Lord Jesus Christ tells us that the proof that we love Him is our obeying Him and keeping His Commandments (Jn 14:21). Abide in the Lord Jesus Christ, by obeying His Word and His Spirit.

The Word of God says that without holiness, no man can see the Lord (Heb. 12:14). Only the pure in heart will see God (Matt. 5:8). The Church that the Lord is coming for is the Church that is without spot, wrinkle, or blemish (Eph. 5:27).

If you, as an individual, have spot, wrinkle, or blemish, you will not be raptured. May your whole spirit, soul, and body be kept blameless until the Coming of the Lord, because it is only those that endure to the end that will be saved (1 Thes. 5:23; Matt. 24:13).

What is holiness? Holiness is being without sin. It is sinlessness. Holiness is to be separated to God, to be consecrated or set apart for Him. Holiness is to be without spot, wrinkle, blemish, or any other thing that offends.

Holiness is complete and absolute obedience to God. The Bible talks of perfecting holiness (2 Cor. 7:1). To perfect holiness is to be complete in holiness; it is to mature in holiness. Some people live their lives confessing the same sins always. They confess, God forgives them, and they go back to it again and again.

Holiness and obedience involve making up your mind to be holy always and to obey God, no matter the cost. Some have chosen the ones they will obey and the ones they won't.

That type of attitude displeases God. Jesus Christ did not come to wash away your sins only: He also came to deliver you from the power of sins. As many as receive Him, to them He gives the power to become children of God (Jn 1:12). The power to become a child of God is the power to overcome sin and live above it.

Do you know that you are not bound to sin again? Don't let yourself to be overcome and enslaved again by the power of sin. If you do, the last state will be worse than the first (2 Pet. 2:20-21). There is nothing to envy in this world. If you gain the whole world and lose your soul, you gained nothing (Mk 8:36).

If you live to please your flesh, if you live according to the lust of the eyes and flesh, you will end in Hell Fire. Beware of the pride of life (1 Jn 2:15-17). God gave you life, but the life you are living is not your own.

We have heard it said that righteousness is right-standing with God. It is standing before God without a sense of guilt. When we are born again, we receive the Righteousness of Jesus Christ that makes us know that we are God's children.

Many have depended on this definition of righteousness alone and they live their lives anyhow, claiming that they have right-standing with God because of Jesus Christ. There are many unrighteous people who claim they are righteous.

When the Lord saves you and washes away your sins, He expects you to live a righteous life. The righteous life is the life that lives right. It is the life that does what it is supposed to do, and avoids what it should avoid. The Bible says that you should neither be deceived nor deceive others (Matt. 24:4; 1 Cor. 3:18; Eph. 5:6; 1 Jn 3:7).

He who does what is right is righteous just as Jesus Christ is righteous (1 Jn 3:7). He that lives in sin, he who sins is of the devil, for the devil has been sinning from the beginning (1 Jn 3:8).

Some believe that once you are saved, you are forever saved. But the Word says that some who are first will be last (Matt. 19:30), and that only those that endure to the end will be saved (Mk 13:13).

All the Israelites were delivered from the Egyptian bondage, all were baptized into Moses; they ate spiritual food and drank from the Rock (Christ) that followed them. Yet God was displeased with many of them and their bodies were scattered in the desert because God killed them.

It pays to serve God. It pays to be holy, righteous, and obedient. Remember that disobedience is like the sin of witchcraft (1 Sam. 15:23). It is better to obey than to sacrifice. God is bigger and greater than all, and He requires our absolute obedience.

Cry out to God concerning any area you find yourself weak in, and He will deliver you. Call to Him and He will answer you (Jer. 29:12-13; Jer. 33:3). If you have any habit you find difficult to break, take some time to fast as the Spirit leads you, and that bad habit will break and crumble.

In your relationship with others, don't repay evil with evil, but rather, reward evil with good. You should also be able to know the Good, the Acceptable, and the Perfect Will of God.

There is a difference between the Permissive and the Perfect Will of God; the Perfect Will of God is the best for anyone. If you diligently obey the Voice of God, you will be the head and not the tail; all people (and even devils) shall be afraid of you.

We operate by the law of liberty; we have been called to liberty, but we must not use our liberty as an occasion for the flesh. We are no more in bondage, but we must not live our lives anyhow, but offer the members of our body as instruments of righteousness to holiness.

God hates complaining, murmuring, and bearing of grudges. God has promised to meet all your needs, and not all your wants. Of course, He gives you your wants as well, but He knows the best for you. If you give a ten-year old boy your car to drive in the highway because he is your child and you love him, do you really love him? Also, God's Time is the best.

The Israelites asked for a king, because they wanted to be like the other nations and God gave them kings, but were they better under those kings? They complained of meat in the wilderness and God gave them quail, but while they ate it, the Anger of the

Lord burned against them; this happened because, instead of asking in faith, they murmured and complained.

God corrects, rebukes, and reproves His children using different means, and for different reasons. He does these to make them better in different areas of their lives. There is nothing that is hidden from God; all the secrets of men are open to Him and they will be exposed at the appointed times.

God hates sensuality. By sensuality, I mean living according to your senses, and not according to the Spirit of God and His Word. Humans have five sense organs of eye, ear, nose, tongue, and skin, which are for sight, hearing, taste, smelling, and feeling respectively. In sensuality, we are concerned with walking by sight, hearing, and feeling.

Learn or study to be quiet. In the multitude of words, sin is not absent. He who can bridle his tongue can bridle his whole body; he who is faithful in money will be faithful in many other areas; and he who can avoid sexual immorality can avoid many other sins. Control your passions and motives, and bring them under subjection to the Word of God.

Sincerity is not enough. That you are sincere (which is very good) does not mean that you cannot make mistakes, that you cannot lose God's Blessings, and that the devil will not have a place in your life. God's people perish and suffer loss due to ignorance. You must, therefore, add knowledge and other Christian virtues to your sincerity.

LED BY GOD AND FOLLOWING HIS LEADING

Questions for Discussion:
1. What does it mean to be led by God?
2. How can we be led by God?
3. In what ways does God lead His people?
4. Is it possible not to follow God's Leading?

In these end times and last days, the need to be led by God cannot be overemphasized, if we must fulfil God's Task and Purpose for us, and avoid the devil's deception. Many times, Divine Plans are different from human plans. The sons of God are led by the Spirit of God (Rom. 8:14).

If you are not led by the Spirit of God, then you have some questions to ask yourself. Of course, the Spirit of God is always there to lead you if you allow Him. You have to follow the Leader to be led.

When the Spirit of God speaks to your heart, when He gives you a witness about something in your heart, it is your responsibility to sense that witness and to follow the witness.

Don't blame God when you refuse to be led. If the Spirit of God, for instance, sees danger ahead of you and gives you a warning, if you refuse to heed the warning and you are caught up in the danger, you are responsible for it.

God loves His children and He will not want them to fall into danger. God will do all He can to help you, but He cannot force His Will on you if you refuse.

Children of God should be sensitive to God's Leading always. Of course, the devil will want to speak to you, as if it is God. Satan parades himself as an angel of light just as his ministers pretend to be ministers of Christ (2 Cor. 11:13-15).

But the Bible tells us to prove all things and hold on to that which is good (1 Thes. 5:21). Believe not every spirit, but test the spirits whether they are of God; many false prophets have gone out into the world (1 Jn 4:1).

There are many voices in the world and none of them is without significance or meaning (1 Cor. 14:10). You need, therefore, to distinguish between the Voice of God and the voice of the devil. There are many ways God leads His people; the devil can fake some of them.

For instance, the devil may fake an audible voice. This is one reason you should be able to recognize the Inward Witness of the Holy Spirit in your spirit, for the devil does not live in your spirit, but the Spirit of God does.

The primary way or the number one way God leads all His children is by the inward witness or inward intuition. It is like a checking on the inside of you, whether your heart (not your mind) is at peace about something or whether you are uncomfortable with it.

If the more you think about or pray about the thing, you feel good about it, the Spirit of God is giving you a go-ahead signal. On the other hand, if you feel bad about it, it is a stop-signal. You know you are saved by an inward witness (Rom. 8:16).

Another way God leads His children is by the still-small voice or inward voice. Your spirit has a voice, just like your physical body. The voice of your human spirit is your conscience, your inward voice.

There is the Authoritative Voice of the Holy Spirit also, and God leads His children that way. For instance, after Peter had the vision of the sheet from Heaven, as he thought about the vision, the Spirit of God told him that three men sought for him. He was directed by the Holy Spirit's Voice to follow them. The Voice may seem audible, but it comes to your spirit (Acts 10:19-20).

God talks by Audible Voice, as well: after Jesus Christ was baptized (and baptism is by immersion: if you were baptized by sprinkling, re-baptize by immersion.

Any baptized Believer can re-baptize you in the Name of the Father, and of the Son, and of the Holy Spirit; in the Name of the Lord), as He came up, God spoke audibly from Heaven (Matt. 3:17). Also, before the Lord went to the Cross, as He spoke to the people in Jerusalem, God spoke to Him from Heaven (Jn 12:23-33).

God can send an angel to direct and guide you; God sent an angel to speak to Mary (Lk 1:26-38). An angel spoke to the high-priest, Zechariah, before the birth of John the Baptist (Lk 1:11-22).

God spoke to Philip through an angel to go to where he would see the Ethiopian eunuch; when Philip obeyed and went there, God changed His Method by speaking to him again by His Holy Spirit (Acts 8:26-39). God has many methods; don't be too rigid.

Joseph, the husband of Mary, was spoken to by means of dreams many times. Through dream, he was told to take Mary as his wife, he was told to take Jesus Christ and Mary to Egypt, and he was told to come back to the land of Israel after the death of Herod (Matt. 1:20; Matt. 2:13; Matt. 2:19-20).

God spoke to King Solomon through dream (2 Chron. 7:12). Even, many of the prophets of the Old Testament received some of the things they said by means of dreams. However, dreams can come from your mind or from the devil.

Another way God speaks to His children is by vision. Of course, the Bible calls dreams 'visions of the night'; that is, the visions you see as you are asleep. There are three types of visions.

There is the inward vision in which your spirit sees things spiritually, while you are still conscious of your physical environment; this will happen even if your eyes are closed.

The vision that Peter had concerning the sheet from Heaven is by trance. Trance is a form of vision in which you see things when your physical senses are suspended (Acts 10:9-17). In a trance, you are not conscious of your physical environment while God speaks to you or shows you things supernaturally.

The last form of vision is the open vision. In the open vision, you are fully aware of your physical environment and yet you see supernaturally. In the open vision, you may see Jesus Christ, an angel, devils, and other beings or things. Many of the God's children are led by visions more often than angelic visitations and audible voices.

God leads by circumstances also. Check the circumstances surrounding you, because God can lead you by them. For instance, when you plan to travel, the circumstances may work out in such a way that the travel may not work out. The same may happen when you are pursuing a business endeavour.

There are angels who minister for the heirs of salvation (Heb. 1:14), and they can make circumstances favourable or unfavourable for you, to protect or guide you.

However, you must be careful to understand your circumstances aright, because the devil can also cause unfavourable circumstances for you. In that case, destroy the works of the devil in the Name of Jesus Christ, and at the Name of Jesus Christ every knee should bow (Phil. 2:10).

As I said, the devil may fake God's Method of leading His children. But don't be afraid, because you have the Word of God and the Spirit of God. You will not be led astray if you follow the Word and the Spirit.

God can also lead by prophecy, by tongues and interpretations, and by other means. He who prophesies speaks to men to exhortation, to edification, and to comfort (1 Cor. 14:3).

God even used a donkey to speak to Prophet Balaam (Num. 22:30). You can't limit God because He is not limited. Many times, the way God will speak to you will depend on you.

For instance, if you are not spiritually sensitive, He may use natural means to speak to you. But depending on natural means is risky, because the devil can easily imitate and fake it.

This is why you don't need to put out a fleece like Gideon did (Jdgs 6:11-40). If you tell God to open that door if He wants you to do something, the devil can open that door. Do you know that the devil can allow you to have good and legal things in order to deprive you of God's Best for you?

Always be sensitive. Don't seek voices, visions, or dreams, so that the devil will not mislead you. Ask God for direction and He will lead you the way He deems good and best.

The Word and the Spirit agree. The Bible, the Word of God, represents the Mind of God. Inasmuch as there are some things you may not find out from the Bible (for instance, which school to attend), nothing from God and His Spirit will contradict the Word of God, when properly interpreted in the right context.

The Word of God was written by the Inspiration of God (2 Tim. 3:16), and the holy men that spoke the Mind of God spoke as they were moved by the Holy Spirit of the Living God (2 Pet. 1:21).

The hardened heart cannot work out the Righteousness of God; the hardened heart will stand against God's Leading and Prompting. Learn to wait on God with open heart and mind. God wants to lead and guide you more than you want Him to lead and guide you.

God reveals secrets to us. The Holy Spirit tells us things to come; He tells us of past things also. The secret things belong to God, but the things that are revealed belong to us. God does nothing without revealing it to His Servants, the prophets.

However, God reveals what He wants us to know. He will reveal what He wants you to know to you; therefore, don't go around for prophecies so that you will not be deceived.

It is one thing to know the Will of God, and it is another to follow it. Many live their lives without knowing the Will of God for their lives. Many people work for God without doing exactly what He wants them to be doing for Him.

There are general things God expects His people to do; and there are specific things He has purposed in His Heart that individuals or groups should do for Him. Unfortunately, many spend their whole lives doing the works of others.

Knowing the Will of God for your life requires seeking His Face in prayer (or in prayer and fasting), and waiting on God until He tells you. He who believes shall not be in haste (Isa. 28:16).

Don't rush in and rush out of God's Presence. Pray in the Spirit and with the understanding. Pray in tongues and in your known language. As you pray in the Spirit, you activate your spirit and he gets more sensitive to the Spirit of God.

Pray long enough and guidance will rise up from your spirit to your mind, and you will know exactly what to do.

The Spirit of God leads the sons of God. The primary way He leads them is by the inward witness or inward intuition. By this means, when He wants you to do something, He will impart a feeling, sense of peace or good feeling inside you concerning that very thing.

But when your spirit feels bad and insecure about something, the Spirit is telling you to avoid that thing or to be careful about it. But many times, people ignore this witness, and they land into trouble later, because they were expecting a voice, a vision, or a prophecy.

This inner witness or feeling is not mental, and it is not physical. Therefore, don't depend on your mental thoughts or your bodily feelings to judge whether God wants you to do something.

Some put a fleece as Gideon did to ascertain the Will of God; but in this dispensation, we don't walk by sight and God doesn't intend to be leading us by our physical senses. Of course, simple sense will help you know what you may have to do, based on what you see, hear, smell, feel, or taste.

But when you say, "Lord God, if you want me to do this, let this door open in the next ten minutes," you are treading on a dangerous ground, because you are operating in the physical realm. We know, from the Bible, that satan is the god of this world (2 Cor. 4:4).

Therefore, satan can open that door of yours, even before two minutes, and you may become happy and believe that God answered you faster than you expected. If you give that testimony in church, you will get ashamed of yourself when you fall into disaster.

Those that worship God, in this New Testament, worship Him in Spirit, and in truth (Jn 4:24). To worship in Spirit, is to worship according to the Spirit's Leading and Prompting. To worship in truth, is to worship according to the Word and Will of God.

Another way the Spirit of God can lead you is by the still-small voice. By that, your spirit won't just give you a witness but will speak to you. The human spirit has a voice, just like the human body.

The Holy Spirit actually lives inside your spirit, and because your spirit lives inside your body, the Holy Spirit also lives inside your body. This is why the Bible says that your body is the Temple of the Holy Spirit. Even your conscience is the voice of your spirit.

There is the more authoritative Voice of the Holy Spirit. By this method, the Spirit of God speaks to you, on your inside, by Himself. You actually hear it with your spiritual ears, even though it may seem to be physically audible.

In the Old Testament, God called Samuel when he was still young, and Samuel thought it was an audible voice from Eli, but it wasn't. Of course, God speaks to us audibly also.

But don't depend on audible voices because the devil can also speak to you audibly. His intention for doing this will be to deceive you or put fear into you.

After Apostle Peter had the trance in which he was told to kill and eat, as he pondered over the vision, the Holy Spirit spoke to him and said, "Three men seek for you." He has a Voice and He speaks internally and audibly too, depending on how He chooses.

But be careful of any external audible voice, because demons can speak to you audibly too. Know your Bible so that you won't be deceived; be sensitive to the Inward Witness of the Holy Spirit in your inside to see whether it agrees with the audible voice.

The Holy Spirit can speak to you by prophecy or tongues and interpretation, either from your own mouth or from the mouth of somebody else. However, be sure that the ones from others are actually from God.

As stated earlier, check your inner witness to see whether it agrees with it. If God has not spoken to you about that; if God does not speak to you about that later; and best of all, if your inner witness is against it, please, think twice.

Do you know that many people could bombard you with 'words' from the Lord, and yet none or only one of those words, actually, came from the Lord?

There are other ways through which God can speak to you. He can speak to you through visions and dreams. He can send an angel to give you a Message. But always remember that satan can also come, pretending to be an angel of light (2 Cor. 11:14).

One of the best things a Christian can do for himself is to know his Bible very well and be sensitive to the inner witness in his spirit by the Holy Spirit. This will make him not to be easily deceived.

But I am not encouraging you to live in fear of the supernatural. God can always top whatever the devil can do. The devil is only imitating and pretending.

Let us consider the issue of following the Will of God. Once you are convinced that God has said this or that, please follow it: do it or avoid it, as the case may be.

God may tell you to do a difficult thing, but He will never tell you to do an impossible thing. Know that the Thoughts of God are higher than your thoughts. God is wiser than all men put together.

Commit your way to the Lord, and do not lean on your own understanding; in all your ways acknowledge Him, and He will bring it to pass (Psa. 37:5; Prov. 3:5-6).

Love the Lord, even to death. If you value your life more than God, you are not worthy of Him. The people that overcame by the Blood of the Lamb and the Word of their Testimony did not love their lives to death (Rev. 12:11).

You may have to pass through a very great opposition and persecution as you follow God's Will for your life. Consider what Apostle Paul suffered in 2 Cor. 11:23-33.

People will criticize you and call you all kinds of names. The opposition may even come from your brothers and sisters in the same church. But never get discouraged; don't give up.

Somebody said, "You can call me crazy, but I am hearing God." Don't expect everybody to understand you. Even your wife may misunderstand you and work against you. But at the end, they will know that you were right and they were wrong.

The Pharisees and the Sadducees opposed and persecuted Jesus Christ. When Jesus Christ left, they faced His apostles and Disciples. The devil will always incite people against you. Also, he will try to frustrate you by attacking your finances and your progress.

Another thing to following the Will of God for your life is that you have to contend and fight with the forces of darkness to make sure that the Plan of God for your life comes to pass.

God may have a good plan and destiny for you, but if you are not prayerful, it may not come to pass. In case you doubt this, Prophet Daniel prayed, and the answer to his prayer was released the first day.

When God sent an angel to deliver the answer, the angel was withstood for twenty-one days by the prince of Persia, and until a stronger warring angel was sent, Daniel did not have his answer.

Therefore, you must be prayerful and know your rights, privileges, and inheritances in Christ Jesus so that the Will of God for your life will come to pass.

We do not wrestle against flesh and blood, but against principalities, against powers, against the rulers of darkness of this world, and against spiritual forces of wickedness in high places (Eph. 6:12-18).

Therefore, put on the whole Armour of God so that you will succeed and prosper spiritually, mentally, physically, financially, materially, and in any other area you may be involved in.

Beware of the devil's alternatives; don't listen to the devil, but insist on God's Will for you. Pharaoh gave Moses and the children of Israel alternatives of how to worship God, contrary to how God Himself wanted it (Exo. 8:28;10:8-11,24-26;12:31).

The enemy gave harsh conditions as terms for peace to the children of Israel, but King Saul was moved and empowered by the Spirit of God so that the enemy was conquered (1 Sam. 11).

Jesus Christ followed the Will of God for His Life, even to death. Abraham left his place at the Command of the Lord. Moses went back to Egypt to face Pharaoh so that he might deliver the children of Israel.

Caleb had to fight with strong armies in order to inherit what God promised him. David had to fight Goliath to be revealed to Israel and be approved by them, even though God had already anointed him king.

Daniel and his friends made up their minds never to offend God, and they followed His Plan for them. Finally, Apostle Paul was greatly opposed as he carried out the Will of God. Know and follow the Will of God!

PROPHECIES, REVELATIONS, VISIONS, AND VOICES

Questions for Discussion:

1. What are prophecies, revelations, visions, and voices?
2. Are there false prophecies, revelations, visions, and voices?
3. What are the harms of following false prophecies, revelations, visions, and voices?
4. How can we avoid the dangers of following false prophecies, revelations, visions, and voices?

God is still in the business of revealing secrets and mysteries to His people. He still speaks to His children. My God is not a dumb God; He speaks even today.

You only have to tune in to the frequency that He speaks, and you will hear Him clearly. Even as God gives revelations and visions, the devil also has been working hard to give counterfeit revelations and visions to people.

The devil, sometimes, comes as an angel of light to deceive people. He can even speak to you to deceive you. All visions and voices are not God's.

This is why the Scripture instructs us to prove all things and hold on to that which is good, true, and Godly. We are told to test every spirit to see whether they are from God. Why? Because many false prophets have gone out into the world (1 Jn 4:1). God is Spirit; the devil is a spirit too.

1 Corinthians 14:22-33 reads thus, "Therefore, tongues are for a sign, not to those who believe, but to unbelievers; but prophesying is not for unbelievers, but for those who believe. Therefore, if the whole church comes together in one place, and all speak with tongues, and there come in those who are uniformed or unbelievers, will they not say that you are out of your mind?

"But if all prophesy, and an unbeliever or an uninformed person comes in, he is convinced by all, is convicted by all. And thus the secrets of his heart are revealed; and so, falling down on his face, he will worship God and report that God is truly among you.

"How is it then, brethren? Whenever you come together, each of you has a psalm, has a teaching, has a tongue, has a revelation, has an interpretation. Let all things be done for edification.

"If anyone speaks in a tongue, let there be two or at the most three, each in turn, and let one interpret. But if there is no interpreter, let him keep silent in the church, and let him speak to himself and to God.

"Let two or three prophets speak, and let the others judge. But if anything is revealed to another who sits by, let the first keep silent. For you can all prophesy one by one, that all may learn and all may be encouraged.

"And the spirits of the prophets are subject to the prophets. For God is not the author of confusion but of peace, as in all the churches of the Saints."

Earlier, Apostle Paul said, "There are, it may be, so many kinds of languages (or voices) in the world, and none of them is without significance. Let him who speaks in a tongue pray that he may interpret (1 Cor. 14:10,13).

"For if I pray in a tongue, my spirit prays, but my understanding is unfruitful. What is the conclusion then? I will pray with the spirit, and I will also pray with the understanding. I will sing with the spirit, and I will also sing with the understanding" (1 Cor. 14:14-15).

We see, from verse 10, that there are many voices in the world. There are also many languages in the world. There are the Voice of God, the voice of an angel, the voice of the devil, the voices of demons, the voices of people, the voice of the mind, etc.

If you speak in tongues, pray that you may also interpret. However, if everybody in the church is praying individually (to be summarized by one person), you are free to speak in tongues or to pray with your understanding.

But the leader can tell you people to stop praying privately at any time; then, obey and be orderly, by stopping. If you must speak in tongues apart from when everyone is praying individually, then there should be an interpreter (which can be you yourself) or else speak silently or quietly.

But the Spirit has a lot to teach us that we might have not known. There are so many things in the Bible that we have not understood. We will understand many later, and we will understand others when the Lord comes.

Speaking in tongues plus interpretation equals prophecy. Interpretation will help others know what you spoke, so that the whole Church may be edified. He who prophesies speaks edification, exhortation, and comfort to men.

He who speaks in a tongue does not speak to men but to God, for no one understands him; however, in the Spirit he speaks mysteries. He who speaks in a tongue edifies himself, but he who prophesies edifies the Church (1 Cor. 14:2-4).

Therefore, brethren, desire earnestly to prophesy, and do not forbid to speak with tongues (verse 39). Let all things be done decently and in order.

Many are so much interested in prophecies, revelations, visions, and voices that they do not pay attention to the Inner Witness of the Holy Spirit Who indwells them and witnesses with their spirit to make them know what to do and what not to do, what to believe and what not to believe, and who to pay attention to and who not to pay attention to.

Many value prophecy, revelation, vision, and audible voice more than they value the Word of God. Ministries and churches established on prophecies, healings, and miracles without a strong base on the Word of God will sooner or later diminish, wane, or stop entirely.

Such ministries can easily be scattered by rumours. Even the deaths of the founders can bring them to stopping ends. To be on a safer side, put the Word of God (the Bible) first, and put the Spirit of God second.

Yes, the Spirit of God inspired the Word (2 Tim. 3:16); He moved the holy men who prophesied in the Old Testament, and the Early New Testament (and even now) (2 Pet. 1:20-21); and the Spirit, the water (the Word), and the Blood agree as one.

The Father, the Word, and the Holy Spirit are One (1 Jn 5:7-8). Man is born again of water (the Word) and of the Spirit (the Holy Spirit).

Apostle Peter said that the Prophetic Word of the Old Testament is surer, in confirming the Personality of Jesus Christ, than their Testimony of being with Jesus Christ on the mountain of transfiguration where Jesus Christ's Countenance changed and shone with light, and the Voice of God spoke to them (2 Pet. 1:16-21).

Brother, the Scripture was given to us so that we may know the Mind and Will of God. If you put the Bible you see behind you, if you don't stick to that Bible, how can you follow the Holy Spirit of the Living God?

Over the years, people have been deceived by visions, dreams, prophecies, revelations, and voices. Even though God still speaks, demons will try to deceive us, as if it is God that is speaking, and it is when we know the Word well and understand the Witness and Promptings of Holy Spirit well, that we can detect His Voice from their voices.

They sincerely believed that they came from God, even when a moderate knowledge of the Bible would have given them a better understanding. People go to camps and retreat grounds, and pray, pray, and pray to hear God's Voice, and they wouldn't even spend one hour a day to study the Bible during that retreat, when they can spend six hours praying daily during the retreat.

Believe me; many of them are deceived by visions and voices. Many can't distinguish God's Leading from devilish voices.

I am not encouraging you to be fearful, because God can always top the devil in everything. But please, pray and ask God to lead, direct, and guide you, and let Him do it the way He wants to do it.

You may be looking for a writing on the sky while the inner witness or the inward voice by the Holy Spirit has always been with you; but because you are not paying attention, you wouldn't get it; and if one devil speaks to you with a shout, you will value it more than that Voice or Leading of God that is in you.

I believe in prophecy, revelation, vision, and audible voice; I like them. But we are not ignorant of the devices of the devil (2 Cor. 2:11). Therefore, you have to know the truth, because it is better to be late than to be late: it is better to delay than to be found dead.

It is also better to follow God some distance behind, than to rush ahead of God and move towards the west, while He is moving towards the north. God loves us and does not want us to be deceived; but the responsibility lies with us.

People run around looking for those who will give them a Word from the Lord. Why not trust in God and get sensitive to the Holy Spirit Who lives inside you? But woe to the man who will say that the Lord said this or that when the Lord has not spoken.

This is how people get preyed by deceivers, hypocrites, and demonic prophets who come as ministers of Christ. Do you not know that even satan comes as an angel of light? (2 Cor. 11: 14-15).

God leads His people by: the inner witness or prompting in their spirit by the Holy Spirit; the inner or inward voice of their spirit by the Spirit of God; the Authoritative Voice of the Holy Spirit; and by visions, dreams, prophecies, audible voices, angelic visitations, and tongues and interpretation.

However He chooses to lead you, be sensitive and submit. It is important to obey God promptly. Obedience is better than sacrifice; and to hearken than the fat of rams (1 Sam. 15:22).

JESUS CHRIST COMES VERY SOON

Questions for Discussion:

1. Will Jesus Christ come again?
2. When will He come again?
3. Who is He coming for?
4. What will He do when He comes?

The Lord Jesus Christ comes quickly, and His Reward is with Him, to give to everyone according to his work (Rev. 22:12). The Lord Jesus Christ is very great and greater than all. He was before all, and He is the End.

It pleased the Father that His Fulness should dwell in Him, and the Father has committed all things into His Hands. The Lord Jesus Christ is the King of kings and the Lord of lords.

But of the times and the season, brethren, you have no need that I write to you. For you yourselves know perfectly that the Day of the Lord so comes as a thief in the night.

For when they say, "Peace and safety!" then sudden destruction comes upon them, as labour pains upon a pregnant woman. And they shall not escape. But you, brethren, are not in darkness, so that this Day should overtake you as a thief (1 Thes. 5:1-4).

The Coming of the Lord Jesus Christ shall be like in the days of Noah. Before the Flood, people were doing normal things; they were doing business, building houses, and enjoying themselves.

People were overtaken with the cares of this life, and they never listened to Noah, who the Bible calls a 'preacher of righteousness,' until the Flood came and took them away. May it not be so with us!

The Day of Judgment is coming. That Day shall overtake the children of men like the thief in the night. When they say, 'Peace and safety,' sudden destruction will overtake them; and they will not escape it.

The Great White Throne Judgment is coming on all the people of the world. Even Christians will be judged by the Lord at His Coming according to their works, so that each will receive his reward according to what he has done.

Beloved, now we are children of God, and it has not yet been revealed what we shall be, but we know that when He is revealed (when He shall appear), we shall be like Him, for we shall see Him as He is.

And everyone who has this hope in Him purifies himself, just as He is pure. Whoever commits sin also commits lawlessness, and sin is lawlessness. And you know that He was manifested to take away our sins, and in Him is no sin.

Whoever abides in Him does not sin. Whoever sins has neither seen Him nor known Him (1 Jn 3:2-6).

When the Lord Jesus Christ ascended to Heaven, while His Disciples stood and watched, two angels appeared to them and told them that He will come back the same way they saw Him go up (Acts 1:9-11).

We are expecting the Coming of the Lord Jesus Christ. However, the most important part to it, is to be ready for His Coming. He will come like a thief in the night.

The Bible says that blessed are the pure in heart for they shall see God. Is your heart pure? Will you see Him? Without holiness, no man shall see the Lord (Heb. 12:14). Holiness is absolute obedience and dedication to God.

The Word says that we must not love the world or anything in the world, because if anyone loves the world, the Love of the Father is not in him.

The Saints will be raptured to meet the Lord in the air. If we believe that our Lord Jesus Christ died and rose again, even so God will bring with Him those who sleep in Jesus Christ. By the Word of the Lord, we who are alive and remain until the Coming of the Lord will by no means precede those who are asleep.

For the Lord Himself will descend from Heaven with a Shout, with the voice of the archangel, and with the Trumpet of God. And the dead in Christ will rise first.

Then we who are alive and remain shall be caught up together with them in the clouds to meet the Lord in the air. And thus we shall always be with the Lord. Therefore, comfort one another with these Words (1 Thes. 4:14-18).

When the Rapture takes place, there will be commotion and crying in this world, for people will run helter-skelter, but then, it would have been too late. Unbelievers will beat themselves and blame one another for their situation. Then, people will seek to die, but death will be far from them.

Even, carnal and worldly Christians will be left behind, and they will say, "Had I known, I would have...." And the Holy Spirit would have gone. Then the devil will torment and persecute those who have been left behind.

The antichrist will deal with people mercilessly; and people will cry and look for death, but death will not be around. Brethren, this is the time anyone can amend his or her ways.

How will you feel if when the Saints leave, you are left behind? How will your unbelieving neighbours see that you were left behind? The Servant who knew His Master's Commandment and did not do it will be beaten with more stripes.

No wonder Apostle Peter said that if after one is born again, and has known the truth, if he gets entangled in sin and overcome by it, his later state will be worse than the former state. It would have been better if he never came to Christ at all (2 Pet. 2:20).

If your hand or foot causes you to sin, cut it off and cast it from you. It is better for you to enter into life lame or maimed, rather than having two hands or two feet, to be cast into the Everlasting Fire.

And if your eye causes you to sin, pluck it out and cast it from you. It is better for you to enter into life with one eye, rather than having two eyes, to be cast into Hell Fire (Matt. 18:8-9). Many are called but few are chosen. Whatever it will cost you, strive to be chosen.

The Coming of Jesus Christ will be as the days of Noah were. For, as in the days before the Flood, they were eating and drinking, marrying, and giving in marriage, until the day came and took them all away; so also will the Coming of the Son of Man be.

Then two will be in the field: one will be taken and the other left. Two women will be grinding at the mill: one will be taken and the other left.

Watch therefore, for you do not know what Hour your Lord is coming. But know this that if the master of the house had known what hour the thief would come, he would have watched and not allowed his house to be broken into. Therefore, you also be ready, for the Son of Man is coming at an Hour you do not expect.

Blessed is that Servant whom His Master, when He comes, will find ready. But if the Servant is not ready, the Master will punish him and appoint him his portion with the hypocrites. There shall be weeping and gnashing of teeth (Matt. 24:37-51).

When Jesus Christ comes in His Glory, and all the holy angels with Him, then He will seat on the Throne of His Glory. All the nations will be gathered before Him, and He will separate them one from another, as a shepherd divides his sheep from the goats.

And He will set the sheep on His Right Hand, but the goats on the Left. Then the King will say to those on His Right Hand, "Come, you blessed of My Father, inherit the Kingdom prepared for you from the foundation of the world.

"For I was hungry and you gave Me food, I was thirsty and you gave Me drink, I was a Stranger and you took Me in, I was naked and you clothed Me, I was sick and you visited Me, I was in prison and you came to Me."

Then the righteous will answer Him saying, "Lord, when did we do those things to You?" And the King will answer and say to them, "Assuredly, I say to you, inasmuch as you did it to one of the least of these My brethren, you did it to Me."

Then He will also say to those on the Left Hand, "Depart from Me, you cursed, into the Everlasting Fire prepared for the devil and his angels. For I was hungry and you gave Me no food,

"I was thirsty and you gave Me no drink, I was a Stranger and you did not take Me in, naked and you did not cloth Me, sick and in prison and you did not visit Me."

Then they also will answer Him, saying, "Lord, when did we see You in those conditions and did not minister to You?" Then He will answer them, saying, "Assuredly, I say to you, inasmuch as you did not do it to one of the least of these, you did not do it to Me."

And these will go away into Everlasting Punishment, but the righteous into Eternal Life (Matt. 25:31-46). Heaven and earth shall pass away, but the Word of the Lord will not pass away.

But of that Day and Hour, no one knows, not even the angels in Heaven, nor the Son, but only the Father. Take heed, watch and pray; for you do not know when the Time is.

It is like a man going to a far country, who left his house and gave authority to his servants, and to each of his work, and commanded the doorkeeper to watch.

Watch, therefore, for you do not know when the Master of the house is coming in the evening, at midnight, at the crowing of the rooster, or in the morning   lest, coming suddenly, He finds you sleeping (Mk 13:31-36).

When Jesus Christ comes, everyone, great or small, will be judged. Anyone not found written in the Book of Life will be cast into the Lake of Fire. He who overcomes shall inherit all things, and the Lord will be his God and he will be His son.

But the cowardly, unbelieving, abominable, murderers, sexually immoral, sorcerers, idolaters, and all liars shall have their part in the Lake which burns with fire and brimstone, which is the Second Death (Rev. 21:8).

He who is unjust, let him be unjust still; he who is filthy, let him be filthy still; he who is righteous, let him be righteous still; he who is holy, let him be holy still. Jesus Christ is coming very soon!

The Lord has given us many warnings in things pertaining to this life, Godliness, and the life to come. God is wiser than all; therefore, let us heed to these warnings and it will be well with us.

Jesus Christ is coming for His Saints and Elects. The Saints of God are His holy and separated people. The Elects of God are those who follow God's Word and Spirit.

Whatever you do in this life, be conscious of life after death; be conscious of eternity. The Saints will be raptured at the Coming of the Lord Jesus Christ, and they will spend eternity in the Presence of God.

The Gospel is the only hope of man: the Good News that Jesus Christ died for the sins of the world so that whoever believes in Him and confesses Him as his Lord and personal Saviour will be saved.

We must send more missionaries into the ends of the world, and we must support the work of missions with all our heart. Whenever Jesus Christ comes, unsaved men will be lost forever.

If we disobey God in the spreading of the Gospel, we are rebelling against God. Disobedience, rebellion, and witchcraft are alike; therefore, we must obey God. Souls mean more to God than any other thing in this world.

There is joy in Heaven over one soul that repents. Jesus Christ came not to condemn the world, but that the world through Him might be saved.

Covetousness and idolatry are alike. Let us not live our lives in greed and covetousness, pursuing the things of this world, that we forget or neglect what the Lord has called us to do.

The more dedicated we are to the Work of the Lord, especially in the spreading of the Gospel, the more reward we will get from God. We will live eternally with Jesus Christ in God's Kingdom.

TESTS, TRIALS, TEMPTATIONS, AND WILDERNESS EXPERIENCES

Questions for Discussion:
1. What are tests, trials, temptations, and wilderness experiences?
2. Who will have them or pass through them?
3. Can a righteous person pass through them?
4. Can being prayerful and holy stop you from experiencing them?

Tests are recommended for promotion, and no teacher or master gives his student or servant tests without a purpose. Tests are to prove someone. God tests His children to prove them so that He can promote them.

A test is a set of questions, exercises, or practical activities to measure someone's skill, ability, or knowledge. A test is a difficult situation, a situation in which the qualities of someone or something are clearly shown. To stand the test of time is to be good enough, strong enough to last for a long time.

Trial refers to a process of testing to find out whether something works effectively and is safe. It is a short period during which you use something or employ someone to find out whether they are satisfactory for a particular purpose or job.

God also tries His people to examine their faithfulness and ability. Afflictions can be trials. God can allow the devil to try His child, as in the case of Job, to prove something to the devil.

Even if someone fails, when tried by the devil, it is because the one chose to fail, and not because he didn't have the ability to withstand.

The former Saints and Servants of the Lord had trials of mockings and scourgings; yes, and of chains and imprisonment (Heb. 11:35-38). Jesus Christ was baptized with the Baptism of Suffering and Shame. Each of us has his own cross (or price, as some call it) to bear (or pay).

You must make the required sacrifice God expects from you. Obedience is better than sacrifice; in fact, the right sacrifice is what God wants from you, and what you give God or deny yourself because of your love for God.

Your faith will be tried to prove the genuineness of it. When you overcome, you will receive praise, honour, and glory at the Revelation of Jesus Christ (1 Pet. 1:7).

Do not think it strange concerning the fiery trial which is to try you, as though some strange thing happened to you; but rejoice to the extent that you partake of Christ's Sufferings, that when His Glory is revealed, you may also be glad with exceeding joy (1 Pet. 4:12-15).

If you are reproached for the Name of Christ, blessed are you, for the Spirit of Glory and of God rests upon you. Count it all joy when you fall into various trials, knowing that the testing of your faith produces patience.

But let patience have its perfect work, that you may be perfect and complete, lacking nothing (Jas 1:2-4). But let none of you suffer as an evildoer; or as a busybody in other people's matters.

Temptation is brought your way by the devil to make you have or do something, even though you know you should not. To resist temptation is to refuse to do something, even though the devil brought the desire for it.

Temptation is an attempt by the devil to try to persuade someone to do something by making it seem attractive. But God will not allow the temptation that is greater than you to come your way.

No temptation has overtaken you except such as is common to man; but God is faithful, Who will not allow you to be tempted beyond what you are able.

If you encounter temptation, God will also make the way of escape, that you may be able to bear it (1 Cor. 10:13). Any temptation that comes your way is common to man, others have experienced it.

Jesus Christ was tempted at all points, yet He did not sin: as a Christian, you can refuse to sin as well. Don't blame the devil if you succumb to temptation. You are to be blamed, because you have the power, right, and authority to be a child of God, and to obey Him.

Blessed is the man who endures temptation; for when he has been proved, he will receive the Crown of Life which the Lord has promised to those who love Him.

Let no one say when he is tempted, "I am tempted by God"; for God cannot be tempted by evil, nor does He tempt anyone. But each one is tempted when he is drawn away by his own desires and enticed.

Then, when the desire has conceived, it gives birth to sin, and sin, when it is full grown, brings forth death. Do not be deceived, my beloved brethren (Jas 1:12-16).

No matter the pressure, don't give in to temptation: tomorrow may be too late; a single sin in your life will keep you from Heaven.

By wilderness experiences (or the university of tears, as someone called it), I mean those experiences that may make you to despise life, the experiences that can make you ask, "Where is the Lord?" But our God is in Heaven, and He knows everything you may be passing through.

He will be with you in trouble (Psa. 91:15) and through the valley of the shadow of death (Psa. 23:4). Don't be discouraged, no matter the test or trial, hold on to God, for He will never leave you nor forsake you (Heb. 13:5).

We must enter the Kingdom of Heaven through many tribulations, persecutions, tests, and trials (Acts 14:22).

Abraham passed through tests and trials. He did not have Isaac until he was very old, and even when Isaac had grown up, God told him to sacrifice Isaac for Him. He obeyed God and it was counted to him for righteousness.

Noah passed his own test also. If he had not built the ark, he would have perished in the Flood, but he obeyed God. Joseph passed through the wilderness experiences, and because he persevered and endured, God made him the prime minister of Egypt.

Moses had his own wilderness experiences. He obeyed God and went to meet Pharaoh. Even when they left Egypt, they spent many years in the wilderness and in tents. Sampson failed and fell into temptation, and this led to the loss of his two eyes.

Gideon obeyed God and passed his test. Jephtah passed his trial when he gave up his daughter according to his vow. David fell into sexual immorality with Uriah's wife and murdered her husband. This brought sword to his own family. Jesus Christ passed His Tests and Trials, and He has been highly exalted.

John the Baptist suffered in the wilderness, eating selected food of honey and locust, and wore camel's hair; he persevered and achieved God's Purpose for his life.

Peter failed by denying Jesus Christ three times. But thanks to God that he repented, wept, and was restored back.

Apostle Paul went through diverse tests and trials, and still overcame and fulfilled his ministry. King Saul failed God by not obeying Him completely, and he lost the throne.

King Solomon allowed riches and wealth to make him disobey God in marriage, and when he was old, his heart was drawn away from God. Jeremiah, Isaiah, Daniel, Shadrach, and many others passed through their wilderness experiences and survived.

Tests and trials are meant to make you mature and strong. Even Jesus Christ learnt obedience by the things He suffered (Heb. 5:8); and those things made Him perfect so that He can serve as the Great High Priest effectively (Heb. 2:10-18).

However, many Believers do not want to pass through hard times; that is to remain immature till death, if God allows it. But when God scourges and disciplines us, it is so that we may partake of His Holiness (Heb. 12:10).

If Apostle Paul could call those sufferings of his 'light afflictions' (you probably have not suffered 10% of what he suffered), you too can endure those small sufferings of yours (Rom. 8:18; 1 Cor. 4:9-13; 2 Cor. 11:23-33).

The Bible says that the Lord knows how to deliver the Godly out of temptations and to reserve the unjust under punishment for the Day of Judgment (2 Pet. 2:9). When the devil tempts you, he will show you the temporal enjoyment your flesh may experience, but he will try to hide the after-effect of the sin from you.

This is why sin is deceitful. Esau sold his birthright for a plate of food, and when he would have got the blessing, he lost it. Consider what he said: he said that Jacob had taken the birthright from him, and then the blessing. But unknown to him, the blessing was connected to the birthright.

According to Jesus Christ, if you suffer for Him, even if you lose your life for Him, He will replace whatever you lost in the process. God allowed the children of Israel to pass through hunger to teach them that man shall not live by bread alone, but by every Word that comes out of the Mouth of God.

If we suffer with the Lord, we will also reign with Him. At the time of the test and trial, it will not be very easy for you: you may be sad at that time, but the fruits that will follow them will be eternal.

Blessed are you when you are persecuted for righteousness' sake, for yours is the Kingdom of Heaven. Rejoice and be exceedingly glad, for great is your reward in Heaven, for so they persecuted the prophets who were before you (Matt. 5:10-12).

Blessed are you when they revile and persecute you, and say all kinds of evil against you falsely for Jesus Christ's Sake. The sufferings you may go through are not comparable to the Glory that will be revealed in us at the Coming of Jesus Christ.

To him who overcomes, Jesus Christ will give to eat from the Tree of Life; he who overcomes shall not be hurt by the Second Death; to him who overcomes, the Lord will give some of the hidden manna to eat.

He who overcomes will be given power over the nations, he will be given the morning star also; he who overcomes shall be clothed in white garments, and his name will not be blotted out of the Book of Life.

He who overcomes, the Lord will make a pillar in the Temple of His God, and he shall go out no more; and he who overcomes, the Lord will grant to sit with Him on His Throne. (Rev. 2 & 3). He, who has ear to hear, let him hear.

Don't allow sorrow, disappointment, and depression lead you away from God's Best for you. When Jesus Christ was about to be crucified, the Disciples, instead of praying and watching with Him slept out of sorrow. You see how powerful sorrow and depression can be.

Bless the Lord, for He is good; His Love and Mercy endure forever. Dry bones shall rise again. No matter the situation you may find yourself in, it shall be well.

The Lord will be with you through the valley of the shadow of death. None of your hairs will fall out without His Permission, and whatever you lose for His Sake, that you will have many folds.

Some wilderness experiences are connected to curses. Curses can come from different sources. Curses, also, operate in different ways.

Remember that, after Job had passed his test, trial, and wilderness experience, God blessed his later end more than the first, by far. The widow of Nain, who had lost her son, thought that all hope was gone until Jesus Christ came and brought the young man back to life.

When the Lord brought back that captivity of Zion, they were like them that dreamt dream. When Lazarus had been in the grave for four days, at the Appearance of Jesus Christ, he was brought back to life, because 'this sickness is not unto death.'

Jesus Christ Himself was in the grave, and the Disciples thought that all hope had been lost; but after three days, He came back to life. Whatever the devil may think he has destroyed in your life, very soon, the Lord will arise for your cause, and all his works in your life will be destroyed.

According to Apostle Paul, "Our light affliction, which is but for a moment, is working for us a far more exceeding and eternal weight of glory." (2 Cor. 4:17). All those things many complain about in their hearts or minds, or even with their mouths, thinking that they are suffering so much are light afflictions! Yes, it will bear on your mind and body, but it is for your promotion and greater glory.

SECRETS TO GOD'S MIRACLE-WORKING POWER

Questions for Discussion:

1. What is a miracle?
2. Does God work miracles?
3. How does God work miracles?
4. How can you have the Miracle-working power of God?
5. What is the importance of miracles?

If you must walk in God's Miracle-working Power, you must have an intimate relationship with Him. I am speaking of walking in that power consistently. An intimate relationship with God will necessitate your knowing and understanding His Word.

His Word will tell you His Character and His Ability. From His Word, you will get to know your rights and privileges as a child of God; you will develop your faith, for faith comes by hearing the Word of God.

Let the Word of God dwell in you richly in all wisdom (Col. 3:16), and study to show yourself approved to God, a workman that needs not to be ashamed, rightly dividing the Word of Truth (2 Tim. 2:15).

When you study the Word well, and compare Scripture with Scripture, you will understand it clearly and put the Word of God where it belongs: you will not misapply the Word. The devil wanted Jesus Christ to misapply the Scripture when he quoted Scripture for the wrong purpose.

To walk in God's Miracle-working Power consistently requires that you maintain a consistent prayer-life. The Lord Jesus Christ communed with the Father daily and always when He was on this earth as a Man.

He rose up very early in the morning and prayed till daybreak. He spent whole nights or almost the whole praying sometimes. He prayed from daylight into the night. He prayed in the public, and he prayed in private.

Prayer is the master-key, and you can't do without it. The more consistent your prayer-life is, the more consistent will be the manifestation of the Power of God through you to people.

The early apostles and Disciples prayed. They prayed in group, and they prayed privately. Even buildings shook when they prayed and sang. Don't get too busy working for God that you do not have time to commune with Him daily.

Another thing that will activate the Power of God in your life is fasting. Fasting helps you put the body under subjection to your spirit so that you can obey God and do His Will better.

You know that the spirit-man desires to do the Will of God, while the flesh (because it is weak) will want its desires to be met. Some of those desires are not sinful and some are.

For instance, the desires for food and sleep are not sinful, but you can eat too much or at the improper times that the fulfilled desire can hinder the Free-flow of the Spirit of God through you.

Also, if you love sleep, it will affect your prayer-life adversely, because you will sleep more than is necessary. Too much sleep will bring weakness and laziness into your life, and these will make you ineffective in your walk with God.

Therefore, you must learn to limit those desires that are not necessarily sinful; and do not yield to the sinful desires of the body at all. There are: absolute fasting, total fasting, partial fasting, fruit or juice fasting, etc. You can even fast from newspapers and televisions, and use the extra time to pray and study the Word.

Then you must walk in love towards God, your brethren, and the rest of the people. Faith works by love, and without love, you are nothing.

Even if you have all faith so that you can remove mountains, if you have the gift of prophecy, and you receive the Revelations and Visions of God, without love, you amount to nothing and God will not allow you into His Kingdom.

Love will enable you to obey God and do the right things to your neighbours. You will need to have compassion for the people you are ministering to; be patient with them and forbear their weaknesses and immature behaviours.

Many of the miracles Jesus Christ performed were done because He had compassion on the people. Compassion will activate the Power and the Gift of God in you. The Spirit of God works with the meek in spirit. You must be gentle and not be ruled by harshness.

Humility is very necessary also. God resists the proud but gives grace to the humble (Jas 4:6). God will not share His Glory with anyone (Isa. 48:11).

Whatever God uses you to do, give all the glory and praise to Him. It is not because you ran or because you willed. No, it is because God showed you mercy. The power that wrought the miracle is His, and you are only a vessel and an instrument.

He that plants and he that waters are nothing; it is God that makes the seed grow and produce that worths all; and we must recognize that God is a Good God.

To walk in signs, wonders, and miracles require total and unreserved obedience. Obedience is better than sacrifice. Don't go by feelings: if God leads you to go and preach when you don't feel high spiritually, obey Him and go. That may be the day you will see the greatest miracle in your life.

We walk by faith and not by sight. You will be able to punish every act of disobedience when your obedience is complete (2 Cor. 10:6). Don't be a hearer of the Word, deceiving yourself; but be a doer of the Word.

God is of Purer Eyes than to behold iniquity (Habk. 1:13). If you hide iniquity in your heart, the Lord will not hear you. Therefore, you must live the life of holiness if you want to see mighty miracles through you. Let no sin or weight remain in your life: sin entangles, and weight hinders.

Get rid of them; let righteousness rule in your life. Above all, know that whatever you may accomplish for God, if you miss Heaven, if you go to Hell, you achieved nothing. Without holiness, no man can see the Lord.

Then you must be perfect as your Heavenly Father is perfect (Matt. 5:48). God cannot tell us to do what we cannot do: God is just. In every area of your life, be perfect.

In words, be perfect; in actions, be perfect; in character, be perfect; in spirit, faith, love, and purity, be perfect; whatever you do, be perfect. Even your thoughts are to be perfect. Perfection has to do with maturity. Even holiness should be perfected (2 Cor. 7:1).

You must not allow any idle word out of your mouth. Let no corrupt word proceed out of your mouth. Fresh water and bitter water do not flow from the same source. Curses and blessings ought not to flow from the same mouth of the child of God.

Be careful how you think because your thoughts will affect your words. Let your words be seasoned with grace, so that your hearers will benefit. In preaching, do not preach wrong things. Teach the Right Doctrines.

If you are going to walk in God's Supernatural Power, you will have to expect persecutions, tests, and trials. Jesus Christ passed through them, and you cannot expect the opposite.

Satan will entice people to persecute you as he did towards Apostle Paul. But don't be discouraged; neither be dismayed. Allow no fear into your heart. Do not fear him who can touch the body but has no power over the soul in Hell. Fear Him who can destroy both the body and the soul in Hell.

Remember to deal with any wrong foundation in your life, for if the foundation is destroyed, what can even the righteous do? For instance, if you live in sin, you have a wrong foundation. Don't think that, by exaggeration, you will glorify God.

No, God hates lies, and you don't help God by lying. If you supplanted your friend, by deceit, to marry her fiancé, go and ask for her forgiveness. Don't waste your life working for God, when you are heading to Hell. Give no place to the devil.

When the apostles and Disciples went out and preached everywhere, the Lord worked with them confirming their Gospel with signs and wonders. If you want to see mighty healings and miracles in your life, you must go out and preach the Gospel.

Preach in buses, preach in markets, preach in streets, preach in houses; go out for early-morning cries, preach in season and out of season, preach everywhere.

If you preach the Gospel of the Kingdom, then God will confirm the Gospel you preach, because God confirms His Word. Don't sit back and wait to preach in your church's pulpit.

There are so many things you can learn from the Bible that will help you manifest God's Power. Among them are: self-discipline, self-denial, wisdom, watchfulness, diligence, honesty, and perseverance.

Don't worry yourself if it seems as though you failed or did not accomplish much at your first outing. Worrying, instead of adding, will remove from you.

Be confident in your God and His Word, and soon, everybody will be looking for you to be prayed for. Elisha persisted and received the double-portion of Elijah's anointing!

Forget the past and mind the future. Beware of bad and evil company; evil association corrupts good manners. Get rid of ignorance, mistakes, and foolishness. Preach and teach the Word of God, in season and out of season. Never walk against God and His Plans, Purposes, and Will.

Godliness with contentment is of great gain, for we brought nothing into the world and it is certain that we can carry nothing with us at our death. Greed and covetousness will hamper the manifestation of the Power of God through you.

David was described by God as a man after His Heart, and Abraham was described as a Friend of God. What will you be described as? You must have the fear of God in your heart; without the fear of God, you can't please God.

Touch not, taste not, and handle not anything that offends God and that is contrary to Godliness and our faith. Give diligence to pressing toward the mark, the prize of the High Call of God in Christ Jesus.

DEVELOPING A STRONG RELATIONSHIP WITH GOD

Questions for Discussion:

1. Can someone have a close, intimate, and strong relationship with God?
2. How can you have a strong relationship with God?
3. What are the benefits of having a strong relationship with God?

There are different levels of relationships. Some relationships are loose, while others are strong. Some are casual, while others are intimate.

In our relationship with God, we should develop a strong and an intimate relationship with Him. This is evident because the first Commandment in the Ten Commandments is that we shall have no other gods before the Living God (Exo. 20:3).

Also, when Jesus Christ was asked about the greatest Commandment, He said that the first and Great Commandment is to love the Lord your God with all your heart, with all your soul, and with all your mind (Matt. 22:36-38).

Hear, O people of God, the Lord our God, the Lord is One. And you shall love the Lord your God with all your heart, with all your soul, with all your mind, and with all your strength. This is the first Commandment (Mk 12:29-30).

Man is tripartite in nature, comprising spirit (or heart), soul (or mind), and body. All these components or natures of man must be fully dedicated to God. No wonder Apostle Paul prayed that the whole spirit, soul, and body be preserved blameless at the Coming of our Lord Jesus Christ (1 Thes. 5:23).

You dedicate your spirit to God by first being born again, so that your spirit is regenerated and made a new creature in Christ Jesus. You then desire the sincere milk of the Word of God so that you can grow thereby.

Also, your spirit should be filled with the Holy Spirit, the Spirit of Power, and you get edified by praying in the Holy Spirit. You build up your most holy faith by praying in the Holy Ghost (Jude 1:20).

Many in the Church need revival. By prayer (sometimes, added with fasting), you get more sensitive to the Holy Spirit, and it will be easier for Him to lead you.

You also renew your mind with the Word of God so that you think as God thinks and make decisions according to His Will and Mind (Rom. 12:1-2).

You are to present your body, which is the Temple of God, a living sacrifice, holy, acceptable to God, which is your reasonable service.

Shall we continue in sin that grace may abound? Certainly not! How shall we who died to sin live any longer in it? Just as Christ was raised from the dead by the Glory of the Father, even so we also should walk in newness of life.

Our old man was crucified with Him, that the body of sin might be done away with, that we should no longer be slaves of sin. Reckon yourselves to be dead, indeed, to sin, but alive to God in Christ Jesus our Lord. Therefore, do not let sin reign in your mortal body, that you should obey it in its lusts.

And do not present your members as instruments of unrighteousness to sin; but present yourselves to God as being alive from the dead, and your members as instruments of righteousness to God.

Sin shall not have dominion over you, for you are not under Law but under grace. Do you not know that to whom you present yourselves slaves to obey, you are the one's slaves whom you obey, whether of sin leading to death, or of obedience leading to righteousness?

But God be thanked that though you were slaves of sin, yet you obeyed from the heart that form of Doctrine to which you were delivered. And having been set free from sin, you became slaves of righteousness.

Just as you presented your members as slaves of uncleanness, and of lawlessness leading to more lawlessness, so now present your members as slaves of righteousness for holiness.

Having been set free from sin, and having become the Slaves of God, you have your fruit to holiness, and the end, Everlasting Life. For the wages of sin is death, but the Gift of God is Eternal Life through Christ Jesus our Lord (Rom. 6).

Without prayer, your relationship with God cannot be strong. Every Christian should pray for at least two hours everyday. Take enough time to worship God. Pray in tongues, so that you can speak mysteries to God and pray for things you may not know about.

Be consistent in your prayer-life. Watch and pray so that you do not fall into temptation. Watchfulness and vigilance should be part of you so that you can know the enemy's plans and stop them.

Having a strong relationship with God requires that you live the life of faith. The righteous is to walk by faith, and not by sight. Without faith, you cannot please God, because he who comes to God must believe that He is and that He rewards those who diligently seek Him. By faith, God called forth the whole creation into existence.

Faith is the substance of things hoped for, the evidence of things not yet seen. Whatever God has promised you, He will give it to you, even though you may not be seeing it physically now. In no distant time, it will be yours. Pray and believe.

The Word of God contains the Mind and Will of God. This is one reason you have to study the Word of God with commitment. Let the Word of Christ dwell in you richly in all wisdom. Faith comes by hearing, and hearing by the Word of God.

It is by the Word of God that you can prove all things so that you can hold on to that which is good. The Word of God is the source of the Blessings of God. One Word from God can change your life forever. The Spirit of God inspired the Word, and two of Them agree.

All Scripture is given by the Inspiration of God, and is profitable for Doctrine, for reproof, for correction, for instruction in righteousness; that the man of God may be complete, thoroughly equipped for every good work (2 Tim. 3:16-17).

No prophecy of the Scripture is of any private interpretation, for prophecy never came by the will of man, but holy men of God spoke as they were moved by the Holy Spirit (2 Pet. 1:20-21). Desire the sincere Word of God so that you may grow and mature.

But be a doer of the Word, and not just a hearer. If you hear the Word without doing it, you deceive yourself. It is not the hearer that is commended, but the doer.

If anything, the more you hear the Word without doing it, the more your punishment will be, also. Obedience is better than sacrifice. Rebellion is like the sin of witchcraft. If you don't mix the Word with faith, it will not avail anything to you, because you will not do it.

As obedient people of God, don't fashion yourselves after the former lust, but as He Who called you is holy, so be holy in all manner of conduct.

If you desire a strong relationship with God, then you must win souls for the Lord Jesus Christ. Jesus Christ came to save sinners. You must preach the Gospel always, even against your time table or schedule.

If you are ashamed of Christ Jesus before men, He also will be ashamed of you before God and the holy angels. He that wins souls is wise.

The wise shall shine like the brightness of firmament, and those who turn many to righteousness like the stars forever and ever (Dan. 12:3). Let God be proud of you.

Giving to God and to men will help you maintain a strong relationship with God. The Bible says that where your treasure is, is where your heart will be also.

As you give to God, you have the confidence that when you get to Heaven, the Lord will reward you abundantly; and it will help you prepare for Heaven. Of course, God will reward you in this world also.

When you give to the people of God in the Name of Jesus Christ, you give to God. When you give to God's Servants, you will be blessed. As you give to the poor, you lend to God and He will repay you abundantly.

Having a strong relationship with God will require self-discipline and self-denial. You don't get taken up by the things of this world; rather, you set your mind on things Above, where Jesus Christ is.

Limit the time you spend on television and films, even for Christian programmes and films. Don't be gluttonous in your feeding. Also, do not sleep too much; sleep to get rest, and when sleep has cleared your eyes, give yourself to profitable and Godly things. The lazy man shall not excel in his endeavour.

To maintain a strong relationship with God, you must be led by the Spirit of God. The Spirit of God is the Spirit of Truth, and He will lead you into all truth. The Holy Spirit will reveal secrets to you, and tell you God's Plan and Purpose for your life.

No man can excel by the strength of the flesh. It is not by might, nor by power, but by the Holy Spirit of the Living God (Zech. 4:6). He is your Comforter, Helper, Advocate, Strengthener, Counselor, Intercessor, and Standby.

He will help you accomplish God's Assignment for your life. But He is a Gentle Spirit; therefore, you must give Him room to lead you.

Make every effort to be more like Jesus Christ our Lord. Jesus Christ had a strong relationship with God, the best any can have; therefore, put God first and every other thing second.

You can't expect to drink from the Lord's Cup and the devil's cup at the same time. You can't eat at the Lord's Table and the devil's table at the same time.

God does not do anything without revealing it to His Servants, the prophets. God seeks for a man who will stand in the gap between God and others, so that the people can receive God's Blessings and Provisions, and also escape God's Judgment.

God is a Jealous God; He will not share His Glory with another. The Spirit of God that dwells in us lusts to envy. God does not want us to be worldly as the people of the world.

He expects that your whole spirit, soul, and body be kept for Him. Your body is the Temple of the Holy Spirit. You can't serve God and satan at the same time.

You need to have a strong hunger and thirst for God and the Things of God. He who thirsts shall be filled, and his thirst shall be quenched. If you hunger and thirst for righteousness, God will satisfy that hunger and thirst. As you hunger and thirst for God, your relationship with Him will be more intimate.

Draw close to God, and the devil will not be your problem. Satan couldn't touch Job of Old Testament or anything that belonged to him without God's Permission. But the problem is that many spend so much time thinking about the devil and fearing him.

People spend a lot of time praying against the devil, his demons, and their works, while they spend smaller time praising, worshipping, seeking, and asking God. Many fear the created being – satan – more than they fear God, the Creator. These are very improper.

Depend on God for whatever thing you may be doing. This is why it is necessary to find out what the Will of God is for your life, because God is committed to whatever He starts.

Except the Lord builds the house, the builders build in vain; except the Lord watches over the city, the watchman stays awake in vain. Commit your ways to the Lord; trust also in Him, and He will bring it to pass.

All the things of this world are vanity. They worth something, when used for the Glory and Will of God, and for the furtherance of His Kingdom.

Don't spend your time pursuing the things of this world, while you have no time for what God wants you to do. It shall profit you nothing to gain the whole world and lose your own soul.

The Whole Duty of man is to fear God and keep His Commandments; and His Commandments are not burdensome. It is when you fear God and keep His Commandments that you can say, with certainty, that you have a close relationship with God. Dare to be a Godly man, woman, youth, boy, or girl!

VESSELS AND INSTRUMENTS OF HONOUR AND DISHONOUR

Questions for Discussion:

1. What do we mean by vessels and instruments?
2. Can a vessel be honourable or dishonourable?
3. What makes a vessel honourable or dishonourable to God?
4. What kind of vessel or instrument does God want for His Service?

The Bible says that in a great house, there are not only vessels of gold and silver, but also of wood and clay; some for honour and some for dishonour. It goes on to tell us what makes you a vessel of honour — sanctification and cleansing of oneself.

Therefore, if anyone cleanses himself from being a vessel of dishonour, he will be a vessel for honour, sanctified and useful for the Master, prepared for every good work (2 Tim. 2:20-21).

Interestingly, going through the second chapter of the second Book of Timothy, you will discover about eleven different things you are. You are God's son (verse 1). You are a soldier of Christ (verse 3).

You are an athlete (verse 5). You are a farmer (verse 6). You are an Elect of God (verse 10). You are a worker or a workman (verse 15). You are God's Own Property (verse 19). You name the Name of Jesus Christ (verse 19).

You are a vessel (verse 21). You are an instrument or a tool of the Master (verse 21). And you are a Servant of the Lord (verse 24).

When you were born again, you became a child of God. You belong to God, and if an earthly father gives good gifts and things to his child, how much more will our Heavenly Father give good things to us when we ask Him?

And you are a soldier of Christ, who is empowered by the Holy Spirit to wage war against the powers of darkness and destroy their works. This is why the Word says that you should give no place to the devil.

Some say that Jesus Christ has won the battle for us and we are to enjoy the victory now. Well, if you apply that correctly, you are right. Jesus Christ defeated the devil, and having spoiled principalities and powers, He made a show of them publicly, triumphing over them in it (Col. 2:15).

Yet the Word says that we wrestle with principalities and powers (Eph. 6:12), and that the weapons of our warfare are not carnal, but mighty through God to the pulling down of strongholds (2 Cor. 10:4). Don't these places tell you that we are to enforce the Victory of Jesus Christ?

Jesus Christ triumphed over the devil and collected the power and authority he had over man (because of Adam's disobedience) from him.

Jesus Christ came up and said, (and I paraphrase) "I have got all authority in Heaven and on earth, and I give you the power and authority to go and teach all nations because I am with you to the end of the age" (Matt. 28:18-20).

Paul said, "Give no place to the devil" (Eph. 4:27). James said, "Resist the devil and he will flee from you" (Jas 4:7). And Apostle Peter said, "Resist the devil steadfastly in faith" (1 Pet. 5:9).

God wants to use the Church to frustrate the plans of the kingdom of darkness; but the Church is not meeting up with God's Expectations.

God wants to make known His Manifold Wisdom by the Church to the principalities and powers in the heavenly places (Eph. 3:10). Even though God told Joshua that He had given him Jericho, Joshua and the people, still had to surround Jericho seven times and blow the trumpets at the seventh time.

When the walls of Jericho crumbled, they still had to go inside and enforce the victory. If the Church doesn't do her work, many more people will spend eternity in Hell Fire.

And you are an athlete. The Word says that if any man competes in athletics, he is not crowned unless he competes according to the rules (2 Tim. 2:5). Even if you come first in a sprint race (100m or 200m race), if you run another person's lane, you will be disqualified.

The same is applicable in the Christian race and in the ministry. Do you not know that they which run in a race all run, but one receives the prize? Run in such a way that you may obtain.

And everyone who competes for the prize is temperate in all things. Now they do it to obtain a perishable crown, but we for an imperishable crown. Therefore run thus: not with uncertainty.

Thus fight: not as one who beats the air. But discipline your body, and bring it into subjection; lest, when you have preached to others, you yourself should become disqualified (1 Cor. 9:24-27).

God told Moses to make sure that he built the tabernacle according to the pattern shown him on the mountain. God has Rules, Commandments, and Standards; they are forever settled in Heaven, and cannot change.

You are a farmer. You may sow and water, or you may sow while another waters. However, when the work is done, God gives the growth and the increase. And each one will receive his own reward according to his own labour.

We are God's fellow workers. The Church is God's Field; she is God's Building. The world is God's Harvest-field.

If a good master-builder has laid the foundation, and another builds on it, let each one take heed how he builds on it. For no other foundation can anyone lay than that which is laid, which is Jesus Christ.

Now if anyone builds on this foundation with gold, silver, precious stones, wood, hay, straw, each one's work will become clear; for the Day will declare it, because it will be revealed by fire; and the fire will test each one's work, of what sort it is.

If anyone's work which he has built on it endures, he will receive a reward. If any one's work is burned, he will suffer loss; but he himself will be saved, yet so as through fire (1 Cor. 3:6-15). You can see from here that you are God's fellow worker.

The hardworking farmer must be first to partake of the crops (2 Tim. 2:6). Therefore, be patient, brethren, until the Coming of the Lord. See how the farmer waits for the precious fruit of the earth, waiting patiently for it until it receives the early and later rain.

You also be patient. Establish your hearts, for the Coming of the Lord is at hand (Jas 5:7-8). As an Elect of God, brethren, be even more diligent to make your call and election sure always. If you do this, you will never stumble.

If you do, an entrance will be supplied to you abundantly into the Everlasting Kingdom of our Lord and Saviour Jesus Christ.

But also for this very reason, giving all diligence, add to your faith virtue, to virtue knowledge, to knowledge self-control, to self-control perseverance, to perseverance Godliness, to Godliness brotherly kindness, and to brotherly kindness love.

If these things are yours and abound, you will be neither barren nor unfruitful in the knowledge of our Lord Jesus Christ. For he who lacks those things is shortsighted, even to blindness, and has forgotten that he was cleansed from his old sins (2 Pet. 1:5-11).

As a workman, be diligent to show yourself approved to God, a worker who does not need to be ashamed, rightly dividing the Word of Truth (2 Tim. 2:15).

You are God's Own Property and the Lord knows those who are His. He watches over His Own Property and children to keep them from any evil.

Let anyone who names the Name of Christ Jesus depart from evil. This is the test for vessels and instruments of honour and dishonour. God is of Purer Eyes than to behold iniquity.

Sin, disobedience, unrighteousness, hypocrisy, and the life of compromise and carelessness, will make you dishonourable. Therefore, cleanse your vessel and your instrument from sin and contamination, and God will use you to an extent you will never expect.

As a vessel, what do you contain? Are you filled with holiness, righteousness, faithfulness, diligence, watchfulness, and integrity? Vessels are containers, and they contain something, even if it is air.

It is either you contain God or you contain the devil: you can't be a vacuum. You are either honourable or dishonourable. You are either cleansed or dirty and impure.

You will not love using a dirty plate to eat your food. Why will you think so with God? Don't be deceived, God cannot be mocked: you reap what you sow!

You are an instrument, a tool for the Master's Use. Machines are supposed to give out high output or work with low input or effort. Don't be rigid and stubborn that the Lord will work and work on you, without your being fruitful and productive in God's Sight.

Finally, you are the Lord's Servant. You are His Bondservant, and your will must be surrendered to His Own Will. God is worthy of our service, praise, honour, glory, and worship.

Beware of exaggeration, flattering, and lying. Man's wisdom does not work out the Righteousness of God. You wouldn't be helping God by saying what does not exist. There is no unrighteousness in God and with God.

The things that God expects in His vessels should abound in you. God expects uprightness, sincerity, trustworthiness, honesty, and faithfulness from His vessels. God expects obedience, righteousness, and holiness from His vessels.

FALSE MINISTERS IN THE CHURCH

Questions for Discussion:

1. Who is a false minister?
2. Are there false ministers in the church-world?
3. What makes one a false minister?
4. What should be our attitude towards false ministers?
5. Can a false minister be approved by God in his state of falsehood?

Take heed that no one deceives you. Many will come in the Name of Jesus Christ, saying, "I am Christ," and will deceive many. Many false prophets will rise up and deceive many (Matt. 24: 4-14).

False christs and false prophets will arise and show signs and wonders to deceive, if possible, even the Elect (Mk 13:22). These were the Words of Jesus Christ when He foretold what will happen at the end of times. And if you have not known it, these things are happening today.

People are using the Name of Jesus Christ and the Bible to deceive many. But thanks to God that it is not possible to deceive the Elect.

Who are the Elects? Has God selected some people and abandoned others? The Elects are those who are led by the Spirit of God, and whose lives are guided by the Word of God.

Some of these false ministers were called by God, but due to sexual immorality, pride, love of the world, and other things, they lost the anointing, and either went after strange gods to get negative powers or began to do wrong things to deceive the simple and exploit men.

False religions, beliefs, and teachings abound in the world today. But if we follow the Word of God and the Spirit of God, we will not be deceived. Even as we know that the antichrist is coming, there are many antichrists in the world today; they are even inside churches.

When you preach and teach things contrary to the Word of God and His Christ, you make yourself an antichrist. When you encourage people, by teaching or practice, to live lives contrary to the Word and Will of God, you are against Christ.

The Word of God says that we should prove all things and hold on to that which is true. We should not believe every spirit, but test the spirits whether they are of God. Let the prophets speak two or three, and let the others judge (1 Cor. 14:29).

We should no longer be children who are deceived easily. Don't run after miracles and prophecies; follow the Spirit of God and His Word so that you will not be deceived. Evil abounds these days. Don't relate with the one you are sure is a false minister.

This is love, that we walk according to His Commandments. This is the Commandment, that as you have heard from the beginning, you should walk in it; for many deceivers have gone out into the world.

Look to yourselves, that we do not lose those things we worked for, but that we may receive a full reward. Whoever transgresses and does not abide in the Doctrine of Christ, does not have God.

He who abides in the Doctrine of Christ has both the Father and the Son. If anyone comes to you and does not bring the Right Doctrine, do not receive him into your house nor greet him; for he who greets him shares in his evil deeds (2 Jn 1:10-11).

According to Apostle Paul, some preach Christ even from envy and strife, and some also from goodwill. People preach Christ out of selfish ambition, not sincerely, but some preach him out of love.

According to him, whether Christ is preached in pretence or in truth, Christ is preached, and he rejoices (Phil. 1:15-18). However, it is not good for you, as a minister, to finish preaching Christ and be cast away into Hell.

Jesus Christ says that in the Day of Judgment, He is going to tell many who prophesied and did mighty works in His Name that He never knew them, for they were workers of iniquity, though they were in the ministry (Matt. 7:21-23).

Don't be marveled because satan himself transforms himself into an angel of light. Therefore, it is no great thing if his ministers also transform themselves into ministers of righteousness, whose end will be according to their works. Such are false ministers, deceitful workers, transforming themselves into ministers of Christ (2 Cor. 10:13-15).

Beware of false prophets, who come to you in sheep's clothing, but inwardly they are ravenous wolves. You will know them by their fruits. Every good tree bears good fruit, but a bad tree bears bad fruit (Matt. 7:15-17).

Another parable Jesus Christ put forth to the people, saying, "The Kingdom of Heaven is like a man who sowed good seed in his field; but while men slept, his enemy came and sowed tares among the wheat and went his way. But when the grain had sprouted and produced a crop, then the tares also appeared.

"So the servants of the owner came to him, and said, 'Sir, did you not sow good seed in your field? How then does it have tares?' He said to them, 'An enemy has done this.'

"The servants said to him, 'Do you want us then to go and gather them up?' But he said, 'No, lest while you gather up the tares you also uproot the wheat with them. Let both grow together until the harvest'" (Matt. 13:24-30). Then there will be separation and burning of the tares.

The coming of the antichrist will be preceded by false prophets and false ministers. The Day of the Lord will not come until the Falling Away comes first, and the man of sin is revealed, the son of perdition.

He opposes and exalts himself above all that is called God or that is worshiped, so that he sits as God in the Temple of God, showing himself that he is God. The mystery of lawlessness is already at work; only He Who now restrains will do so until He is taken out of the way.

The coming of the lawless one is according to the working of satan, with all power, signs, and lying wonders, and with all unrighteous deception among those who perish, because they did not receive the love of the truth, that they may be saved (2 Thes. 2:3-10).

Miracles and prophecies are not proofs that the Spirit of God is with somebody. You need to go beyond them to checking their fruits and comparing their sayings and works with the Word of God. He, who has an ear, let him hear what the Spirit of God says to the Church.

False ministers are bent to deceive and they compromise God's Word. They are sent by satan, directly or indirectly, whether or not they are aware of it; and people like what satisfies their flesh. People like to come to church and still live the way they like.

They may not have problem with you when you tell them to come to church (they even want to be regarded as good persons because they go church), but when you speak against sin in their lives, many of them will get offended.

Some will go church for as long as ten years and yet not be born again. Some desire to be teachers when they understand neither what they say nor the things which they affirm.

Now the Spirit expressly says that some have departed (and others will still depart) from the faith, giving heed to deceiving spirits and doctrines of demons, speaking lies in hypocrisy, having their own conscience seared with a hot iron (1 Tim. 4:1-2).

These days are perilous times, when men love themselves, love money, boast, are proud, blaspheme, and do all sorts of ungodly things. They have the form of Godliness, but deny its power. Turn away from such people (2 Tim. 3:1-5).

Preach the Word! Be ready in season and out of season. Convince, rebuke, exhort, with all longsuffering and teaching.

For the time has come when they do not endure Sound Doctrine, but according to their own desires, because they have itching ears, they heap up for themselves teachers; and they turn their ears away from the truth, and are turned aside to fables.

But you be watchful in all things, endure afflictions, do the work of an evangelist (evangelists preach the Gospel and get sinners saved by the demonstration of God's Power), fulfill your ministry (2 Tim. 4:2-5).

Many are sent to churches from the kingdom of darkness as agents of darkness to do one thing or the other there. Many of them operate as prophets, pastors, elders, deacons, musicians, departmental leaders, interpreters, choristers, organizers, and other functions.

They may appear to be zealous for God, but they are after one assignment or the other. They can pretend so much, to deceive, because they are after specific Christians or ministers to bring them down. But thanks to God that we have God's Word and His Spirit, and we know that they are there.

We should never be afraid of false ministers, but avoid them when we recognize them because we will be wasting our time following them. Remember also that evil company corrupts good manners.

Attack them by prayer and fasting, if perhaps they happen to maneuver their ways to positions of authority in your church. You have the host of Heaven behind you. God is with you, in you, and for you. Greater are they that are with us than they that are with them.

The Church is marching on and the gates of Hades will not prevail against it. We have power and authority to trample on serpents and scorpions and over all the powers of the enemy; and nothing shall by any means harm us. There is neither divination nor enchantment against us.

Be sensitive to the Holy Spirit's Promptings, Urges, and Witness. Always obey the Voice of the Spirit of God instantly; never argue because He knows better than you do know.

False ministers are servants of corruption and bondage. They live to please the devil and themselves. Their minds have been corrupted and held in bondage by the devil, the wicked one.

Be careful who you allow to lay hands on you because, by the laying on of hands on you by a minister operating with a wrong spirit, you can be enslaved or affected by wrong spirits. This is why you must be prayerful and maintain a red-hot Christian life and spirituality.

Just as a good minister can impart something from the Spirit of God in him on you, a false minister can also do the same if you are not red-hot spiritually.

THE MINISTRY GIFTS AND HELPS

Questions for Discussion:
1. What are the ministry-gifts?
2. Why did Jesus Christ give these ministry-gifts to His Church?
3. Which ministry is more important than the other?
4. What is the ministry of helps?

When we speak of the ministry gifts, we are speaking of the offices of the apostle, the prophet, the evangelist, the pastor, and the teacher.

When we speak of the ministry of helps, we are speaking of such ministries as that of musicians, intercessors, financial sponsors, programme-organizers, and others that make or enable the five-fold ministry-offices function effectively.

When an evangelist comes to town and ministers under a strong anointing, people seem to ascribe all the work to him, but what of the organizers: those that arranged the seats, pasted the posters, arranged the vocal equipment, etc? All the glory must go to God.

Actually, when people speak of having deliverance, prayer, and healing ministries, they are just talking about what God has committed into our hands. Every Believer should cast out demons, and so is a deliverance minister.

Also, apostles, prophets, evangelists, pastors, and even teachers, should minister deliverance and healing to others. Also, we should all pray always.

There are diversities of gifts, but the same Spirit. There are differences of ministries, but the same Lord. And there are diversities of activities, but it is the same God Who works all in all.

But the Manifestation of the Spirit is given to each one for the profit of all. But one and the same Spirit works all these things, distributing to each one individually as He wills.

For as the body is one and has many members, but all the members of that one body, being many, are one body, so also is Christ.

For, in fact, the body is not one member but many. If the whole body were an eye, where would be the hearing? If the whole were hearing, where would be the smelling? But now God has set the members, each one of them, in the body just as He pleased.

And if they were all one member, where would the body be? A body is the embodiment or the existing together of different or many parts that function together as one. But now indeed there are many members, yet one body.

And the eye cannot say to the hand, "I have no need of you"; nor again the head to the feet, "I have no need of you." No, much rather, those members of the body which seem to be weaker are necessary.

And those members of the body which we think to be less honourable, on these we bestow greater honour; and our unpresentable parts have greater modesty, but our presentable parts have no need.

But God composed the body, having given greater honour to that part which lacks it, that there should be no schism in the body, but that the members should have the same care for one another.

And if one member suffers, all the members suffer with it; or if one member is honoured, all the members rejoice with it. Now you are the Body of Christ, and members individually (1 Cor. 12).

Do you know that the body can survive without an eye for twenty years? But the same body will not survive without an anus for a year, except on a specialized medical care. How the eye boasts as if it is more important than the anus!

But to each one of us grace was given according to the measure of Christ's Gift. Jesus Christ gave some to be apostles, some prophets, some evangelists, and some pastors and teachers.

The Bible tells us why these gifts were given: for the equipping of the Saints for the work of the ministry, for the edifying of the Body of Christ, till we all come to the unity of the faith and of the knowledge of the Son of God, to a perfect man, to the measure of the stature of the Fulness of Christ.

God gave them to us that we should no longer be children, tossed to and fro, and carried about with every wind of doctrine, by the trickery of men, in the cunning craftiness of deceitful plotting, but, speaking the truth in love, may grow up in all things into Him Who is the Head   Christ (Eph. 4).

As each one has received a gift, minister it to one another, as good stewards of the Oracles of God. If anyone speaks, let him do it as with the ability which God supplies, that in all things God may be glorified through Jesus Christ (1 Pet. 4:10-11).

Do not think of yourself more highly than you ought to think, but think soberly, as God has dealt to each one a measure of faith.

Having gifts differing according to the grace that is given to us, let us use them: if prophecy, let us prophesy in proportion to our faith; or ministry, let us use it in our ministering; he who teaches, in teaching; he who exhorts, in exhortation.

Let him who gives do it liberally; he who leads with diligence; he who shows mercy, with cheerfulness. Let love be without hypocrisy. Abhor what is evil. Cling to what is good (Rom. 12:3-9).

God has appointed these in the Church: first apostles, second prophets, third teachers, after that miracles, then gifts of healings, helps, administrations, varieties of tongues.

Are all apostles? Do all have gifts of healings? Do all speak with tongues? Do all interpret? But earnestly desire the best gifts (1 Cor. 12:28-31).

The ministry of the apostle is the ministry of someone who is sent by God for specific purposes, especially for the establishment of new works and/or churches.

The apostles are endowed with strong anointing, and they seem to have the ability to stand in the other remaining offices, at least to a level.

Of course, no apostle will carry all the other gifts with the magnitude and frequency like those who occupy those specific offices. Apostles do not necessarily carry all the other offices' abilities.

Apostle Paul started as a prophet and a teacher, while Apostle Barnabas started as a teacher (Acts 13:1-2). However, they still operated in those offices, to a level, in their apostolic works. Often, but not always, apostles have spectacular encounters with Jesus Christ and His Holy Spirit.

Novices cannot stand fully in the apostolic ministry. Some pastors do apostolic works of establishing new churches. Modern-day missionaries, if called by God for that purpose, are apostles.

The prophet operates more in the areas of visions, revelations, and prophecies. A real prophet will have at least two of the gifts of the word of wisdom, the word of knowledge, and discerning of spirits, plus the gift of prophecy operating consistently in his ministry.

People operate in different offices with different levels of anointing, and you can stand in two or more offices at a time. You can also move from one office to the other, as God wills.

The evangelists are endowed with the special gifts of the working of miracles and the gifts of healings, plus other gifts, as the Spirit of God deems necessary for each individual.

Any person who neither has the gift of working of miracles nor the gifts of healings is not a New Testament evangelist, even if he takes the title. Many use the title because they would not write 'Pastor...' or 'Bro....'

Pastors have the special gift of nurturing, taking care of, and getting the Believers matured in Christ. If you don't have a pastoral or shepherd heart, the heart of patience, tolerance, and compassion, you are not a pastor.

Teachers have the ability to explain and expound the Bible with clarity. Many of the other offices' occupiers have the ability to teach, though there are specific teachers. Some ministers are both preachers and teachers, while others are either preachers or teachers.

To preach is to proclaim the Gospel or the Good News; to teach is to explain or expound the Word of God. Find your place in the Kingdom and in the ministry, and don't envy anyone.

Musicians play important roles in the Kingdom of God. They aid in the praise and worship of the Almighty, and their ministry can either increase or decrease the anointing on the life of the minister: apostle, prophet, evangelist, pastor, and teacher.

It is true that some unbelievers develop and sing Gospel music; some even use occult powers to make their musical albums sell well in the market. However, musicians have an important place in the ministry.

So also are the intercessors and the prayer-warriors. Of course, every child of God should be an intercessor and a prayer-warrior, but God has given specific works of prayer to some people.

Those that sponsor ministers, churches, and ministries financially have a very great place in the Kingdom. They make the ministers happier, and God's Works progress more rapidly.

Then there are the organizers: those that sweep the halls, arrange the seats, do advertisements, and those that do other things. There are other forms of ministry of helps that help the ministers, churches, and ministries expand and function well, but the glory for everything must go to the Lord God.

In ministry, don't neglect the days of little beginnings. However small the thing you are doing for the Lord is, be committed to it, be diligent in it, and God will multiply it exceedingly. Don't be inconsistent. Don't say in your heart, "Let me be doing this, but if it doesn't work out, I will quit."

Once you are convinced it is what the Lord wants you to be doing, don't worry about it, because very soon, there will be a multiplication. Also, note that if you pay the right sacrifice or price of obedience, that multiplication will come sooner than you may expect it.

God will send an abundance in every area of your life and ministry, if you are faithful and obedient to Him. The hardship you may be seeing now may be a trial of your faith.

After Job's trial, his later end was better than his former days. God knows how to turn your defeat to victory, and how to restore the days the locust, cankerworm, and the palmerworm have eaten.

The Acts of the Apostles is still being written today, because there are many acts of the Believers and the ministers going on today. As the early apostles and Disciples affected their generation for good, we too have the same, and even greater, impact to make in our generation.

PRAYING ALWAYS WITH ALL KINDS OF PRAYER

Questions for Discussion:

1. When should we pray?
2. What does it mean to pray always?
3. What are the different kinds of prayer?
4. Which kinds of prayer are necessary to the Believers?

Satan is afraid of the Gifts of the Holy Spirit; satan is afraid of good preaching and right teaching; yet, satan fears prayer more than all of them. It is prayer that holds all these things together and makes them effective.

Without prayer, even your spiritual activities will fail, be unproductive, or be less productive. Yet, remember that fasting increases the power and effectiveness of prayer many folds.

Prayer is very powerful, and we have to pray always with all kinds of prayer. The effectual fervent prayer of the righteous avails much and is powerful. Prayer is a force that many have refused to use, even though it is within their reach. Men of all ages and nations have been praying.

In fact, man has that instinct within him; man has the desire to communicate with His Creator; hence, even unbelievers pray. But the prayer of the wicked is an abomination to God (Prov. 15:8).

However, God (being a Good God) gives His rain, sun, children, air, etc to all men; and if they were to buy them, with what will they buy them? He will also hear the cry of the needy!

God gave man authority over the earth, though man lost that authority to the devil when he sinned against God by disobeying Him; hence, the Bible calls the devil the god of this world (2 Cor. 4:4).

This is why the devil can cause pains, sufferings, sicknesses, earthquakes, and such things. But when the Lord Jesus Christ rose up from the dead, He said that all authority in Heaven and on earth has been given to Him and He gave that authority to the Church, His Body, who represent Him on earth (Matt. 28:18-20).

We, the Church, individually and as a group, have authority over the earth and we exercise that authority by prayer. There are different kinds of prayer, and we will take them up later.

We are commanded to watch and pray that we do not fall into temptation (Matt. 26:41). To watch is to be alert, sober, and vigilant. We have to open our eyes and ears (physically and spiritually) to know what is happening around us so that we can pray intelligently and effectively.

It is not enough to just pray; you've got to pray to receive results. Hence, Apostle Paul said that he doesn't fight aimlessly like the one beating the air (1 Cor. 9:26).

When you know the strongholds and plans of the enemy, you will fight against him more effectively. And the devil, many times, does not want to be recognized so that his plans and purposes will neither be thwarted nor destroyed.

Ask, and you shall receive; seek, and you shall find; knock, and the door shall be opened to you. For he who asks, receives; he who seeks, finds; and to him that knocks, the door will be opened (Matt: 7:7-8).

You do not have, because you do not ask. When you ask, you do not receive because you ask amiss that you may spend them on your own pleasures (Jas 4:2-3). Asking or praying in doubt and with double-mind will also hinder your answers.

Another thing that can hinder your prayer is sin and disobedience. God's people suffer because of ignorance (Hos. 4:6); and ignorance leads to unbelief which is a great obstacle to receiving your answers.

This is why you have to study the Word of God for yourself, so that you may know what the Lord Jesus Christ purchased for you, and you will pray more effectively.

The Bible says that we are to pray always or without ceasing (1 Thes. 5:17). We are to be instant in prayer (Rom. 12:12). No one should be forcing you to pray, but you have to make prayer a habit and a duty; and you will have to discipline yourself to pray as supposed.

If you show a careless attitude to prayer, that is how your prayer-life will be: inconsistent. Therefore, just as athletes train to perform well, you have to discipline yourself and pray till you make it your lifestyle.

One condition to receiving answers to your prayer is faith, believing that God has answered your prayer. Whatever you ask of when you pray, believe that you receive it and you shall have it (Mk 11:24).

Another condition is to pray according to the Will of God (1 Jn 5:14). Another is to do those things that please Him. And you have to bear fruit, that whatever you ask the Father, He will give it to you (Jn 15:16). And don't live in sin, for the prayer of the sinner is abominable to God.

Throughout the Bible, we see the records of people who prayed. Abraham interceded for Sodom and Gomorrah, though at last, ten righteous people couldn't be found there (Gen. 18:32); Moses interceded for the children of Israel so that God did not wipe them out as He had intended (Exo. 32:7-14).

Elijah prayed, and it did not rain for three and half years, and when he prayed afterwards, it rained (1 Kgs 17 & 18). Jesus Christ prayed a lot. Apostle Paul prayed and showed us an example.

Now, we will consider the different kinds of prayer. There is praying in the Holy Ghost. Praying in the Holy Ghost includes praying in tongues, praying prophetically, and groaning in the Spirit (1 Cor. 14:14-15; Rom. 8:26). You build up your most holy faith by praying in the Holy Ghost (Jude 1:20).

And there is the prayer of intercession. In the prayer of intercession, you stand to intercede on behalf of others, especially in trying to keep them from being punished.

There is the prayer of supplication, which is to ask for God's Help, Supply, Provision, and Intervention on your behalf and on the behalf of others, especially Christians.

When you petition God, you are telling God to do this or that for yourself and others, according to His Word; hence, the Word says that you should plead your case (Mic. 6:1; Mic. 7:9; Isa. 41:21). Of course, many kinds of prayer are related, but they need to be separated for better understanding.

There is the prayer of faith. The prayer of faith is the prayer that you pray because God has specifically promised you or others something, and you stand on that provision and pray, believing that you receive; and you shall have it.

No matter how the situation may appear not to have changed, hold on to your belief and confession, and instead of praying again for it, keep on thanking God for the answer and you will see the manifestation in no distant time.

We now consider the prayer of consecration. This kind of prayer needs to be prayed always by every Christian, submitting himself/herself to the Will of God for his or her life as Jesus Christ did (Matt. 26:38-42).

Be willing and ready to do the Will of God, no matter how hard it may look like. I will consider the prayer of confession. First, confess your sins to God, for he that covers his sins shall not prosper, but he that confesses and renounces them shall find mercy (Prov. 28:13). This is very important for every Christian.

Of course, a Christian should not live in sin, but many don't repent of their sins and continue to pray. You are deceiving yourself. And you know that you have to forgive others for God to forgive you (Matt. 6:14-15).

Next is to confess or declare what you want to be, what you want to happen, without doubting. Whoever says to this mountain, "Be removed, and be cast into the sea," and does not doubt in his heart, but believes that those things he says will be done, he will have whatever he says (Mk 11:23).

There is the prayer of agreement, which involves two or more people praying together in agreement over this or that thing. The people involved will need to believe and not doubt, for maximum result; and the prayer can be made even if they are not together physically.

The prayer of binding and loosing involves destroying the works of devils by speaking directly to the devils responsible for them, and to their works, to pull down and to root out, to destroy and to throw down, to build and to plant (Jer. 1:10).

And the Lord says that whatever you bind on earth, will be bound in Heaven, and whatever you loose on earth, will be loosed in Heaven (Matt. 18:18). There is the prayer of commitment in which you cast your cares to the Lord (1 Pet. 5:7).

The prayer of worship involves showing respect and love for God. It is the prayer of adoration. Pray always with all kinds of prayer!

BEING ESTABLISHED IN FAITH

Questions for Discussion:

1. What is faith?
2. What does it mean to be established in faith?
3. How can we be established in faith?
4. What is the relationship between faith and the Word of God?

Faith is the substance of things hoped for, the evidence of things not seen. (Heb. 11:1). Faith is believing that God exists and that His Word is true and sure. It is being confident that what the Lord promised, He will perform without failure.

Faith is obedience to the Word of God in any area, because you believe that you are committed to obey Him as your Lord and Master. Faith is acting on the Word, taking action as directed by His Word.

But faith comes by hearing the Word of God (or as Apostle Paul put it, "Faith comes by hearing and hearing by the Word of God" (Rom. 10:17). When you hear the Gospel, the Gospel tells you that Jesus Christ suffered and died for you, and that if you receive Him, He will wash away your sins and save you.

When you submit to the Gospel, you receive faith by the Gospel (the Good News or the Word of God concerning salvation); and through the faith, you are saved when you confess Jesus Christ.

Then you don't stop at that level of the knowledge of the Word of God; you progress by hearing, reading, studying, meditating on, and confessing the Word of God; and you increase your faith through those means. The Bible says that we should be filled with the Word of Christ in all wisdom (Col. 3:16).

The Word should dwell in us richly so that our faith will be stronger. We resist the devil steadfastly in faith, and faith is our shield that protects us from all the fiery arrows of the enemy. The righteous shall live by faith.

Faith works by love (Gal. 5:6). The Word of God says that if you have all faith that you can remove mountains, but have not love, you are nothing (1 Cor. 13:2). Among faith, hope, and love, the greatest is love.

Therefore, no matter the level of faith you may be operating in, you must love: first, love God with your all, so that you can keep His Commandments; second, you must love others as yourself, so that you can do to them as you would have them do to you, as you desire they do to you.

The Word of God commands us to have faith in God (or literally, to have the Faith of God). We ought to have absolute confidence in our God, so that even if the seas roar, though the mountains may crumble, though the earth may quake, we should never be afraid, because we are confident that the Lord is with us and will shield us.

This is why we have to obey God absolutely, because it is sin and disobedience that brings guilt.

The Faith of God is the faith that calls those things that do not exist by name as though they do exist. God Who gives life to the dead and calls those things which do not exist as though they did, told Abraham that He has made him a father of many nations, when, as yet, he didn't even have a son.

But thanks to God that Abraham, contrary to hope, in hope believed, so that he became the father of many nations. And not being weak in faith, he did not consider his own body, already dead (since he was about a hundred years old), and the deadness of Sarah's womb.

He did not waver at the Promise of God through unbelief, but was strengthened in faith, giving glory to God, and being fully convinced that what He had promised He was also able to perform.

And, therefore, it was counted to him for righteousness (Rom. 4:17-22). It was through the God-kind of faith that He created the heavens and the earth. Even though they were not in existence, God declared that they should be, and they came to be.

By faith we understand that the worlds were framed by the Word of God so that the things which are seen were not made of things which are visible (Heb. 11:3).

Whoever says to this mountain, "Be removed and be cast into the sea," and does not doubt in his heart, but believes that those things he says will be done, he will have whatever he says.

Whatever things you will ask when you pray, believe that you receive them, and you will have them (Mk 11:23-24). If you have faith, and do not doubt, if you say to a mountain, "Be removed and be cast into the sea," it will be done. And whatever thing you ask in prayer, believing, you will receive (Matt. 21:21-22).

Some people have thought that Jesus Christ went about healing anyone He wanted to heal, but this is not true. Even though Jesus Christ was anointed without measure, people received their miracles both by the demonstration of the anointing upon Him, and by the exercise of their own faith.

The woman with the issue of blood, for example, received her healing by exercising her faith, and Jesus Christ told her, "Your faith has made you whole." He told another that he will receive if he had faith, for all things are possible to him that believes (Matt. 9:22; Mk 9:23).

When He came to His Own place, His people despised Him, saying, "Is this not Jesus whose parents and brethren we know?" Their unbelief prevented Jesus Christ from doing mighty works among them (Matt. 13:54-58; Mk 6:1-6).

Unbelief, doubt, sin, disobedience, and fear are obstacles to faith. You must get rid of those things if you are going to excel in the faith-life, because the righteous one will live by faith. Faith will keep you free from the arrows and plans of the devil; and without faith, you give the devil a place in your life.

Faith and works go together. Faith without works is dead, and works without faith is self-righteousness and cannot save you or fulfil God's Purpose for your life.

If you believe that God will protect you and provide for you, then you must be prayerful and learn to give; and if you fail in prayer and in giving, you will be disappointed.

You believe that there is one God. You do well. Even the demons believe and tremble! Abraham was justified by works when he offered Isaac his son on the altar, and by works faith was made perfect (Jas 2:19-22).

Your faith is activated by prayer and confession. With the heart one believes to righteousness, and with the mouth confession is made to salvation (Rom. 10:10).

Whatever you believe God can do for you, pray for that: and when you ask, you receive; when you seek, you will find; and when you knock, the door will be opened to you (Matt. 7:7). Don't joke with prayer; it is one of the most important things in your life.

There is the gift of faith which the Holy Spirit imparts to a Spirit-filled Believer to help him receive a miracle from God. It is distinguished from the gift of the working of miracles in that the working of miracles works miracles actively, while the gift of faith receives miracles passively.

When Daniel was not hurt by the lions in the den, it was the gift of faith that was in operation, but when Jesus Christ commanded the waves of the sea and the wind to cease, it was the working of miracles that was in operation. But the gift of faith is given to Believers as the Spirit of God wills.

Faith is perfected through practice. It is like taking part in athletics or sports; you have to train and practice so that you can perfect in your area and be able to win the game. It is like lifting weights; you start with lighter ones, and you progress to heavier ones.

Even though you would be able to lift heavy objects in future, you wouldn't be able to lift them at the beginning. The Lord says that if you have faith as small as the mustard seed, you can remove mountains.

The practice is not necessarily to get more faith (and you need more faith; the Bible speaks of great faith), but to strengthen and activate the faith.

The elders of old, the Saints and Servants of old, received good reports or testimonies by faith. Without faith, it is impossible to please to God, for he who comes to God must believe that He is, and that He is a Rewarder of those who diligently seek Him (Heb. 11:2,6).

Abel gave to God by faith. Noah obeyed God by faith. Moses chose to suffer affliction with the people of God than to enjoy the passing pleasures of sin, esteeming the reproach of Christ greater riches than the treasures in Egypt.

Faith purifies the heart; the Word of God which is the truth sanctifies us; by the Word, we are made clean (Acts 14:9; Jn 17:17; Jn 15:3). There is strong faith (Rom. 4:17-20). There is weak faith (Rom. 14:1). There is shipwrecked faith (1 Tim. 1:19). There is unfeigned faith (1 Tim. 1:5).

Anything not done in faith is sin (Rom. 14:23). We walk by faith, and not by sight (2 Cor. 5:7). Don't deny the faith, and don't cast off your first faith. Do not err from the faith, but earnestly contend for the faith once delivered to the Saints (Jude 1:3).

Jesus Christ is the Way, the Truth, the Life, and the Door. He is the Way to God and anything you may desire. He is the Truth, and any other thing opposed to him is fake. Jesus Christ is the Source of life for anybody who desires life. Also, He is the Door to the Treasures of God.

BEING SUCCESSFUL IN LIFE

Questions for Discussion:

1. What does it mean to be successful in life?
2. How can one be successful in life?
3. In what areas is a Christian supposed to be successful?

To be successful in life is to fulfill God's Purpose and Plan for your life. This is why the Lord says that life is not in the abundance of what a man possesses (Lk. 12:15).

This is why the poor members of the Church of Smyrna were told by the Lord that they were rich (Rev. 2:9), and the rich members of the Church of the Laodiceans were told that they were poor and wretched (Rev. 3:17).

God sees differently from how men see. Do you know that, even as a minister, you can have the largest church and organize the biggest crusade, and still not be following God's Plan for your life?

What people call 'success' is no success at all. If you become the wealthiest, richest, most famous, most powerful, or most educated person of all ages, and you lose your soul in Hell at last, you were very unsuccessful.

Material blessings, academic blessings, marital blessings, ministerial blessings, and many others are good and necessary; after all, without money, how can the Gospel go to the ends of the earth?

But let me tell you the truth, true success is obedience to the Word of God, and the achievement of God's Purpose for your life.

Abraham was successful in life, even though he had only one son after many years (apart from the son of the bondwoman   Ishmael). Moses was successful; even though he did not make it to the land of Canaan, he made it to Heaven.

Joshua and Caleb were successful; of all the adults that left Egypt, only two of them made it to Canaan, and they fulfilled God's Purpose for their lives. Samuel, David, Isaiah, Daniel, Jesus Christ, Peter, Paul, and many others were successful. David was rich and Daniel was famous, but all of them fulfilled God's Plans for their lives.

Most of the adults that left Egypt at the exodus of the Israelites did not make it to Canaan, and to Paradise. Sampson lost his ministry and his eyes due to irresponsibility.

Solomon lost the kingdom of Israel after his death, because his heart was estranged from God, though he was very wise and rich. Judas Iscariot fell by the way. King Asa did not end well. These and many others were unsuccessful in life. They displeased God and lost their missions.

What does it mean to be successful in life? The word 'success' means the achieving of something you have been trying to do, with a good result. If you do very well in what you want to do or in what you are to do (like your Christian life, your ministry, or your job), you are a success.

However, Godly success is not always the same with human success. What humans regard as success may be seen by God as destruction. What humans may regard as foolishness may be seen by God as success.

Concerning success, I will like to speak about Apostle Paul. This holy and fiery apostle of the Almighty God had a great success in his ministry. This is not to say that he did not make mistakes; of course, he made some mistakes.

This holy apostle and prophet of Jesus Christ suffered dearly in the ministry. He traveled by foot and by ship; he was stoned and beaten with rod and whips; he suffered hunger and rejection. Nevertheless, he called all those things, and many more, light afflictions (2 Cor. 4:17).

Apostle Paul wanted and desired to succeed in the ministry and be faithful to the Lord that he despised the pains and the shame he encountered, and pressed for the prize of the High Call of God.

He did not have internet services, aircraft, cars, duplexes, cathedrals; yet he decided to preach the Gospel where Christ had not been named. He did not collect tithes and offerings to enrich himself, and keep a lot in store.

He used what he collected for the Work of God. Today, many have removed their focus from Jesus Christ, Heaven, and souls; they are interested in money.

Let me talk about other areas of success before I go back to the real success spiritual success. But the spirit-realm controls the physical realm; therefore, spiritual success is supposed to show physically.

However, if you are not rich yet, it does not necessarily mean that you have a problem spiritually, even though you may have to check your life of obedience and faith; your unwillingness to get rich will affect God's Supply for you (Isa. 1:19). God's Divine Power has given us all things we need for life and Godliness.

Also, God's people suffer due to ignorance (Hos. 4:6). Some don't even know that it is God's Will for them to prosper materially and financially. The earth is the Lord's and the fullness of it (Psa. 24:1).

Silver and gold is God's; a thousand cattle by the hill are His (Psa. 50:10). God did not create these things for the devil and his children, but for God's people, even though Adam sold out his inheritance to the devil when he disobeyed God and sinned against Him.

Thus satan became the god of this world (2 Cor. 4:4). But Jesus Christ came to bring that inheritance back to us and we are gods and kings of the Great God and King (Psa. 82:6; Rev. 1:6).

Jesus Christ became poor so that through His poverty, we might be made rich (2 Cor. 8:9). It is God's Will for us to prosper in material things. Of course, many of the early apostles, prophets, and Disciples were not rich materially.

One reason this was so is because they were committed to winning souls: we must be committed to winning souls like them; they won souls in the face of fierce persecutions. We live more peaceably now.

Another reason is that many of them were ignorant of God's Will in this area. They didn't have the entire Bible as we have today; we can compare one part with another. Nevertheless, they pursued the substance, and today many of us seem to be pursuing the shadows   riches and material blessings.

No wonder they were more spiritual than many today. However, never set your mind on temporal things, things that perish and do not have eternal value. Riches and wealth have eternal value when used for God's Glory.

Physical prosperity or success is very necessary. I am speaking of health and healing here. No matter how much you have, if you are sick and can't work or stand, it is a very big problem. In that case, you wouldn't even enjoy your meals.

But God has provided health and healing for us. Jesus Christ carried our sicknesses and diseases, and it is God's Will for us to be healthy. If you choose to be sick, you are just giving the devil a place in your life. God is not responsible for it.

Abraham was very rich in cattle, in silver, and in gold (Gen. 13:2). He had 318 trained servants, and more than that, for he couldn't have used all for the war he fought (Gen. 14:14). The Lord blessed Abraham in all things (Gen. 24:1).

Isaac reaped a hundred-fold of what he planted. He waxed great, and went forward, and grew until he became very great (Gen. 26:12-13). Isaac had possession of flocks, and possession of herds, and great store of servants: and the Philistines envied him (Gen. 26:14).

Jacob increased exceedingly, and had much cattle, and maidservants, and menservants, and camels, and asses (Gen. 30:43). Job was blameless and upright, and one who feared God and shunned evil. He had so much that he was the greatest of all the people of the east (Job 1:1-3).

David was righteous and feared God, yet he was a king and prepared for the House of the Lord a hundred thousand talents of gold, and a thousand talents of silver, and of brass and iron without weight for it was in abundance: timber also and stone he prepared (1 Chron. 22:14).

Even in the New Testament, people of God were rich. That is why Apostle Paul told Timothy to charge the rich to do good (1 Tim. 6:17). Talking of promotion and power, Daniel and his three friends were high in positions in the Babylonian government.

They were blessed academically also, for they were ten times wiser than the others. God blessed them in appearance also. (Dan. 1:15,19-21; Dan. 3:29-30; Dan 6:1-3). Mordecai was highly promoted and honoured by God (Esth. 6:1-14). God delivered the Israelites with a strong hand (Exo. 12:29-33). Joseph was the prime minister of Egypt for God was with him (Gen. 41:38-44).

But, Brethren, do not love the world or anything in the world. The love of money is the root of all evil. He who loves silver will not be satisfied with silver. Whatever God gives you, use it for His Glory and to expand the Church on earth.

Heaven should be your main goal, and you must strive to please God. The Word of God shall not depart from your mouth, but you shall meditate on it day and night, that you may do all His Word. For then you will make your way prosperous, and then you will have good success (Josh. 1:8).

Curses and spiritual attacks can hinder somebody's progress in life. Be sensitive to the Spirit, because He will give you a signal, by any way He chooses, of the existence of any of them in your life. Then, break them in the Name of Jesus Christ.

God has given you the power to decree a thing and it will be established. Whatever you decree will come to pass; don't doubt. You may need to add fasting to your prayer.

The Power, Presence, and Favour of God bring increase and multiplication in all areas of life: spiritual, mental, physical, and otherwise. God is a Good God!

DIVINE HEALTH AND HEALING

Questions for Discussion:

1. What is Divine Health?
2. What is Divine Healing?
3. How can we receive Divine Health and Healing?
4. Are Christians free from sicknesses and diseases?

When God formed His man, Adam, he was healthy. God never intended that we suffer sicknesses and diseases. Sicknesses and diseases came from satan, and their influences on men were made possible by sin and disobedience.

God told His healthy Adam to keep to certain Rules. However, Adam disobeyed God, and God became angry with man. Man fell short of the Glory of God, and was then open to satanic attacks. Sicknesses and diseases are forms of those attacks. There are many other ones.

Sickness is the state of being ill. Illness is a disease of the body or mind. Disease is an unhealthy condition in the body, especially one caused by infection. We can see that illness or disease is related to the mind.

Apart from the germs and micro-organisms like bacteria, fungi, and viruses that cause sicknesses and diseases, stresses (both of the mind and of the body) and anxieties cause sicknesses and diseases also.

However, no disease-causing micro-organism could have any effect on man if man had not sinned and fallen short of God's Glory (Rom. 3:23).

Divine Health is God's Perfect Will for His people. Divine Health is the state of existence whereby God's Power keeps one from sickness and disease. It is different from Divine Healing.

Divine Healing is the situation where God's Power expels sickness and disease from someone. Divine Healing is God's Permissive Will, as opposed to His Perfect Will, which is Divine Health.

The Word of God says that the Lord Jesus Christ bore our griefs, and carried our sorrows. The chastisement of our peace was upon Him, and with His Stripes we are healed (Isa. 53:4-5). That is the Old Testament report of what Christ did for us.

After He had come and done them, Apostle Peter said that by His Stripes we were healed (1 Pet. 2:24). Sickness and disease represent grief and sorrow. Sicknesses, diseases, and pain are the handiwork of the devil, and God is not happy seeing people in those conditions.

Jesus Christ Himself took our infirmities and bore our sicknesses (Matt. 8:17). As Christ Jesus has borne them, we don't need to bear them again. However, many of us open the door to sicknesses and diseases, and they come in because that is what the devil wants.

We should never break the hedge; for if we break it, the serpent will come in (Eccl. 10:8). Give no foothold, no place to the devil (Eph. 4:27).

There are many ways sicknesses and diseases can come into the life of a Christian. One way is by sin and disobedience. Too much stress, both on your body and your soul can cause them also. Worrying causes illness more than some of us have realized.

Another cause of illness is lack of rest and exercise; even our feeding habit and what we eat have a lot to do with our health. In fact, the best hospital in the world is taking good care of what you eat and how you eat them.

The Word of God is a medicine for Divine Healing, and it also keeps you in Divine Health. God sent His Word to heal His people (Psa. 107:20). The Word of God is spirit and life (Jn 6:63).

The Word of God is the Sword of the Spirit and it pierces and destroys every disease-causing micro-organism (Eph. 6:17; Heb. 4:12). The Word will give you peace, and keep you from worrying which causes sickness. Perfect peace have they that love God's Word (Isa. 26:3; Psa. 119:165).

Give attention to God's Word; incline your ear to His Sayings. Do not let them depart from your eyes; keep them in the midst of your heart, for they are life to those who find them, and health to all their flesh (Prov. 4:20-22). That is very clear!

When you read, study, meditate on, and confess the Word of God, you are activating Divine Healing and Health in your life. He sent forth His Word, the topic notwithstanding, and His Word healed His people.

The Word of God says that there was no feeble or sick person among the children of Israel at a particular time (Psa. 105:37). That is God's Will for us. No wonder He gives gifts of healings to His children so that they can minister healings, supernaturally, to God's people and the people of the world.

Of course, God, in His Love, gave us medical science so that those who don't know about Divine Healing and those don't have faith may be healed thereby. That is not to say that any Christian who patronizes hospitals and medical technology has sinned or does not have faith; understand that faith has different levels and layers.

But, how will you be bold to tell an unbeliever that God healed you, when you used the same medicine he used: we should develop our faith?

But Divine Healing is preferable with God to medical healing. I would rather die, believing God, than die, depending on science and technology. Some say that they may die if they trust God; have you not been seeing or hearing of many deaths, right in the hospitals?

Some don't even know that many sicknesses and diseases are as a result of direct demonic attacks. Medicine does not solve spiritual problems. Therefore, if you have been bewitched because you opened doors to the devil, and you depend on medical science, you may die like a dog.

The Lord was not pleased with a certain king of Israel (King Asa) who, in time of sickness, trusted in physicians and doctors, instead of trusting in the Lord (2 Chron. 16:12).

Learn to pray against the works of the devil in the form of sicknesses and diseases. At the Name of Jesus Christ, every knee should bow, including sicknesses and diseases (Phil. 2:10).

Is any sick among you? Let him call for the elders of the Church, and let them pray over him, anointing him with oil in the Name of the Lord: and the prayer of faith shall save the sick, and the Lord shall raise him up.

And if he has committed any sin, they shall be forgiven him. Confess your faults (sins) one to another, and pray for one another, that you may be healed. The effectual fervent prayer of the righteous man avails much (Jas 5:14-16).

You can notice that some sicknesses are connected with sins. That is why you need to forgive others, and ask God to forgive you your sins. There are some sins you will need to confess to the people praying for you, if you want to be healed.

Jesus Christ told the sick man that his sins were forgiven, and later told him to take up his bed and go (Matt. 9:2-8). You can readily see that forgiveness and healing go together, where sin is the cause of the sickness, because not all sicknesses are caused by sins.

Also, it is not always that you will receive healing through the operation of the gifts of healings in the life of a Believer or a minister. It is not always that you need someone to pray for you to be healed. There are many Promises of God concerning Divine Healing in the Bible; stick to the Word of God and claim your healing.

No matter the symptoms you may be feeling, don't be like Peter who looked at the waves of the sea, away from looking to Jesus Christ, and started sinking.

If God has said it, He will do it. God can neither lie nor fail to perform His Word. He created the whole universe by the power of His Word, and His Word is just as effective today as it has always been. He is the Lord that heals and healed you (Exo. 15:26).

If God can heal cancer, He can heal HIV also, for nothing is impossible with God. The problem is that many prefer that the devil steal their money through medical bills to receiving healing from God by faith. Others prefer medicine because they are attended to free of charge, or are given medical allowances.

Learn to fellowship with other brethren, because when the corporate anointing is in manifestation, you can receive your healing, even without specific prayer. The Lord wants you to be healthy always.

Be very cautious of what you eat and how you eat. Healthy eating will sustain your health. If you can eat more of fruits and vegetables, you will have stronger health.

FASTING, DISCIPLINE, AND SELF-CONTROL

Questions for Discussion:

1. What is fasting?
2. What is discipline?
3. What is self-control?
4. What are the benefits of fasting, discipline, and self-control?

Fasting is going for some time without food. Water may or may not be taken for that space of time. Actually, fasting for a long time should go along with the drinking of water.

I will call the case of fasting while drinking only water complete or total fasting, and fasting without food and water absolute fasting. There is a partial fasting which involves taking certain kinds of food while fasting. Dieting is not the fasting we are talking about.

Self-discipline is the ability to discipline or make yourself do what you are to do and avoid what you are to avoid. Many make great plans and resolutions but don't carry them out due to lack of discipline.

Apostle Paul said that he disciplined himself, and brought his body under subjection. Bringing your body under subjection is self-discipline. People that run races, people that take part in athletics, discipline themselves, and train well to be able to win the prize (1 Cor. 9:24-27).

In Christianity, a Christian must discipline himself to do well in his Christian life. If you don't discipline yourself to pray, you will not have a consistent prayer-life.

If you don't discipline yourself and get rid of all obstacles, you will not study your Bible as you are supposed to; you will not evangelize as you are supposed to evangelize. When people hear good messages and read good books, they take decisions to do what they have heard and read, but how many of them do them?

Your ability to bring your fleshly desires and lusts under control or subjection is self-control. Self-control is a fruit of the recreated human spirit which the Book of Galatians calls the Fruit of the Spirit (Gal. 5:22-23).

When you are born again, your human spirit is recreated or regenerated, and he becomes a new creature. You build your spirit by reading, studying, and meditating on the Word of God.

As you read, study, and meditate on the Word of God, your mind and thinking is renewed, and you start thinking as God thinks, because the Word of God is God's Mind. Your mind or soul is where you take decisions of what to do.

Your spirit wants to please God, but your flesh may develop bad desires (you may be tempted with the lust of the eyes and the lust of the flesh), then your renewed mind takes side with your spirit to do the Will of God; if you discipline yourself to do it, that is self-control.

There are many examples of fasting in the Old Testament. Moses fasted for forty days and forty nights with neither food nor water (Exo. 34:28). Joshua and the elders of Israel fasted till evening after they were defeated by Ai, and God revealed the problem with them to them (Josh. 7:1-15).

Even King Ahab that was wicked, fasted and put on sackcloth, and God did not pour His Judgment on him the time He wanted (1 Kgs 21:27-29). Daniel fasted for twenty-one days, and had a breakthrough (Dan. 10:1-21).

Even in the New Testament, John the Baptist lived a fasted life (Matt. 3:4). Jesus Christ fasted for forty days and forty nights before He began His Public Ministry (Matt. 4:1-11). The Disciples fasted and the Holy Spirit spoke to them as they fasted and prayed (Acts 13:1-4).

When Apostle Paul and the others were entrapped in the sea, they kept on fasting till fourteen days before they ate, after God had encouraged Paul (Acts 27:9-29). There are other examples of fasting both in the Old and New Testaments.

You can fast to bring your body under subjection. You can fast to be able to pray more effectively. Fasting in times of danger is good. You fast to receive guidance from God.

It is good not to eat or eat much before preaching or teaching as a minister, and before singing as a musician. Fasting will make you become more sensitive to the Holy Spirit. Fast as a group and fast individually.

The devil will try to make you stop fasting by saying that you are looking pale and sick. He will use people to suggest it, even Christians and your close relations.

When you fast, do not be like the hypocrites, of a sad countenance. For they disfigure their faces, that they may appear to men to fast. They have their reward.

But when you fast, anoint your head, and wash your face, that you appear not to men to fast, but to your Father Who is in the Secret Place and your Father who sees in secret will reward you openly. The same applies to praying and giving (Matt. 6:1-18).

The length of fasting and how the fasting should be done will be influenced by many factors: the need, your physical condition, your commitment, how you are led, etc.

Don't compete with anybody as far as fasting is concerned. You don't have the same assignment in life. Always be conscious of the fact that obedience is better than sacrifice, and to listen better than burnt offerings (1 Sam. 15:22).

Before I go on with fasting, I want to speak on self-discipline. Many people can spend two, three, or more hours watching football or films on the television. But how many of them can spend two hours daily in prayers?

Many will go around visiting this or that person, but when they want to pray, they will start feeling sleepy, even before twenty minutes. Just as you trained yourself to watch television, you have to train yourself to pray and do other necessary things.

You will not be perfect at first time; but keep on pressing and doing them, and they will, as well, become easy.

Do not love the world or anything in the world; if any man loves the world, the Love of the Father is not in him.

All that is in the world: the lust of the flesh, the lust of the eyes, and the pride of life do not come from the Father but from the world; and the world passes away and its lusts, but he who does the Will of God endures forever (1 Jn 2:15-17).

I said this in respect of self-control. Present your body a living sacrifice to God, holy and pleasing to Him, and renew your mind by the Word of God (Rom. 12:1-2).

From the fifty-eight chapter of Isaiah, we see many things about fasting. People fast and afflict their souls without receiving the results they want because on the day of their fast, they do as they want and exploit their workers.

Some fast for strife and debate, and to strike with the fist of wickedness. You cannot fast like that and expect to be heard by God. God's Intention in fasting is not for you to afflict your soul for the period, and after that to go back to your old ways.

The fast that God has chosen is to loose the bonds of wickedness, to undo the heavy burdens, to let the oppressed go free, and to break every yoke.

It is to share your food with the hungry, and to bring to your house the poor who are cast out; when you see the naked, to cover him, and not hide yourself from your fellow human beings.

It is to take away the yoke from your midst; the pointing of the finger, and speaking wickedness. If you extend your soul to the hungry and satisfy the afflicted soul, if you serve the Lord as you are supposed to, obeying Him,

Then your light shall break forth like the morning, your healing shall spring forth speedily. Your righteousness shall go before you, and the Glory of the Lord shall be your rear guard.

Then the Lord will hear you when you call. The Lord will guide you continually, and satisfy your soul in drought and strengthen your bones; you shall be like a watered garden, and like a spring of water, whose waters do not fail.

Those from among you shall build the old waste places; you shall raise up the foundations of many generations. And you shall be called the repairer of the breach, the restorer of streets to dwell in.

Then you shall delight yourself in the Lord, and the Lord will cause you to ride on the high hills of the earth and give you what Jesus Christ has purchased for you (Isa. 58).

You can see that there are so many things to benefit from fasting. You will not die if you fast moderately, if you fast as the Lord leads you. Also, you can achieve anything you want by self-discipline. And as you control your fleshly passions; your Christian life will be superb.

The best way to fast is to fast as you are led by the Spirit of God. This does not mean that you must hear an audible voice telling you how long or how to go about the fasting.

Fast as you are moved by your spirit-man; don't be in competition with anybody, and don't fast to show God or people how long you can fast.

GIVING TO GOD AND TO MEN

Questions for Discussion:

1. What does it mean to give to God?
2. Does God need our gifts?
3. In what ways can we give to God?
4. In what ways can we give to men?
5. What do we gain by giving to God and to men?

The Bible says that it is more blessed to give than to receive (Acts 20:35). This Statement from God should make us develop our minds, to fashion our minds in such a way that we will be willing to give. This, according to the Scripture, will make us to be more blessed.

When we receive gifts from people, we feel happy; how much happier we should be to give. But when we give, many times, we feel sad and loosing. This is because we see, with our natural eyes, what we give out, while we don't see, with the same natural eyes, what we receive.

But the Bible says that what we see naturally were made from what we don't see (Heb. 11:3). God spoke the world into existence by saying, "Let there be..." (Gen. 1:1-31).

However, many of us don't see things from God's Perspective. Many of us believe what we see more than what we don't see. But this is not a good attitude.

The Lord Jesus Christ tells us that blessed are those who have not seen but yet have believed (Jn 20:29). The Word of God says that we walk by faith and not by sight (2 Cor. 5:7).

Brethren, it is time for us to know that the spiritual controls the physical. Many unbelievers understand this principle, and this is why many of them visit witch-doctors for charms and divination.

The Word of the Living God, Who is blessed forever more, says that you receive more blessings giving than receiving. Of course, your receiving has something to do with the attitude of your heart.

This is because the Bible says we should not give by compulsion; we should not give grudgingly, for God loves a cheerful giver (2 Cor. 9:7). Whenever you give to God or to man, do it willingly and because you want to obey God out of a sincere heart.

Also, bear it in mind that your reaping or receiving has to do with how you give, because when you give bountifully, you receive bountifully; when you give sparingly, you also receive sparingly (2 Cor. 9:6).

But giving sparingly or bountifully doesn't necessarily have to do with the amount given. You remember the woman that gave only two dimes, and yet the Lord Jesus Christ affirmed that she gave more than the others? (Mk 12:41-44).

The Lord said that the others gave out of their abundance, while the woman gave all that she had. The person who has N1,000.00 and gave God N100.00, gave more than the person who has one million naira and gave God one thousand naira. Do you understand?

When you hide and squeeze your offering money so that others may not see how small it is, God knows your abundance or your lack.

The Lord Jesus Christ has declared that when we give, it will be given back to us in a good measure; the measure that is pressed down, shaken together, and running over. In that measure will men give to you (Lk. 6:38).

It is noteworthy that Jesus Christ indicated that God will use men to give back to you; therefore don't expect God to rain down currency notes from Heaven, because God is no counterfeiter.

But this does not necessarily mean that God cannot give you physical cash by Himself. For instance, if God wants to give you N1,000.00 physically by Himself, an angel can appear in human form and collect that money from a willing person; the angel can then drop the money physically in your house for you.

God provided physical cash for Jesus Christ and Peter by directing Jesus Christ to tell Peter to cast a line into the river so that, catching a fish, he will find the needed coin in its mouth (Matt. 17:27).

You can't beat God in giving because the more you give God, the more He blesses you in return. Apart from the physical reward you will receive, you will also have an eternal inheritance and reward reserved for you in Heaven (Rev. 22:12).

He can repay you with a good job, a good salary, a promotion, a physical gift from someone, and through many other ways. So make up your mind to give because the more you give, the more you receive.

Now, how do you give God? You give God in tithes and offerings. God says that people rob Him, not only in tithes, but in tithes and offerings (Mal. 3:8). Therefore, give a quality offering to God.

When someone visits you, you buy him a bottle of soft drink; but when you want to give God an offering, you give Him money that will not even buy Him a half bottle of the same drink. Is it fair? Make up your mind today that you will not rob God again.

How do you give God? You give God your time, your energy, your talent, and many other things that you possess. In Acts of the Apostles, people sold their lands and gave God all (Acts 2:41-47; Acts 4:32-37)).

Nothing is too much to give God. If you build a cathedral for God, you did not do too much for Him; after all, He gave His Only Son, Jesus Christ, to us.

When Jesus Christ came, He gave His Life for us; and He says that if you love your life more than Him, you are not worthy of Him (Matt. 10:37-39, Lk. 14:26-30).

Tithe is 1/10 or 10% of your income. While some find it difficult to give God tithe or tenth part of their income, some have given 20% or more of their income to God because of their love for God.

Jesus Christ talks of giving God with 'the measure' (the tithe is a good measure) (Lk 6:38). Apostle Paul taught that Jesus Christ receives (not 'received') tithe in Heaven (Heb. 7:8).

In the Old Testament, God spoke of paying and bringing (not just 'giving') your tithe (Heb. 7:9; Mal. 3:10; Gen. 14:20; Lk. 18:12; Deut. 14:28; Matt. 23:23). Don't argue whether you need to pay or give tithe now, because it is not too much for God.

If you can't give God your tithe, can you surrender your life for Him? Apart from tithe, there are different kinds of offerings you can give God, as the Spirit of God leads you.

If you give God your first salary, you did not give Him too much. That is not to say that you must give Him your first salary, but if you have the courage, it will give you a better base. The Bible speaks of first-fruit offerings.

You have heard of the seed-faith offering. It is good. However beware of those who go around exploiting people with, 'Sow seed.' Let the Holy Spirit lead you.

It is a good thing to give to the poor and the needy. He who gives to the poor lends to God, and God will reward or repay him abundantly (Prov. 19:17).

Remember the widows and the orphans. Remember the sick, the naked, and the prisoners. The Lord Jesus Christ says that what you do to the Believers, you do to Him (Matt. 25:31-46).

When you make the lives of people better, you are doing the Will of God, because it is satan that brought poverty, sickness, and hardship to this world.

Remember to give to your pastor and other men of God. He who gives to the prophet will receive a prophet's reward (Matt. 10:41). Whatever you do to God's people in the Name of Jesus Christ, you do to God (Matt. 10:40-42).

If ministers have sown spiritual things to you, it is not a big thing for them to receive physical things from you (1 Cor. 9:11). As you give to God and to men, God Himself will bless you; even people will appreciate you and praise God!

Give what you have. Don't say you don't have anything, because there is a seed in your hand which you can sow if you want to. God will not require what you don't have from you, for He is a Just God. Don't eat your seed, because if you do, you will lose your harvest.

CONCERNING SPIRITUAL GIFTS

Questions for Discussion:
1. What are spiritual gifts?
2. Mention and discuss the nine Gifts of the Holy Spirit, as recorded in First Corinthians, chapter twelve.
3. Which gift is most important?
4. How do we get the gifts?
5. Can one person have all the gifts?

Spiritual gifts are the Manifestations of the Holy Spirit in the life of whom He has filled or come upon. The Holy Spirit fills and comes upon Believers when they are baptized in the Holy Spirit, and maintain His In-filling Presence.

Actually, the many different Manifestations of the Holy Spirit in the lives of Believers that make them minister, walk, or live supernaturally are Spiritual Gifts of the Holy Spirit, in a sense, because it is the Holy Spirit that manifests the Power of God and carries the Presence of God throughout the earth and the universe.

For the purpose of this study, we will be concentrating on the nine Gifts of the Holy Spirit, as recorded in the twelfth chapter of First Corinthians.

Before we start discussing them, the Bible tells us that the signs that will follow the Believers include: casting out devils in the Name of Jesus Christ; speaking in new tongues; taking up serpents without being hurt; drinking deadly things and not being hurt; and laying hands on the sick so that they may recover (Mk 16:17-18).

The Lord Jesus Christ tells us that He gives the Believers the power and authority to trample on serpents and scorpions, and over all the power of the enemy, and nothing shall by any means hurt them (Lk. 10:19).

When the apostles and Disciples went out and preached everywhere, after the Ascension of Jesus Christ, the Lord worked with them and confirmed the Word or the Gospel through the accompanying signs (Mk 16:20).

The Believers are to do the works that Jesus Christ did, even greater works because He went to the Father (Jn 14:12). We are told that God bears witness of the Word both with signs and wonders, with various miracles, and Gifts (or Distributions) of the Holy Spirit (Heb. 2:4).

All those demonstrations of the Power of God, all those miracles, signs, and wonders are Manifestations of the Holy Spirit. Of course, all the gifts come under revelation gifts, inspirational or vocal gifts, and power gifts.

We will still look at them in more details. However, we will see other Gifts and Enablements of the Holy Spirit in the lives of the Believers.

Do not be ignorant of spiritual gifts. However, know that no one speaking by the Spirit of God calls Jesus Christ accursed, and no one can say that Jesus Christ is Lord except by the Holy Spirit.

There are diversities of gifts, but the same Spirit. There are differences of ministries, but the same Lord. There are diversities of activities, but it is the same God Who works all in all.

But the Manifestation of the Spirit is given to each one for the profit of all. But one and the same Spirit works all these things, distributing to each one individually as He wills (1 Cor. 12).

Having then gifts differing according to the grace that is given to us, let us use them: if prophecy, let us prophesy in proportion to our faith, or ministry, let us use it in our ministering,

He who teaches, in teaching, he who exhorts in exhortation, he who gives with liberality, he who leads, with diligence, he who shows mercy, with cheerfulness (Rom. 12:6-8).

As each one has received a gift, minister it to one another, as good stewards of the Manifold Grace of God. If anyone speaks, let him speak as the Oracles of God. If anyone ministers, let him do it as with the ability which God supplies (1 Pet. 4:10-11).

We see a five-fold ministry gifts of apostles, prophets, evangelists, pastors, and teachers (Eph. 4:11). These gifts are persons with those ministries which the Lord gave to His Church for the equipping of the Saints so that the Saints will do the work of the ministry (the Work of Christ), and for the edifying of the Body of Christ.

If you are called into these ministries, you have been called to full-time ministry, and not part-time; but this does not necessarily mean you can never work or do business. However, when you are able, ready, willing, or determined, full-time ministry is the best, and any extra work (as God may permit), should be extra indeed.

Apostle Paul gives us more light when he stated that God has appointed these in the Church. First apostles, second prophets, third teachers, after that miracles, then gifts of healings, helps, administrations, varieties of tongues (1 Cor. 12:28).

Evangelists often go with the working of miracles and gifts of healings; pastors go with administrations and helps. Even though there are ministries of helps, pastors (as shepherds) help the sheep in their weaknesses, and forbear with them till they mature.

Now, we will go to the nine Gifts of the Holy Spirit. For to one is given the word of wisdom through the Spirit, to another the word of knowledge through the same Spirit, to another faith by the same Spirit, to another gifts of healings by the same Spirit,

To another the working of miracles, to another prophecy, to another discerning of spirits, to another different kinds of tongues, to another the interpretation of tongues (1 Cor. 12:8-10).

These gifts are what we know, basically, as the nine Gifts of the Holy Spirit, and they are part of the signs, wonders, and miracles that God gives to Believers and shows to unbelievers.

These gifts are necessary for the evangelization of the world, and for the comfort and edification of the Saints. Apostle Paul told Pastor Timothy to stir up the Gift of God in him (2 Tim. 1:6). The Kingdom of God is not in word but in power (1 Cor. 4:20).

Apostle Paul said that his speech and his preaching were not with persuasive words of human wisdom, but in demonstration of the Spirit and of power (1 Cor. 2:4).

Even their Gospel did not go to the Thessalonians in Word only, but also in power, and in the Holy Spirit and in much assurance, as they behaved themselves well among them (their character was right and Godly) (1 Thes. 1:5).

The nine gifts are divided into revelation gifts: the word of wisdom, the word of knowledge, and the discerning of spirits; inspirational gifts: prophecy, different kinds of tongues, and interpretation of tongues; and power gifts: the gift of faith, the gifts of healings, and the working of miracles.

With the revelation gifts, we know the enemy's strategies; with the inspirational gifts, we build ourselves up; and with the power gifts, we destroy the works of the devil.

The gift of the word of wisdom is the gift by which God reveals His Plans and Purposes for the future to us. Through it, we prepare for what the devil has planned or will plan in the future, and we also get a part of God's Wisdom to solve issues.

The gift of the word of knowledge is the gift through which we know what has happened in the past, and what is happening presently. It can come through vision, audible voice, prophecy, etc.

The discerning of spirits is the ability God gives His people, which enables them to see and hear, supernaturally, the things happening or existing in the spirit-realm; by this gift, we can perceive both good and bad spirits.

The gift of faith is the gift by which the Spirit of God imparts faith, supernaturally, to us to enable us receive miracles or solutions, passively.

On the other hand, through the working of miracles, we work and command miracles and solutions, actively. The gifts of healings give us the ability to destroy sicknesses and diseases, supernaturally, under the anointing.

The gift of prophecy is an utterance gift in a known tongue or language, and it is useful for edification, comfort, and exhortation.

The gift of different kinds of tongues gives the holder the ability to minister in different kinds of tongues; he can speak different kinds of languages consecutively in a meeting to reach out to different people of different languages.

It is different from the simple gift of tongues. The tongues spoken are not known to the speaker naturally. The gift of the interpretation of tongues is the ability to interpret unknown tongues to a known tongue or language by the help of the Holy Spirit.

Freely you have received, and freely you should give. You are given these gifts according to the Will of God when or after you are baptized or filled with the Holy Spirit. You can have more than one gift, and you can get more gifts with time.

These gifts are weapons against the enemy. You have to desire the gifts, individually and as a group; but the Spirit will still distribute them as He wills. Gifts can be misused and abused, and you will give account to God how you used your gift(s).

All the gifts, except tongues and interpretation of tongues, operated in the Old Testament. The prophets of Old operated in these gifts. Think of Moses, Elijah, Elisha, Isaiah, and Ezekiel.

The Lord Jesus Christ's Life was characterized by these gifts, and that is why multitudes followed Him. Even the early apostles and Disciples proved that Jesus Christ is alive, having resurrected from the dead, by these gifts. Even today, you can operate in these gifts!

FAITHFULNESS AND DILIGENCE IN STEWARDSHIP

Questions for Discussion:

1. What does it mean to be faithful?
2. What does it mean to be diligent?
3. How should we do God's Work?
4. Is there any gain of being faithful and diligent?

In stewardship, it is expected that a man be found faithful. Stewardship refers to the way in which someone controls and looks after an event or an organization. A steward is a man whose job is to look after a place with the things in it, like a farm, an estate, etc.

In Christianity or ministry, stewardship refers to looking after or taking control of what God has committed to your hands: His Assignment for you, the ministry He has committed to your trust.

How do you take care of your churches, as an apostle? How do you manage or administer the words or revelations God has given you for others, as a prophet? How do you dedicate yourself to the salvation of souls, as an evangelist?

How do you take care of or shepherd your flock, your members, as a pastor? How do you dedicate yourself to studying and teaching, as a teacher? How much time do you give to intercession as an intercessor? As a musician, how do you prepare yourself before you sing?

No matter what God has committed to your hands, be diligent in doing it, and make sure He finds you faithful in it.

Now is the time for action and service. Stop delaying; whatever your hands finds to do, do it now with all your strength. Preach in season and out of season. The Lord Jesus Christ is coming very soon, and He will reward each one according to his work.

It is not men that will judge you. It is not even Christians or your pastor that will judge you.

Some people have succeeded in buying or winning the favour of people so that whatever they do, the people applaud and support them. Some pastors buy the conscience of their deacons. But God is the One that will judge.

All men shall stand before God and give account to Him of all He has committed to their trust. Even sinners and unbelievers will tell God how they handled or lived the life that He gave to them.

How have you handled the health that God has given to you? How do you appreciate and praise Him for it and use it for His Glory? Many are in the hospitals and cannot walk or work as you do.

The Bible says that Moses was faithful in all His House (Heb. 3:5). Moses was faithful to what God called him to do. In going to Pharaoh, in demonstrating the Power of God, he was faithful.

Moses was faithful in teaching the people the Commandments of the Lord; he was faithful in keeping the things God told him to do. Moses built the tabernacle exactly as he was shown. He interceded for the children of Israel so that God did not wipe them away as He had intended.

Moses walked with God. Even though the people provoked him, that he used the rod on the rock, instead of speaking to the rock, as God directed him. God forgave him and took him to Heaven.

Faithfulness is among the Fruit of the Spirit as recorded in the fifth chapter of the Book of Galatians. Faithfulness means trustworthiness.

Can God trust you with the assignment He has for you? Will you be faithful to what the Lord has called you to do? Have you been faithful to what He had committed to your trust?

He that is faithful in small things will be faithful in big things. If you are not faithful in the little God gave you, how can you be faithful in the big things you want to do for Him?

In the parable of the talents, the one that received five talents traded with it, and got five more talents. The one that received two talents got two talents extra as well. But the one that received one talent buried it, for whatever reason he considered, and was punished at last.

Don't despise anything that the Lord has given to you, and don't be proud of whatever big thing He may commit to your trust. Be faithful in it and let Him be proud of you as he was with Jesus Christ and with Job (Matt. 17:5; Job 1:8).

It is he that endures to the end that shall be saved. You may start well, but if you don't finish well, you will regret at last. Don't say, "Had I known…." It will be too late.

Don't think that the devil will not fight you or bring temptations to your way. You are not greater than Jesus Christ or Paul. But don't drift back because of trials and temptations.

As a minister the devil will fight you through your wife, children, neighbours, and even colleagues. But never mind, all will be well. God is with you in trouble and out of trouble.

The Call of God is a high call. God gave His Only Son to die for the sins of the world. He made Him a Soulwinner. The Lord Jesus Christ accomplished the Task that the Father had for Him. He did the Assignment faithfully.

As Christians, we are supposed to be Christ-like; therefore, we should be faithful in God's Assignments for us. Apostle Paul was happy towards the end of his ministry and until his death. He said that he had fought the good fight and finished the race. (2 Tim. 4:6-8).

No matter what it takes, answer the Call of God for you. It may not be easy for you; in fact, you will have to suffer persecutions for the Cause of Christ. You must have to take up your cross daily and follow Him.

There will be rewards for obedience and punishments for disobedience. God will neither leave you nor forsake you. God helped the holy Saints of Old, His past holy Servants, to fulfill the ministry He had for them, and yours will not be an exception.

Be strong in the grace that is in Christ Jesus. You, therefore, must endure hardship as a good soldier of Jesus Christ.

No one engaged in warfare entangles himself with the affairs of this life, that he may please him who enlisted him as a soldier. And also, if anyone competes in athletics, he is not crowned unless he competes according to the rules.

The hard-working farmer must be first to partake of the crops. Consider these things and may the Lord give you understanding in all things.

If we die with Him, we shall live with Him; if we endure, we shall also reign with Him. If we deny Him, He will also deny us. If we are faithless, He will remain faithful; He cannot deny Himself.

Be diligent to present yourself approved to God, a worker who does not need to be ashamed, rightly dividing the Word of Truth (2 Tim. 2:3-15).

Giving all diligence, add to your faith virtue, to virtue knowledge, to knowledge self-control, to self-control perseverance, to perseverance Godliness, to Godliness brotherly kindness, and to brotherly kindness love.

For if these things are yours and abound, you will be neither barren nor unfruitful in the knowledge of our Lord Jesus Christ. For he who lacks these things is short-sighted, to blindness and has forgotten that he was cleansed from his old sins.

Therefore, brethren, be even more diligent to make your call and election sure, for if you do these things, you will never stumble; for so an entrance will be supplied to you abundantly into the Everlasting Kingdom of our Lord and Saviour Jesus Christ (2 Pet. 1:5-11).

Keep your heart with all diligence, for out of it spring the issues of life (Prov. 4:23). If you lead, do it with diligence (Rom. 12:8).

God is not unjust to forget your work and labour of love which you have shown towards His Name, in that you have ministered to the Saints and do minister. Show the same diligence to the full assurance of hope until the end (Heb. 6:10-11).

If you diligently heed the Voice of the Lord your God and do what is right in His Sight, give ears to His Commandments, and keep all His Statutes, He will remove sickness and disease from you (Exo. 15:26).

You shall diligently keep the Commandments of the Lord your God, His Testimonies and His Statutes which He has commanded you (Deut. 6:17). Follow good works diligently (1 Tim. 5:10).

God rewards those that diligently seek Him (Heb. 11:6). He who has a slack hand becomes poor, but the hand of the diligent makes rich (Prov. 10:4). The hand of the diligent will rule, but the lazy man will be put to forced labour (Prov. 12:24).

The soul of the diligent shall be made rich. The plans of the diligent lead surely to plenty. Have you seen a man diligent in his works, he shall stand before kings, and not before ordinary men (Prov. 22:29).

Be diligent to know the state of your flocks, and attend to your herds; for riches are not forever, nor does a crown endure to all generations (Prov. 29:23-24).

Be diligent in whatever the Lord has given you to do and be found faithful in it. God has not called you to serve Him for nothing. He will reward you abundantly.

But know that there is punishment for laziness and unfaithfulness. Diligence and faithfulness shall be our watch-word.

Do not rob God. Robbing God is not in tithes and offerings alone. To rob someone is to deprive or relieve him of what belongs to him in his presence. It is distinct from stealing, in that stealing is done in the absence of that person.

God is ever present, and when you deny Him of what belongs to him, you are robbing Him. When you don't give God the time that belongs to Him, it is robbery.

THE ANOINTING AND POWER OF THE HOLY SPIRIT

Questions for Discussion:

1. What is the Anointing and Power of the Holy Spirit?
2. What is the importance of the Anointing and Power of the Holy Spirit?
3. How can we get the Anointing and Power of the Holy Spirit?
4. To what level should we receive the Anointing and Power of the Holy Spirit?

All power in Heaven, on the earth, and in the whole universe belongs to God. God is omnipotent, He is all-powerful. The power of satan and his cohorts is nothing, and is powerless before God.

The Psalmist said that God has spoken once, and twice he has heard it, that power belongs to God (Psa. 62:11). Power belongs to God indeed.

Do you know that God did not fight satan and his fallen angels directly when they rebelled against God? God sent Archangel Michael and His warring angels to fight the devil and send him out of Heaven.

Even when the devil will be put into the bottomless pit, it will still be an angel that will do it; and angels will banish satan and his host from this universe into their eternal abode and place of torment.

However, it is the Spirit of God, Who is the Holy Spirit or Holy Ghost, that empowers the angels of God to do God's Assignments for them. Even in this present age, God has empowered the Church to deal with the devil and his cohorts, and to destroy their works.

God is too much to fight the devil directly. How will a Creator fight His creature? Stop fearing the devil or man, for they can do you nothing without God's Permission. The devil is powerless before God, and God has given you power over all devils.

The Power of God is infinite. Not even the chiefest of the angels knows all about the Power of God, though they know some things about His Power.

This is one reason satan rebelled against God: at that time, the angels had not seen God deal with anyone as He dealt with satan and the fallen angels later.

The same is applicable to His Wisdom and Knowledge. The Presence of God fills the whole universe; God is everywhere and He knows all that are happening in the whole of the universe.

There are Three Persons in One God: God the Father, God the Son (Jesus Christ), and God the Holy Spirit. The Bible says that these Three are One (1 Jn. 5:7). This is a mystery.

Many times, we try to explain things based on our thinking or the small revelation we had; but there are so many things we will not understand fully now; but we will understand more, later.

It is true that the Holy Spirit reveals many things to us, but He can't reveal everything to us, but the things that God has chosen that we know. There are many things in the Bible we haven't understood yet.

When God moves to the ends of the universe, He moves By His Spirit. No wonder the prophet prophesied that the Glory of God (the Spirit of God) will fill (fills) the whole earth as the waters cover the sea (Habk. 2:14; Isa. 11:9).

God the Father sits on His Throne in Heaven, and Jesus Christ sits at His Right Hand. The Spirit of God manifests in different Forms in the Throne-room. He manifests as a River of Water.

It is the Spirit of God that carries God's Presence and Power to everywhere. If God's Spirit comes upon you, power has come upon you.

You receive power when the Holy Spirit comes upon you, and you are empowered to witness for the Lord Jesus Christ, from where you are to the ends of the earth (Acts 1:8).

This is why the Lord told His apostles to tarry in the city of Jerusalem until they are endued with power from on High (Lk. 24:49). Human power and knowledge cannot do God's Work effectively.

The Lord gives His people power and authority over the devil and all his demons. They are empowered to destroy their works, and nothing shall by any means hurt them (Lk. 10:19).

We are commanded to go into all the world and preach the Gospel to every creature. He who believes and is baptized will be saved, but he that believes not will be condemned.

And these signs shall follow those who believe: in the Name of Jesus Christ, they will cast out devils; they will speak with new tongues; they will take up serpents; if they drink anything deadly, it will by no means hurt them; and they will lay hands on the sick, and they will recover (Mk 16:15-20).

After the Lord had left, the Disciples went out and preached everywhere, the Lord working with them and confirming the Word through the accompanying signs.

The Kingdom of God is not eating and drinking, but righteousness, peace, and joy in the Holy Spirit. He, who serves Christ in these things, is acceptable to God and approved by men (Rom. 4:17-18).

The Kingdom of God is not in word but in power (1 Cor. 4:20). Apostle Paul spoke and preached in the demonstration of the Spirit and of power, that the faith of his hearers should be in the Power of God, instead of the wisdom of men (1 Cor. 2:1-5).

The burden of the enemy will be taken away from your shoulder, and his yoke from your neck, and the yoke will be destroyed because of the Anointing of God's Spirit (Isa. 10:27).

God anointed Jesus Christ of Nazareth with the Holy Spirit and with power, Who went about doing good and healing all who were oppressed by the devil, for God was with Him (Acts 10:38).

It is the devil that brings sicknesses, diseases, pains, sorrow, sufferings, poverty, disappointments and death; but the anointing will drive them and any other works of his out of men's lives.

The Spirit of God comes upon Believers to anoint them to preach the Gospel to the poor. He anoints them to heal the broken-hearted, to proclaim liberty to the captives and recovery of sight to the blind, to set at liberty those who are oppressed, to proclaim the Acceptable Year of the Lord (Lk. 4:18-19).

When the Holy Spirit fills you, He produces the flow of rivers of living water out of your heart (Jn 7:38). Nothing is impossible with God; there is nothing that cannot be done when the anointing comes.

The Anointing of the Holy Spirit teaches us the truth about God. The Holy Spirit teaches us all truth. He leads us in the way of righteousness, and shows us things to come.

The Spirit of God brings to our remembrance the things that God has taught us. The sons of God are led by the Spirit of God. The anointing in us is greater than the devil that is in the world (1 Jn 4:4).

Don't grieve the Holy Spirit; don't quench His Fire, either. The Holy Spirit will tell you the things that are freely given to us by God (1 Cor. 2:12). He is your Comforter and Helper.

The Holy Ghost is your Comforter, Counselor, Helper, Intercessor, Advocate, Strengthener, and Standby. What can you do without Him? The Holy Spirit helps your weaknesses and infirmities, and He makes intercession for us with groanings which cannot be uttered (Rom. 8:26).

Pray in the Holy Spirit; pray in tongues to build yourself up spiritually. Whether you turn to the left or the right, your ear will hear a Voice behind you, saying, "This is the way; walk in it" (Isa. 30:21). This is the Voice of the Spirit of God as He leads you.

The Holy Spirit is the Angel of God's Presence, the Carrier of God's Presence (Isa. 63:9-10). Moses knew the importance of God's Presence that he did not want to go without it (Exo. 33:15).

The Holy Spirit will lead you into all truth for He speaks what He hears God speak (Jn 16:13). The Spirit of God upon you will make you prophesy, see visions and dream dreams (Acts 2:17).

The Holy Spirit reproves the world of sin, and of righteousness, and of judgment (Jn 16:18). The Holy Spirit will refresh you and give you rest.

The Holy Spirit, when poured upon us, from on High, turns the wilderness into a fruitful field and the fruitful field into a forest (Isa. 32:15). The Holy Spirit will bring excellence into your life (Dan. 6:3).

The Holy Spirit makes you bring forth your fruit in your season, your leaves will not wither, and whatever you do shall prosper (Psa. 1:3). He will give you understanding (Job 32:8).

The Holy Spirit teaches us to profit (Isa. 48:17). The Holy Spirit will cause you to do God's Word (Ezek. 36:27). The Holy Spirit will give life to your whole being (Rom. 8:11).

Jesus Christ, Moses, Joshua, Elijah, Elisha, Daniel, the prophets, Apostles Peter and Paul, and the early apostles, prophets, and Disciples walked in the Power and Anointing of the Holy Spirit, and that was why they could turn the city upside down and the people that were against them feared them.

Even these days, we are to walk in the Power and Anointing of the Holy Spirit of the Living God. We live in the dispensation of power and authority, and the glory of the latter house shall be greater than that of the former (Hag. 2:9).

God promised to send the Later Rain and the Former Rain together in our day (Joel 2:23). The Rain is a type of the Holy Spirit. We are to walk in greater power and anointing than the early apostles and Disciples, because we are the generation that will prepare the world for the Coming of the Lord.

But you must pray, consistently and daily. You can't make it without being prayerful. Increase your knowledge of God and His Word, for God doesn't give big responsibilities to novices.

You will need to fast consistently and regularly, as the Spirit leads you. You will not, necessarily, need to fast for forty days and nights; but even if you are led to do it, you will not die doing it. Christ has already won the battle for us.

The anointing and power in the Life of Jesus Christ drew great multitude of people to Him, and even today, when the anointing in your life is strong enough, great multitudes of people will be drawn to you.

As a Christian who is filled with the Holy Spirit, the Seven Spirits of God or layers of anointing should be seen in you. These are the Spirit of the Lord, the Spirit of Wisdom, the Spirit of Understanding, the Spirit of Counsel, the Spirit of Might, the Spirit of Knowledge, and the Spirit of the Fear of the Lord.

INDECENT DRESSING AND OUTWARD APPEARANCE

Questions for Discussion:

1. What is indecent dressing?
2. How should Christians appear?
3. What are the benefits and the disadvantages of indecent dressing?
4. What are the benefits and the disadvantages of dressing decently?

People dress indecently and seductively these days, especially girls, ladies, and women. Of course, some men dress indecently also.

But whereas even unbelieving men dress decently, many ladies who claim they are Christians, who go to different churches and call on the Name of the Lord, dress indecently to work, school, shopping, and even church.

Most of them will tell you that it doesn't matter, if they want to speak with respect to that. But doesn't it matter? It may not matter with you; but does it not matter with God?

No wonder the Lord Jesus Christ asks, "Why do you call Me, Lord, Lord and do not do what I say?"(Lk. 6:46).

He says that many will say to Him on the Day of Judgment, "Lord, Lord, have we not prophesied, cast out demons, and did mighty miracles in Your Name?" But He will tell them, "I never knew you, depart from Me, you workers of iniquity" (Matt. 7:21-23).

What will happen to you on the Day of Judgment if you realize that many of the things you thought didn't matter actually matter? Then, there will be no second chance.

How will you feel if you are cast into Hell Fire, where the fire does not quench, and the worms do not die? What will be your experience when a demon or your unbelieving neighbour asks you, "So you later came here?"

The Lord Jesus Christ tells us that if we love our lives more than Him, then we are not worthy of Him (Lk. 14:26). If you can't sacrifice your dressing for the Lord, can you sacrifice your life for Him? Don't be foolish but understand what the Will of the Lord is.

The dressing and outward appearance of Christians must be different from those of unbelievers. If a Muslim will value covering herself well, how much more should you value it?

The problem is that many people will find it easier to manage bondage than liberty. But do not use your liberty as an opportunity for sin and disobedience (Gal. 5:13).

The Bible tells us that man looks at outward appearance (1 Sam. 16:7). Even in the secular world, appearance can decide your acceptability in many areas of life.

Escape for your dear life; run before it is too late. The five foolish virgins lost their target. Remember that they were virgins, but they lacked something they didn't remember or deem necessary.

Please, open your eyes well, well; the devil has intruded into the Church: his ministers now parade themselves as ministers of Jesus Christ, to deceive and destroy the souls of the children of men.

Be careful of any church where people are allowed to dress anyhow to, no matter how anointed you may think the preacher is or how knowledgeable he is concerning the Bible. It is a different case when unbelievers dress anyhow to crusades, maybe, for the first time.

The Bible says that out of the abundance of the heart, the mouth speaks. Your actions and your words show what is on the inside of you. Your physical appearance reveals your inner man.

If you don't care about what people think about your indecent dressing, then your spirit has a serious problem, and your mind has been corrupted. I don't care what you may think about it.

Even unbelievers will find it difficult to believe you are a Christian when you dress indecently as they do. There must be a difference between the dressing of a Christian and a non-Christian.

Many ladies think that they attract marriage partners by dressing seductively. Well, you can only attract a carnal man when you dress that way. How can a reasonable spiritual man decide to marry someone that is worldly in appearance?

Even Queen Esther who was in a heathen nation of Babylon asked nothing but what Hegai the king's eunuch, the custodian of the women, advised. Yet she obtained favour in the sight of all who saw her, and the king loved her more than all the other women.

It is true that she took part in the compulsory preparations and purifications that all of them underwent; however, besides what their custodian advised, she requested for nothing (Esth. 2:15-17).

Esther took part in those things because they were in a foreign heathen land. In fact, they were captives, and Mordecai had charged her not to reveal that she was a Jew. Even if she had not used them, she would have been chosen, except that it might have revealed her identity.

It was the beauty that God gave her, it was God's Favour and Glory that attracted the king to her. The Glory of God will attract your husband to you.

Apostle Paul asked that women should adorn themselves in modest apparel with propriety and moderation, not with braided hair or gold or pearls or costly clothing, but which is proper for women professing Godliness with good works (1 Tim. 2:9-10).

Did you notice that there is an appearance that is proper for women professing Godliness? But many people will want us to believe that all that God looks at is your heart. The lie is from the devil, the father of lies.

The heathen of their days spent their time, money, and energy in decorating themselves to look charming and expensive. However, Paul discouraged that among Christians; and they were to do everything in moderation.

The word 'propriety' means the correctness of social or moral behaviour. Whatever Godly women do should be what is morally accepted among Godly Christians.

I am not speaking about what is accepted among people who have departed from the faith, giving heed to deceiving spirits and doctrines of demons; they speak lies in hypocrisy, having their own conscience seared with a hot iron (1 Tim. 4:1-2).

I am not speaking of what is accepted among those who do not endure Sound Doctrine, but according to their own desires, because they have itching ears, heap up for themselves teachers who teach them what they want to hear (2 Tim. 4:3).

Apostle Peter said, "Do not let your adornment be merely outward   arranging the hair, wearing gold, or putting on fine apparel   rather let it be the hidden person of the heart, with the incorruptible beauty of a gentle and quiet spirit which is very precious in the Sight of God (1 Pet. 3:3-4).

In the first place, the word 'merely', is not in the original text, and that is why it is italicized in the New King James Version. The King James Version says, "...whose adorning let it not be that of outward adorning of...."

Well, Apostles Paul and Peter are not necessarily saying that you should neither arrange your hairs, wear costly dresses, nor put on fine apparels. If you can't go to work, school or church without a costly dress or fine apparel, something is wrong with you; you now love the world.

There is a level you may be and what is costly to others may not be costly to you; however, even at that level, position, or wealth, never put your mind on costly things. Whatever God gives you, use it for His Glory and don't allow it enter your head.

Understand what I am saying here. You can use a costly car without putting your mind on costly things. If you are in a position to use costly things, use it to the Glory of God, and not for pride or to show off.

Concerning the dressing or arranging of the hair, using of weavons and attachments is devilish and worldly. Many of those weavons are actual human hairs that were cut and sold. Many of the weavons and attachments are manufactured with demonic materials to enslave the children of men.

Also, when you use weavons and attachments, when you perm and jerry curl your hair, you are saying that God is stupid to have made your hair the way He made it. When people refuse to cover their hairs, they resort to worldly means of weavons for a covering.

Much of those things women use for their hair, in perming and jerry-curling, is manufactured from alantoin extracted from aborted babies. The worst is that some men even fry their hair.

Satan has entered the Church and has deceived many. Many are sincerely deceived. Those cortexes, lipsticks, make-ups, and many other painting materials, apart from being worldly, are manufactured from demonic materials, aborted babies' placentas, and human blood.

This is a mystery that many have not realized. When people use those things, they get demonic problems they don't know where they came from.

Blouses that show too much of your back; tight-fitting and revealing dresses; mini-skirts; spaghetti or line-sleeve and transparent dresses; blouses showing your breast; cobweb and body-hug dresses; blouses revealing your belly; and any such dresses are devilish, satanic, demonic, and worldly.

Sagging your trousers and dread-locking your hair are satanic also. Women shouldn't put on trousers because they look more decent in skirts and gowns. In biology, when women mature, their buttocks get enlarged, this is why when they wear trousers, they reveal their body contours and look seductive.

Any attire or dress that glorifies the devil and does not glorify God is worldly and devilish. There are no two ways about this matter.

We now come to the issue of earrings, necklaces, and bangles. These things are worldly also. God made you look fine, what advantage is it in decorating your body, which is the Temple of the Holy Spirit, with those things?

We wear cloths and dresses to cover our nakedness. Before Adam sinned, we didn't even need dresses, for God's Glory covered us. Earrings were classified among foreign and ungodly things when Jacob purified his household (Gen. 35:1-15). The knowledge of God advanced from Abraham, Isaac, to Jacob.

Even though you may argue, can you prove to me why you need them when God made you beautiful? The problem is that many of these things have continued for so long that many don't even know why they do what they do. Personally, I don't see those things as beauty, and God does not like them.

Take it to the whole world and quote me: these sleeveless or very short-sleeved blouses which women and ladies wear, which show their arm-pits when they raise their hands are satanic, worldly, seductive, and deceptive. It is deceptive because many assume that since it is for fresh air and not for direct attraction, nothing is wrong with it.

That is why you say you want to worship and praise God while you show the men your arm-pits. That is why you wear skirts and gowns that will show the men that came to worship God your laps as you sit down, because you want to look sharp and modern. Many are deceived with the thought that since God touched me, nothing is wrong with me.

Don't you know that God touches unbelievers also? Is it not written in your Bible that God gives sun and rain to the evil and the good, to the just and the unjust? (Matt. 5:45). Don't you know that even unbelievers fall down under the anointing? Maybe you have never seen where God spoke to Prophet Balaam through an ordinary donkey (Num. 22:15-35). The Spirit of the Lord came upon Prophet Balaam in Num. 24:2.

Many read the Bible, and it appears that they don't understand simple and clear language. No wonder the Holy Spirit, through Apostle Paul, said that some will depart from the faith, giving heed to deceiving spirits and doctrines of devils, speaking lies in hypocrisy... (1 Tim. 4:1-2).

No wonder God spoke through Apostle Paul to tell us that the time will come when they will not endure sound doctrine, but according to their own desires, because they have itching ears, they will heap up for themselves teachers; and they will turn their ears away from the truth... (2 Tim. 4:3-4).

Look at what I mean: many are so much interested in miracles, prophecies, signs, and wonders that they seem never to have seen it in their Bible that the Lord Jesus Christ will tell many that prophesied, cast out demons, and did mighty works in His Name that He never knew them, because they were workers of iniquity (Matt. 7:21-23). This situation pains the Lord so much that He asks, "Why do you call Me 'Lord, Lord,' and not do the things which I say? (Lk 6:46).

Even you young men that want to appear however you want to appear. You don't want restrictions. God put the tree of the knowledge of good and evil in the Garden of Eden to teach man the need for restrictions and obedience. When you want unlimited access and unrestricted freedom, you are not ready for Heaven.

That is why some of you men wear earrings and noserings. I have seen a church in America where men wear those things. They even wear caps right inside church programmes. God has become your mate: is it not so? These have nothing to do with civilization and modernization as far as God is concerned. Have you not seen ladies that follow men so that people will not take them as uncivilized? You want to look like a Rastafarian?

Young men dress and unbutton their shirts to show people their chests. I went to one church, and it was their youth day. During their mass choir, their leader flied his shirt and unbuttoned it to show his chest. Neither the bishop nor any of their pastors said anything, at least to my hearing.

I think many people don't really believe in Heaven and Hell. Forget about what they claim; if they really believed that the Word of God is unchangeable and forever settled in Heaven, if they really believe in Heaven and Hell in their innermost beings, we wouldn't have been seeing many of the things we see. God is waiting for many people at His Judgment Seat!

Many ladies appear to be stubborn when it comes to how they will dress. Many are bent on having what they want, and don't care about what God or people think about them. And the devil has succeeded in making many indecent ways people dress look harmless. Have you ever seen how indecently many dress during wedding, in the name of wedding gowns?

THE BELIEVER SHOULD NOT PERISH

Questions for Discussion:

1. Who is a Believer?
2. Can a Believer perish?
3. How can a Believer perish?

For God so loved the world that He gave His Only Begotten Son that whoever believes in Him should not perish but have Eternal Life (Jn 3:16).

I want you to notice, particularly, that the verse declares that the Believer should not perish and not that the Believer shall not perish. The one that believes on the Lord Jesus Christ should not perish.

If you believe on the Lord Jesus Christ, if you are born again, you are not supposed to perish. When someone or something should not perish, it means that the person or thing ought not to (is not supposed) to perish. It also means that the person or thing may perish.

If you are hanging on a strong and stable crane, high above the ground level, you should not fall down and crash by the influence of the force of gravity. However, if you separate yourself from the crane, you will crash on the ground.

People of God perish because of lack of knowledge (Hos. 4:6). Ignorance of God and His Ways will make you perish; though, in this case, the perishing is not applicable to perishing in Hell Fire alone; in fact, this place is talking about losing God's Provisions for you, among other applications.

The devil is no good entity; if you don't know your rights and privileges in Christ Jesus, he will steal from you, kill you, and even destroy you (Jn 10:10).

Don't allow the enemy to succeed in prevailing over you. Let none of his works come to pass in your life. Give no place to the devil (Eph. 4:27).

This is why you have to study the Bible, because, in reading and studying it, in meditating on and speaking forth its contents (the things applicable to you), you overcome the devil and his devils. You are sitting with Christ at the Right Hand of God (Eph. 2:6).

Well, my topic is that the Believer should not perish in Hell Fire. However, many Believers will perish in Hell Fire. Casual reading of the New Testament will reveal this truth to you. God does not intend that it should be so, but it will be so to many.

The Bible says that it is not the Will of God that any soul should perish, but those that refuse Jesus Christ will perish in Hell Fire. Those that live in sin and disobedience will perish in Hell Fire.

As a matter of fact, God is not the one that sends people to Heaven or Hell; actually, people choose where they will go, even without their knowledge. Where you go is dependent on what you do with Jesus Christ, His Holy Spirit, and God's Word.

God sets before you life and death, blessing and curse (good and bad), and you choose the one you want (Deut. 30:19). God does not force anyone. Of course, He can change circumstances and conditions around you to help you take the decision to obey; however, He still, will not force you.

Hell Fire was not made for man. Hell was made for satan and his fallen angels, his demons. Why? Because they rebelled against God.

However, the man that rebels against God is putting himself in the same position as the devil, and the Bible says that he will suffer the same condemnation and punishment in Hell Fire. The punishment of Hell Fire is everlasting and eternal.

The fire of Hell does not quench and its worms do not die. If all the sufferings in this world are put together, and one person is made to carry them and bear them, yet it will not equal what someone will suffer in Hell for 24 hours.

My brother, run from the damnation of Hell Fire while there is time. After death, there is no room for repentance; neither is there room for forgiveness.

The Lord Jesus Christ asks, "Why do you call Me, Lord, Lord, and do not do what I say?" (Lk. 6:46). Many will say to Him on that Day, "Lord, Lord, have we not done this or that in Your Name?" But He will tell them that He never knew them (Matt. 7:21-23).

Notice that many of them even prophesied. It is only those that do the Will of the Father that will enter the Kingdom of Heaven (verse 21). You may be baptized and confirmed in your church, but that is not the answer.

If you want to enter the Kingdom of Heaven, you must be born of water and of the Spirit (Jn 3:5). That is a higher level of "I am born again" (Jn 3:3). The water is the Word of God (Eph. 5:26), and the Spirit is the Holy Ghost.

You must obey the Word of God, and you must listen to the Spirit of God. Many who are first will be the last, and the last first (Matt. 19:30). Let this not be your portion.

Some people argue and say that God knows those who will go to Heaven and those who will go to Hell. In other words, they say that some are meant for Heaven and some are meant for Hell. This is no truth.

Of course, the Bible says that God will have mercy on whom He would have mercy (Rom. 9:14-20). The Bible says that God loved Jacob and hated Esau (Rom. 9:9-14). But you've got to interpret that Scripture well, in order not to misdirect yourself.

The Bible says that it is those that endure to the end that will be saved (Matt. 24:13). In other words, if you fall by the wayside, you will not be saved. He who despises God, He will despise (1 Sam. 2:30).

The end of a matter is better than the beginning (Eccl. 7:8). It is one thing to start well, but it is another to end well. Don't fall by the roadside. Many are called but few are chosen (Matt. 20:16).

Why were they chosen? It is because they were faithful. Count yourself to be death with Christ and alive for Him. The life that you live now should be for Him.

The Word of God talks of the children of the Kingdom being cast away into the Outer Darkness wherein is gnashing of teeth (Matt. 8:12). Those children were meant for the Kingdom of Heaven, but due to sin, disobedience, and unrighteousness, they lost their place in it.

God, after saving the children of Israel from the Egyptian bondage and allowing them to have many spiritual and mighty experiences, destroyed those that sinned and did not believe (1 Cor. 10:1-13).

The Word of God says that because iniquity shall abound in the last days, the love of many shall wax cold; however, some people's love will not wax cold and they will endure to the end (Matt. 24:12-13).

It is those that endure to the end that will be saved. Without holiness, no man can see the Lord (Heb. 12:14). Blessed are the pure in heart, for they shall see God (Matt. 5:8). If you are not holy and pure, forget Heaven.

However, whatever you might have done, repent now; confess your sins to God and make the necessary restitutions; and God will wipe away your sins and unrighteousness.

If you confess your sins, He is faithful and just to forgive your sins and cleanse you from all unrighteousness (1 Jn 1:9). There is no hard-man with God.

All your pride and boasting is because your time is not up. When your time expires, God will judge you and He is no respecter of persons (Rev. 2:20-23). God says, "Return to me, you backslider!" Obey Him now so that you will not say, "Had I known...."

This is not a question of whether you are an apostle, a prophet, an evangelist, a pastor, a teacher, a bishop, or an archbishop, a president and founder, a general overseer, an elder, a deacon or a deaconess, a men's or women's leader, a Sunday School teacher, a singer, an intercessor or whatever you may be; if you don't obey God and His Word, forget Heaven and prepare to live with the devil eternally.

Abstain from the lust of the flesh which war against your soul. Flee youthful lusts. God will not allow any temptation that is greater than you to come to you, but don't go where angels fear to tread on. Man can never be wiser than God; when God says, 'Flee,' do just that.

When you are enticed, do not give in to the enticement or temptation. Don't get entangled with sin and disobedience. There are many errors among Believers today; avoid those errors so that it will be well with your soul.

Examine yourself to see whether you are still standing in the faith. If you judge yourself, you will not be judged. Beware of hypocrisy and compromise. All hypocrites will end in eternal separation from God.

Unfaithful servants will be cast into the Outer Darkness. Those who compromise the Word and Standard of God will find themselves in the Lake of Fire which burns with fire and brimstone.

Wives, submit to your husbands, in the Lord; husbands, love your wives as your own bodies. If you put a stumbling block to your spouse, so that your words and actions cause him or her to live contrary to the Word and Will of God, God will require it from you: you will give account of your relationship with your spouse to God.

Abhor what is evil; cling to that which is good and true. You must forgive others so that God will forgive you your own sin. Awake to righteousness and shun sin and immorality.

Many have already been corrupted by the lust of the flesh, the lust of the eyes, and the pride of life. The minds of many have already been polluted by demonic suggestions.

He who overcomes will inherit all things. The overcomer will be blessed forever. Let your inward man direct and control your outward man, and not vice versa.

If you live according to your flesh, you shall die; but if through the Spirit, you put to death the deeds of the flesh, you shall live.

God did not call us to serve Him for nothing. He will reward our obedience and punish the disobedient. Cease to do evil, learn to do well.

If you live your life anyhow, you will be devoured by the sword of God's Judgment. If you judge yourself, you will not be judged. Walk in the highway of righteousness, the way that pleases God and does His Good Will.

RECEIVING, THINKING, BELIEVING, CONFESSION, AND POSSESSION

Questions for Discussion:

1. How do we receive the things that enter into us?
2. What should we think on?
3. What should we believe?
4. What should we confess?
5. What do we possess?

Man is made up of the human spirit, the soul, and the body (1 Thes. 5:23). Many people are more conscious of their body than they are of their spirit, but the truth is that man was made in the Image and Likeness of God (Gen. 1:26-27).

If man was made in the Likeness of God and God is Spirit (Jn 4:24), man must of necessity be a spirit also. You are, actually, a spirit, and you have a soul (the soul is the seat of reasoning, emotions, thoughts, etc).

Your body accommodates both your spirit and your soul. Your spirit exists within your heart, your belly position (Prov. 20:27). On the other hand, your soul (that is your mind) is within your brain area.

However, what is most important is that you know that you consist of these three parts or areas, and for you to be conscious of the fact that your spirit-man is the main man. Your spirit-man is your inner man (1 Pet. 3:4) or your inward man (2 Cor. 4:16).

When Adam disobeyed God, his spirit died and he got separated from God and became His enemy, even though God still loved him. God made provision for Adam's restoration which was consummated at the Coming, Death, and Resurrection of the Lord Jesus Christ.

When someone believes and confesses Jesus Christ, his spirit is regenerated or made alive by the Holy Spirit of the Living God.

This is what is meant by being born again; and the Lord says that except a man is born again, he can neither see nor enter the Kingdom of Heaven (Jn 3:3,5).

If any man be in Christ, he is a new creature, old things are passed away and all things have become new (2 Cor. 5:17). It is your spirit that was born again and became a new creature.

It is not your mind, your soul, that is born again. You may still think imperfect thoughts even after you are born again. That is why the Word of God tells born again, Spirit-filled Believers to renew their minds (Rom. 12:2).

Your mind is renewed, is saved, by the Word of God (Jas 1:21). The more you read or hear the Word, the more you meditate on it and believe it, the more your mind is renewed; you see yourself thinking and speaking like God   God's Word is God.

It is not your body that is born again. Your body remains the same: the same height and complexion. Some have tried to change their complexion by bleaching their skin. That is satanic.

What will you tell God when you stand before His Judgment Seat on the Judgment Day and He asks you, "Why did you call Me an imperfect Creator?" Some have changed their hair, face, and other parts of the body.

The Word of God tells us to present our bodies a living sacrifice, holy, acceptable to God which is our reasonable service (Rom. 12:1). Presenting your body is a good sacrifice; it involves self-denial and self-control.

We are to present our members, parts of our body as instruments of righteousness and obedience to holiness and pleasing God (Rom. 6:13,19). Your body is the Temple of the Holy Spirit and you must keep it holy for the Lord.

Our topic is about receiving, thinking, believing, confession, and possession. Our body has five sense-organs. The organs include: the eye (for sight), the nose (for smelling), the tongue (for taste), the skin (for touch), and the ear (for hearing).

It is actually from these senses that we receive information into our brains (our brain is a giant and complex computer: it receives, stores, processes, and gives out information). God is a Wonderful God!

You must be careful of what you receive, especially through your eyes and your ears. What you receive and keep receiving will influence your beliefs. Your beliefs will influence your actions, confession, and possession.

Actually, your actions are a form of your confession. Your confession is your available action, and your action is your visible confession.

The impure images and information you receive and keep receiving will tempt you with impure thoughts and actions. Godly words and information will make you think Godly thoughts.

Be careful of what you allow into your mind, for it will greatly influence your thoughts, beliefs, confessions, and actions; and they, in turn, will influence your possessions and your ability to fulfill your destiny.

God has a great destiny for you. Receive the grace to fulfill your destiny in Jesus Christ's Name. Amen.

When you spend your time in pornographic images, messages full of unbelief and doubt, and gossiping, your Christian life will be messed up. Evil communication and company corrupts good manners (1 Cor. 15:33).

Don't be wiser than God. The Bible says that you must flee from youthful lusts (2 Tim. 2:22). You must pursue God and Godliness also.

Don't stay in a locked room, in a dark room, alone with somebody of the opposite sex because you think you are very much anointed. The man may force you, and the lady may seduce you.

The Word of God tells us to think on good, pleasant, loving, truthful, praiseworthy, and Godly things (Phil. 4:8). Don't spend your time meditating on evil and ungodly things because they will mar you. What you ponder on will make or mar you.

Think on the Word of God. Meditate on God's Word day and night (Josh. 1:8). Keep looking at the Word (Prov. 4:20-21). Keep your eyes on Jesus Christ and you will never sink (Matt. 14:28-31; Heb. 12:2).

Also, have absolute confidence and belief in the Word of God. God can neither lie nor fail to perform His Word (Heb. 6:18). He is the Almighty Jehovah, the Maker of all things and there is nothing impossible with Him (Lk. 1:37).

They that trust in the Lord shall be like Mount Zion, which cannot be removed but abides forever (Psa. 125:1). Believe and don't doubt in your heart. When you pray, believe that you receive and you shall have your request (Mk 11:24).

Your confession will expose your belief, for out of the abundance of the heart, the mouth speaks (Lk. 6:45). Even in salvation, believing is to righteousness, while confession is to salvation (Rom. 10:10).

Keep confessing the Word of God, no matter how dark and difficult your path and situation may be like. Always be positive and never be negative, no matter what you may be seeing or hearing. Always be moved by what you believe, by what God says.

Coming to your possession, the Lord God Almighty has given us all things that pertain to life and Godliness through our knowledge of Jesus Christ Who has called us by His Own Power and Glory (2 Pet. 1:3,4).

We are given exceeding great and precious promises, and all the Promises of God in Christ Jesus are 'Yes,' and 'Amen' (2 Cor. 1:20).

If you maintain the confession of your faith, no matter how bad the circumstance may look like, you will overcome and have your expectations.

The Word tells us to fight the good fight of faith, to lay hold on Eternal Life (1 Tim. 6:12). Eternal Life is the Life and Nature of God.

Even when it seems you are seeing the opposite of what you expect, if you don't waver, if you don't doubt but believe, I tell you, you will have all that you need, all that you require, and all that Christ Jesus has provided for you.

Check whether your plans, desires, purposes, and pursuits correspond with those of the Lord over your life. God's Plans and Will for our lives are always the best. But you get to know about them by waiting on God and listening to Him, by prayer and meditation.

Don't harden your heart, but be open to God, so that you will receive His Direction. Don't say that you have made up your mind on this issue, and can't change it. Also, don't wait to have God stamp your decision; let Him, rather, direct you on what to do, so that demons will not deceive you by stamping it for you.

MANIFESTING GOD'S GLORY

Questions for Discussion:
1. What is God's Glory?
2. How can we manifest God's Glory?
3. What can stop, hinder, or limit our manifesting God's Glory?

The Glory of God is the Presence and Power of God being manifested or demonstrated. God's people have been called to manifest the Glory of God. This is one reason that God puts His Spirit in and upon His people.

The Holy Spirit manifests the Glory of God, and God wants the earth to be filled with the Glory of God as the waters cover the sea (Psa. 72:19). The Manifestation of the Holy Spirit by the Gifts of the Holy Spirit in the lives of Believers is a way that God manifests His Glory. There are many other ways.

After Moses had been in the mountain for forty days and forty nights, his face radiated physically, so that people could see it. That was the Glory of God. Even now, though you may not see the light or radiation physically, yet in the spirit-realm, devils and their agents see it.

On the mountain of transfiguration, the Face of Jesus Christ was changed so that the three apostles that were with Him saw His Face radiating light. That was the Glory of God. Even in this dispensation, whenever God chooses, the radiation can be seen physically.

When you preach the Gospel, when you teach the Word of God, the Spirit of God backs the Gospel and Word you speak, and you will see signs, wonders, and miracles. The signs, wonders, and miracles are the manifestations of the Glory of God.

The Lord Jesus Christ, in His Earthly Ministry, manifested the Glory and Power of God in His Life and Ministry in signs, wonders, and miracles. He tells us in the Word that we who believe in Him will do the same works that He did, even greater works (Jn 14:12).

Moses demonstrated the Power and Glory of God to the Egyptians. Even in the wilderness, God demonstrated His Glory in bringing water out of a rock, in sending manna and quail to them, and in protecting them. The fall of Jericho was a demonstration of the Power and Glory of God.

Elijah brought fire down from Heaven, and he also withheld rainfall for three and half years. Elisha prayed to God and the army that came to arrest him could not see again; even at death, his bone raised the dead.

The children of Israel observed the Glory of God as a devouring fire on the top of the mountain. While they saw it as a devouring fire, Moses saw it as a glory-cloud and walked into the cloud.

Before the time, the people had seen the Glory of the Lord in the cloud at the time they complained about bread. When Moses finished building the tabernacle as the Lord commanded him, the cloud covered the tabernacle of meeting, and the Glory of the Lord filled the tabernacle.

And Moses was not able to enter the tabernacle of meeting, because the cloud rested above it, and the Glory of the Lord filled the tabernacle (Exo. 16:7,10; Exo. 24:16-17; Exo. 40:34-35).

The Word of God says that all the earth shall be filled with the Glory of the Lord (Num. 14:21). Often, the Glory of the Lord appeared to the children of Israel in the form of the cloud (the glory-cloud).

When King Solomon finished building the Temple, it came to pass, when the priests came out of the holy place, that the cloud filled the House of the Lord, so that the Glory of the Lord filled the House of the Lord (1 Kgs 8:10-11).

According to the record in 2 Chronicles 5:11-14, it came to pass when the priests came out of the most holy place (for all the priests who were present had sanctified themselves, without keeping to their divisions),

And the Levites who were singers…clothed in white linen, having cymbals, stringed instruments and harps, and…priests sounding with trumpets – indeed it came to pass when the trumpeters and singers were as one, to make one sound to be heard in praising and thanking the Lord,

And when they lifted up their voice with the trumpets and cymbals and instruments of music, and praised the Lord, saying, "For He is good, for His Mercy endures forever" that the House, the House of the Lord, was filled with a cloud.

When the House was filled with the cloud, the priests could not continue ministering because of the cloud, for the Glory of the Lord filled the House of God.

Whenever you want the Glory of the Lord to manifest in your midst, let the people there sanctify themselves, let them confess any sins to God and be washed in the Blood of Jesus Christ.

Then, as you pray, praise, and worship God in one accord, the Glory of God will fall in your midst; and it can even be noticed physically. When the glory falls, people will get saved, healed, and filled with the Spirit, even when no one has prayed for them.

In the Book of Acts of the Apostles, as the Disciples were all with one accord in one place, suddenly, there came a sound from Heaven, as of a rushing mighty wind, and it filled the whole house where they were sitting.

Then there appeared to them divided tongues, as of fire, and one sat upon each of them. And they were all filled with the Holy Spirit and began to speak with other tongues, as the Spirit gave them utterance (Acts 2:1-4). That was the Glory of God in manifestation.

The reason many meetings, gatherings, or fellowships don't see this (or see it more often) is because many gather together but their hearts and minds are not together. In fact, some harbour bitterness, wrath, unforgiveness, and hatred in their hearts.

After Peter and John had been persecuted for preaching to the people in the Name of Jesus Christ, they were allowed to go. When they met the other apostles and Disciples, and reported to them all that the chief priests and elders had said to them, when they heard that, they raised their voice to God with one accord and said, "Lord, you are God…."

And when they had prayed, the place where they were assembled together was shaken, and they were all filled with the Holy Spirit, and they Spoke the Word of God with boldness (Acts 4:18-31).

Another place where the Power and Glory of God fell was in the prison where Paul and Silas had been imprisoned. When they had laid many stripes on them, they threw them into prison, commanding the jailer to keep them securely.

Having received such a charge, he put them into the inner prison and fastened their feet in the stocks. But at midnight Paul and Silas were praying and singing hymns to God, and the prisoners were listening to them.

Suddenly, there was a great earthquake, so that the foundations of the prison were shaken, and immediately all the doors were opened and everyone's chains were loosed (Acts 16:22-32).

There are many places where the Glory, Power, and Presence of God were revealed in the Bible. Ezekiel saw the Glory of God in a vision and fell on his face. Like the appearance of rainbow in a cloud on a rainy day, so was the appearance of the likeness of the Glory of the Lord (Ezek. 1:28).

The Glory of the Lord was revealed to Prophet Ezekiel again and again. When you see the Glory of the Lord, you will fall down as Ezekiel did.

The Lord will not share or give His Glory with/to another (Isa. 48:11). God was not happy when He said, concerning His people, "Has a nation changed its gods, which are not gods? But My people have changed their glory for what does not profit.

"Be astonished, O heavens, at this, and be horribly afraid; be much desolated. For My people have committed two evils: they have forsaken Me, the Fountain of Living Waters, and hewn themselves cisterns – broken cisterns that can hold no water (Jer. 2:11-13).

People of God leave the real things for the shadows; people can go to churches for years and not have one single deep experience with God.

When people worship idols, they change the Glory of the Incorruptible God into an image made like creeping things (Rom. 1:23). Covetousness and greed are forms of idolatry, according to the Word of God.

When you sin, you fall short of the Glory of God. (Rom. 3:23). You can be restored to the Glory of God by repentance and confession. Whether you eat or drink or whatever you do, do all to the Glory of God.

Give no offence to anyone or the Church of God. Please all men in all things, not seeking your own profit, but the profit of many, that they may be saved (1 Cor. 10:31-33).

Christ in us is our Hope of Glory (Col. 1:27). We have been blessed with all spiritual blessings through Christ, because we are in Him and He is in us.

If we abide in Jesus Christ and His Word abides in us, we shall bear much fruit, and when we ask God anything, we will receive it. When Christ Jesus died and rose again, He defeated the devil for us and gave us the victory.

Believers receive power and authority from Him to tread on serpents, scorpions, devils, and their works; nothing shall hurt them.

Even at His Coming, we shall be glorified with Him forever. We all, with unveiled face, beholding as in a mirror the Glory of the Lord, are being transformed into the same image from glory to glory, just as by the Spirit of the Lord (2 Cor. 3:18).

The Work of the Holy Spirit is to glorify the Lord Jesus Christ, and He does it as we allow ourselves to be used by Him!

Manifesting the Glory of God is also in destroying the works of the devil. The reason the Son of God was made manifest was to destroy all the works of the devil.

We have been empowered to carry on with the Work of the Lord and we must destroy the works of the devil. God wants to use us to prove to the devil that He is all-powerful and above all.

God instructed His Adam and Eve to have dominion. God intends that we, as born-again Spirit-filled children of His, have dominion over the created things in this world. We also have dominion over the works of the devil.

We have been called and set over the nations and over the kingdoms, to root out and to pull down, to destroy and to throw down, to build and to plant. These are how we manifest God's Glory.

It is the Will of God that you excel both in life and in Godliness. As you excel in life and in Godliness, you manifest the Glory of God. He that is anointed demonstrates the Power and Glory of God. The anointing breaks every yoke of the devil, and lifts every burden of the enemy.

Arise and shine for your light has come and the Glory of God is risen upon you. For behold, the darkness shall cover the earth, and deep darkness the people; but the Lord will rise over you, and His Glory will be seen upon you.

Manifesting the Glory of God requires you pay some price. Of course, the Lord has already paid the Ultimate Price for all of us. But whoever will come after Jesus Christ must deny himself, take up his own cross, and follow Him.

The price is the price of obedience: doing what God wants you to do. If the Lord tells you to preach to that your neighbour, do it; if He tells you to sacrifice that your job, do it; if He tells you to fast for seven days, do it. He is our Lord and Master, and He deserves our obedience and reverence.

As a Believer, you need a fresh anointing. Don't depend on the glory of yesterday; don't relax to celebrate the manifestations of yesterday. God has so much provision for you today that you will be marveled, if you keep in pace with God. Live a power-filled life always. Be on fire for the Lord always.

Put your angels to work by being prayerful, holy, and by maintaining a heart full of faith, praise, and thanksgiving. When you praise and worship God, God Himself comes to fight for you, and you will be delivered from all the works of the devil.

Trouble whatever troubles you. Use the Name of Jesus Christ against anything that works against you; at the Name of Jesus Christ, every knee should bow. Don't lie low for the devil to have his way in your life. Resist the devil, his demons, and his agents, and they will flee from you.

The Lord is my Strength and my Salvation, of whom shall I be afraid? The Lord shall keep us from all the plans of the wicked one; therefore, our victory is assured. What can man do to us? Live your life with the consciousness of the fact that God and His angels are with you.

You've got to draw water out of the wells of salvation. The wells are there; there is enough provision and room for us in Christ Jesus our Lord. But we must draw out and take those inheritances of ours by prayer, faith, and praise. If we are faithless, God will remain faithful, for He cannot deny Himself.

Declare the Lord's Doings among the people, both by testimony and by action (present reality). The signs, wonders, and miracles that God does are to bless people and draw their attention to God, so that they will obey and reverence God.

We are the mighty ones of God, who have been called to show forth His Praise. The prophet said, "Lord, who has believed our report? And to whom has the Arm of the Lord been revealed?" When the Power, Glory, and Word of God are revealed to people, they believe our report about God and His Son Jesus Christ.

There are different levels of the anointing; therefore whatever level you may be operating from, aspire and go for the next level. The more the level of your anointing and faith, the more will be the manifestation of the Glory and Power of God through you.

Elisha struck the river and asked, "Where is the Lord God of Elijah?" The river divided because the Lord God Almighty answered. The Lord God is there with you. Believe His Word, and speak according to His Word in faith, and you will see the result that you need.

Do not doubt the Word of God because of what you may be seeing. John the Baptist asked whether or not Jesus Christ was the Expected One, possibly because the Lord did not deliver him, contrary to his expectation. We must be moved by what the Word says, instead of what we see or hear.

AGENTS OF SATAN IN CHURCHES AND IN THE WORLD

Questions for Discussion:

    1. Who are the agents of the satan?

    2. Where can they be found?

    3. Can we find them in the midst of Christians?

There are people who serve the interest of the devil in this world. Just as God needs people to work with Him, the devil needs people to work with him also.

The devil (satan) comes to steal, to kill, and to destroy. However, Jesus Christ came to give us life and more abundant life (Jn 10:10).

The Word of God says that we wrestle not against flesh and blood but against principalities, against powers, against rulers of the darkness of this world and against spiritual wickedness in high places (Eph. 6:12).

The devil and his associates (his fallen angels and demons) have ranks in their operation, the highest being the spiritual wickedness in high places. Those kinds operate in the heavenlies, and they direct the rulers of the darkness of this world who, in turn, give orders to the powers.

The principalities receive instructions from the powers. Apart from these spiritual entities, there are human beings that work with them to achieve their purposes.

The human agents are the witches and the wizards. Though the witches refer to the female agents while the wizards refer to the male agents, for the purpose of our study, the witches will serve for both of them.

Even the human agents also operate in ranks, and there are different cults and secret societies: some operate in the air, some operate in the water, and others operate on the land. They do travel to the outer space through astral projections and soul-travels.

Even though there is the likeliness that there are more female agents of satan than there are the male agents, especially in the marine kingdom, the male agents occupy higher positions often. Of course, there are many female agents who occupy greater positions than many male agents, depending on the society or cult one operates in.

This can also happen due to their levels of advancement. However, there are levels they don't allow females to pass, except in few instances; because they recognize that females are weaker and may expose their higher secrets easily, more than males.

As noted earlier, the devil comes to steal, kill, and destroy. The devil, his fallen angels and demons, and his human agents have those three things in mind, directly or indirectly. They fight the ministers of the Gospel.

They tempt them with different things and in different ways to make them sin. They also try to harm them physically. They are sworn enemies of Christians; they do whatever they can to pull the Christians down, hurt them, and, if possible, to kill them.

They take Christians as criminals and ministers as their most wanted criminals. This is because the ministers are leaders who are followed by many, and when one minister falls or dies, many are affected. They are in different arms of churches.

The devil and his agents use ministers' spouses and children against them. This is why some minister's wives will pick up quarrels often with their husbands to get their husbands angry, and maybe overreact.

For women-ministers, their husbands can also be used to frustrate their ministries, though the devil's usage of wives in this connection is more. Also, they try to make ministers' children ungodly and stubborn to frustrate them and give them bad image in the public.

This is why you must pray and study the Bible with your family always. Pray for each member of your family in your private prayer-life.

In churches, they pretend to be children of God and carry out their assignments under cover. Of course, some may be more evident to be agents of darkness, depending on their assignments and works.

Some of the assignments may be to cause sicknesses, sleep, lukewarmness, sexual immorality and lust, strife and quarrels, and such things.

Some agents appear violent while others appear quiet. Therefore, don't be deceived by appearance, let the Holy Spirit lead you concerning this.

This is why you, individually or as a group, need the gifts of the word of knowledge and the discerning of spirits so that the devil won't deceive you easily.

However, even without the gifts, your knowledge of God and His Word, and your being able to be sensitive to the Inward Witness of the Holy Spirit in your spirit will safe-guard you.

Never be afraid of witches, for, before the Holy Spirit in you, they are powerless. The Fire of the Holy Spirit, the Blood of Jesus Christ, and the angels of God are there for you, so that no evil will harm you.

Witches cause accidents to take human lives. They do this to send more people to Hell and to get enough blood in their blood-banks, because they feed on blood. They cause poverty and calamities in the lives of people.

During their initiations, their original God-given heart is removed and a stony heart is given them spiritually, so that they begin to desire and feel like the devil with great passion. This is why someone can turn very wicked overnight.

Therefore, parents, be careful with the type of associations your children keep, because children and youths are easily initiated through different things like gifts, borrowing, and lending.

They do this in nursery, primary, secondary, and tertiary schools. They do this in churches, markets, streets, clubs, and everywhere. You must always pray for your children and cover them with the Blood of Jesus Christ.

This is why you should train them in the Way of the Lord, so that when they are old, they will not depart from it. Make sure they are committed Christians, even at early age.

Some people use the gifts or alms given them to make some incantations in their covens and enslave the activities of their donors. They may come to you as beggars or those in need.

This doesn't mean that you should not give or lend, but always cover the gifts with the Blood of Jesus Christ before you give them out. Remember that when you give or lend in the Name of the Lord, you are doing it for the Lord Jesus Christ Himself.

If they lend money to you or sell goods to you in credit, they can use the credit-contact to remote-control your money and business, except you are prayerful. He who goes on borrowing will go on sorrowing. Also, the borrower is a servant to the lender (Prov. 22:7).

Pray over the food and meat you take; bless them in the Name of Jesus Christ, and they will be blessed by prayer and by the Word of God (1 Tim. 4:5). Be careful how you allow people touch you; but, don't be afraid.

Even, many rulers of different categories in the government of the nations are in different cults, and they use them to frustrate the economies of the nations of the world.

This is why many of them are very wicked and are uncaring; because when people are frustrated, many look for negative powers to solve their problems and go into robbery, prostitution, pursuit of money, wrong company, and others.

To this end, the Word of God says that we should pray for all men, especially those in authority, that we may live a Godly and peaceable life (1 Tim. 2:1-4). It is only the prayers of Christians that can save their countries.

Satan appears as an angel of light, and it is no wonder if his agents and ministers do the same (2 Cor. 11:14-15). Many of the false brethren in churches, ministries, and fellowships are nothing but agents of satan, and they cause confusion there.

Actually, if you serve the will of satan, you make yourself his agent, whether you are a witch or not. Therefore, husbands, wives, children, friends, pastors, members, do not allow the devil to use you fulfill his work.

When you speak lies in hypocrisy, you are serving the interest of the devil. When you preach and teach things that are contrary to the Word of God, you are serving the interest of the devil.

Many have been deceived, and many are deceiving others. Demons deceive people, even Believers, so that those who have been deceived will be used to deceive others.

Jezebel was used by the devil to cause God's children commit immorality (Rev. 2:20). False apostles of the Ephesian Church were tested and found liars (Rev. 2:2).

He who believes shall not be in haste (Isa. 28:16). Try the spirits and prove all things. Before you marry, make sure you are spiritually sensitive to God's Direction and Leading. Favour is deceitful and beauty is vain.

Even many products in markets are produced in the demonic world and sold to our world, physically. They include: cosmetics, dresses, food items, and many others; therefore, pray over the things you use before using them.

Some say we should not talk about the devil; however, if their eyes are opened, they will not say so. How would a demonic lady lure a highly anointed man of God into sexual immorality, without the man recognizing it?

Be prayerful always; add fasting to your prayers. Also, increase in your knowledge of God and His Word. Fellowship with other sincere Believers and let the Peace of God be with you. Amen.

When you cause strife and division in the House of God, you are serving the interest of the devil. Therefore, as a Believer, don't allow the devil to use you fulfil his purpose.

BEING AN EXAMPLE TO THE BELIEVERS

Questions for Discussion:

1. How can we be examples to the Believers?
2. In what ways should we be exemplary in our lives?
3. Is it possible to show bad examples to other Believers?
4. What are the advantages of being good examples to the Believers?

Believers believe in the Lord Jesus Christ. The Disciples were first called Christians in Antioch (Acts 11: 26). To be a Christian is to be like Christ.

However, it is a well-known fact that many Believers fall short of the Likeness of Christ, even to a great gap. But God wants His people, the Believers, to be like His Son, Jesus Christ, because Jesus Christ came to bring many sons to glory.

Due to this, God, through Apostle Paul, commands us to be examples to the Believers. Do you know that many believe that no one can be like Christ in this present world? But the Lord tells us to be perfect just as our Heavenly Father is perfect (Matt. 5:48).

Be holy for the Lord God is holy (1 Pet. 1:15). Be holy, be perfect in your life; whatever you do, in word or in actions, be perfect and holy.

The Bible says that without holiness, no man can see the Lord (Heb. 12:14). If you are not pure in heart, you cannot see God (Matt. 5:8); and out of the abundance of the heart, the mouth speaks (Matt. 12:34).

Where your treasure is, is where your heart will be (Lk. 12:34). Out of the heart proceeds the issues of life (Prov. 4:23).

Even, life and death are in the power of the tongue, the mouth (Prov. 18:21). Your words and actions are a reflection of what is in your heart.

You must love God with all your being, and more than all beings and things. If you love anything or anyone more than the Lord Jesus Christ, you are not worthy of Him.

Be an example to the Believers in word, in conduct, in love, in spirit, in faith, in purity (1 Tim. 4:12). In your school, be an example; in home, be an example; in market, be an example; in church, be an example; wherever you may be and whatever you may do, be an example.

Let not the Name of the Lord be blasphemed among the heathen for your sake (Rom. 2:24). Let God be proud of you; let Him have confidence in you as He had in Job.

In word, be an example to the Believers: let no corrupt word come out of your mouth but that which is good (Eph. 4:29). Some people can destroy others with their words. Don't tell your brother that he is a fool (Matt. 5:22).

Refrain from gossip, slander, back-biting, and jesting. Learn to encourage people with your words, instead of destroying them with the same. Remember that men shall give account of every idle or careless word they speak on the Last Day (Matt. 12:36).

Don't judge your brother, because there is only one Judge: Jesus Christ. By the way, why do you pay attention to the speck in your brother's eye, while you do nothing about the plank in your own?

Be an example to the Believers in conduct also. Be careful how you behave yourself. Conduct yourself in a Godly manner.

As a minister, be trustworthy in your conduct. If you are a civil servant, don't expect a bribe before you do your work. As a student, you must not get involved in an examination malpractice, either by helping somebody or by receiving help from another during examinations.

Your behaviour should be worthy of emulation. People should speak well of you, though they may persecute or be against you. But this does not mean that all men will speak well of you.

Another area that the Bible commands us to be examples in is in love. All the Law is summed up in your loving God with all your heart, with all your soul, and with all your strength. The extension of it is in loving your neighbour as yourself (Matt. 22:35-40).

If you love Jesus Christ, then keep His Commandments (Jn 14:15), and His Commandments are not burdensome (1 Jn 5:3). God can tell you to do a hard thing, but not an impossible thing.

If God tells you to pray, pray; if He tells you to study His Word, do just that. If the Lord tells you to evangelize, evangelize; follow the Leading of the Holy Spirit, because the Holy Spirit speaks the Mind of God.

If you follow God's Spirit, He will lead you out of trouble and take you to a good place. God's Commandments are to make us; they are for our good, and they are not meant to destroy us.

There is so much more to love than we have realized. Have your ever wondered why the Lord Jesus Christ stated that He left us with a New Commandment, which is to love one another? (Jn 13:34).

Though you speak with the tongues of men and of angels, though you have the gift of prophecy and receive revelations, though you have all faith so that you could remove mountains, you are nothing if you don't have love.

What then is love since the Bible says that you can bestow all your goods to feed the poor, give your body to be burned, and still not have love? Well, the Bible tells us what love is.

Love suffers long and is kind; love does not envy; love does not parade itself, is not puffed up; love does not behave rudely, does not seek its own, is not provoked, thinks no evil; love does not rejoice in iniquity, but rejoices in the truth (1 Cor. 13:1-8).

Love bears all things, believes all things, hopes all things, and endures all things. Love never fails. You see that if you live your life in love, you are a super-human. Of course, the life of love will get you to Heaven.

God is Love and we are children of God. Therefore, we are a people of love. No wonder the Love of God is shed abroad in our hearts by His Holy Spirit (Rom. 5:5). Use the love that God has given you; increase and multiply it, and it will be well with your soul.

You must be an example to the Believers in spirit. We are sprit-beings who have souls and live in physical bodies. The Life of God, the Eternal Life that we received when we were born again is a life in the Spirit of God.

Even, the Word of God that gets us born again, that makes us grow and mature, is life and spirit. The spiritual controls the physical. God spoke the physical world into existence using His Spiritual Power. Be filled and be being filled with the Spirit of God; don't stop at the Holy Ghost baptism; go on.

Life in the Spirit is wonderful. Smith Wigglesworth said that he would rather have the Spirit of God upon him for five minutes than to have a million dollars. What a great statement!

The Anointing and Power of the Holy Spirit is what we must thirst and hunger after. We must live our lives, and we must minister, in the Holy Ghost.

Allow yourself to be led by the Holy Spirit; soak yourself in the Word of God, because the Word of God is power. Let the Fruit of the Spirit be abundant in your life.

Be an example to the Believers in faith. The fathers received good report by faith (Heb. 11:2). Without faith, it is impossible to please God. You must believe that God exists and that He will reward you, to be able to please Him.

Faith is the substance of things hoped for, the evidence of things not seen. Faith comes by hearing the Word of God (Rom. 10:17). Abel offered to God a more excellent sacrifice by faith. Enoch walked with God by faith. Noah obeyed God by faith; Abraham obeyed God by faith.

Moses chose to suffer with the people of God by faith. The prophets of the Old Testament and the early Disciples and ministers of the New Testament pleased God by faith. You must be a man of faith.

Nothing is impossible to him that is with God. God can neither lie nor fail to perform His Word. Has He said it? He will perform it. All power belongs to our God (Psa. 62:11). Neither the devil, his cohorts, nor his works can stand before God.

Lastly, we are commanded to be examples in purity. As a man, be pure; as a lady, be chaste. Don't be immoral in your life. Avoid sexual immorality. Your body is the Temple of God. Don't sell your birthright for a five-minute sex like Esau (Gen. 25:29-34; Heb.12:16-17).

Flee youthful lust and avoid being in a closed dark room alone with the opposite sex. Don't help the devil get you into sin, and don't be wiser than God.

Of course, there are many other ways we have to be exemplary. Run your Heavenly and Christian race in such a way as to obtain the reward and prize. Learn to be orderly, for God loves orderliness.

Whatever you do, in word or in deed, do all in the Name of the Lord, giving glory to the Father. Always put God first in everything you do. Amen.

We are Bondservants of the Lord, and we must sacrifice all for the Lord, even our lives as the Lord needs them. Others should see self-sacrifice and self-denial in us so that they too can lay down their substances, treasures, and lives for the Lord.

The Bible is the Book of books, and it contains the best examples of both faithfulness and unfaithfulness. Study it to know what the people that went before you did.

Learn from their victories, obedience, faith, and exploits. Avoid their mistakes. The things of the past were written for our admonition, so that we can learn from them.

MY FATHER'S BUSINESS

Questions for Discussion:

    1. What is the Father's Business?

    2. What part are we to play in the Father's Business?

    3. What happens when we don't do the Father's Business?

My Father's Business is the assignment that the Lord God Almighty has for me. It is the Work of the Lord that must be accomplished. In the Business of the Father, each of us has one thing or the other to do.

This is why the Word of God says that the Lord gave some to be apostles, and some prophets, and some evangelists, and some pastors, and some teachers.

These ministry gifts are given to the Church to prepare and equip the Saints so that the Saints (the people of God) might do the work of the ministry. The work of the ministry is the Father's Business.

In secular companies, there are divisions of labour, because one man will not do it all. The same is applicable in the Kingdom of God. No one man (no matter how anointed you may be) can do it all.

Everybody has his place; of course, some have the ability to occupy more than one place. We need each other to fulfill the Purpose of the Lord in this world.

We should dedicate our time, effort, energy, ability, wisdom, and mind to the Father's Business, so that the business will not suffer.

When the Lord arose from the dead, He said, "All authority has been given to Me in Heaven and on earth. Go, therefore, and make Disciples of all the nations, baptizing them in the Name of the Father, and of the Son, and of the Holy Spirit, teaching them to observe all things that I have commanded you; and lo, I am with you always, even to the End of the Age."

Making Disciples of all the nations, baptizing the Believers, and teaching them, are forms of the Business of the Father God.

According to Mark's Report, the Lord Jesus Christ said, "Go into all the world and preach the Gospel to every creature. He who believes and is baptized will be saved, but he who does not believe will be condemned.

"And these signs will follow those who believe: In My Name, they will cast out demons; they will speak with new tongues; they will take up serpent; and if they drink anything deadly, it will by no means hurt them; they will lay hands on the sick, and they will recover."

So then after the Lord had spoken to them, He was received up into Heaven and sat down at the Right Hand of God. And they went out and preached everywhere, the Lord working with them and confirming the Word through the accompanying signs. Amen (Mk 16:15-20).

Preaching the Gospel to every creature, casting out demons in His Name, and laying hands on the sick so that they will recover are forms of the Father's Business.

When the Lord said that His Followers should pray that the Will of God be done on earth as it is in Heaven, part of what He was saying, is that the Will of the Father and His Business ought to be done on this earth.

The task of taking the Gospel to the ends of the earth was given to the Believers, and not the angels. Therefore, if we are not committed to preaching the Gospel, many more souls will troop into Hell Fire, and God will be greatly displeased.

For whoever calls on the Name of the Lord shall be saved. How then shall they call on Him in Whom they have not believed? And how shall they believe in Him of Whom they have not heard? And how shall they hear without a preacher? And how shall they preach except they are sent? (Rom. 10:13-14).

You must preach the Good News wherever you are; and you should help in sending people to wherever you may not go. You can send by praying to the Lord of the harvest to send labourers to His Field (Matt. 9:38); and you can send by supporting missionary works financially.

Be committed to the Cause of the Lord, even if it means laying down your life for Jesus Christ. If you love your life more than Him, you are not worthy of Him (Lk. 14:26).

Whoever puts his hands to the plough and looks back is not fit for service in the Kingdom of God. Whoever loses his life for the Sake of Jesus Christ will have it back (Matt. 10:39).

Actually, we got the term 'My Father's Business' from the second chapter of Luke when Jesus Christ had gone to Jerusalem at the age of twelve. The parents looked for Him after they did not see Him, because He had stayed back.

When they found Him, his mother asked Him, saying, "Son, why have You done this to us? Look, Your father and I have sought You anxiously." And He replied, saying, "Why did you seek Me? Did you not know that I must be about My Father's Business?"

But they did not understand the Statement which He spoke to them (Lk. 2:42-52). Even today, many still don't understand. Many Christians give most of their time and energy, pursuing the things that don't have eternal value.

Christ Jesus saw Peter and Andrew casting a net into the sea; for they were fishermen. Then He said to them, "Follow Me, and I will make you fishers of men." They immediately left their nets and followed Him.

Going on from there, He saw James and John in the boat with Zebedee their father, mending their nets, He called them, and immediately they left the boat and their father, and followed Him (Matt. 4:18-22).

They left their own businesses for the Lord's Business immediately, according to the Commandment of the Lord. Whatever the Lord tells you to do, do it no matter how hard it may be.

Jesus Christ Himself went about all Galilee, teaching in their synagogues, preaching the Gospel of the Kingdom, and healing all kinds of sicknesses and all kinds of diseases among the people.

Then His Fame went throughout all Syria, and they brought to Him all sick people who were afflicted with various diseases and torments, and those who were demon-possessed, epileptics and paralytics, and He healed them. Great multitudes followed Him (Matt. 4:23-25).

According to the Gospel of Luke, Jesus Christ returned in the Power of the Spirit to Galilee and News of Him went out through all the surrounding region. And He taught in their synagogues, being glorified by all.

Then He went down to Capernaum, and was teaching them on the Sabbaths. And they were astonished at His Teaching, for His Word was with authority. Report about Him went out into every place in the surrounding region.

When the sun was setting, all those who had any that were sick with various diseases brought them to Him, and He laid His Hands on every one of them and healed them. And demons also came out, crying out.

Now when it was day, He departed and went into a deserted place. And the crowd sought Him and came to Him, and tried to keep Him from leaving them, but He said to them, "I must preach the Kingdom of God to other cities also, because for this purpose I have been sent" (Lk. 4).

Jesus Christ was always committed to the Business of the Father till His Death. He did not loved His Life, even to death. He preached, taught, healed the sick, cast out devils, and did many other things.

After Jesus Christ had died and resurrected, Simon Peter told the others with him that he was going to fish. They replied that they will also go with him. As they fished, having caught nothing in the night, Jesus Christ came to them in the morning.

He directed them on what to do, and when they did it, they were not able to draw their net in, because of the multitude of fish. As they fed later, Jesus Christ asked Apostle Peter, saying, "Simon, son of Jonah, do you love Me more than these?"

Do you prefer the Father's Business to any other business or commitment you may have? Of course, you have to follow the Lord's Leading step by step.

Apostle Paul is someone we can look up to, after Jesus Christ. This great apostle wrought great signs, wonders, and miracles, as he preached and taught the Word.

He pursued the Work of the Lord with great zeal and passion, and he was ready to die for Jesus Christ. He suffered dearly in the ministry.

He refused to marry for the sake of the Gospel (however, that was personal decision, and it is better to marry than to burn with lust); he worked to sustain himself in the ministry (though it is better not be hindered or burdened by anything in the ministry).

He was hard-pressed on every side; he was perplexed; he was persecuted, struck down, always carrying about in the body the Dying of the Lord Jesus Christ.

He worked in much patience, in tribulation, in needs, in distresses, in stripes, in imprisonments, in torments, in labours, in sleeplessness, in fasting, in dishonour, by evil report.

He was beaten five times with thirty-nine stripes; he was beaten three times with rods; he was stoned once; he was shipwrecked three times; he suffered from journeys, robbers, Jews, Gentiles, wilderness etc. (1 Cor. 9; 2 Cor. 4, 6 & 11).

WATCHFULNESS, VIGILANCE, AND SOBRIETY

Questions for Discussion:

1. What does it mean to be watchful, vigilant, and sober?
2. What will happen if we are not watchful, vigilant, and sober?
3. Why should we be watchful, vigilant, and sober?

To be watchful is to be careful to notice what is happening, in case anything bad happens. To watch is to look carefully, in order to avoid any danger.

To be vigilant is to give careful attention to what is happening, so that you will notice any danger. Sobriety refers to behaviour that shows a serious attitude to life.

These three words require seriousness; that is, to be watchful, vigilant, and sober, you've got to be sensible and quiet. We live in evil days; therefore, you must be watchful, vigilant, and sober.

The Word of God tells us to watch and pray so that we will not enter into temptation. The reason is that the spirit is willing, but the flesh is weak (Matt. 26:41).

You can watch without praying, and you can pray without watching. You must watch and pray. If you watch without praying, you can know of danger, but you may not avoid it.

If you pray without watching, you can pray amiss, and you can be caught up in the temptation or danger. Be sober, be vigilant, because your adversary, the devil, walks about like a roaring lion, seeking whom he may devour.

Resist him, steadfast in the faith, knowing that the same sufferings are experienced by your Brotherhood in the world (1 Pet. 5:8-9).

To be sober is to have a serious attitude to life; it is not to take things or life for granted, but to be careful and sensitive. The devil is looking for any loophole in your life so that he may strike.

Therefore, don't create any loophole for him. Your faith (steadfast faith) is the shield with which you can stop all the arrows of the devil.

The parable of the wheat and the tares tells us the need for watchfulness (Matt. 13:24-30). A man sowed good seeds in his field; but in the night, because he had no watchman who was watching, an enemy went to that field of his and sowed tares and left.

Neither the man nor his servants knew about the tares until when they sprouted and grew alongside the wheat. Without watchfulness, vigilance, and sobriety, the devil can spoil the good things you are doing for God.

Their unwatchfulness led to a loss; because, for fear of damaging the wheat, the owner advised his servants to allow both of them to grow together till the harvest. The wheat and the tares, therefore, had to share the soil nutrient in the field.

The wheat would have grown better if the competition for the available nutrients and conditions was not there. This same thing is happening in churches today.

Due to carelessness, agents of the kingdom of darkness have entered many churches to do their destructive and bad works among the Believers while posing as fellow Believers.

There are many bad and sinful doctrines and ways of life that have been introduced into churches because satanic agents entered among Christians.

For instance, let's consider the issue of Christian ladies using weavons. There are many reasons why Christians should not use weavons. Using weavon is like telling God that He is stupid and imperfect for giving you the kind of hair you have.

It is like bleaching which many do; they feel that God should have made them fair in complexion instead of dark. But on the Day of Judgment, you will find out that you tried to degrade God.

Also, many of those weavons are real human hair which were cut and sold. How can you be wearing another person's hair as a Christian lady or woman? This is worldliness; this is satanic and demonic; sister, the ground you are treading on is dangerous.

Then, even though some of those weavons may be synthetic or artificial (which the first point still condemns), many of those weavons ladies use are manufactured in the water-kingdom of darkness and brought to this earth for sales to contaminate the people of the world.

The thing that some people don't know is that some companies which exist physically on this earth came from the dark kingdom of satan, especially the water-world of the devil.

It may surprise you to know that an occult man who wants to construct a building can do it using workers from the dark kingdom who will manifest physically. Occult companies use satanic agents as workers and people wouldn't know.

In fact, many things we see physically came from the dark kingdom. Even many legal and morally good things we see are manufactured in the dark kingdom, some of which I wouldn't mention here.

This is why you need to pray over and sanctify the things that you use, especially edible things. But how will you want to sanctify things that the Lord has rejected and condemned?

Everything is not demonic, don't misunderstand me; don't live in fear either, because greater is He that is in us than he that is in the world.

The anointing breaks every yoke of the enemy. But many Christians create loopholes for the devil through sin, disobedience, and worldliness.

You need to be watchful and sober, because if you are not, the devil can lead you into sin and worldliness, and if the Lord Jesus Christ meets you in that state at His Coming, or you die in that state, you will miss Heaven and go to Hell.

But that is not God's Plan for you, and He did not bring you out of the world to condemn you later. Therefore, don't condemn yourself. You condemn yourself by despising His Word and the Promptings His Spirit.

The Bible recommends that a bishop must be vigilant (1 Tim. 3:2). Every minister of the Gospel must be vigilant. As a pastor, you need to walk with God.

You need to be vigilant and watchful; and you need to know the Voice or Leading of the Spirit of God. Do you know that somebody can be sent to your church or ministry by the powers of darkness to pull you down?

That person may come in and become very zealous in your activities, and you may start promoting the person to responsible positions. After some months or years, he or she may do or say things that can destroy your ministry.

The fellow can lie against you, and may say things that you may not be able to explain. People, even your members, may believe him or her, saying that if he or she was fake and lying, he or she wouldn't have been with you for so long.

This is why you don't need to believe everything you hear about someone. Don't believe every good or bad thing people say about a minister, except you have the witness inside you.

Watch, for you do not know what Hour your Lord is coming. But know this, that if the master of the house had known what hour the thief would come, he would have watched and not allowed his house to be broken into (Matt. 24:42-43).

Take heed, watch and pray; for you do not know when the Time is. It is like a man going to a far country, who left his house and gave authority to his servants, and to each his work and commanded the doorkeeper to watch.

Watch, therefore, for you do not know when the Master of the House is coming in the evening, at midnight, at the crowing of the rooster, or in the morning, lest coming suddenly, He finds you sleeping (Mk 13:33-36).

The Bible tells us to be watchful in all things (2 Tim. 4:5). Watch your tongue, watch your words, watch your actions, watch your relationships, watch your life, watch your ministry.

Watch your environment, watch your commitments, and watch in everything. Don't be taken by surprise unnecessarily.

Remember that the Spirit of God will tell you things to come. The Word says that we should not sleep, as others do, but should watch and be sober.

For those who sleep, sleep at night, and those who get drunk are drunk at night. But let us who are of the day be sober, putting on the breastplate of faith and love, and as a helmet the hope of salvation (1 Thes. 5:6-8).

Therefore, gird up the loins of your mind, be sober, and rest your hope fully upon the grace that is to be brought to you at the Revelation of Jesus Christ;

As obedient children, not conforming yourselves to the former lusts, as in your ignorance; but as He Who called you is holy, you also be holy in all your conduct (1 Pet. 1:13-15).

But the end of all things is at hand; therefore, be serious and watchful in your prayers. And above all things have fervent love for one another, for love will cover a multitude of sins (1 Pet. 4:7-8).

God doesn't want us to be at a disadvantage at any time and in any thing. No wonder Apostle Paul declared that we are not ignorant of the devices of the devil (2 Cor. 2:11).

If you are ignorant, he will take advantage of you; and he does not come, but to steal, kill, and destroy. God's people perish because of ignorance; therefore, go for more and right knowledge.

Remember that you are a watchman; therefore, watch in all things. The souls of men are tied to you; if you don't watch over their souls, they will perish. Therefore, give diligence to being committed to winning souls for the Lord.

Know your friends, and be careful of your enemies. It is good to keep friends, but know that your friends will either make or mar you. Therefore, be careful with the type of friends you keep. Also, know that your enemies may be looking for the slightest opportunity to strike. Therefore, watch always.

We are in the End Time; you must be watchful the more as you see the Day of the Lord approaching. There are many End-time realities, things that the Lord told us will happen before He comes.

As He has warned us ahead of time, so that the Day of the Lord will not overtake us unexpectedly, we must be more alert. We must prepare for the Lord's Coming; we must be ready to welcome Him.

FROM GLORY TO GLORY

Questions for Discussion:

1. Can we carry God's Glory?
2. What does it mean to carry the Glory of God?
3. To what extent should we grow in carrying the Glory of God?

We are changed from glory to glory by the Spirit of the Lord (2 Cor. 3:18). Now the Lord is the Spirit and where the Spirit of the Lord is, there is liberty.

After Moses had been in the mountain for forty days and forty nights, the children of Israel noticed that his face shown with the Glory of God. They could see visible radiation of God's Glory in his face.

But Moses had seen God's Glory before, and he had moved in God's Glory before (remember that God had appeared to him, and he had demonstrated signs and wonders); however, in this place, he moved to another level of God's Glory.

That was Old Testament, and we are in the New Testament which is established upon better promises (Heb. 8:6). If the ministry of death was glorious, which glory was to be done away, how will the Ministry of the Spirit not be more glorious?

For if the ministry of condemnation had glory, the ministry of righteousness excels much more in glory. For even what was made glorious had no glory in this aspect, because of the glory that excels.

For if what is passing away was glorious, what remains is much more glorious. This means that all those mighty things that we read about in the Old Testament are not comparable to the things that are available to us in the New Testament.

The Glory of God is the Presence and Power of God. It is the Manifestation of the Spirit of God to people and through people. The Spirit of God manifests through God's people and can manifest even to unbelievers. You need the Glory of God in your life.

No wonder Moses told God not to send them forward without His Presence. It is the manifestation of the Glory of God through you that distinguishes you from the others. When you see His Glory, you will not remain the same!

We change from glory to glory; we are moved from one level of glory to another level of glory. Don't settle down at the level of glory you have; go for the next.

After the glory of being born again, go for the glory of being baptized and filled with the Holy Spirit. After speaking in tongues, move to the next level of the demonstration of the Power of God through healings and miracles. Progress to other levels!

I will use the account or story in Exodus to describe the Glory of God to you. Moses went up with Aaron, Nadab, and Abihu, and seventy of the elders of Israel, and they saw the God of Israel.

And there was under His Feet as it were a paved work of sapphire stone and it was like the very heavens in its clarity. But on the nobles of the children of Israel He did not lay His Hand. So they saw God and they ate and drank.

Then the Lord said to Moses, "Come up to Me on the mountain and be there, and I will give you tablets of stone and the Law and the Commandments which I have written, that you may teach them."

So Moses arose with his assistant Joshua, and Moses went up to the Mountain of God. And he said to the elders, "Wait here for us until we come back to you. Indeed, Aaron and Hur are with you. If any man has a difficulty, let him go to them."

Then Moses went up into the mountain and a cloud covered the mountain. Now the Glory of the Lord rested on Mount Sinai, and the cloud covered it six days. And on the seventh day He called to Moses out of the midst of the cloud.

The sight of the Glory of the Lord was like a consuming fire on the top of the mountain in the eyes of the children of Israel. So Moses went into the midst of the cloud and went up into the mountain. And Moses was on the mountain forty days and forty nights (Exo. 24:9-18).

You can notice varying levels of glory and relationship with God here. The other people couldn't go up except Moses, Joshua, Aaron, Nadab, Abihu, Hur, and seventy of the elders of Israel.

After going for an extent up the mountain, they saw the Glory of God. Then Moses and Joshua left them up the mountain for another level of glory. Finally, Moses left Joshua after some extent and moved up into the mountain for a higher level of glory and relationship with God.

It is interesting to note that the level of glory you witness and the relationship you have with God will determine your position or the responsibility God will give you, for Joshua replaced Moses at his death.

The same varying levels of glory and relationship with God are seen in the Ministry of Jesus Christ. Many people followed Jesus Christ, and they were so many that, sometimes, they trod on one another.

Out of the multitude that followed Him, Jesus Christ selected a seventy that He sent out for missionary work. He also had His twelve special people. Out of the twelve, He had a special three of Peter, John, and James.

Then out of the three came the closest to Jesus Christ – John. Also, out of the three came the leader of the apostles   Peter. Where do you belong? Your dedication to God and level of obedience to Him will determine your position with Him.

We will yet look at another story in Exodus. Moses experienced and demonstrated the Glory of God so much. And it came to pass, when Moses entered the tabernacle, the pillar of cloud descended and stood at the door of the tabernacle, and the Lord talked with Moses.

All the people saw the pillar of cloud standing at the tabernacle door, and all the people rose and worshiped, each man in his tent door. So the Lord spoke to Moses Face to face, as a man speaks to his friend.

And he would return to the camp, but his servant Joshua the son of Nun, a young man, did not depart from the tabernacle.

Then Moses said to the Lord, "See, You say to me, 'Bring up this people.' But You have not let me know whom you will send with me. Yet You have said, 'I know you by name, and you have also found grace in My Sight.'

"Now therefore, I pray, if I have found grace in Your Sight, show me now Your Way, that I may know You and that I may find grace in Your Sight. And consider that this nation is Your people."

And He said, "My Presence will go with you, and I will give you rest." Then he said to Him, "If Your Presence does not go with us, do not bring us up from here. For how then will it be known that Your people and I have found Grace in Your Sight, except You go with us?

"So we shall be separate, Your people and I, from all the people who are upon the face of the earth." So the Lord said to Moses, "I will also do this thing that you have spoken; for you have found grace in My Sight, and I know you by name."

And he said, "Please, show me Your Glory," and He said, "I will make all My Goodness pass before you, and will proclaim the Name of the Lord before you. I will be gracious to whom I will be gracious, and I will have compassion on whom I will have compassion."

But He said, "You cannot see My Face; for no man shall see Me, and live." And the Lord said, "Here is a place by Me, and you shall stand on a rock. So it shall be, while My Glory passes by,

"That I will put you in the cleft of the rock, and will cover you with My Hand while I pass by. Then I will take away My Hand, and you shall see My Back; but My Face shall not be seen (Exo. 33:9-23).

Can you imagine what happened here? God had been appearing and speaking to Moses, and Moses had done so many miracles and wonders; yet, here, he said, "Show me Your Way, that I may know You."

Moses was still humble enough to desire to know God's Way. Some have not even seen one-tenth of what Moses saw, and they boast of so many things.

They wouldn't even take enough time to read or study their Bible again, and they listen to wrong spirits and teach wrong doctrines and messages.

Also, Moses told God that it is His Presence that will make them separate or distinguished from the other people. Brother, the Power and Glory of God will distinguish you.

The problem is that many have settled for lower levels of glory, and many are bound by the traditions of men and conventional ways that they have chosen not to give up. But the Glory of the Lord makes the difference: the Spirit makes the difference.

God is glorious in power (Exo. 15: 6), and He is glorious in holiness (Exo. 15:11). He is glorious in name also. Glorious things are spoken of God (Psa. 87:3). The Church, which is the Body of Christ, is a glorious Church of a Glorious Jesus Christ.

Jesus Christ moved from glory to glory while He was on earth; and we are to move from glory to glory also, for what He did, we shall do also. We shall do even greater works than He did (Jn 14:12).

In Christ Jesus, we have available to us an exceeding abundant life. There is an exceeding abundant grace available to us through Christ our Lord.

We are to receive this grace actively; we must not lie low and suffer unnecessarily when the grace and power to overcome and be victorious is there. Fight the good fight of faith and lay hold on Eternal Life.

There are many things we can learn from the eagle. The Bible says that those that wait on the Lord shall renew their strength; they shall mount up with wings like eagles, they shall run and not be weary, they shall walk and not faint.

Eagles eat fresh meat; they soar on the wind, and don't fly; and if they notice something wrong with them, they separate themselves to correct it. This separation, normally, takes a long time of about a month, until their strength is renewed.

The Lord gives strength to the weak, and to those who have no might He increases strength. We are to renew the Glory of God in us as we move from one level of glory to another level.

Get involved in retreats, camps, and other special programmes and meetings, both personal and in group. This will help increase the Power and Glory of God upon you, and you will move from glory to glory, from one level of power and authority to another level.

The faithful will be rewarded with Eternal Glory and unconceivable bliss. Spending eternity with God is another level of glory, which, no matter the anointing you may carry now, if you miss it you are a great loser.

There is the Spirit upon you, Who came upon you to anoint you with different levels of the anointing, as you obey and follow Him. As you pay the right sacrifice in obedience, discipline, and self-control, the anointing in your life will increase.

The earth shall be filled with the knowledge of the Lord as the waters cover the sea. This is the day that we have to manifest and show the Power, Might, and Glory of our Lord and Christ in order to bring glory to the Father.

PURSUE, OVERTAKE, AND RECOVER

Questions for Discussion:

    1. What do we mean by pursue, overtake, and recover?

    2. Do we have any ability to overpower the enemy?

    3. When and how should we pursue the enemy?

A time came in David's life that the Amalekites invaded Ziklag, and burned it with fire, taking captives their women (wives), their sons, and their daughters.

David and the people that were with him lifted up their voice and wept, until they had no more power to weep. What a calamity! Have your sufferings reached that extent?

David's two wives were taken captive. And David was greatly distressed; for the people spoke of stoning him, but David encouraged himself in the Lord his God.

David enquired of the Lord, saying, "Shall I pursue after this troop? Shall I overtake them?" And He answered him, "Pursue, for you shall surely overtake them, and without fail recover all."

So David went, he and his men. But David pursued, even though some of them who were very weak stayed behind when they could not cross the Brook Besor.

Along the way, they found someone who had not eaten for three days and fed him. When he had got his strength back, he directed David and his men to where the invading troops were.

Then David attacked them and recovered all that they had taken away. What would have happened if David had not pursued and attacked them? He would have lost all.

What would have happened if he had not enquired of the Lord? He might have not had the courage to pursue and attack them. God knows of your losses and predicaments, and He will make a way for you.

Even the Amalekite's servant that fell sick so that his master abandoned him (he directed David) was in God's Plan for the whole thing (1 Sam. 30:1-20).

This was also demonstrated by Abraham when he recovered Lot. When Sodom and other cities were attacked, the invading army took all the goods of Sodom, and all their provisions, and went their way.

They also took Lot, Abraham's brother's son who dwelt in Sodom, and his goods and departed. Then one who had escaped came and told Abraham, the Hebrew. When Abraham heard that his brother was taken captive, he armed his men and pursued the captors.

Abraham armed his three hundred and eighteen trained servants, who were born in his own house, and went in pursuit as far as Dan. He divided his forces against them by night, and he and his servants attacked them and pursued them.

So he brought back all the goods, and also brought back his brother Lot and his goods, as well as the women and the people (Gen. 14).

After his return, he gave tithe to Melchizedek who blessed him and said, "Blessed be Abram of God Most High, possessor of Heaven and earth; and blessed be God Most High, Who delivered your enemies into your hand."

Abraham would have lost Lot if he had remained in his place comfortably and not pursued. But he refused to remain at ease, and chose rather to act; and when he acted, he brought glory to the Name of the Lord.

The Word of God says that we should occupy till the Lord comes (Lk. 19:13). To occupy is to take charge and control of what you have been given to oversee. It is to enter a place and keep control of it. For example, by a military force.

In this case, the Lord wants us to oversee and do what He has entrusted into our hands, and keep it from interference by an enemy.

Then, even if due to one reason or the other, an enemy invaded our ground and took away anything, we should pursue, overtake, and recover all. To occupy is to do the Father's Business (the Lord's Business).

Some reason that since their income is enough, they will be buying medicine to control the disease they are passing through, which might have been termed 'incurable.'

Some may say, "Since I have this church or ministry, even if it is not flourishing well, at least let me maintain it." Inasmuch as we should give thanks to God in any situation we find ourselves in, yet it is the Lord's Will that you enjoy the fullness of His Provisions for you.

However, we must recognize that some deprivations and harsh states are brought about or allowed by the Lord Himself for different purposes.

What I am saying is that you should know when to pursue and when not to pursue. Even David enquired of the Lord and pursued when the Lord told him to pursue.

Some harsh conditions may be a test or a trial for you, and in that case, pursuing will not help matters, because it will not change it.

God told me that it is not every time that you have to bind and loose in prayers to correct a negative situation. He cited the case of Abraham whose wife was barren. Abraham prayed to God about the situation and God gave him a son, without binding and loosing (or dealing with demons).

If you study your Bible well, you will come to know that the prayer of binding and losing (or casting out demons) will not solve some undesirable conditions. For example, do you think that Prophet Jonah would have cast out that big fish that swallowed him?

His was a case of sin and disobedience, and what he needed to do to be free was repentance, confession, and mercy. Some will not come out of their conditions until their knowledge and wisdom have been developed to a level that God is satisfied.

Some will not come out until they learn humility and despise pride. You may not like the situation, but God allowed it for your own good, for your development and promotion.

There is a case in the Bible where the Israelites said, "The time has not come, the time that the Lord's House should be built." The Lord asked them, saying, "Is it time for you yourselves to dwell in your paneled houses, and this Temple to lie in ruins?"

The Lord went on, "Consider your ways! You have sown much, and bring in little; you eat but do not have enough; you drink, but you are not filled with drink; you clothe yourselves, but no one is warm; and he who earns wages, earns wages to put them into a bag with holes."

The Lord told them, "Consider your ways! Go up to the mountains and bring wood and build the Temple, that I may take pleasure in it and be glorified. You looked for much, but indeed it came to little; when you brought it home, I blew it away."

"Why? Because of My House that is in ruins, while every one of you runs to his own house. Therefore the heavens above you withhold the dew, and the earth withholds its fruit.

"For I called for a drought on the land and the mountains...on whatever the ground brings forth, on men and livestock, and on all the labour of your hands" (Hag. 1).

However, whatever the enemy, who comes not but to steal, kill, and destroy, might have taken away from you will be restored to you. But you have to pursue him and overtake him so that you can recover all.

When you believe, you speak and confess so that you can possess your possession. Confront your confrontations! Pray through; pray until you have a witness that you have prayed through.

Some prayers require fastings. You may have to do some days or weeks of night-vigils, maybe some three hours every night.

The violent takes his inheritance and possession by force. The Spirit of God lifts up a standard against the devil. Greater is He that is in you than he that is in the world. Confront the devil. God has not given you a spirit of fear, but of power and of love and of sound mind (2 Tim. 1:7).

The Lord is with you, and He will never leave you. They that are with you are more than they that are against you. One angel destroyed one hundred and eighty-five thousand Assyrian soldiers in one night (2 Kgs 19:35).

Be glad then, you children of Zion, and rejoice in the Lord your God; for He has given you the former rain faithfully, and He will cause the rain to come down for you the former rain and the later rain in the first month.

The threshing floors shall be full of wheat, and the vats shall overflow with new wine and oil. So the Lord will restore to you the years that the swarming locust has eaten, the crawling locust, the consuming locust, and the chewing locust, His great army which He sent among you.

You shall eat in plenty and be satisfied, and praise the Name of the Lord your God, Who has dealt wondrously with you, and God's people shall never be put to shame.

Then you shall know that He is in the midst of Israel. He is the Lord your God and there is no other. God's people shall never be put to shame (Joel 2: 23-27).

Learn to distinguish when to wait on God and when to pursue and overtake the invaders and spoilers.

We must understand the strategies of the enemy, so that he will not gain an advantage over us. God's people perish because of ignorance.

We should not even give him the opportunity to strike in the first place, to take away anything from us; however, if he succeeds in depriving us of anything, we must pursue him and recover all by force.

Are you possessing your inheritance in Christ Jesus the way you should? How will you feel, if when you get to Heaven, you realize that you deprived yourself of many things the Lord purchased and provided for you?

Whatever you have lost shall be found. Whatever the enemy has stolen or robbed from you shall be found and recovered. But you have your part to play; and you know that God cannot fail to fulfil His Own Part.

The Kingdom of God suffers violence, and the violent take it by force. Don't sit back and watch the devil deprive you of God's Blessings for you without doing anything. Pursue, overtake, and recover all!

THE IMMUTABILITY OF GOD'S WORD AND STANDARD

Questions for Discussion:

1. What is God's Word and Standard?
2. Is it true that God's Word and Standard is impossible to change?
3. Who can God change His Word and Standard for?

The Word of God is forever settled in Heaven. God is not a man to lie, and He is not a son of man to change His Mind. Has He spoken and shall He not bring it to pass? Instead of one Word from God to fail, heaven and earth shall pass away.

People try to change the Word of God to suit their desires. They use the Bible to defend themselves, when it is actually the devil that is quoting the Scripture to them wrongly, as he did to Jesus Christ. But God cannot be mocked; whatever you sow, that you will reap.

Brethren, contend earnestly for the faith which was once for all delivered to the Saints. For certain men have crept in unnoticed who long ago were marked out for this condemnation, ungodly men who turn the Grace of our God into lewdness, and deny the only Lord God and our Lord Jesus Christ.

But remember that the Lord, having saved the people out of the land of Egypt, afterward destroyed those who did not believe.

All the fathers of the Israelites were under the cloud, all passed through the sea, all were baptized into Moses in the cloud and in the sea, all ate the same spiritual food, and all drank the same spiritual drink.

But with most of them, God was not well-pleased, for their bodies were scattered in the wilderness. Now, these things became our examples, to the intent that we should not lust after evil things as they also lusted.

And do not become idolaters, as were some of them. Nor let us commit sexual immorality, as some of them did, and in one day twenty-three thousand fell; nor let us tempt Christ, as some of them also tempted, and were destroyed by serpents; nor complain, as some of them also complained, and were destroyed by the destroyer.

Now all these things happened to them as examples, and they were written for our admonition, upon whom the ends of the ages have come. Therefore, let him who thinks he stands take heed lest he fall.

No temptation has overtaken you, except such as is common to man; but God is faithful, Who will not allow you to be tempted beyond what you are able, but with the temptation will also make the way of escape, that you may be able to bear it (1 Cor. 10:1-13).

Therefore, we must give the more earnest heed to the things we have heard, lest we drift away. For if the Word spoken through angels proved steadfast, and every transgression and disobedience received a just recompense or reward, how shall we escape if we neglect so great a salvation;

Which at the first began to be spoken by the Lord, and was confirmed to us by those who heard Him. God also bearing witness both with signs and wonders, with various miracles, and Gifts of the Holy Spirit, according to His Own Will? (Heb. 2:1-4).

Beware, brethren, lest there be in any of you an evil heart of unbelief in departing from the Living God, but exhort one another daily, while it is called "Today," lest any of you be hardened through the deceitfulness of sin.

For we have become partakers of Christ, if we hold the beginning of our confidence steadfast to the end, while it is said "Today, if you will hear His Voice, do not harden your hearts, as in the rebellion." For who, having heard, rebelled? Indeed, was it not all who came out of Egypt, led by Moses?

Now, with whom was He angry forty years? Was it not with those who sinned, whose corpses fell in the wilderness? And to whom did He swear that they would not enter His Rest, but to those who did not obey?

So we see that they could not enter in because of unbelief. Therefore, since a promise remains of entering His Rest, let us fear, lest any of you seem to have come short of it. For indeed, the Gospel was preached to us, as well as to them;

But the Word which they heard did not profit them, not being mixed with faith in those who heard it. For we who have believed do enter that rest (Heb. 3:12-4:3).

The angels who did not keep their proper domain, but left their own abode, He has reserved in everlasting chains under darkness for judgment of the Great Day. For God did not spare the angels who sinned, but cast them down to Hell; and delivered them into chains of darkness to be reserved for judgment.

God did not spare the ancient world, but saved Noah, one of eight people, a preacher of righteousness, bringing in the Flood on the worlds of the ungodly.

As Sodom and Gomorrah, and the cities around them, in a similar manner to these, having given themselves over to sexual immorality and gone after strange flesh, are set forth as an example, suffering the vengeance of Eternal Fire.

God turned the cities of Sodom and Gomorrah into ashes, condemned them to destruction, making them an example to those who afterward would live ungodly; and delivered righteous Lot, who was oppressed by the filthy conduct of the wicked (for that righteous man, dwelling among them tormented his righteous soul from day to day, by seeing and hearing their lawless deeds).

These dreamers defile the flesh, reject authority, and speak evil of dignitaries. They speak evil of whatever they do not know; and whatever they know naturally, like brute beast, in these things they corrupt themselves. Woe to them!

This is because they have gone into the way of Cain, have turned greedily in the error of Balaam for profit, and perished in the rebellion of Korah.

These are spots in your love-feasts, while they feast with you without fear, serving only themselves. They are clouds without water, carried about by the winds; late autumn trees without fruit, twice dead, pulled up by the roots.

These are raging waves of the sea, foaming up their own shame; wandering stars for whom is reserved the Blackness of Darkness forever.

Behold, the Lord comes with ten thousand of His Saints, to execute judgment on all, to convict all who are ungodly among them of all their ungodly deeds, which they have committed in an ungodly way, and of all the harsh things which ungodly sinners have spoken against Him.

These are grumblers, complainers, walking according to their own lusts; and they mouth great swelling word, flattering people to gain advantage. Many walk according to their own ungodly lusts. These are sensual persons, who cause divisions, not having the Spirit.

But you beloved, building yourselves up on your most holy faith, praying in the Holy Spirit; keep yourselves in the Love of God. On some have compassion, making a distinction, but others save with fear, pulling them out of fire.

There were false prophets among the Israelites of Old, just as they are false teachers among the Church today, who secretly bring in destructive heresies, even denying the Lord Who bought them, and bring on themselves swift destruction.

And many follow their destructive ways, because of whom the way of truth is blasphemed. By covetousness, they exploit you with deceptive words. The Lord knows how to deliver the Godly out of temptations and to reserve the unjust under punishment for the Day of Judgment.

The Lord will judge those who walk according to the flesh in the lust of uncleanness and despise authority. They are presumptuous, self-willed. They are not afraid to speak evil of dignitaries.

They speak evil of the things they do not understand, and will utterly perish in their own corruption, and will receive the wages of unrighteousness.

They are spots and blemishes, carousing in their own deceptions while they feast with you, having eyes full of adultery and that cannot cease from sin, enticing unstable souls.

They have a heart trained in covetous practices, and are accursed children. They have forsaken the right way and gone astray. While they promise them liberty, they themselves are slaves of corruption; for by whom a person is overcome, by him also he is brought into bondage.

For if after they have escaped the pollutions of this world through the knowledge of the Lord and Saviour Jesus Christ, they are again entangled and overcome, the latter end is worse for them than the beginning.

For it would have been better for them not to have known the way of righteousness, than having known it, to turn from the Holy Commandments delivered to them (Jude 1 and 2 Pet. 2).

God cannot change His Word and Standard for anyone. God is of Purer Eyes than to behold sin, disobedience, unrighteousness, and iniquity.

If God could turn His Face away from Jesus Christ Himself when He was carrying the sins of the world on the Cross of Calvary, who are you that God will allow you into His Kingdom with sin? All the ungodly, the unrighteous, and sinners will be cast into the Lake of Fire, Hell Fire.

God can never lie nor fail to fulfil His Word. God has promised that He will provide all that you need. He has also promised to protect you. Therefore, do not worry; do not be anxious for anything. Anyway, worrying will not solve the problem. Commit your cares to the Lord for He cares for you.

By the Stripes of Jesus Christ you have been healed. The Bible says that you were healed by the Stripes of Jesus Christ (1 Pet. 2:24). That means that even when you may be feeling the symptom of the sickness, you were healed.

Learn to walk by faith, and don't accept the package of the devil. Speak according to the Word of God, and believe the same, and the plans of the devil will fail to come to fruition in your life. The Promises of the Almighty can never fail; hold on to anything He has promised you.

Preach and teach the Gospel of the Kingdom of God. Don't preach or teach human wisdom and reasoning. Don't preach psychology, philosophy, or faithlessness. God's Word can never fail, and if you preach and teach it, you will see outstanding results of it, both in your life and in the lives of those who hear you.

HAVE YOU APPLIED WHAT YOU KNOW?

Questions for Discussion:

1. Are we supposed to apply what God has taught us?
2. What happens if we don't apply what we know?
3. Who is to be blamed if we suffer for not applying what we know?

If many Christians apply half of what they know now, satan, his demons, and his human agents will be so afraid of them, that they will relate with them from afar.

But the devil operates almost freely in the lives of many Christians without much fear. God has told and taught many people many things and yet they don't apply them. It is applied knowledge that brings results.

If you know all and apply nothing, instead of gaining, you will lose, because the Servant that knows His Master's Commands and does not do them will be beaten with more stripes (Lk. 12:47-48).

There is a level of lack of knowledge, and that is a more terrible level, because you will not apply the things you don't know. Hence, the Word of God says that God's people perish for lack of knowledge (Hos. 4:6).

Ignorance of God, His Word and Ways, and the ways of the devil will lead to loss, death, and destruction.

Of course, no one knows everything about God or the devil, but you can increase your knowledge by the study and reading of the Bible and other Godly Christian materials.

Some people listen to their pastors or general-overseers only. Though that approach has a positive side of being in a better position to avoid error and intrusion of false teachings, yet it has the negative side of not receiving what God may want to pass to you through other ministers.

There are many people that the Lord has called, and they have different ministries, abilities, and areas of calling. All you need for your Christian life can never be passed to you by any one preacher.

However, as you listen to anybody or read their materials, be careful to follow God's Spirit and His Word. This is why you must be sensitive to the Anointing that teaches you all things (1 Jn 2:20,27).

And you must be full of the Word of God so that you can test and prove the teachings you hear. If you are sincere, God will lead you into the truth and lead you away from the spirit of error.

This is not to say that you must listen to everybody. Don't listen to those you are convinced (without bias) are not teaching the truth.

Remember that a little leaven leavens the whole lump. Small error can cause great havoc to your Christian faith.

I am saying this because we know that there are many false prophets and false teachers who use the Bible and the Name of Jesus Christ to extend the thoughts, plans, and works of the devil. There are many false ministers.

However, we are speaking about knowing what to do and not doing it. Whoever knows the good he should do and does not do it, to him it is sin (Jas. 4:17). God commands us to be doers of the Word, and not just hearers alone.

He tells us that if we hear and do not do what we hear, we are deceiving ourselves (Jas 1:22). But don't deceive yourself nor let another person deceive you. God can never be mocked.

God loves obedience, and doing His Word proves to Him that you love Him (Jn 14:15). Absolute complete obedience is holiness, and without holiness, no man can see the Lord.

Even when you might have not reached perfection, make up your mind that whatever you are sure God wants you to do, you will do. That state of mind is consecration and dedication to God, and it is holiness.

God will then increase your knowledge and help you do what you are to do in order to perfect holiness (2 Cor. 7:1). The grace and ability to obey Him is there; use it!

Prayer is one area people don't apply what they know. When they listen to good messages about prayer, they decide to be consistently prayerful, but many never make it, for they go back after few days.

Some go back because of discouragement, but you don't need to be discouraged; you only need to be persistent. Think about this: those that take part in games train and discipline themselves in order to succeed, and many of them make mistakes and fail along the line.

But it is persistence and consistence that produce champions. A winner or a champion had made many mistakes before.

Some principles of God's Word don't produce fruits overnight; and God doesn't always settle His Account with people every twenty-four hours.

Some principles take a very long time to mature and produce the needed fruits. Others may take a short or shorter time, but make up your mind to achieve the results.

The Word of God is a seed and you know that some seeds or trees (crops) produce within a year (annual crops); some produce within two years (biennial crops); and some produce after many years (perennial plants).

Even pregnancy among animals takes different lengths of time. Some can produce within a short period (like insects); others within nine months (like human beings); and others after more than a year (like elephants).

In building construction, the bigger and taller the building, the deeper and more solid the foundation (of course, the nature of the ground or soil matters a lot; rocky basement will require a shallower foundation than sandy or clayey soil). Some foundations can cost what you may use to finish a five-storey building, like foundations for sky-scrappers.

You must apply what you know and wait patiently to reap its results. The devil has no mercy, and ignorance is no excuse to him.

In fact, he will want you to be ignorant of him and his devices; but we are not ignorant of his devices, and he will not get an advantage over us. In battle, if you don't know of your enemy's strategy, you may be destroyed in a split-second.

How can you use a machete to attack someone coming against you with a gun? And why will you use a gun to fire someone throwing bombs on you from fighter-jets? Be wise as serpents and harmless as doves (Matt. 10:16).

Demonic works and strongholds need confrontation. You must confront demonic conditions with God's Power. It may require fasting, and you have to do it (as led by the Holy Spirit).

Only counseling will not do the work. That is why people are counseled often, and they remain in their problems. Of course, if someone submits to counseling under God's Word and Anointing, he will receive result because God's Word is anointed.

The five foolish virgins should have carried extra oil; but they didn't, either by ignorance or by carelessness, and missed the bridegroom (Matt. 25:1-13). Let this not be your portion in any area in the Name of Jesus Christ. Amen.

Renew your mind by the Word of God and think the Way God thinks, and you will do God's Will. You need more information from the Word of God to increase your faith and function more effectively.

Some don't apply what they know because of unbelief. There are two kinds of unbelief: unbelief that comes by lack of the knowledge of the Word of God, and the unbelief that exists, not because you don't know, but because you are not persuaded by the Word that you know.

The second one is what the other ten spies, apart from Joshua and Caleb, exhibited. God had told them that Jericho will fall for their sake, but because of what they saw with their physical eyes, they doubted the Word of God (Num. 13 & 14).

The secret of receiving what you want is obedience, and obedience is the application of what you know. It is the application that produces the results and not just the knowledge.

Science without technology amounts to nothing. Science is the finding and the knowledge, and technology is the application of scientific findings and knowledge to solve the existing needs. This is true in medical, biological, chemical, engineering, and agricultural fields.

The same is applicable in Christianity. God's Word is meant to solve needs. If you want people to believe in your God, then your God will have to solve their problems.

Many Christians wonder why unbelievers go to witch-doctors for this or that solution. Preach and teach the real Word of God and allow God manifest Himself through you; if you do, more souls will accept our Lord and Christ.

Abraham was told to leave his country, and he left in obedience to God's Voice. Noah was directed to build an ark, with specifications, and he did it. Moses was told to build the ark of covenant and the tabernacle exactly the way he saw them, and he did it so.

Jesus Christ followed God's Plan for His Life and succeeded in His Earthly Ministry. Follow God's Word and Leading for you, as an individual, and what you will see will blow your mind!

.

PROSPERITY IN EVERY AREA

Questions for Discussion:
1. What is prosperity?
2. In what area are we to prosper?
3. Is it possible for us to fail to prosper?

Prosperity is the Will of God for all of His children. God wants His children to prosper in every area of their lives. They are to prosper spiritually, mentally, emotionally, and physically.

God's children should prosper ministerially, financially, academically, materially, health-wise, in business, and in every other area they may find themselves, according to the Will of God for their individual or collective lives.

Hence Apostle John prayed that Elder Gaius might prosper in all things and be in health just as his soul prospered (3 Jn 1:2).

That is God's Will for all of His children, even till date. However, we see many of Gods' people who are not prospering in many areas of their lives. There are many reasons why this can be so.

How can a child of God not prosper when the earth is the Lord's and the fullness of it? Why do many Christians not prosper when silver, gold, and the cattle belong to God? What makes them to fail when the Lord God can do all things?

Jesus Christ is the Door to God and His Blessings. He is the Way, the Truth, and the Life. Speaking to the Church at Philadelphia, Jesus Christ said, "See, I have set before you an open door, and no one can shut it...."

He is the Door, and the Way through the Door. He holds the key of David. When He opens, no one can shut; and when He shuts, no one can open (Rev. 3:7-8).

If you are willing and obedient, you shall eat the good of the land (Isa. 1:19). You must be willing to prosper in order to prosper. Any area you are unwilling to prosper will not go smoothly for you. You may prosper in one area and not prosper in the other.

However, God will sustain you as His child in any area, though you may not prosper in that area. Someone said that he neither wants riches nor poverty, but God's Provisions and Sustenance (Prov. 30:8).

In the scale of wealth, you have: the poor, the comfortable, the rich, the wealthy, and the flourishing. To flourish is the highest level of wealth, and the righteous shall flourish (Prov. 11:28).

Those that flourish lend to many nations and don't need to borrow from any. But you must be willing to flourish to flourish, and you can flourish in any area of your life and ministry.

However, always have it in mind that life does not consist in the abundance of what you have. This is why the Lord tells us to beware of covetousness. If you have all the money, wealth, fame, power, certificate, etc, and you don't please God, or you end in Hell, you gained nothing.

It will be better for you to be poor and wretched in this world and make Heaven at last, than to be the richest, most famous, powerful, and educated person, and be cast into Eternal Punishment.

Also, you must be obedient to prosper. Any prosperity (in human eyes) that is achieved through the life of sin and disobedience has a comma and a question mark. Obedience, righteousness, and holiness will bring true prosperity to you.

"But, what of unbelievers or unfaithful Believers that prosper?" you may ask. In the first place, you are talking of material prosperity, for you cannot prosper spiritually in sin and disobedience. In the second place, that is in the eyes of the natural man.

Any prosperity that leads you to Hell Fire is no prosperity at all. What shall it profit a man if he gains the whole world and loses his own soul?

Also, people see people with flashy cars and of high social status, but they don't know what those people pass through. Many of them will find it very difficult to sleep for two hours a day because of fear and anxiety; others have different health problems that keep them sad, internally.

Still, others have made different sacrifices and commitments that have brought heavy losses to them. Some used their body parts or family members to sacrifice to the spirits that gave them money.

Others are involved in gross corruption and bribery, and because of their practices, they are always afraid. But the Blessings of the Lord make rich and add no sorrow to the blessed.

Spiritual prosperity requires a good knowledge of the Word of God and being prayerful. It involves faith and spiritual exercise.

Spiritual prosperity affects, to a great extent, other areas of life, for the spiritual controls the physical. How you prosper spiritually will affect you health-wise, maritally, and financially.

I know there are people who prosper spiritually but not financially: many of them are unwilling, because they think financial prosperity will lead them into sin and compromise.

Financial prosperity comes from God. In fact, no matter what you do, if God has made up His Mind that you will never prosper financially, you cannot prosper financially.

If you like, go to the strongest secret society or witch-doctor, if God says you will die today, you cannot see tomorrow. Even, all the things satan boasts of cannot be if God says, "Enough is enough."

He who trusts in the devil or in man is a fool. He who says that the Lord does not see has no understanding.

Financial prosperity is a product of obedience, faith, hardwork, giving, and diligence. You cannot maintain these five virtues permanently and not prosper financially.

Faith will bring what does not exist to existence. Obedience will make you follow God's Plan for your life and to obey His Word.

Hardwork will make you invest your resources and energy to the cause you are pursuing; Giving will bring multiplication and increase to your seed and offerings; and diligence will produce consistency.

Physical prosperity is a function of Divine Intervention and obedience to physical laws. God's Word is medicine to your body. He sends forth His Word, and His Word heals the sick.

By the Stripes of Jesus Christ, we were healed. No matter the type of sickness (even when medical science has no solution for it), God can heal you if you believe.

But to pass from the level of healing to the level of health, you must feed on God's Word and meditate on it; you must be prayerful; you must maintain a healthy eating-habit; you must exercise bodily; and you must have adequate rest.

A student who wants to do well in his academics must be studious and diligent. The lazy man, no matter how he wants good things, will not have them, except someone gives him by charity. An idle mind is the devil's workshop.

The reason many students go into cultism is because many of them are not very committed to their studies. Others go into it because of bad friends, fear, and threats. But why should a hardworking student be a friend to a lazy and uncommitted student?

Do not be deceived, evil communication (wrong company) corrupts good manners. Influence is stronger than information. This is why a boy that was brought up in a Christian home can change into something else when he starts associating with bad friends.

Emotionally, many are disorganized and not stable because of fear, disappointment, and anxiety. Why worry about your life or tomorrow? God is faithful and He will bring His Will to pass in your life.

Commit your cares to Him, for He cares for you (1 Pet. 5:7). Get rid of pondering on past disappointments, because God has a brighter tomorrow for you.

Do not be afraid of him who can touch the body but not the soul. Worry and anxiety cause physical sicknesses. Get rid of bitterness, hatred, and unforgiveness from your heart.

No matter how your marital life may be, commit it to God and He will bring peace and joy to your family. God can change your husband, wife, children, mother, sister, and brother. The problem with us is that we try to please people without pleasing God first.

If you spend enough time with God in prayer and listening to Him, He will remove satanic barriers and obstacles along your way, and He will give you directions on how to relate with your family members, and you will find happiness.

No matter how hopeless the ministry God has given you may look like, the Lord that commissioned it will prosper it. No matter how the devil fights your ministry, God's Spirit and His angels will fight for you. You only have to be faithful in what the Lord called you to do.

Find out exactly what He wants you to do so that you will not run along the wrong track. God is committed to His Cause, and the gates of Hades will not prevail against the Church of Jesus Christ.

If you do not let the Word of God depart from your mouth, but you meditate on it day and night, and do what it says, your way will be made prosperous, and you will have a good success (Josh. 1:8).

God is the Source of the security and protection that you need; don't go after strange gods, and even if you use police or military escort (Apostle Paul used in Acts 23:12-32 and Acts 28:16), don't put your trust on them, because if God leaves you, a bomb can destroy you along with those security men.

Poverty is not good. However, each person has or will go through lack, hardship, and adversity. God allows those things for different purposes. Some people will not pay attention to God's Leading or Prompting until they enter into hard and difficult situations, and then they will seek God like never before.

The Lord has declared that if you are willing and obedient, you shall eat the good of the land. Two things are involved here: willingness and obedience. If you conform to two of them, you will enjoy the good things that the Lord has provided for you.

THE NARROW AND THE BROAD WAYS

Questions for Discussion:
  1. What is the narrow way?
  2. What is the broad way?
  3. Which of them are we to follow?
  4. What are the benefits of following the narrow way?
  5. What are the outcomes of following the broad way?

Enter by the narrow gate; for wide is the gate and broad is the way that leads to destruction, and there are many who go in by it. Because narrow is the gate and difficult is the way which leads to life, and there are few who find it.

Every good tree bears good fruit, but a bad tree bears bad fruit. A good tree cannot bear bad fruit, nor can a bad tree bear good fruit. Every tree that does not bear good fruit is cut down and thrown into the Fire.

Not everyone who says to the Lord Jesus Christ, 'Lord, Lord,' shall enter the Kingdom of Heaven, but he who does the Will of His Father, Who also is our Father in Heaven.

Many will say to Him on that Day, "Lord, Lord, have we not prophesied in Your Name, cast out demons in Your Name, and done many wonders in Your Name?" He will then declare to them, "I never knew you, depart from Me, you who practice lawlessness" (Matt. 7:13-23).

A good man out of the good treasure of his heart brings forth good, and an evil man out of the evil treasure of his heart brings forth evil. For out of the abundance of the heart his mouth speaks.

But why do you call Him 'Lord, Lord,' and do not do the things which He says? (Lk. 6:45-46). Some people, after giving their lives to the Lord Jesus Christ, turn back to be the lords of their own lives. Many worship the Lord with their lips, but their hearts are far from Him.

Many will not do evil things when fellow Christians are around, but they will do those things when no one is watching. What about God Who sees in secret, whose Eyes run to and fro the earth?

Many Christians live the life of 'it-doesn't-matter'. They choose what they will give up and what they wouldn't give up. No wonder someone said, "Not just decisions, but Disciples."

People go to the altar-calls, and yet their hearts are far from God. Do you know that, even agents of the kingdom of darkness go out for altar-calls in pretence, just to deceive?

People stay in churches for years, and even rise up to hold positions of authority in the churches, and yet are either not born again or live in iniquity.

No matter how corrupt a generation may be, anyone who sincerely wants to please God will please Him. Take, for instance, the time before the Flood: Enoch walked with God and pleased Him that God had to take him away to Heaven, and he did not see death (Gen. 5:24).

Though the earth was very corrupt in the days of Noah, yet Noah found favour in the Eyes of God, because he was a just man and blameless in his generation (Gen. 6:9).

Abraham followed God in his generation. Though Lot lived in Sodom, yet, he was a righteous man (2 Pet. 2:6-9). They followed the narrow road!

You are the salt of the earth; but if the salt loses its flavour, how shall it be seasoned? You are the light of the world. A city that is set on a hill cannot be hidden.

Nor do they light a lamp and put it under a basket, but on a lampstand, and it gives light to all who are in the house. Let your light so shine before men, that they may see your good works and glorify your Father in Heaven.

Whoever breaks one of the least of God's Commandments, and teaches men so, shall be called least in the Kingdom of Heaven; but whoever does and teaches them, he shall be called great in the Kingdom of Heaven.

For unless your righteousness exceeds the righteousness of the hypocrites, who show outward righteousness, but are corrupt inside, you will by no means enter the Kingdom of Heaven.

Whoever looks at a woman to lust for her has already committed adultery with her in his heart. If your right eye causes you to sin, pluck it out and cast it from you; for it is more profitable for you that one of your members perish than for your whole body to be cast into Hell.

Whoever divorces his wife for any reason, except sexual immorality, causes her to commit adultery; and whoever marries a woman that is divorced commits adultery. Let your 'Yes' be 'Yes' and your 'No,' 'No.'

Give to him who asks you, and from him who wants to borrow from you do not turn away. Love your enemies, bless those who curse you.

Do good to those who hate you, and pray for those who spiteful use you and persecute you: that you may be sons of your Father in Heaven; for He makes His sun rise on the evil and on the good, and sends rain on the just and on the unjust.

For if you love those who love you, what reward have you? Do not even sinners do the same? You shall be perfect, just as your Father in Heaven is perfect (Matt. 5).

When you do a charitable deed, do it in secret; and your Father Who sees in secret will Himself reward you openly.

When you pray, go into your room, and when you have shut your door, pray to your Father Who is in the secret place, and your Father Who sees in secret will reward you openly.

Also, when you fast, anoint your head and wash your face, so that you do not appear to men to be fasting, but to your Father Who is in the secret place, and your Father Who sees in secret will reward you openly.

Do not lay up for yourselves treasures on earth, where moth and rust destroy and where thieves break in and steal.

But lay up for yourselves treasures in Heaven, where neither moth nor rust destroys, and where thieves do not break in and steal. For where your treasure is, there your heart will be also.

No one can serve two masters. For either he will hate the one and love the other, or else he will be loyal to the one and despise the other. You cannot serve God and mammon.

Do not worry about your life, what you will eat or what you will drink; or about your body, what you will put on. Is not life more than food, and the body more than clothing?

But seek first the Kingdom of God and His Righteousness, and all these things shall be added to you. Do not worry about tomorrow, for tomorrow will worry about its own things. Sufficient for the day is its own trouble (Matt. 6).

If you hear the Word of God and do it, you are like a wise man who built his house on the rock, and the rain descended, the floods came, and the winds blew and beat on that house, and it did not fall, for it was founded on the rock.

But if you don't do what you hear, you are a foolish man, and when those things come on your house, which is built on the sand, it will crash. Be doers of the Word, and not just hearers, deceiving yourselves.

Pursue peace with all people, and holiness, without which no one will see the Lord (Heb. 12:14). Do not love the world or anything in the world (1 Jn 2:15).

All the fathers of the people of Israel were under the cloud, all passed through the sea, all ate the same spiritual food, and all drank the same spiritual drink. But with most of them, God was not well-pleased; for their bodies were scattered in the wilderness.

Now these things became our examples, to the intent that we should not lust after evil things as they also lusted.

And do not become idolaters as were some of them. Nor let us commit sexually immorality, as some of them did, and in one day twenty-three thousand fell.

Nor let us tempt Christ, as some of them also tempted, and were destroyed by serpents, nor complain, as some of them also complained, and were destroyed by the destroyer.

Now all these things happened to them as examples, and they were written for our admonition, upon whom the ends of the ages have come.

Therefore, let him who thinks he stands take head, lest he fall. No temptation has overtaken you, except such as is common to man; but God is faithful, Who will not allow you to be tempted beyond what you are able, but with the temptation will also make the way of escape, that you may be able to bear it (1 Cor. 10).

They are ways that seem good and right to men, but the ends of them all are Eternal Destruction, loss, and shouts of 'Had I known!'

There is a highway we must all follow, and that is the highway of holiness. The highway of holiness and the narrow gate that leads to life are friends. We must be holy in all our conduct. Instead of guiding our lives, we should allow the Word of God and His Spirit guide and lead us!

LOVE AND FORGIVENESS

Questions for Discussion:
1. What is love?
2. What is forgiveness?
3. What are the benefits of love and forgiveness?
4. What happens if we don't love and forgive?

Love is the Great Commandment: to love the Lord your God with all your heart, with all your soul, and with all your strength; and to love your neighbour as yourself. This is the summary of the Law (Matt. 22:36-40).

The Word of the Lord commands us to love one another fervently, for love covers multitude of sins (1 Pet. 4:8). Let brotherly love continue (Heb.13:1). Be kindly affectionate to one another with brotherly love, in honour giving preference to one another (Rom. 12:10).

Let love be without hypocrisy. Abhor what is evil. Cling to what is good (Rom. 12:9). And let us not grow weary while doing good, for in due season, we shall reap, if we do not lose heart.

Therefore, as we have opportunity, let us do good to all, especially to those who are of the Household of Faith (Gal. 6:9-10).

People may not appreciate you, or even thank you, but God will reward you; you do it to God when you do it in the Name of God.

Love your enemies, bless those who curse you, do good to those who hate you, and pray for those who spitefully use you and persecute you, that you may be the sons of your Father in Heaven; for He makes His sun to rise on the evil and on the good, and sends rain on the just and on the unjust.

For if you love those who love you, what reward have you? Do not even the sinners do the same? (Matt. 5:44-46). If you kill your enemy by prayer, and he dies and goes to Hell, is it God or the devil that gained?

Of course, Peter spoke by the anointing, and Ananias and Sapphira dropped dead, but it was as the Spirit led him. You don't just go about declaring that all your enemies die; if they die, the devil using them against you will leave and enter new people who will start to oppress you again.

Be a strong and prayerful Christian who is full of faith and the enemy will never harm you. But the problem is that many Christians are lukewarm.

Apostle Paul put temporary inability to see on Elymas by God's Power, and that led to getting the attention of the governor more (Acts 13:8-12). I like this style!

The Word of God speaks of the love of many waxing cold because of the abundance of iniquity (Matt. 24:12). The Ephesian Church was rebuked by the Lord because they had left their first love (Rev. 2:4).

They left it by failing to do the first works. The Laodicean Church was neither cold nor hot; they were lukewarm. If you are lukewarm, the Lord will spew you out of His Mouth (Rev. 3:15-16).

Get hot in your Christian life and maintain a red-hot Christian life. Be fervent in spirit, maintain the spiritual glow (Rom. 12:11).

The test or proof that you love the Lord is that you keep His Commandments (Jn 14:15; 1 Jn 2:4), and His Commandments are not burdensome (1 Jn 5:3).

They may look difficult, but they are not impossible, for God is a Just God. If you say that you love the Lord, and don't keep His Commandments, you lie and the truth is not in you.

If you say that you love the Lord and yet hate your brother, you are a big liar (1 Jn 4:20). Jesus Christ laid down His Life for us, and we too ought to lay down our lives for the brethren.

Love is a Fruit of the Spirit. The Love of God, having been shed abroad in our hearts by the Holy Spirit, we should bear the fruit of love and mature in it. We ought to be rooted and grounded in love (Eph. 3:17).

And we should forbear one another in love. Walk in love, as Christ also loved us. Faith and love represent our breastplate in the spiritual warfare (1 Thes. 5:8).

As many as the Lord loves, He rebukes so that they will not be disapproved and condemned (Rev. 3:19). Therefore, open rebuke is better than secret love. Rebuke evil and wrong-doing in love.

Do not love the world or anything in the world. If any man loves the world, the Love of the Father is not in him; for all that is in the world: the lust of the eyes, the lust of the flesh, and the pride of life come not from the Father, but from the world. And the world passes away with its lusts, but he who does the Will of the Father abides forever (1 Jn 2:15-17).

The love of money is the root of all evil, for which some have strayed from the faith in their greediness and pierced themselves through with many sorrows (1 Tim. 6:10).

Love suffers long and is kind; love does not envy; love does not parade itself, is not puffed up, does not behave rudely, does not seek its own, is not provoked, thinks no evil, does not rejoice in iniquity, but rejoices in the truth; bears all things, believes all things, hopes all things, endures all things.

Love never fails, even though spiritual gifts will fail and pass away. And now abide faith, hope, love, these three, but the greatest of these is love (1 Cor. 13).

Forgiveness is a term used in connection with sin and offence. We receive forgiveness from God when we repent of our sins and confess them to Him. If we confess our sins, He is faithful and just to forgive our sins, and to cleanse us from all unrighteousness (1 Jn 1:9).

He who covers his sins shall not prosper, but he who confesses and renounces them shall find mercy (Prov. 28:13). Take note of the renouncing factor; don't confess your sins with the intention to go back to it when you are tempted again.

As high as the heavens are above the earth, so great is the Father's Love. As far as the east is from the west, so far has He taken our sins from us (Psa. 103:11-12).

Our sins, He will forgive and remember them no more. The Blood of Jesus Christ is able to cleanse the vilest sinner who repents of his sins. And he that comes to God will not be cast away.

Consider the parable of the prodigal son; when the prodigal son was still afar off, as he was coming back, the father ran and embraced him, forgiving him his sins and making a big feast for him (Lk. 15:11-32).

There is no forgiveness in death. It is now that you have an opportunity to repent and be cleansed. Once death comes, a sinner goes straight to Hell, and all sinners belong to the devil.

Whether they are bishops, apostles, prophets, evangelists, pastors, teachers, musicians, prayer-warriors, clergy, laity, rich, poor, great, small, male, female, old, young, president, professor, director, or whatever position or title they may hold or have, all sinners are cursed forever.

Also, you must forgive others of the wrong they do to you. We are forgiven if we forgive others. If we don't forgive others, our Heavenly Father will not forgive us also (Matt. 6:14-15).

No matter the number of times he or she may sin against you, forgive him or her as he or she comes to you and says that he or she is sorry (Matt. 18:21-22).

Let no bitterness, hatred, and unforgiveness remain in your life, for they will block your blessings and make you spiritually wanting. Don't even hold grudges against the one that refuses to apologize.

Even, bitterness can cause sickness and heart-attack, just as worry and anxiety can cause heart-attack. Mental confusion will cause spiritual and physical problems to you.

Don't be like that unmerciful servant who was forgiven of a big debt, but when he saw his fellow servant who owed him a little, he sent him to the prison. His master punished him, calling him a wicked servant (Matt. 18:23-35). Mercy transcends over judgment.

Also, learn to forgive yourself of your past mistakes. Many are being overcome by their past mistakes because they do not forgive themselves, but allow their past sins and mistakes to hunt them, even when they would have confessed them to God.

Is God unfaithful to forgive your sins as He promised? You are not being more righteous by rejecting God's Word and doubting His Forgiveness. God cannot lie, and He has promised to forgive you when you confess your sins to Him.

God is Light and in Him is no darkness. If we say that we have fellowship with Him, and walk in darkness, we lie and do not practice the truth.

But if we walk in the light as He is in the light, we have fellowship with one another, and the Blood of Jesus Christ His Son cleanses us from all sin (1 Jn 1:5-7).

He who says he abides is Him ought himself also to walk just as He walked. He, who says he is in the light, and hates his brother, is in darkness until now.

Learn and train yourself to forgive others and forbear with men. Men are hard to deal with. Somebody can come to you saying one thing, while his mind is on another thing entirely.

Men hurt, but God heals and encourages. Learn to trust in the Lord always, and don't depend on men because they can fail you. But you, why not be trustworthy?

THE ABUNDANCE OF THE HEART

Questions for Discussion:

1. What is the human heart?
2. What is the importance of guarding our hearts?
3. Where do our actions and words come from?

The words spoken by people, their conduct and actions, their character and habits, come from their inside. What fills the inside of a man is what he will bring forth, in words or in actions.

This is one reason that when people misbehave, you may have to look beyond that singular misbehaviour. If you can do some evil things, you can do many others, because they come from the same heart.

If you can do some good things, you don't need to fear to do many others, because they also come from the same heart. I am not talking of words and actions brought about by pretence.

The Lord Jesus Christ tells us this when He stated that you will know false prophets by their fruits. Every good tree bears good fruit, but a bad tree bears bad fruit. A good tree cannot bear bad fruit, nor can a bad tree bear good fruit (Matt. 7:5-18).

A good man out of the good treasure of his heart brings forth good, and an evil man out of the evil treasure of his heart brings forth evil. For out of the abundance of the heart his mouth speaks (Lk. 6:45).

Either make the tree good and its fruit good, or else make the tree bad and its fruit bad; for a tree is known by its fruit. How can you, being good, speak evil things? How can you, being evil speak good things? For out of the abundance of the heart, the mouth speaks (Matt. 12:33-34).

The Bible says that we should guard our hearts with all diligence, for out of it are the issues of life (Prov. 4:23). The things you see in this life are what you speak or what others speak concerning you. But you have power with God!

The Word says that you are to do the guarding. It is not God the Holy Spirit that will do it for you. He is your Helper, and He will help you do all things; but you must give Him free access.

Guard your heart by being careful of what enters your mind, because your mind is the doorway to your heart. Fill your heart with the Word of God; let the Holy Spirit fill you continually. Don't give space for the devil to occupy.

Some people feed their hearts and minds with sensual things. Some watch anything they see on television. They spend so much time on cables and videos, and spend little time with God. Some so-called Christians enjoy listening to worldly music, and say that it is not a problem.

Many have even produced music having Biblical quotations, and the Name of Jesus Christ in them, but even an unbeliever will notice that something is wrong with the music. They call them Christian reggae, Christian blues, Christian makosa, and Christian disco.

Cursed is the man who trusts in man and makes flesh his strength, whose heart departs from the Lord. Blessed is the man who trusts in the Lord, and whose Hope is the Lord. The former shall be like a shrub in the desert, and shall not see when good comes.

The later shall be like a tree planted by the water which spreads out its root by the river, and will not fear when heat comes, but its leaves will be green, and will not be anxious in the year of drought, nor will cease from yielding fruit (Jer. 17:5-8).

The Bible says that the heart is deceitful above all things and desperately wicked, who can know it? The Lord searches the heart, and tests the mind, even to give every man according to his ways, according to the fruit of his doings (Jer. 17:9-10).

Man works against God; this is because man fell when Adam (the first man) disobeyed the Word of God. Man went into more sin and disobedience that the Lord saw that the wickedness of man was great in the earth, and that every intent of the thoughts of his heart was only evil continually.

This state of man, made the Lord to become sorry that He had made man on the earth, and He was grieved in His Heart. And the Lord said, "I will destroy man whom I have created from the face of the earth." However, Noah found favour in the Eyes of the Lord (Gen. 6:6-8).

But what is the state of the unregenerated man these days? They despise and scorn God. Even many people who had been born again have backslidden in their hearts, and live for themselves.

The Lord knows the secrets of the heart (Psa. 44:21). The Bible speaks of secrets of a man's heart (1 Cor. 14:25). All things that are hidden will be revealed and made manifest at the Coming of the Lord Jesus Christ.

What is it that you are hiding in your heart? If you hide lies, hypocrisy, sin, and lust in your heart, it will be exposed at last, and you will find yourself in the Lake which burns with fire and brimstone. You can receive forgiveness now by repenting, confessing your sins, and making the right restitutions.

Let the Word of Christ dwell in you richly all wisdom (Col. 3:16). The Word of God shall not depart from your mouth, but you shall meditate in it day and night, that you may observe to do according to all that is written in it. For then you will make your way prosperous, and then you will have good success (Josh.1:8).

Meditate on the Word of God; give yourself entirely to the Word, that your progress and profiting may be evident to all (1 Tim. 4:15). You have got to be so full of the Word that the fire of the Word will pursue devilish things out of you.

It is very necessary to be filled with the Holy Spirit, and to maintain the fullness of the Spirit always. The men that were to serve as deacons were to be full of the Holy Spirit (Acts 6:3).

Do not be unwise, but understand what the Will of the Lord is. And do not be drunk with wine, in which is dissipation, but be filled with the Holy Spirit, singing and making melody in your heart to the Lord.

Give thanks always for all things to God the Father in the Name of our Lord Jesus Christ, submitting to one another in the fear of God (Eph. 5:17-21).

Blessed are the pure in heart, for they shall see God (Matt. 5:8). As a Christian, you must purify your heart and keep it pure. Pursue peace with all people, and holiness, without which no one will see the Lord.

Look carefully lest anyone fall short of the Grace of God; lest any root of bitterness springing up cause trouble, and by this many become defiled, lest there be any fornicator or profane person like Esau, who for one morsel of food sold his birthright (Heb. 12:14-16).

Blessed are the poor in spirit, for theirs is the Kingdom of Heaven. Blessed are the meek, for they shall inherit the earth. Blessed are those who hunger and thirst for righteousness, for they shall be filled.

Blessed are the merciful, for they shall obtain mercy. Blessed are the peacemakers, for they shall be called sons of God. Blessed are those who are persecuted for righteousness' sake, for theirs is the Kingdom of Heaven.

Blessed are you when they revile and persecute you, and say all kinds of evil against you falsely for the Sake of Jesus Christ (Matt. 5:3-11).

It is necessary that your whole spirit, soul, and body be preserved blameless at the Coming of our Lord Jesus Christ. He Who called us is faithful, and He will do it (1 Thes. 5:23-24).

Your spirit is your heart; don't pollute it with the love of the world or the pleasures of the flesh. Renew your mind with the Word of God so that your way of thinking will change, and instead of thinking like the natural man, you start thinking the Way God thinks.

His Thoughts are higher than our thoughts, and His Ways than men's ways. Don't pollute your body, but use the members of your body to serve God effectively.

Above all, love God fervently with your whole heart. This will make it easy for you to obey Him. The proof of your love for God is your obedience to His Word and Commandment.

Also, you must love your neighbour as yourself. This will help you to do to them as you would desire that they do to you. Love is the end of the Law. There is no fear in love, but perfect love drives away fear (1 Jn. 4:18).

The Lord pleads that you give Him your heart. When you give Him your heart, you have given Him everything, because all other things spring forth from the heart. Give God your heart (Prov. 23:26)

If anyone is born again, he is a new creature, old things have passed away, behold all things have become new (2 Cor. 5:17).

Men shall give account of every idle word they speak on the Day of Judgment. By your words you will either be condemned or justified (Matt. 12:36-37). And words proceed from the heart.

THE POWER OF THE TONGUE

Questions for Discussion:

1. What do we mean by the tongue?
2. What is the significance or value of the tongue?
3. What is the relationship between what we speak and what we have or receive?

Many have not realized the power of the tongue. This is why many of them speak the way they do. If people realize the importance, the value, or the power of the tongue, they will be careful and weigh their words before they speak.

Unfortunately, even those who have been taught along this line have offended in words, at one time or the other, and have reaped the negative impacts of their negative words.

The Bible says that life and death are in the power of the tongue (Prov. 18:21). Words, even words spoken by them, have killed many, more than we have realized.

When someone feels some symptoms of sickness or disease, and speaks with his own mouth, saying, "I am sick," that person is accepting the sickness or disease that the devil wants to bring upon him.

The spiritual controls the physical. But someone may ask, "What of when I already have the sickness?" Or, "What of when I have the symptoms?"

When you are tempted to steal, have you stolen simply because the thought came to your mind? No, you steal when you take that thing or when you have made up your mind to take it, and you are waiting for an opportunity or when you will not be caught.

In the later case, even when you have not touched that thing, God sees you as a thief; but the simple thought or temptation does not make you a thief.

The same is applicable to sickness, even though you may not see it that way. The devil will throw an arrow of sickness at you; you must reject that sickness, and confess health in the Name of Jesus Christ.

By the Stripes of Jesus Christ we were healed (not that we shall be healed) (1 Pet. 2:24). He carried our sicknesses and diseases (Matt. 8:17). Learn to speak according to the Word of God: this is faith.

But the problem is that many people want sympathizers. Those people that sympathize with you are not God, and if you want sympathy, it will destroy your faith.

In fact, the devil will use the words of those sympathizers to keep your eyes off Jesus Christ, the Author and Finisher of our faith, and keep you looking at the problems.

And if you look at the problems and you look away from your God, you will sink as did Peter. When he saw the wind boisterous, he began to sink (Matt. 14:30), and if not because he cried for help, he might have sunk, got drowned, and died.

Jesus Christ tells us that for every idle word men may speak, they will give account of it in the Day of Judgment. For by your words you will be justified, and by your words you will be condemned (Matt. 12:36-37).

Your words can justify you, and it can also condemn or mar you. You can receive healing, financial breakthrough, marital well-being, and spiritual success by your words; and those areas of life can be cursed by your words.

Many people speak too much; they speak when it is not necessary. The Word says that sin is not absent in the multitude of words (Prov. 10:19).

Do you want to be perfect in words? Then learn when to speak and when not to speak. We should be quick to hear and slow to speak. Be slow to anger as well (Jas 1:19-20). Man's anger or wrath does not work out the Righteousness of God.

When you want to defend yourself, you will speak too much. I am not saying that you should not defend yourself, but know what to say to defend yourself when necessary, and learn to leave the rest to God.

Even Jesus Christ was criticized; who are you not to be criticized? Even when men may not believe you, God will justify you. Anyway, God is the Final Judge and not any man. Learn to be quiet and leave things to God (1 Thes. 4:11).

The Bible says that those who love the tongue, those who don't mind what they say, will reap the fruit of their work or word (Prov. 18:21). There are spiritual laws, just as they are natural laws.

When you speak against someone who is greater than you or who has authority over you, the person may punish you, and that will be your reward. If you curse someone who is on a higher spiritual level than you, the curse may return to you. When you say good or bad things about yourself, good or bad things will come to you.

The Bible says that the Servant of God must not quarrel (2 Tim. 2:24). I know, from experience, that if you make up your mind not to quarrel, the enemy will bring so much pressure and many temptations to lure you to quarrel, so that you will say bad things and offend God.

But, thanks to God that the devil will not have any place in your life, unless you let him, and he is not going to seize your mouth and speak with it. Hold fast to that which is good without wavering.

Some people say things that they neither understand nor are convinced of. People even affirm things they are not sure of, and this is not good. Reject profane and old wives fables. Do not rebuke an older man and an elder, but exhort him as a father.

Don't be a busybody in other people's affairs, or a gossip, saying things you should not say. Avoid the profane and idle babblings, and contradictions of what is falsely called knowledge. Speak evil of no man.

Do not strive about words to no profit, to the ruin of the hearers; shun profane and idle babblings, for they will increase to more ungodliness. Avoid foolish and ignorant disputes, knowing that they generate strife.

Beware of pride and boasting, shun blasphemy and slander. Speak the truth in love; let each one of you speak truth with his neighbours. Let no corrupt word proceed out of your mouth, but what is good for necessary edification, that it may impart grace to the hearers.

Let all bitterness, wrath, anger, clamour, and evil speaking be put away from you, with all malice. Refuse filthiness, foolish talk, and coarse jesting, which are not fitting, but rather giving of thanks. Remove filthy language out of your mouth.

Avoid foolish disputes, genealogies, contentions, and striving about the Law, for they are unprofitable and useless (Tit. 3:9). Do not allow negative confession out of your mouth, no matter how the situation may look like.

Speak the things which are proper for Sound Doctrine (Tit. 2:1). Speak sound speech which cannot be condemned. If any man does not stumble in word, he is a perfect man, able also to bridle the whole body. Bits in horses' mouths make them obey men, and men can turn their whole body.

Even though ships are very big, and are driven by fierce winds, they are turned by a very small rudder wherever the pilot desires. A forest is set on fire by a little fire. And the tongue is a fire, a world of iniquity.

No man can tame the tongue. It is an unruly evil, full of deadly poison. Don't bless God with your tongue and curse men with it also. Let the Spirit direct your tongue.

Use your tongue for effective prayer. Many will rather go about visiting and gossiping than pray. Preach and teach the Word of God, as God enables you. Don't be ashamed to speak of Jesus Christ.

Declare the Gospel in the public: blow the horn, let all men hear it! The Great Commission or world evangelism is still a priority with God and with us His children. Men, and not angels, are sent to preach the Gospel.

The tongue is so powerful that God created the heavens and the earth by His Words. God calls those things that do not exist by name as though they existed, and when He calls them, they come to existence. You are a god (Psa. 82:6).

Therefore, speak the Way God speaks, and you will see great results that will blow your mind. Maintain the profession or confession of your faith without wavering. If you believe, speak out what you believe, because it is the speaking that brings the physical manifestation!

GOD IS NOT FROM ANY NATION

Questions for Discussion:

1. Who created all men?
2. To Whom will all men give account to?
3. Who determines how men should live?
4. Has God given us any Commandments on how we should live?

God is the Maker of the whole universe and everything in it. God is omnipotent, omnipresent, and omniscient. He is my God and Father. God is in the Heaven of heavens, from where He oversees the whole universe.

That is not to say that God is responsible for everything that happens in the universe; He may permit what happens, even when it is not His Perfect Will. For instance, it is the Will of God that all men be saved (1 Tim. 2:4), but for you to be saved, you must have to submit your will to the Message of the Gospel.

God declares that He has set before men life and death, good and bad, and He has encouraged you to choose good and life (Deut. 30:19). However, what you choose will affect what you become.

God may allow the devil to cause an earthquake which may claim many lives, even though He doesn't want their death, because of sin, prayerlessness, faithlessness, and non-dependence on God.

There is the Good and Acceptable and Perfect Will of God in everything, just as the good, the better and the best in things. If men co-operate with God, His Will will come to pass on earth.

The more we co-operate with Him, the more His Will will be done on this earth. We co-operate with God through obedience, prayer, and faith. No matter how God may want to help us, our beliefs, actions, and confessions can stop Him.

God is not from any nation and He owns all nations. Though we know, from the Bible, that God has a special link with the nation of Israel, yet, He is not from Israel; Israel cannot dictate for Him, and He will not change His Standard because of Israel.

God cannot change His Standard for anyone and for any church. No matter how anointed you are, no matter what you may have, all came from God.

Many people do the things they do because they think that since this or that nation does the same things, they must be right; but this is not true in the ultimate sense. The thing that many fail to understand is that the devil is working in every nation of the earth.

No matter the nation you may come from, the devil had been working in your nation before you were born, and he will continue to work there. The devil has succeeded to work in many nations without being recognized.

There are many things that are being done in some nations of the world which people don't see as having come from the devil. For instance, when a country legalizes abortion, whether or not they know it, the work of the devil is being fulfilled in their midst.

God hates abortion; for no one has right to take any other person's life. No matter the theory or proposition medical science may make to make abortion look good, they are just dancing to the tone of the devil's deception. Once the zygote has been formed, a human being has come.

Let us consider the issue of women liberation movements. Have you noticed the rate of divorce and juvenile delinquencies these days? These are the long-term effects of women liberation movements.

When women decide to abandon their basic responsibilities in pursuit of secondary issues, the devil is at work, whether they recognize it or not. Women have the responsibility to be helpers suitable to their husbands.

I am not saying that women must not work, but most women have worked at the expense of their families. They get jobs that do not give them time to train their children well. Many cannot make their husbands happy because of their commitment to work and business.

Even if your husband is happy because of the money you are making, when your children are living however they want, both of you are wrong. I know many men don't take up their responsibilities, but allow the wife to fend for the family; this is wrong.

It is the responsibility of the husband to fend for the family, even though both of them should put their trust in God for their provisions.

This is why the devil has worked so hard, and he is still working, to frustrate the economy of the nations of the world so that what the man will get will not be able to support his family well, and the wife will start working (on her own) as well.

I know some women work to avoid idleness, and this is good, if the work doesn't stop you from doing your elementary job well. Every woman should spend at least two hours everyday in prayer and Bible study, apart from the normal family prayer-time.

You won't even be idle if you do your house work well. But many have left the maids to do what they should do. Why does a woman want to be the president of her country? Some will ask about Deborah. She was a prophetess who judged and God was their King.

Many women hide under the shadow of avoiding idleness to work, when, in fact, their real motive is to make money. Inasmuch as making money is good, what will it profit you if you make big money and your house (husband, children) is not in order?

Women should find enough time to pray for their husbands and children, even though the husband should pray as well. I tell you, even if your husband is a multimillionaire, the devil's attack through a witch or a wizard can reduce him to a poor man in a short while. But your diligence in prayer can avert it.

We will now consider the issue of whether it is good for women to put on trousers. One thing about dresses is that they are meant to cover the person putting them on, whether they are men or women.

Gowns, wrappers, skirts, blouses, trousers, shirts, etc are to cover the person wearing them. I want you to know that over the years, in every continent (America, Europe, Africa, Asia, etc), there have been changes in the modes of their dressing.

However, any dressing or change in dressing that does not glorify God is satanic and demonic, no matter what any person may think or say, even though you may not have it in mind as you put them on. That is the truth. The devil prefers to work under cover and without being noticed.

When women put on sleeveless blouses, mini-skirts, tight-fitting and partly transparent (revealing) dresses, they are glorifying satan, and helping him to fulfil his purpose, whether or not they know it.

Considering the biological features of women, I believe that women should not use pairs of trousers. Why? When a woman is matured sexually, one of the features that biologists tell us will be noticed in her is enlarged buttocks. Have you never noticed that trousers show their body contours for everybody to see? Trousers reveal their buttocks and laps seductively.

Now, don't say that you are going to allow your children wear pairs of trousers and when they mature, they will stop using them. If you train them up that way, when they are old, they will not depart from it (Prov. 22:6).

I know some may not be happy with me for saying this; but think of this, the Bible says that if doing something will cause your brother sin, you should avoid it (Rom. 14:15-23).

Of course, anyone can decide to sin because of what you did or do, even when the situation shouldn't have warranted it. You know that the Jews spoke against Jesus Christ and the Holy Spirit, even though Jesus Christ was just doing the Assignment God had given Him.

But seductive dresses or dressing seductively helps the devil spread his lust wave, and people get into the sins of lust, fornication, adultery, etc. Some will say that whoever wants to fall will fall, but you and I know that some things can make someone fall, when he wouldn't have fallen without them.

Let the Spirit of God lead you, and do not be led by your mind and thought. Trousers are neither an American culture nor a British culture.

It started at a time and got so much opposition there then; but over so many years later, the opposition has waned so much that some think it is their culture. After all, was there anything like America until Amerigo sailed past the Atlantic Ocean and found the land which was later developed to be America?

My conclusion is this: any dressing that helps the devil fulfil his will, plan, and purpose is from him. If you can't stop dressing this or that way because of Jesus Christ, can you lay down your life for Him? (Matt. 10:39).

KEYS TO FINANCIAL PROSPERITY

Questions for Discussion:
1. What is financial prosperity?
2. How can someone prosper financially?
3. What are the advantages of prospering financially?

Financial promotion does not come from the west, the east, or the south; it comes from God. All that you have came from God. Think of it, if you were never born, you could possibly become nothing in this world.

Many children never saw the light of the day, they were never born. Some died from miscarriages, and others by abortion. Some were born dead and some died shortly after their birth, but you have stayed till now by the Grace of God.

Some of you think that it is because of the security agencies that you are still alive; of course, the security agencies have done well, but do you know that even army generals can die while still in office?

Others think that the reason they are alive today is because of one cult or secret society, because of one charm or talisman from one witchdoctor or the other. Who protected you before you had enough knowledge to think of satanic and demonic protection?

No matter how reinforced and protected you may think you are, if God takes His Protection from you, if God decides to take away your life now, you are a dead man.

King Herod was struck by an angel of God and was eaten by worms, because he did not give glory to God, but received the glory (Acts 12:23). The rich man whose business, company, productivity, or farm increased and multiplied did not live to see those riches, even though he had planned to enjoy them (Lk. 12:16-21).

Going back to the issue of unborn babies, abortion is devilish and from the devil. No one has the right to take away another person's life, for that is murder.

Once the zygote (newly formed baby) has been formed by the conjugation or meeting together of the male sperm and female ovum (egg), a human being has been formed. Any law legalizing abortion in any country came from satan.

Also, most of the miscarriages associated with pregnancies are demonic; they were caused or induced by devilish powers. Many have been made or convinced to believe that those miscarriages were natural and caused by stress or other medical interpretations.

The truth is that the devil prefers not to be noticed many times. This is one reason you should be prayerful and not allow sin and disobedience into your life.

One key to financial prosperity is diligence. Have you seen a man diligent in his business? He shall stand before great people; he will not stand before ordinary men (Prov. 22:29).

If you are a trader, be diligent in it; if you are a farmer, be diligent in it. If you are employed, be diligent in your job, and God will lift you up. If you are not faithful in another man's business, who will give you your own business? (Lk. 16:12).

Many ministers of the Gospel, whether they are apostles, prophets, evangelists, pastors, or teachers, are lazy, and not diligent and hardworking in the ministry. That is why many of them are suffering, and some of them blame our Righteous and Just God in their hearts.

God has no room for laziness; Jesus Christ was not lazy, but traveled here and there preaching, teaching, casting out devils, healing the sick, and doing other Assignments God had for Him.

Imagine a situation where a pastor, after conducting the Sunday service, goes home to watch television, listen to news, sleep, play game, and do other normal things, waiting for the Tuesday Bible class.

After the Tuesday Bible class, he goes home to eat, visit his relatives and friends, read newspapers and magazines, waiting for the Thursday prayer meeting, after which he goes home to wait for the next Sunday service. That pastor is lazy; let him not blame God if he is suffering.

If you are a pastor, give adequate time to prayer, Bible study, evangelism, fasting, and visitation (if assistants wouldn't do it), and you will prosper.

Lack of knowledge and wisdom has made others not to prosper financially. Some don't know how to invest and do business. Others do not recognize good opportunities when they come their ways.

Ask God to give you wisdom, knowledge, and understanding. Others are not willing to prosper financially. They say that money is the root of all evil. But the Bible says that it is the love of money that is the root of all evil (1 Tim. 6:10).

Money is a defence and wisdom is a defence (Eccl. 7:12). Money answers all things, solves many things (Eccl. 10:19). Of course, they are many things money cannot do. But my God can do all things!

You must be willing and obedient to eat the good of the land (Isa. 1:19). If you are obedient to God's Word and the call, but are not willing to prosper, it will hinder your prosperity, and you will be complaining to God.

Also, note that the devil does not love you, and he will do all he can to keep you miserable. You have to exercise your right and authority over him in the Name of Jesus Christ and command him to remove his hands off your finances. Remember that Prophet Daniel's angel was resisted for 21 days.

The Word of God says that when you give, it shall be given back to you in good measure, pressed down, shaken together, and running over (Lk. 6:38). He who gives sparingly, will also reap sparingly; but he who gives bountifully, shall also reap bountifully.

But you must give with a cheerful heart, and not out of persuasion or bearing grudge (2 Cor. 9:6-7). Give to God and to men, and you will be blessed. Give to your pastors, your brothers, and your sisters in the Lord.

Give God your tithes and offerings. Give God quality-offering; nothing is too much for God. Give or pay your tithe; don't say, "I will give next time," for you are robbing God and robbing yourself of your blessings.

When you give God your tithe, He will rebuke the devourer for your sake and open the windows of Heaven and rain down blessings on you that you will not have enough room to contain them. Test God in this and see that you can't beat Him in giving (Mal. 3:8-12).

When you give to a prophet in the name of a prophet, you will receive a prophet's reward. When you give to a righteous man in the name of a righteous man, you will receive a righteous man's reward (Matt. 10:41).

When you give to a Believer in the Name of the Lord, you are giving to God, and He will repay and reward you (Matt. 25:31-46). When you give to the orphan, the widow, and the poor, you are giving and lending to their Maker, and God will reward you and replenish it (Prov. 19:17).

The key to financial prosperity is obedience. You can't live in sin and expect to prosper God's Way. There are many in churches who give testimonies of how God blessed and prospered them.

If God opens your eyes to see how they received the so-called blessings, you will realize that the means is crooked and evil. When a woman sleeps with another man to have a child because her husband is medically impotent, is it God that blessed her?

God wants us to prosper and be in good health, even as our souls prosper (3 Jn 1:2). The Blessings of the Lord make rich and add no sorrow to it (Prov. 10:22). You can notice that it is as your soul prospers.

If you want financial, material, academic, business, or marital blessings, have you considered the most important blessing: spiritual blessing? That is the prosperity of the spirit and the soul.

Many rich men you see don't sleep as you do in the night. You can see that God's Prosperity and good health are related.

If you have not prospered now, pray for God to prosper you. You may need to add fasting to your prayer. Be patient enough to wait for your time of prosperity. God is never late.

Some people, because of impatience, have done many wrong things to get rich. But the material or financial prosperity that sends you to Hell Fire is not prosperity at all, but the blindness the devil has used to keep you from seeing your end. May God deliver you. Amen.

WHERE IS YOUR HEART?

Questions for Discussion:

1. Where do men put their hearts on?
2. Where should we put our heart and mind on?
3. Why should we put our hearts on the right Person, Place, and things?

Where is your heart? This is one of the most important questions anyone can ask you. Where your heart is, has a lot to do with you.

No wonder the Bible says that if you were raised with Christ, seek those things which are Above, where Christ Jesus is sitting at the Right Hand of God. Set your mind on things Above, not on things on the earth.

If you do that, when Jesus Christ Who is our Life appears, then you also will appear with Him in Glory (Col. 3:1-4).

Where do you put your treasure? Is it in banks, in property-development, or in investments? The Lord Jesus Christ tells us that where your treasure is, is where your heart will be also (Lk. 12:34).

If you don't labour for the Lord, how will your heart be in Heaven? If you seek the praise of men, instead of that of God, how will your heart be in Heaven? If you don't win souls for the Lord, if you don't support the Work of the Lord, if you don't obey the Lord, your heart will not be in Heaven.

Where your heart is has a lot to do with you. This is because the Word of God says that out of the abundance of the heart the mouth speaks (Matt. 12:34). Your words and actions are a reflection of what is in your heart.

If your heart is filled with good things, your heart will produce words and actions that will prepare you for Heaven. If your heart is full of the Word of God (Col. 3:16), and you are obedient to the Word you know, your reward will be abundant in Heaven and your heart will be there.

Those who are rich in this present age should not be haughty and proud, nor trust in uncertain riches but in the Living God, Who gives us richly all things to enjoy.

They should do good, be rich in good works, ready to give, willing to share, storing up for themselves a good foundation for the time to come, that they may lay hold on Eternal Life (1 Tim. 6:17-19). Then will their hearts be in Heaven.

The Bible teaches that it is easier for a camel to pass through a needle's hole than for a rich man to enter the Kingdom of Heaven (Mk 10:24-27). With men, that is impossible, but not with God; for with God, all things are possible (verse 27).

If a rich man will submit to the Word of God, the Word of God will remove his heart from the things of this world, and he will begin to set his heart on things Above, which only can make him please God. Do you remember the rich young ruler who could not obey Jesus Christ? (Matt. 19:16-26).

The rich man went away sorrowful because his heart was on his riches. If you are rich, God gave you the riches; therefore, instead of trusting on the riches, trust the Giver. Remember that riches have wings, and they do fly away (Prov. 23:5).

Some may trust in horses and some may trust in chariots, but we will trust in the Name of our God (Psa. 20:7). Cursed is the man that puts his trust on men and on money (Jer. 17:5-6).

The Bible says that if you lay up treasures for yourself in this world, you may lose them to the hands of thieves and robbers. Even, rust and moth do destroy material things.

However, if you lay them up in Heaven, be sure that neither thieves, robbers, rust, nor moths are there (Matt. 6:19-21).

Furthermore, in nakedness you came and in nakedness you will go at death (Job 1:21). Remember the rich man that died the night after he had made plans to enjoy his riches and wealth. The Lord called him a fool (Lk. 12:20).

He was called a fool because he had no heart for God. To have a heart for God is not to come to church and make a donation of one million dollar when you have no plan to serve and obey God.

No matter how rich you may be, you will have one room, one car, one pair of shoes at a time; and finally, you will have one grave. Don't allow the riches that the Lord has given you or allowed you to possess lead to your Eternal Destruction.

Some people's hearts are on their past mistakes, the disappointments of the past, their past sins and hurts they received from people. Some people have vowed not to forgive this or that person.

If you don't forgive, God will not forgive you also; and you will remain a sinner, no matter how you confess (Matt. 6:15). Bitterness in your heart will hinder your spiritual life and can result to mental or physical sickness.

The Bible says that if you confess your sins, God is faithful and just to forgive your sins and to cleanse you from all unrighteousness (1 Jn 1:9).

If you repented and confessed your sins, God has forgiven you: go ahead and live the good life that Christ Jesus has provided for you. Putting your heart and mind on your past sins will greatly affect your Christian walk; forgive yourself.

Your past mistakes and disappointments can be turned into a great future. Even though the devil steals from you (and you can stop or could have stopped it through prayer), know that all things work together for good to them that love God, to them who are called according to His Good Purpose (Rom. 8:28).

The Lord God is able to restore the years that the cankerworm and the palmerworm have eaten (Joel 2:25-26). Nothing is impossible with God (Mk 10:27).

Some people's hearts are on education and certificates. Education is good, and certificates are good; but they should not stop you from doing what you are supposed to be doing for God.

I tell you, there are many people in institutions of higher learning, like universities, polytechnics, and colleges of education, today who the Lord would have they had entered Theological schools (and note that there are many wrong and bad Theological schools) and prepare for ministry immediately after high or secondary schools.

God pleads with you to give Him your heart (Prov. 23:26). If He has your heart, He has your all. Walk with God in perfect heart, the perfect heart that says, "Since God has said that this should be this way, it should be this way."

Walking with God in perfect heart made God to add fifteen more years to King Hezekiah, when he prayed (2 Kgs 20:1-7). Your heart is your spirit-man. Apostle Paul said that he has always walked with (or followed) God with all pure conscience since his youth (Acts 23:1).

Did you notice that he was saying that even when he was killing and imprisoning Christians, he did what he did with a perfect heart? No wonder he told us later that he did what he did ignorantly in unbelief (1 Tim. 1:13).

And we know that God forgave him when he repented and submitted to God. Even though you may still be making some mistakes now, don't be discouraged: follow God with a perfect heart and make every effort to know God and His Word the more so that you can avoid those mistakes.

The heart of a sinner is deceitful and desperately wicked (Jer. 17:9). All the ways of a man seem right to him, but the Lord tries and weighs his heart (Prov. 21:2).

If men disappoint or hurt you, know that they are men. If they criticize, slander, or back-bite you, learn to swallow up the negative effects the devil will want to bring your way through them. Don't allow any stumbling block of the enemy knock you down.

God loves you very much. Give Him your all; give Him your heart. If He has your heart, it will be easy to correct and instruct you. Don't say that you know everything. When you get to know more, you will realize that you had known little.

Don't let the devil have your heart. Don't sell your soul to the devil for anything. Don't be like Esau, who for a single meal sold his birthright and lost it forever.

MISERABLE PEOPLE OF GOD

Questions for Discussion:
1. Who are God's people?
2. How can God's people become miserable?
3. How can we avoid being miserable?

The Bible says that if our hope in Christ is only in this world, we are of all men the most miserable (1 Cor. 15:19). Do you understand that?

It means that if the reason you are a Christian, if the reason you serve God is because of what He would do for you in this life only, you are miserable. No wonder the Bible says that if you gain the whole world and lose your soul, you profited nothing (Lk. 9:25; Mk 8:36).

What shall a man give in exchange for his soul? (Mk 8:37). The Lord that we serve has given us so many precious promises and inheritances both in this life and in the life to come (life after death) (1 Tim. 4:8).

If you were raised together with Christ Jesus, set your mind on things Above, and not on earthly things (Col. 3:1-2). When Christ Who is your Hope shall appear, you will reign with Him in Glory (Col. 3:4). The Word of God says that where your treasure is, is where your heart will be also (Matt. 6:21).

This is one reason you should labour for Christ. You should evangelize and win souls to the Kingdom of God. If you are ashamed of Jesus Christ and refuse to confess Him before men, He will be ashamed of you also when He will appear in Glory with His holy angels (Lk. 9:26).

If you are afraid that you will be persecuted or killed for preaching Jesus Christ, that means that you love your life more than Him. In that case, the Lord says that you are not worthy of Him (Lk. 14:26).

When many people come to church for healing, they are not interested in other things but the healing they need. They would want you to stop all other things so as to attend to them.

Whether you, as a pastor is talking about commitment, dedication, holiness, righteousness, prayer, the study of the Word, or whatever, you are on your own to them. All they want is for you to finish your preaching or teaching and give them their healing so that they can go.

God has given us and will give us so many good things. Every good and perfect gift comes from Above (Heaven); it comes from the Father (Jas 1:17). His Divine Power has given us all things we need for life and Godliness through our knowledge of Him Who has called us by His Power and Glory (2 Pet. 1:3-4).

The earth is the Lord's and all its fulness (Psa. 24:1). Silver and gold are His; even a thousand cattle by the hills belong to our God (Hag. 2:8).

There is nothing the Lord cannot give you. There is nothing that is impossible, either to God or with God. 'To God' because He has the Ability to do all things, having created the whole universe by His Word and Power (Gen.1).

'With God' because nothing is impossible to him that co-operates with God, to him who believes and does what God tells him to do (Mk 10:27). However, never you put the blessing before the Blesser.

Many go to the wrong churches, ministries, and ministers, because they are seeking for miracles instead of the God that works miracles.

Even when the Spirit of God may be prompting them and witnessing in their spirits that they are either in the wrong places or going to the wrong places, they do not pay attention to Him because they are following their minds that are bent on having what they want.

How can a pastor allow people to dress anyhow they want to his church if he doesn't have a hidden agenda? People wear mini-skirts and seductive dresses to some churches and the pastor tells them that it doesn't matter.

The men in the churches are seduced and lured into lust and fornication, and the atmosphere becomes non-conducive for the Spirit of God to operate, and the pastor is not touched. Beware of such pastors, prophets, and ministers.

What many people don't know is that many preachers and ministers are serving the interest of satan instead of that of God. Some do it without their conscious knowledge, while others do it consciously.

There are many satanic and occult churches, ministries, and ministers in the world today. Does this marvel you? You shouldn't be marveled because the Bible tells us that satan masquerades or poses as an angel of light when, in fact, he is the angel of darkness (2 Cor. 11:13-15).

It is, therefore, no big thing if his ministers come as ministers of Christ. In the Book of Revelation, the Lord Jesus Christ commended the Ephesian Church because the false apostles that claimed that they were apostles of Christ were tested by them and found out to be liars, fake, and impostors (Rev. 2:2).

The Word of God tells us to prove all things and to hold on to that which is good and true (1 Thes. 5:21). We are to test every spirit (1 Jn 4:1).

The issue is that no matter what you may receive from God, if you don't spend eternity with God, you lost everything. The Bible speaks of the children of the Kingdom of God being cast out to the Outer Darkness (Matt. 8:12).

These were people who were meant for Heaven, but because of sin and disobedience, they didn't make it. Because they wanted to please their fleshly passions, they were disapproved.

No wonder the man of God, Apostle Paul, after having been in the ministry for many years and having done mighty exploits through the Name of Jesus Christ and by the Power of the Holy Spirit of the Living God, still said that he beat his body and brought his body under subjection, so that after preaching to others, he will not be disqualified (1 Cor. 9:27).

Our hope in Christ Jesus is mainly in the life to come. No matter what He gives you or is able to give you, don't set your mind on them. God is able to give you healing and health; He is able to give you job and money.

The Lord will give you admission into institutions of learning so that you will obtain the certificates and qualifications that you want. Do you need children, wife, or husband? It is a small thing with God. He is able to do exceeding abundantly above all you can ask or imagine (Eph. 3:20).

"Ride on, pastor!" That statement or something like that is heard in churches often. However, the apostle, the prophet, the evangelist, the pastor, or the teacher is not the Judge. The Judge is the Lord Jesus Christ. He has said that you must be changed by His Word and His Spirit (Jn 3:5).

He has given you the Bible; and He told you that His Word (the Bible) will judge you on that Day (Jn 12:48). The Lord Jesus Christ says that the proof of the love you have for Him is that you obey Him (Jn 14:15).

His Commandments are not burdensome (1 Jn 5:3). They are meant to make you, and not to mar you. Why do you call Him, Lord, Lord, and do not do what He says? (Lk. 6:46). Only those who do the Will of the Father will enter the Kingdom of Heaven (Matt. 7:21).

God is no respecter of persons (Acts 10:34). Our God is a Consuming Fire, and it is a fearful thing to fall into His Hands (Heb. 10:31).

Make up your mind that whatever it takes, you are going to please God. You have not resisted to bloodshed, striving against sin (Heb. 12:4).

If your right eye will lead you to Hell, pluck it out; for it is better to enter the Kingdom of Heaven with one eye than to land into Hell with full body (Matt. 5:29).

SEXUAL IMMORALITY

Questions for Discussion:

1. What is sexual immorality?
2. Why must we avoid and flee from sexual immorality?
3. What will happen if we indulge in sexual immorality?

The Bible says that all other sins that a man commits are outside the body, but he that commits fornication sins against his own body. The Word of God tells us to flee fornication. It did not say that we should avoid fornication, but that we should flee fornication.

To flee is to run away from something as though you are afraid (in fear) of it. Do you not know that your body is the Temple of the Holy Spirit, Who is in you, Who you received from God, and you are not your own? (1 Cor. 6:18-20).

You were bought with a Price; therefore, glorify God in your body, and in your spirit, which are God's. The body is earthly and physical. With my spirit, I contact the spiritual realm; with my soul, I contact the mental realm; and with my body, I contact the physical realm.

You should always allow your spirit, who is born again, to rule your life. Your body is not born again, and if you allow the dictates and desires of the body to govern you, you will be a carnal Believer.

The body wants three basic things which are: food, sex, and comfort. Comfort is connected to rest, relaxation, and sleep. All those appetites were given us by God, and we have to use them the right way.

Food is good, but if you are not careful, you will become gluttonous. Love of food will keep you from fasting, and you will become less sensitive spiritually.

Sleep and relaxation can make you become lazy if you love them. Too much sleep will affect your prayer-life and your obedience to God. Of course, he who loves sleep will not be rich.

You must work to excel in life and in ministry. Don't be idle, for the idle mind is the devil's workshop: when he is through with the mental planning and luring, he will execute it.

Sex has its moral and legal use. Let's forget about the legal use, for now, because many laws existing in many countries of the world were inspired by the devil and his demons. When a country approves same-sex marriage, the devil is at work in that country.

When a country says that nothing is wrong with sex outside marriage, if both partners give their consent, that is satan at work. Christians should pray against the approval of sinful bills or laws in their nations.

However, there is the moral and Biblical use of sex, and that is that sex must be within marriage. Do you know that some people are living together as husbands and wives without marriage?

The Samaritan woman that Jesus Christ had conversation with was living with someone who was not her husband (Jn 4:16-19). My dear, if you are like that, you better get married before you end in Hell Fire.

Sexual immorality is a sin against God, and it has many forms and associates. They include: fornication, adultery, masturbation, lust, lesbianism, homosexuality, incest, voyeurism, pornography, bestiality, necrophilia, orgies, paedophile, bisexuality, heterosexuality, etc.

If you indulge in any of these, you are heading towards Hell. No sexually immoral person will inherit the Kingdom of God and of Christ (Eph. 5:3-6).

Fornication is to have sex with someone you are not married to. Adultery is for a married person to have sex with someone he or she is not married to. Masturbation is to make yourself sexually excited by touching or rubbing your sexual organs.

Lust is to have very strong sexual desire for someone even when you have not actually had the physical intercourse. Lesbianism is for a woman to be sexually attracted to another woman.

Homosexuality is a man being attracted sexually to another man. Incest is illegal sex between people who are closely related, like a brother and his sister, or a father and his daughter. Voyeurism is getting sexual pleasure from secretly watching other people's sexual activities.

Pornography is the treatment of sexual acts in pictures, film, or writing in a way that is intended to make people feel sexually excited. Bestiality is sexual relations between a person and an animal.

Necrophilia is sexual interest in dead bodies. Orgy is sexual activity in a group; that is, having sex with more than one person at a time. Paedophile is someone who is sexually attracted to small children. Bisexuality is to be sexually attracted to both men and women. Heterosexuality is to be sexually attracted to people of the opposite sex.

The Word of God tells us to flee fornication. Don't say that you cannot fall and remain in a closed dark room with the opposite sex.

In the Bible, sexual immorality made people to lose their God-given purposes. Reuben who was the first son of Jacob lost his first place because of sexual immorality (Gen. 49:3-4). King David brought immorality and sword to his family by adultery and murder (2 Sam. 11 & 12).

Because of lust and pride, King Solomon despised the Law of God and married foreign women who turned his heart from following the Lord in his old age. Sampson, that Old Testament strong man, lost his power and mission due to sex (1 Kgs 11; Jgs. 16).

There are many diseases associated with sexual immorality or sex. The sexually transmitted diseases (STD's) include: syphilis, gonorrhea, HIV/AIDS, and others. Do you see that God loves you when He tells you to flee fornication?

Joseph fled from fornication when Portiphar's wife tried all she could to get Joseph into that sin. Joseph said that to do that would amount to sinning against God and Portiphar (Gen. 39:4-23). If you deny God because of sexual urge, can you lay down your life for Him?

Many ladies dress indecently and seductively. Many say that they are Christians and your appearance does not matter but your heart. But man looks at outward appearance (1 Sam. 16:7). Woe to him or her that will cause a brother or a sister to fall (Matt. 18:6).

Dress decently and you will receive the Acceptance of God and of men. Body-hugs (tight-fitting dresses), sleeveless blouses, revealing dresses, mini-skirts, hanging blouses that show your belly, the ones that reveal your breasts, and many others are satanic, devilish, and demonic.

The Bible says that because iniquity shall abound, the love of many shall wax cold (Matt. 24:12). Some even get involved in sexual immorality so that people will not say that they are not civilized and matured.

Do not give your strength to women (Prov. 31:3). He that keeps company with harlots spends his substance (Prov. 29:3). There is the attire of a harlot (Prov. 7:10). Do not let your heart decline to the harlot's paths.

The immoral woman has cast down many wounded: yea, many strong men have been slain by her. Her house is the way to Hell, going down to the chambers of death.

Don't sell your birthright and inheritance for sex, no matter the pressure and urge. God is able to help you overcome. Depend on the Holy Spirit, and not on the strength of the flesh. By the arms of the flesh shall no one prevail (1 Sam. 2:9).

Some sexually immoral tendencies are as a result of demonic strongholds. If you find that you won't overcome the urge to have sex, please, take some time and fast, pray, study the Bible, and wait on God.

Let's mean business here; if you fast for three days and nights straight, you will not die. If you fast till 3:00 p.m. or 6:00 p.m. for seven days, you will not die either. Many want a quick-fix method.

Inasmuch as there is deliverance that can be received by prayer, many have gone into the hands of false ministers in the name of deliverance ministries. What about telling your pastor?

SIN AND DISOBEDIENCE

Questions for Discussion:

1. What is sin?
2. What is disobedience?
3. What are benefits and dangers of sin and disobedience?
4. How does sin come?
5. How can we avoid sin and disobedience?

Sin is going contrary to the Word of God. Sin is disobedience, and disobedience is sin. When God tells you to do something, if you don't do it, it is sin. If He tells you to avoid something, if you don't avoid it, if you do it, it is sin.

Sin entered the world by one man (Adam), and one Man (Jesus Christ) came to take away sin. Sin came from the devil but righteousness, peace, and joy came from the Lord.

There are three basic definitions of sin, as found in the Bible. Sin is lawlessness, the transgression of the Law (1 Jn 3:4). Sin is anything not done in faith (Rom. 14:23). Sin is knowing what you should do and not doing it (Jas 4:17).

These three definitions of sin are comprehensive and they touch many different things. God hates sin, though He loves the sinner. God is of Purer Eyes than to behold sin (Habk. 1:13).

Sin will keep you far from God. God will do everything to save the sinner, but if he refuses, he bears the consequences.

Sin is the transgression of the Law. To transgress the Law is to go against the Law. When the Law is mentioned, some think that the Law has been done away with. This needs proper interpretation. Jesus Christ came to fulfil the Law and the Prophets, and not to destroy them (Matt. 5:17).

The ritual Laws of the Old Testament have been done away with, but not the moral Laws. Today, instead of resting and worshipping God on the Sabbath (Saturday), we rest and worship on the first day of the week (Sunday) (1 Cor. 16:2; Acts 20:7).

The important thing there, is that God loves us and wants us to rest. He gives His beloved rest. It is not because we work every time that we succeed. God is able to supply all our needs.

Actually, we are supposed to worship God everyday. So, everyday is our day of worship. But unlike in the Old Testament where they couldn't even cook on the Sabbath, we know now that the Law was made for man and not man for the Law (Mk 2:27).

But we know that "You shall have no other god before Me" still exists. "You shall honour your father and your mother," "You shall not commit adultery," etc still exist today. But even when we do these things, we do them out of love for God and for man.

All the Law is summed up in love: you shall love the Lord God with all your heart, with all your mind, and with all your strength, and you shall love your neighbour as yourself (Deut. 6:5; Matt. 22:37).

We live by the Law of Liberty (Jas 1:25; Jas 2:12), and we do not use our liberty as an opportunity for the flesh (Gal. 5:13).

Sin is anything not done in faith. The Bible says that if you do something in doubt, it is sin, and sin leads to condemnation (Rom. 14:23). Think of the many it-doesn't-matters among Christians today.

I have snapped pictures in a university and you see a lot of things with respect to dressing in the environment. In fact, a time came that I stopped snapping normal pictures except passports, apart from special cases, there. In the university environment, you see a lot of indecent dressings, both among ladies and among young men.

Even among people who call themselves Believers, you see a lot of indecent dressings. People dress indecently to many campus fellowships and churches.

People paint themselves and look like unbelievers, and yet these are people who had been born again and washed with Christ's Precious Blood. Later, they despised the Blood, and live however they want in the name of it-doesn't-matter.

They wear body-hugs and transparent dresses. The worst is that when many of them came in newly in their first year, they used to dress decently, but as time went on, they disappointed both God Who gave them the admission and their parents who sponsor them.

There are many other areas where people live in doubt and say that it makes no difference. Right in their heart, they are not confident of what they are doing, even though many people tell them that it is sinful.

Students live the life of examination malpractice, and yet they are Believers. Do you know why, after Jesus Christ had talked about regeneration in John 3:3, He talked of living by the Word and the Spirit in John 3:5?

The last definition of sin is not doing the good that you know that you should do. In the Epistle of James, James speaks of a case in which a brother comes to you for help and you know that you can and should help him, but instead of helping him, you tell him to go in peace (Jas 2:14-17).

This definition of sin holds many Christians. For instance, if the Spirit of God speaks to your heart to go out for evangelism or to preach to a particular person, if you don't do it, it is sin and disobedience.

No wonder the Word of God says that if the Christian refuses to preach to and warn the sinner, and that sinner dies in his sin, the sinner will go to Hell Fire for his sins, but his blood will be required from the Christian (Ezek. 33:6-9).

If the Spirit witnesses to your heart to pray, then pray; if He tells you to study the Bible, do just that. Preach the Word of God. Be prepared in season and out of season (2 Tim. 4:2). If you know you should love your wife and refuse to love her, it is sin to you.

Of course, I had said that sin is disobedience and disobedience is sin. When God gives us His Commandments, He expects us to obey them. Our obedience to God's Word is for our own good. If we obey Him, He will bless us.

Also, our obedience to the Word of God will keep us from harms. For instance, when God tells you not to commit fornication, He expects you to obey Him, and He will bless you for obeying Him. However, apart from that, it will save you from many venereal diseases.

Disobedience to the Word of God will receive punishment, both in this life and after death. It is true that because of Jesus Christ's Intercession for us at the Right Hand of the Father, God's Judgment does not fall on us immediately like in the Old Testament.

However, when the time of grace God gives you expires, you will be judged (Rev. 2:21). Furthermore, Hell Fire is reserved for sinners and the disobedient.

Has the Lord as great delight in burnt offerings and sacrifices, as in obeying the Voice of the Lord? Behold, to obey is better than sacrifice, and to hearken than fat of rams. Rebellion is as the sin of witchcraft; and stubbornness is as iniquity and idolatry (1 Sam. 15:22-23).

Those were the Words Prophet Samuel spoke to King Saul, after the king disobeyed God's Commandment to him. What is worthy of note in this place is that the king obeyed God but his obedience was partial.

We can then deduce, from God's Reaction, that partial obedience is disobedience. His disobedience cost him the kingdom of Israel, for he was dethroned as a king without an offspring to succeed him. Apart from that, he died in the battle field.

The devil wants to destroy you, he wants to kill you and steal from you. Don't give him a place through disobedience (Eph. 4:27). He that breaks the hedge shall be bitten by the serpent (Eccl. 10:8).

The problem is that many don't value our inheritance in Christ Jesus. Many Christians have despised Esau and spoken badly of him. But do you know that many have behaved and acted worse than Esau?

Some have sacrificed their souls and inheritance for an employment. Some have lost their destinies for a ten-minute sex. Can you lose your life for the Cause of Christ? (Heb. 12:16-17; Matt. 10:39).

Shadrach, Meshach and Abed-Nego told King Nebuchadnezzar that their God was able to deliver them, and He will deliver them. However, they went on to tell the king that they will not bow to his golden image, they will not disobey their God, even though their God refuses to deliver them (Dan. 3:16-30).

You have not yet resisted to bloodshed, striving against sin (Heb. 12:4). Jesus Christ was tempted at all points, and yet He did not sin. You are a Christian; therefore, be like Christ!

True freedom is freedom from sin and disobedience. True gain is making Heaven at last and receiving abundant reward from God in His Eternal Kingdom. If you say you are free, when you are still bound by sin and disobedience, you are in bondage.

If you gain the whole world and lose your soul at last, you gained nothing. Make up your mind to obey God at all time, no matter the cost and sacrifice.

GOD'S UNCHANGING STANDARD IN A CHANGING WORLD

Questions for Discussion:

1. How can we know God's Standard?
2. Can God's Standard change?
3. How is the world changing?

The world is changing very fast, especially now. Many modern inventions and technologies have amazed all of us. Of course, the Lord God told us that knowledge will increase in the last days (Dan. 12:4).

The inventions in aircrafts, computers, electronics, digital communications, medicine, and many other fields are noteworthy. While many of the advancements in science and technology are great, some serve good purposes, while some serve bad purposes.

Think of the advancement in the production of weapons of war: a whole city can be wiped out within a small space of time by using weapons of mass destruction.

While computers and the television are good for the storage, processing, and retrieval of data and information, and for communication, think of the pornography that is associated with them. Many have run after the things of this world so much so that they have little or no time for God.

Many pursue after flashy cars, attractive buildings, education, and certificates, and they give their time, energy, and mind to these things, but have no time for God.

However, when I talk of a changing world, I am not talking about these inventions, even though many of them have something to do with what I am talking about.

The advancement in cosmetics which make people to paint their faces and other parts of the body that they look horrible and worldly is part of what I am talking about.

God says that we should fear Him and not to mingle with those who are given to change. Their calamity, according to God, shall come quickly (Prov. 24:21-22).

If you look at many churches today, you see a lot of worldliness among people who go to church. Even Believers are not left out; many Believers live like the people of the world. Many of them dress and appear like unbelievers.

There must be a difference between the Believer and the unbeliever. Their lives must be different; their desires and priorities must be different; and their appearances should be different.

You can't dress like a harlot and expect me to believe that you are a Christian. Man looks at outward appearance; and I am a man, even though I am not an ordinary man, I still look at outward appearance.

But you must know that God sees the outward appearance too. The Word of God says that out of the abundance of the heart, the mouth speaks (Matt. 12:34). As a man thinks in his heart, so is he (Prov. 23:7).

If you dress and appear anyhow before the public and you don't care about what people think of you, something is seriously wrong with you. You need to repent and change, and God will forgive you (Acts 3:19).

I tell you that God is not an American. He is not a European either. God is not from any nation, rather all men in all nations are from God, because He created and formed them. However, God is not a Father to all men.

He is a Father to those who have accepted the Lord Jesus Christ as their Saviour. If you are not born again, ask the Lord Jesus Christ to come into your life as your Lord and personal Saviour.

Having recognized that you are a sinner who cannot save himself, believe that Jesus Christ came to this world, died for your sins, and was raised again for your justification (Rom. 4:25). He who comes to God, God will not cast him away (Jn 6:37).

No matter how dirty or sinful you may be, He is able to wash you and remember your sins no more (Isa. 1:18; Isa. 43:25). Don't wait till tomorrow, because you may not see tomorrow (Heb. 3:7-8).

If God is not pleased with you, He is not pleased with you. Simply because Believers in America or in London do those things do not make them right. Just as perversion in dressing is a problem in Nigeria today, the same had applied to them some years ago, even today.

After many years, some have thought that this or that is their culture, but the devil introduced those things over there some years back, even as he is doing today.

God is no respecter of persons. Whether you are an apostle, a prophet, an evangelist, a pastor, a bishop, an archbishop, a reverend or what, if you disobey God's Word and His Holy Spirit, you are disobedient.

Of course, because of Jesus Christ's Intercession for us at the Right Hand of the Father, God's Judgment and Punishment may not come on you now, but once the time God gave you is gone (as He gives time to everybody), God's Punishment will catch up with you.

Remember that no sinner will ever enter the Kingdom of Heaven (Eph. 5:5; 1 Cor. 6:9-10). A minister of the Gospel who lives in sin is a sinner, and all sinners will inherit Hell Fire. Many have said that many things don't matter.

What of if on the Day of Judgment, you find out that they finally mattered, and by that time, I tell you, it will be too late. Then, no matter how you repent, confess, and plead for mercy, God's Ears will not be open to your cries.

Some say that God never said that you should not drink alcohol at all, but that you should not drink it too much. But think of it, how could Apostle Paul tell Timothy to use little wine for his stomach's sake instead of using only water if he was already drinking little.

Certainly, Apostle Paul needed to advise him to take a little for medicinal purpose since he was taking none of it, because the other Believers were not taking it. Of course, their level of medical development those two thousand years ago was crude and unrefined.

Give strong drink to those who are perishing (Prov. 20:1; Prov. 31:3-7). Medical science and technology have advanced today that you don't need alcohol, even for stomach ache.

If alcohol will make your brother to stumble, why drink it? Even, the unbelievers will doubt your repentance or faith when they see you drink or buy it.

Let the Spirit of God lead you always and don't be overcome by the lust of the flesh. Don't do something, simply because someone else is doing it. Anything not done in faith is sin (Rom. 14:23).

Some sects or groups of Christians or Believers despise some other sects of Christians, saying that the others are legalistic and conscious of the Law. Well, Jesus Christ came not to destroy the Law and the Prophets, but to fulfil them (Matt. 5:17).

They say that the others are religious. Well, inasmuch as I don't believe in religion, but in Christianity (in a life changed by the Word and the Spirit of God, because someone has accepted Jesus Christ and the authenticity of the Word of God), yet "pure and undefiled religion before God and the Father is this..." (Jas 1:26-27, KJV & NKJV).

You've got to know the difference between the ritual Laws which have been done away with and the moral Laws which still stand today. Rightly divide the Word of Truth!

God can neither lie nor change His Mind (Num. 23:19) God's Standard has never changed and can never change for any people. Therefore, don't deceive yourself and don't deceive others, for we must all stand before the Judgment Seat of Christ to give account of ourselves (Rom. 14:10-12).

Don't be deceived by anyone (Eph. 5:6). He who does what is right is righteous just as God is righteous; he who lives in sin, he who does unrighteousness belongs to the devil (1 Jn 3:7).

But no matter what you might have done, contrary to the Word of God, repent now and ask for His Forgiveness and He will abundantly cleanse and pardon you. Remember that there is a Heaven to gain, and there is a Hell to shun. The Peace of the Lord Jesus Christ be with your spirit. Amen.

WISDOM, KNOWLEDGE, AND UNDERSTANDING

Questions for Discussion:

1. What is wisdom?
2. What is having knowledge?
3. What does it mean to be understanding?
4. What are the benefits of wisdom, knowledge, and understanding?

Wisdom refers to good sense and judgment. Wisdom is knowledge gained over a period of time through learning and experience. Wisdom comes from God; the Word of God is the source of wisdom.

The Spirit of God Who is the Spirit of Excellence gives us the wisdom that we need for Godliness, and to deal with the things of this life. The Lord created the whole universe by His Wisdom, and He saw that they were good. The fear of God is the beginning of wisdom (Psa. 111:10).

Knowledge has to do with the facts, skills, and understanding that you have gained through learning or experience. Knowledge refers to the information that you have about a particular situation, event; etc.

The fear of the Lord is the beginning of knowledge (Prov. 1:7). God's people are destroyed for lack of knowledge (Hos. 4:6).

The Bible is the Book of knowledge: knowledge of God and His Ways, knowledge of the devil and his ways, knowledge of the universe and the things in it, knowledge of yourself and your inheritance in Christ Jesus. Study it to increase your knowledge.

Understanding refers to knowledge about something based on learning or experience. It is the way in which you judge the meaning of something. Understanding is the ability to know and learn. Lean not on your own understanding, but apply your heart to understanding in God's Way.

Do not be children in understanding, but in malice be children (1 Cor. 14:20). You need to have a clear understanding of the Scripture and Way of God in order to apply it aright, so that you can please God.

If anyone lacks wisdom, let him ask of God, Who gives to all liberally and without reproach, and it will be given to him. But let him ask in faith, with no doubting, for he who doubts is like a wave of the sea driven and tossed by the wind.

For let not that man suppose that he will receive anything from the Lord; he is a double-minded man; unstable in all his ways (Jas 1:5-8). Whatever it is that you need from God, ask in faith, believing that you receive, and you shall have it.

Who is wise and understanding among you? Let him show by good conduct that his works are done in the meekness of wisdom. But if you have bitter envy and seeking in your hearts, do not boast and lie against the truth.

This wisdom does not descend from Above, but is earthly, sensual, and demonic. For where envying and self-seeking exist, confusion and every evil thing are there.

But the wisdom that is from Above is first pure, then peaceable, gentle, willing to yield, full of mercy and good fruits, without partiality and without hypocrisy (Jas 3:13-17).

The Spirit of God is the Spirit of Wisdom, Knowledge, and Understanding. This is why, concerning Bezalel, the son of Uri, God said, "...and I have filled him with the Spirit of God, in wisdom, in understanding, in knowledge, and in all manner of workmanship."

No matter the work God has for you or the area that you find yourself (that is good and acceptable), if you have the Spirit of God, if you are filled with the Spirit of God, then you have access to wisdom, knowledge, and understanding (Exo. 31:3).

The lives of Daniel, Shadrach, Meshach, and Abed-Nego tell us the impact of having the Spirit of God in you. The Word of God says that Daniel distinguished himself above the governors and satraps, because an Excellent Spirit was in him; and the king gave thought to setting him over the whole realm (Dan. 6:3).

How come? First, they were Jews, God's people. In our case or dispensation we will say that they were born again. That made them candidates for the Spirit's Presence.

Daniel purposed in his heart that he would not defile himself with anything (Dan. 1:8). If you want to excel in Christianity, Godliness, and ministry, then make up your mind that whatever it takes you, you will not defile and pollute yourself with the desires of the flesh and worldliness.

Though we are in the world, yet we are not of this world. Do not love the world or anything in the world. If anyone loves the world, the Love of the Father is not in him.

For all that is in the world   the lust of the flesh, the lust of the eyes, and the pride of life   is not of the Father but is of the world. And the world is passing away, and the lust of it, but he who does the Will of God endures forever (1 Jn 2:15-17).

Even when the king had apportioned special delicacies: food and drink, for them, because they knew that they will be defiled by them (according to the Law God gave them), they refused eating or drinking them.

Faithfulness, holiness, and obedience produce power and God's Presence by God's Spirit. Because they refused to be defiled, when they were tested for ten days and given vegetables to eat and water to drink, they appeared better and fatter in flesh than all the young men who ate the portion of the king's delicacies.

As for these young men, God gave them knowledge and skill in all literature and wisdom, and Daniel had understanding in all visions and dreams.

When their training was over, the king interviewed them, and among all those that were trained, none was found like those four; therefore, they served before the king.

And in all matters of wisdom and understanding about which the king examined them, he found them ten times better than all the magicians and astrologers who were in all his realm (Dan. 1).

Going through the Book of Daniel tells us that they continued with the Lord their God even after their appointments. Many backslide when God puts them in high positions.

Some will not have extra-marital affairs now that they are still average in wealth and riches; but when God gives them abundant wealth, they start going after women and drinking alcohol.

Many will be dedicated to the Lord and His Work when God has not blessed their businesses. Some will even sleep in the church, doing tarry-nights and night-vigils; but when their businesses grow, they will not have time for God, His Word, and prayer again.

Riches have wings and they do fly away. If God removes His Protection from you, the devil can reduce you from a millionaire to a beggar in just few days. But Daniel, instead of abandoning God, kept on being obedient to Him and God lifted him to higher levels.

David and Solomon prayed for understanding (Psa. 119:34,73,125,144,169; 1 Kgs 3:9-12) and the Lord gave it to them.

God leads us in the ways of wisdom, knowledge, and understanding, in Godliness, in things of this life, and concerning the life which is to come.

Sometimes, Christians behave in ways that do not depict wisdom and understanding. However, God did and does all things by His Wisdom and Understanding and we are the children of God and are to be like God (Godly).

BECOMING A PRAYER-WARRIOR

Questions for Discussion:

1. What does it mean to be a prayer-warrior?
2. Who can become a prayer-warrior?
3. How can we become prayer-warriors?
4. What can stop us from becoming prayer-warriors?

Jesus Christ told us a parable to the intent that we know that men ought always to pray and not faint (Lk. 18:1). The Word of God says that we should pray without ceasing, we should pray always (1 Thes. 5:17).

We are commanded to watch to prayer (1 Pet. 4:7), and to watch and pray (Matt. 26:41). Why should we pray? Because the Word of God says that we receive when we ask, we find when we seek, and we have an open door when we knock (Matt. 7:7).

If your son asks you of bread, you do not give him a stone; if he asks of a fish, you don't give him a snake. In the same vein, if he asks for an egg, you do not think of giving him a scorpion.

If we know to give good things to our children, how much more will our Father in Heaven give good things to us? (Matt. 7:9-11; Lk. 11:11-13). Do you trust man more than God? Cursed is he that puts his trust in man instead of in God (Jer. 17:5).

God, the Maker of all things, is able to do all things. He can neither lie nor fail to perform His Word (Heb. 6:18). Instead of one thing that has gone out of the Mouth of God not to come to pass, heaven and earth shall pass away (Matt. 24:35).

Has He said it? He will do it also. This is one reason we should obey the Instruction of the Lord that we should study the Word of God (2 Tim. 2:15) and be full of it (Col. 3:16).

If you know the Word of God, you will know His Provisions for you. If you are full of God's Word, you will know your rights, privileges, and inheritances in the Kingdom.

This will make you receive from God the things that you need, and to stop the works of the devil from coming to pass in your life. You will also be able to overcome tests, trials, and temptations.

The problem is that many Believers don't pray. Many don't maintain a consistent prayer-life. Many have made many decisions and resolutions which they failed to keep.

They decided that they will pray this long or that long every day, but they went back to prayerlessness after a short while. A prayerful Christian is a powerful Christian whereas a prayerless Christian is a powerless Christian.

Of course, everybody prays; even powerless Christians pray. But God has declared that the prayer of the sinner is an abomination to Him (Prov. 15:8). If you are a sinner, if you are not born again, the prayer that God wants from you right now is the prayer of repentance and acceptance of the Lord Jesus Christ into your life as your Lord and Saviour.

He came down from Heaven, suffered, died, and resurrected again for your sins, so that you may be justified and made righteous before God (Jn 1:12; Rom. 3:24).

Why don't people pray? Many don't pray because of laziness. They sleep too much and find it easier to do many other things than to pray.

Many don't pray because they feel, on the inside of them, that it really makes no difference whether or not they pray. They say that whatever will be, will be, and whatever will not be, will not be. But that is not true; the devil has subtly told people that.

Some don't pray because of business. My own definition of business is whatever makes you busy. Your job can keep you busy; your relationship can keep you busy; even preaching can keep you so busy that you won't pray as you are supposed to.

Ignorance of God and His Ways makes people not to pray as they are supposed to. Some don't know what the Bible teaches about prayer. Some teach about prayer very well and yet don't pray.

Satanic or demonic strongholds and obsession are other factors that make people not to pray. Have you ever wondered why you start feeling sleepy and weak when you want to pray or when you are praying?

You may see someone that will start sleeping when he starts praying, but when the same person wants to watch a football match in the television, the sleep leaves him. That is demonic remote-control.

This is one reason you don't need to eat too much (or even at all) in the night. When your body feels fasted in the night, it will be easier for you to overcome sleep in the night.

Also, eat at least three hours before going to bed. This will minimize or remove the ability of demons and their human agents to make you sleep and sleep and sleep. It will also make it hard for demons to force you have the experiences that you don't like in dreams.

Some people wake up early in the morning, and instead of rising up to pray, they decide to sleep a little more and they find out that they never wake up until it is late.

Some people decide to lie down on their beds and pray, and before long, they start sleeping and end up not praying effectively. To pray effectively, you must discipline yourself. You will need to plan and implement your prayer-time.

It is one thing to pray, and it is another thing to maintain a steady prayer-life. Some people, after listening to good messages or reading books on prayer, decide that they are going to pray two, three, or more hours everyday.

Some may do it for one, two, three, or more days, and before you know it, they get back to inconsistent prayer-life. Praying long is good, but if it is one or two hours you are able to pray everyday, maintain it and make it consistent: but increase the time, as you are able.

I recommend that every Believer should pray for at least two hours everyday, but it is not specifically written in the Bible. Take a day or more to do some personal fasting. Regular fasting with prayer will make you a spiritual giant.

Prayer should be very important to you as a Christian. Jesus Christ prayed effectively and always. Apostle Paul told us to pray always and without ceasing.

There are many conditions to receiving answers to your prayers. One condition is to pray in faith (Jas 1:6-8); another is to pray without doubting and wavering; another is to pray in the Name of Jesus Christ (Jn 16:24); another is to bear fruit that will remain (Jn 15:16); still, another is to do those things that please God (1 Jn 3:22).

Of course, prayer will not work in an unforgiving heart, because if you don't forgive, God will not forgive you also, and you will be sinful when screened spiritually (Mk 11:25-26). Pray according to the Will of God (1 Jn 5:14-15).

There are other conditions, but one thing you must realize is that the bottom-line lies in the fact that what we receive from God is as a result of the Sacrifice that Jesus Christ performed for us.

It is not of him that wills nor of him that runs, but of God that shows mercy (Rom. 9:15-16). Time and chance happen to everything on earth (Eccl. 9:11). Therefore, you should wait patiently for your answer if it delays. Delay is not denial, and God knows the best for you.

This is why it is necessary you pray according to the Will of God. Prayer is not "Give me this or that" only. Prayer is talking to God and waiting for Him to speak to you also.

Don't rush out of the Presence of God. Also, learn to pray in the Holy Ghost. Pray in tongues always and everyday. The Holy Spirit helps us to pray for the right things in the right way (Rom. 8:26-27).

We are a triumphant people, a triumphant Church, and we enforce the victory that the Lord has won for us by prayer and speaking forth of words of faith.

Learn to stay alone with God, praying to Him. Wait on God patiently. Speak to God and allow Him speak to you by listening and being quiet before the Lord.

PSALMS CONCERNING THE WORD OF GOD AND GOD'S GUIDANCE

"How can a young man cleanse his way? By taking heed according to Your Word. With my whole heart I have sought You; Oh, let me not wander from Your Commandments! Your Word I have hidden in my heart, that I might not sin against You.

"Blessed are You, O Lord! Teach me Your Statutes. With my lips I have declared all the Judgments of Your Mouth. I have rejoiced in the way of Your Testimonies, as much as in all riches. I will meditate on Your Precepts, and contemplate Your Ways. I will delight myself in Your Statutes; I will not forget Your Word.

"Deal bountifully with Your Servant, that I may live and keep Your Word. Open my eyes, that I may see wondrous things from Your Law. I am a stranger in the earth; do not hide Your Commandments from me. My soul breaks with longing for Your Judgments at all times.

"You rebuke the proud – the cursed, who stray from Your Commandments. Remove from me reproach and contempt, for I have kept Your Testimonies. Princes also sit and speak against me, but Your Servant meditates on Your Statutes. Your Testimonies also are my delight and my counselors.

"My soul clings to the dust; revive me according to Your Word. I have declared my ways, and You answered me; teach me Your Statutes. Make me understand the way of Your Precepts; so shall I meditate on Your Wonderful Works. My soul melts from heaviness; strengthen me according to Your Word.

"Remove from me the way of lying, and grant me Your Law graciously. I have chosen the way of Truth; Your Judgments I have laid before me. I cling to Your Testimonies; O Lord, do not put me to shame! I will run the course of Your Commandments, for You shall enlarge my heart.

"Teach me, O Lord, the way of Your Statutes, and I shall keep it to the end. Give me understanding, and I shall keep Your Law; indeed, I shall observe it with my whole heart. Make me walk in the path of Your Commandments, for I delight in it. Incline my heart to Your Testimonies, and not to covetousness.

"Turn away my eyes from looking at worthless things, and revive me in Your Way. Establish Your Word to Your Servant, who is devoted to fearing You. Turn away my reproach which I dread, for Your Judgments are good. Behold, I long for Your Precepts; revive me in Your Righteousness.

"Let Your Mercies come also to me, O Lord – Your Salvation according to Your Word. So shall I have an answer for him who reproaches me, for I trust in Your Word. And take not the Word of Truth utterly out of my mouth, for I have hoped in Your Ordinances. So shall I keep Your Law continually, forever and ever.

"And I will walk at liberty, for I seek Your Precepts. I will speak of Your Testimonies also before kings, and will not be ashamed. And I will delight myself in Your Commandments, which I love. My hands also I will lift up to Your Commandments, which I love, and I will meditate on Your Statutes.

"Remember the Word to Your Servant, upon which You have caused me to hope. This is my comfort in my affliction, for Your Word has given me life. The proud have me in great derision, yet I do not turn aside from Your Law. I remembered Your Judgments of old, O Lord, and have comforted myself.

"Indignation has taken hold of me because of the wicked, who forsake Your Law. Your Statutes have been my songs in the house of my pilgrimage. I remember Your Name in the night, O Lord, and I keep Your Law. This has become mine, because I kept Your Precepts.

"You are my portion, O Lord; I have said that I would keep Your Words. I entreated Your Favour with my whole heart; be merciful to me according to Your Word. I thought about my ways, and turned my feet to Your Testimonies. I made haste, and did not delay to keep Your Commandments.

"The cords of the wicked have bound me, but I have not forgotten Your Law. At midnight I will rise to give thanks to You, because of Your Righteous Judgments. I am a companion of all who fear You, and of those who keep Your Precepts. The earth, O Lord, is full of Your Mercy; teach me Your Statutes.

"You have dealt well with Your Servant, O Lord, according to Your Word. Teach me Good Judgment and Knowledge, for I believe Your Commandments. Before I was afflicted I went astray, but now I keep Your Word. You are good, and do good; teach me Your Statutes.

"The proud have forged a lie against me, but I will keep Your Precepts with my whole heart. Their heart is as fat as grease, but I delight in Your Law. It is good for me that I have been afflicted, that I may learn Your Statutes. The Law of Your Mouth is better to me than thousands of coins of gold and silver.

"Your hands have made me and fashioned me; give me understanding, that I may learn Your Commandments. Those who fear You will be glad when they see me, because I have hoped in Your Word. I know, O Lord, that Your Judgments are right, and that in faithfulness You have afflicted me.

"Let, I pray, Your Merciful Kindness be for my comfort, according to Your Word to Your Servant. Let Your Tender Mercies come to me, that I may live; for Your Law is my delight.

"Let the proud be ashamed, for they treated me wrongfully with falsehood; but I will meditate on Your Precepts. Let those who fear You turn to me, those who know Your Testimonies. Let my heart be blameless regarding Your Statutes, that I may not be ashamed.

"My soul faints for Your Salvation, but I hope in Your Word. My eyes fail from searching Your Word, saying, 'When will You comfort me?' For I have become like a wineskin in smoke, yet I do not forget Your Statutes. How many are the days of Your Servant? When will You execute judgment on those who persecute me?

"The proud have dug pits for me, which is not according to Your Law. All Your Commandments are faithful; they persecute me wrongfully; help me! They almost made an end of me on earth, but I did not forsake Your Precepts. Revive me according to Your Lovingkindness, so that I may keep the Testimony of Your Mouth.

"Forever, O Lord, Your Word is settled in Heaven. Your Faithfulness endures to all generations; You established the earth, and it abides. They continue this day according to Your Ordinances, for all are Your Servants.

"Unless Your Law had been my delight, I would then have perished in my affliction. I will never forget Your Precepts, for by them You have given me life. I am Yours, save me; for I have sought Your Precepts.

"The wicked wait for me to destroy me, but I will consider Your Testimonies. I have seen the consummation of all perfection, but Your Commandment is exceedingly broad.

"Oh, how I love Your Law! It is my meditation all the day. You, through Your Commandments, make me wiser than my enemies; for they are ever with me. I have more understanding than all my teachers, for Your Testimonies are my meditation.

"I understand more than the ancients, because I keep Your Precepts. I have restrained my feet from every evil way, that I may keep Your Word. I have not departed from Your Judgments, for You Yourself have taught me. How sweet are Your Words to my taste, sweeter than honey to my mouth! Through Your Precepts I get understanding; therefore I hate every false way.

"Your Word is a lamp to my feet and a light to my path. I have sworn and confirmed that I will keep Your Righteous Judgments. I am afflicted very much; revive me, O Lord, according to Your Word. Accept, I pray, the freewill offerings of my mouth, O Lord, and teach me Your Judgments.

"My life is continually in my hand, yet I do not forget Your Law. The wicked have laid a snare for me, yet I have not strayed from Your Precepts. Your Testimonies I have taken as a heritage forever, for they are the rejoicing of my heart. I have inclined my heart to perform Your Statutes forever, to the very end.

"I hate the double-minded, but I love Your Law. You are my Hiding Place and my Shield; I hope in Your Word. Depart from me, you evildoers, for I will keep the Commandments of my God! Uphold me according to Your Word, that I may live; and do not let me be ashamed of my hope.

"Hold me up, and I shall be safe, and I shall observe Your Statutes continually. You reject all those who stray from Your Statutes, for their deceit is falsehood. You put away all the wicked of the earth like dross; therefore I love Your Testimonies. My flesh trembles for Fear of You, and I am afraid of Your Judgments.

"I have done justice and righteousness; do not leave me to my oppressors. Be surety for Your Servant for good; do not let the proud oppress me. My eyes fail from seeking Your Salvation and Your Righteous Word. Deal with Your Servant according to Your Mercy, and teach me Your Statutes.

"I am Your Servant; give me understanding, that I may know Your Testimonies. It is time for You to act, O Lord, for they have regarded Your Law as void. Therefore I love Your Commandments more than gold, yes, than fine gold! Therefore all Your Precepts concerning all things I consider to be right; I hate every false way.

"Your testimonies are wonderful; therefore my soul keeps them. The entrance of Your Words gives light; it gives understanding to the simple. I opened my mouth and panted, for I longed for Your Commandments. Look upon me and be merciful to me, as Your Custom is towards those who love Your Name.

"Direct my steps by Your Word, and let no iniquity have dominion over me. Redeem me from the oppression of man, that I may keep Your Precepts. Make Your Face shine upon Your Servant, and teach me Your Statutes. Rivers of water run down from my eyes, because men do not keep Your Law.

"Righteous are You, O Lord, and upright are Your Judgments. Your Testimonies, which You have commanded, are righteous and very faithful. My zeal has consumed me, because my enemies have forgotten Your Words. Your Word is very pure; therefore Your Servant loves it.

"I am small and despised, yet I do not forget Your Precepts. Your Righteousness is an everlasting righteousness, and Your Law is Truth. Trouble and anguish have overtaken me, yet Your Commandments are my delights. The righteousness of Your Testimonies is everlasting; give me understanding, and I shall live.

"I cry out with my whole heart; hear me, O Lord! I will keep Your Statutes. I cry out to You; save me, and I will keep Your Testimonies. I rise before the dawning of the morning, and cry for help; I hope in Your Word. My eyes are awake through the night watches, that I may meditate on Your Word.

"Hear my voice according to Your Lovingkindness; O Lord, revive me according to Your Justice. They draw near who follow after wickedness; they are far from Your Law. You are near, O Lord, and all Your Commandments are Truth. Concerning Your Testimonies, I have known of old that You have founded them forever.

"Consider my affliction and deliver me, for I do not forget Your Law. Plead my cause and redeem me; revive me according to Your Word. Salvation is far from the wicked, for they do not seek Your Statutes. Great are Your Tender Mercies, O Lord; revive me according to Your Judgments.

"Many are my persecutors and my enemies, yet I do not turn from Your Testimonies. I see the treacherous, and am disgusted, because they do not keep Your Word. Consider how I love Your Precepts; revive me, O Lord, according to Your Lovingkindness. The entirety of Your Word is Truth, and every one of Your Righteous Judgments endures forever.

"Princes persecute me without a cause, but my heart stands in awe of Your Word. I rejoice at Your Word as one who finds great treasure. I hate and abhor lying, but I love Your Law. Seven times a day I praise You, because of Your Righteous Judgments.

"Great peace have those who love Your Law, and nothing causes them to stumble. Lord, I hope for Your Salvation, and I do Your Commandments. My soul keeps Your Testimonies, and I love them exceedingly. I keep Your Precepts and Your Testimonies, for all my ways are before You.

"Let my cry come before You, O Lord; give me understanding according to Your Word. Let my supplication come before You; deliver me according to Your Word. My lips shall utter praise, for You teach me Your Statutes. My tongue shall speak of Your Word, for all Your Commandments are righteousness.

"Let Your Hand become my help, for I have chosen Your Precepts. I long for Your Salvation, O Lord, and Your Law is my delight. Let my soul live, and it shall praise You; and let Your Judgments help me. I have gone astray like a lost sheep; seek Your Servant, for I do not forget Your Commandments (Psa. 119:9-176).

"Blessed is he whose transgression is forgiven, whose sin is covered. Blessed is the man to whom the Lord does not impute iniquity, and in whose spirit there is no deceit. When I kept silent, my bones grew old through my groaning all the day long. For day and night Your Hand was heavy upon me; my vitality was turned into the drought of summer. Selah

"I acknowledged my sin to You, and my iniquity I have not hidden. I said, 'I will confess my transgressions to the Lord,' and You forgave the iniquity of my sin. Selah

"For this cause everyone who is Godly shall pray to You in a time when You may be found; surely in a flood of great waters they shall not come near him. You are my Hiding Place; You shall preserve me from trouble; You shall surround me with songs of deliverance. Selah

"I will instruct you and teach you in the way you should go; I will guide you with My Eye. Do not be like the horse or like the mule, which have no understanding, which must be harnessed with bit and bridle, else they will not come near you.

"Many sorrows shall be to the wicked; but he who trusts in the Lord, mercy shall surround him. Be glad in the Lord and rejoice, you righteous; and shout for joy, all you upright in heart! (Psa. 32).

"Sing aloud to God our Strength; make a joyful shout to the God of Jacob. Raise a song and strike the timbrel, the pleasant harp with the lute. Blow the trumpet at the time of the New Moon, at the full moon, on our solemn feast day.

"For this is a statute for Israel, a Law of the God of Jacob. This He established in Joseph as a testimony, when He went throughout the land of Egypt, where I heard a language I did not understand.

"I removed his shoulder from the burden; his hands were freed from the baskets. You called in trouble, and I delivered you; I answered you in the secret place of thunder; I tested you at the waters of Meribah. Selah

"Hear, O My people, and I will admonish you! O Israel, if you will listen to Me! There shall be no foreign god among you; nor shall you worship any foreign god. I am the Lord your God, Who brought you out of the land of Egypt; open your mouth wide, and I will fill it.

"But My people would not heed My Voice, and Israel would have none of Me. So I gave them over to their own stubborn heart, to walk in their own counsels. Oh, that My people would listen to Me, that Israel would walk in My Ways! "I would soon subdue their enemies, and turn My Hand against their adversaries.

"The haters of the Lord would pretend submission to Him, but their fate would endure forever. He would have fed them also with the finest of wheat; and with honey from the rock I would have satisfied you (Psa. 81).

As a general rule, you should be able to know the difference between the Old Testament and the New Testament. There are some things that were allowed in the Old Testament dispensation, which are not allowed in the New Testament dispensation.

For instance, whereas people were rewarded according to their works in the Old Testament, we are not to reward evil with evil in the New Testament. The Bible says, "You have heard that it was said, 'An eye for an eye and a tooth for a tooth.' But I tell you not to resist an evil person. But whoever slaps you on your right cheek, turn the other to him also.

"If anyone wants to sue you and take away your tunic, let him have your cloak also. And whoever compels you to go one mile, go with him two. Give to him who asks you, and from him who wants to borrow from you do not turn away.

"You have heard that it was said, 'You shall love your neighbour and hate your enemy.' But I say to you, love your enemies, bless those who curse you, do good to those who hate you, and pray for those who spitefully use you and persecute you,

"That you may be sons of your Father in Heaven; for He makes His sun rise on the evil and on the good, and sends rain on the just and on the unjust. For if you love those who love you, what reward have you? Do not even the tax collectors do the same?

"And if you greet your brethren only, what do you do more than others? Do not even the tax collectors do so? Therefore you shall be perfect, just as your Father in Heaven is perfect" (Matt. 5:38-48).

Also, in the Old Testament, they lived by their righteousness; but in the New Testament, even though we are to live in holiness and obey God, as a prove that we truly love Him, yet we live by the Righteousness and Sacrifice of Jesus Christ. To this end, the Bible says, *"For Christ is the End of the Law for righteousness to everyone who believes.*

"For Moses writes about the righteousness which is of the Law, 'The man who does those things shall live by them.' But the righteousness of faith speaks in this way, 'Do not say in your heart, "Who will ascend into Heaven?"' (that is, to bring Christ down from Above) or, *'"Who will descend into the abyss?"'* (that is, to bring Christ up from the dead).

"But what does it say? 'The Word is near you, in your mouth and in your heart' (that is, the Word of Faith which we preach): *that if you confess with your mouth the Lord Jesus and believe in your heart that God has raised Him from the dead, you will be saved.*

"For with the heart one believes unto righteousness, and with the mouth confession is made unto salvation. For the Scripture says, 'Whoever believes on Him will not be put to shame.' For there is no distinction between Jew and Greek, for the Same Lord over all is rich to all who call upon Him. For 'whoever calls on the Name of the Lord shall be saved'" (Rom. 10:4-13).

In this New Testament, we operate with the spirit of love, mercy, forgiveness, and love, unlike in the Old Testament, where they operated with the spirit of judgment. This why the Bible says, *"Now it came to pass, when the time had come for Him to be received Up, that He steadfastly set His Face to go to Jerusalem, and sent messengers before His Face.*

"And as they went, they entered a village of the Samaritans, to prepare for Him. But they did not receive Him, because His Face was set for the journey to Jerusalem. And when His Disciples James and John saw this, they said, 'Lord, do You want us to command fire to come down from Heaven and consume them, just as Elijah did?'

"But He turned and rebuked them, and said, 'You do not know what manner of spirit you are of. For the Son of Man did not come to destroy men's lives but to save them.' And they went to another village (Lk. 9:51-56).

"If it is possible, as much as depends on you, live peaceably with all men. Beloved, do not avenge yourselves, but rather give place to wrath; for it is written, 'Vengeance is Mine, I will repay,' says the Lord.

"Therefore 'if your enemy is hungry, feed him; if he is thirsty, give him a drink; for in so doing you will heap coals of fire on his head.' Do not be overcome by evil, but overcome evil with good" (Rom. 12:18-21).

DEMONIC AND SATANIC ACTIVITIES TODAY

The Bible says that the works of satan and his hosts are stealing, killing, and destroying (Jn 10:10). And the reason Jesus Christ came was that He might destroy the works of the devil (1 Jn 3:8). Therefore, our work, as Christians, is to destroy the works of the devil.

In these days of concentrated satanic and demonic activities, we have to be wise and operate according to the Word of God in order to be free from the plans, purposes, and works of the devil and his hosts. Yes, Jesus Christ has freed us from the power of the devil; but the Bible tells us what to do in order to maintain and enjoy that freedom and victory that our Lord got for us.

This is why the Bible says, "Nor give place to the devil" (Eph. 4:27), and "Resist the devil and he will flee from you" (Jas 4:7). This is talking of the responsibility that God gave you as a Christian: it is not God that will resist the devil for you, but you yourself. And He has given you the resources you need to resist the devil. If you give the devil a place in your life, then the devil will gladly have that place.

Yet, "Behold, I give you the authority to trample on serpents and scorpions, and over all the power of the enemy, and nothing shall by any means hurt you" (Lk. 10:19). And, "No weapon formed against you shall prosper, and every tongue which rises against you in judgment, you shall condemn. This is the heritage of the Servants of the LORD, and their righteousness is from Me," says the LORD (Isa. 54:17).

Also, "And these signs will follow those who believe: in My Name they will cast out demons; they will speak with new tongues; they will take up serpents; and if they drink anything deadly, it will by no means hurt them; they will lay hands on the sick, and they will recover" (Mk 16:17-18). These and many others are God's Provisions for us as His children; but we must also take up our responsibilities, so that we will enjoy the things that Jesus Christ has provided for us to the fullest.

In these end-times, learn and get used to studying the Word of God (in order to know your rights, privileges, power, and authority as a Believer in Christ Jesus); and apply what you know, because it is applied knowledge that brings the desired results. Learn to fast and pray in these days of concentrated demonic activities. But don't be afraid, for God is with you and for you! Flies do not perch on boiling oil, even as serpents do not coil around red-hot iron. Therefore, maintain a red-hot spiritual life always.

Learn to pray over and bless your food and water. The Bible says, "For it is sanctified by the Word of God and prayer" (1 Tim. 4:1-2). Many products in the market are polluted by witches and demons. Pray and bless the things you buy in the market, especially edible things and pre-packed and canned foods. Pray over yourself when you go for such services as barbing and hair-keeping. Be sensitive to know who you should not patronize, even for things like dry-cleaning.

Please, no matter how I may sound, before you take any drug or medicine (for those who like taking drugs/medicine), pray over them. There are satanic and demonic products in the form of drugs and medicine; and there are also satanic, demonic, and occult doctors, pharmacists, and nurses in many hospitals, whether public or private, local or foreign. If you want to go to hospital, pray over yourself and cover yourself with the Blood of Jesus Christ before you go. You may also tell a trusted person to pray for you; but never forget to pray by yourself.

No matter how urgent the case may be, if you can't pray, then don't go! Many people have lost their lives in hospitals, not because of the sickness or disease that attacked them, but because of satanic medicine and medical practitioners. It will even be difficult for police to detect these practices, because they are spiritually remoted and performed. And you know that many policemen are not spiritually sensitive; therefore, even if a policeman is there, the doctor can do what he wants to do, and the security agent can't even notice it.

Please, pray over the clothes and wears you buy, especially the second-hand ones, because many of them actually come from the underworld. Someone may doubt the possibility; but do you know that the Bible says that God created the physical world from the spiritual world (things that exist from things that do not exist)? (Heb. 11:3). The spiritual controls the physical, whether the good realm or the bad realm. Even unbelievers believe that after performing some demonic rituals, they can disappear and reappear at will.

In geography, we are told that the 70% of the earth's surface is covered with water. Do you know the vastness of the expanse of water in the Atlantic Ocean, for example? If a ship appears from the mermaid kingdom in that great expanse of sea and sails to the seaport, how do you know where it came from? Yes, it can carry any national flag they want it to carry.

And you know that there are submarines which go under water and come up when they want; so if the one from the underworld appears as a submarine, how do you know where it came from? They will come with whatever paper for the goods that you may want at the seaport, and they can interfere with whatever signal you may send or receive. Yes, they can operate physical shipping industries that will carry their goods at whatever point in the sea. Even if you may argue that the signal or information says that the ship came from another physical seaport, it makes no difference, because they can always outsmart you.

Don't be deceived: they will still have physical clearing agents for the goods, and distributing or marketing companies and agents for their materials. You may even work in a physical satanic company without your knowledge; and you will say, "I know how these things are produced." Do you also know how they got many of the 'imported' chemicals and materials they use in the factory?

Pray over your meat and fish. Please, pastor, when people bring life-animals for thanksgiving and gifts, pray over them and sanctify them. As odd as I may sound, some of those animals are more than animals. And even many of those ones which are normal animals might have been dedicated to devils (with different proclamations and curses) before they bring them to you. This is also applicable to the ones you buy in the market by yourself, even the ones you use for general cooking in camps, ceremonies, and retreats.

Before you travel, pray. Many of the accidents you hear of are not mechanical, but spiritually remote-controlled. Many plane-crashes, motor-accidents, and shipwrecks, which are blamed on mechanics, vehicle producers, and transport companies are actually caused by witches and devils. This is not for you to be afraid, because angels are guarding you; in fact, fear can open a way for the devil. Entertain no fear, because satan is nobody before your Almighty God!

Pray for your children and family, because witches want to enslave and initiate them if they have the opportunity. There are many conscious agents of satan in nursery schools, primary schools, secondary schools, universities, work-places, streets, and markets. Train your children to refuse edible things from strangers, and to pray over what they eat and drink. Pray over gifts you receive and the things you buy in the market. During/after your ceremonies and weddings, pray over the gifts you receive.

The devil and his devils are desperate these days more than before, because he knows that his time is short. If he can't destroy you, he will want to kill you; and if he can't kill you, he will want to steal from you. Therefore, watch and pray, lest you enter into temptation (Matt. 26:41).

The Bible says, "Owe no man anything..." (Rom. 13:8) and, "...the borrower is servant to the lender" (Prov. 22:7). It is not that it is sinful to borrow, because the Word also says, "...and from him who wants to borrow from you do not turn away" Matt. 5:42). But to borrow and refuse to pay is evil. It is also not good to postpone paying your debts when you are in the position to pay the debt.

Also, debt has spiritual significance; therefore, if you are not prayerful, somebody can use the credit-contact to drain your money or influence your life financially. He who goes on borrowing, goes on sorrowing. Learn to trust in God, instead of trusting in men and creditors. Also, the time, energy, and effort you put in to borrow and think on how to pay can bring stress and shame on you.

Pray for your newborn child and children; cover them with Blood of Jesus Christ. Pray over what you give out to strangers like beggars: cover it with the Blood of Jesus Christ.

Pray and cover yourself, your family, business, occupation, and property with the Blood of Jesus Christ. Believers need to pray a lot these days (and also fast), especially in group prayers.

Pray before you embark on journeys by land, air, or water. And if you have an uneasy feeling as you want to travel, then pray through before traveling. But this is not to tell you to live in fear, because angels are already guarding you. However, be prayerful generally.

DIVINE REVELATIONS AND NEAR-DEATH EXPERIENCES (NDE'S)

If it is contrary to the Word of God, then it is from satan – the devil and God's archenemy – who deceived Eve (from the beginning) with: "Did God really say…." That which is against God and His Word cannot be from God, the Maker of all things, Who holds the whole world in His Hand, because God's Word and His Spirit agree. The Lord Jesus Christ, Who defeated satan on the Cross of Calvary about two thousand years ago, is the Same – yesterday, today, and forever. He is coming very soon; get ready to meet Him: Heaven and Hell are real; let no one deceive you.

And the Word says, "Beware of false prophets, who come to you in sheep's clothing, but inwardly they are ravenous wolves. You will know them by their fruits. Do men gather grapes from thornbushes or figs from thistles? Even so, every good tree bears good fruit, but a bad tree bears bad fruit. A good tree cannot bear bad fruit, nor can a bad tree bear good fruit. Every tree that does not bear good fruit is cut down and thrown into the Fire. Therefore by their fruits you will know them.

"Not everyone who says to Me, 'Lord, Lord,' shall enter the Kingdom of Heaven, but he who does the Will of My Father in Heaven. Many will say to Me in that Day, 'Lord, Lord, have we not prophesied in Your Name, cast out demons in Your Name, and done many wonders in Your Name?' And then I will declare to them, 'I never knew you; depart from Me, you who practice lawlessness!'" (Matt. 7:15-23).

To tell you the truth, a lot of the noise made by many Believers means little or nothing to God. Many Believers and ministers cause God more pain and heartbreak than unbelievers. Many ministers preach and teach what God never thought of, not to talk of saying it: Many of them preach, teach, and practice the mind of the devil. Many Believers live however they want, while shouting, "Praise the Lord!" and "The Lord is good!" Well, let all of us amend our ways while there is still time, because God cannot change His Word for any person.

One time, I went to an open-air crusade which was titled: Mega Fire Crusade with one celebrated evangelist. It was a two-day crusade. I went the last day; and I stayed from the beginning of the preaching till the closing of the crusade. Brethren, the man didn't even mention or pray about either receiving Jesus Christ or avoiding sin. But he mentioned and prayed about car, building, marriage, factory, business, healing, and giving.

And he took two sets of offerings/donations, and invited people to the church that organized the crusade, telling them that he would anoint them during the church service. I was so unhappy that I met him after he came down, while they were about carrying him to his hotel room. He asked what my problem was, thinking that I came for prayer. I told him what I observed in his ministration, telling him that I am an evangelist and the primary aim of crusades should be to draw souls to Jesus Christ.

Guess what? He never even regretted or apologized, but defended himself, saying that sometimes it is like that. But, brethren, the crusade was only for two days. This is not a story that somebody told me, but what I experienced myself.

When I walk along the street and see how many ladies and women dress, I weep. And when you pass through beer parlours and joints, and see our young men, you will wail. What about the things happening among Believers, ministries, and churches?

Jesus Christ is coming very soon: Heaven and Hell are real. Let us get ready for His Return, knowing that the Christian race and God's Judgment are individual, and not collective. There is Only One Jesus Christ; and there is only one Bible. If you love the Kingdom of Heaven, then start reading and studying your own Bible for yourself, so that when those who teach you lies are condemned by God, you will not be condemned alongside with them.

It is not every place that is called by the name of church, ministry, fellowship, or mission that is preparing people for Heaven. Many of them are preparing people for Hell Fire. You will come to terms with the reality in the end. And the great regret is that by then, there will not be a second chance.

It is not just a matter of, "Thank You Jesus!" It is a matter of obeying His Word and Commandments, not being hypocrites who claim to be Believers, but live and act however we want, not regarding the things contained in the Bible, which He gave us. God is no respecter of any person; He will judge all men using His Word as His Standard. Remember that the righteous Lucifer became His archenemy by sin, and the holy Adam became separated from Him by disobedience.

Someone can accuse others of spreading the 'gospel of sin', and of making people sin-conscious. Read 1 Cor. 10:1-14, and see who the 'gospel' of sin is meant for (even though there is no such thing as 'the gospel of sin'). But beware, that you do not run and labour in vain! Also, know that idolatry does not only mean the worship of carved and molten images (Jas 4:4-5). Refer to Rom. 6:1 and 2 Cor. 6:1. May God open the eyes of your understanding, so that those who follow you may enter the Kingdom of Heaven!

NOW, I AM NOT JUDGING ANYONE, NOR AM I ENCOURAGING JUDGING ANYONE; but we must speak to warn those who are derailing, not to judge them; because they can still repent, as long as they are still alive, if they open themselves to the Holy Spirit's Promptings. And this applies to both the leaders and the led!

Read: Matthew 7:15-27; 2 Corinthians 11:13-15; 2 Peter 2:1-22; 1 John 4:1; Jude 1:3-13; and see that Jesus Christ, Paul, Peter, John, and Jude spoke against false preachers, teachers, prophets, and ministers. Did they do it to condemn them? No; rather, they did it to warn their followers and those who may be deceived by them.

Many people speak against Divine Revelations from God (including the testimonies of those who had Near-death Experiences) about Heaven and Hell. God has chosen to do it His Own Way, as He had been doing before. Why not believe God? Revelations like these are meant to encourage the faithful and warn the faithless (unfaithful). "The Bible is our standard and guide"; but, many people use this statement to trample on and work against the Will and Purpose of God.

The true testimony-bearers did not say that dressing a particular way alone will take you to Heaven; they emphasized on salvation, holiness, and total obedience to the Word of God. And be mindful that holiness and righteousness is both inward (of the heart and the mind) and outward (of the body). Refer to 2 Corinthians 7:1 and Romans 12:1-2.

And as for whether they should sell the testimonies, they are to allow God lead them in that area. By the way, if a true man of God is invited to preach to people (or teach them), inasmuch as he has his transport fare (or can get there) or is transported to the place of the ministration, he goes there and preaches free of charge to all who are there to listen; and he does so joyfully to win and establish souls for the Lord. If you give him some money after the ministration, and he collects it, is it evil?

Even if you don't give him, God will take good care of him; but if he comes with compact discs (CDs), DVDs, books, or tapes, must he give them to you free of charge? Your buying (willingly) any material, is it not for your own good and future use/revision? Can you mention one man of God that gives all his materials free of charge to people, except where (in some instances) the minister himself, someone else, a group of people, or the ministry/church pays for them (or for some of them)? Or, are they selling them at exorbitant prices?

And if the compact discs, tapes, and books are not produced, how will those within the vicinity of the programme who didn't attend the programme hear from the man of God directly? Or, is it better for them to hear misinterpreted and misinformed reports from those who attended the programme? And what about the areas the man of God may not speak on for that time; is it not from the materials he came with (or his materials that are sold by traders) that people will learn? By the way, the Bible you have and read, did you get it free of charge?

Unbelievers and businessmen spend money to buy or get what they want; should Christians complain, because they paid small money to get books, CDs, and tapes? Many

Believers/Christians will spend a lot of money on food, clothes, schools and certificates, and other physical and mental things; but when it comes to spending money for spiritual things, they will hypocritically complain. Don't they know that "man shall not live by bread alone, but by every Word that comes out of the Mouth of God"?

And on the case of knowing who is in Heaven or in Hell (after having died), even the person you think you know may have a hidden (inward) sin or a grave 'mistake' which you will not know. By the way, the finally dead person has died, and cannot change his or her situation of everlasting friendship or separation from God.

When Apostle John heard something(s) in the Book of Revelation and wanted to write it (them) down, he was commanded not to write it (them) (Rev. 10:4). When Apostle Paul went to Heaven (Paradise), there were things he heard and saw, which he was not allowed to say or write (2 Cor. 12:4). Prophet Daniel was told to seal up part of the revelations he got (Dan. 12:4). Even Jesus Christ Himself knew many things which He didn't tell His apostles, as at the time He was with them (Jn 16:12).

However, they all revealed and said many of the things that they heard, saw, and knew! And read what was told Prophet Daniel in that place: he was told to seal it up until the time of the end. This means that at the appointed time, maybe in the time of the end (the last days), they will no longer be sealed up, but be revealed. Also, remember that it also says that knowledge will increase in the last days.

Apostle John, in the Book of Revelation, chapters 2 & 3, mentioned the names of specific churches. Except you want to deceive yourself, Apostle John, mentioning: the church of Ephesus, the church in Smyrna, the church in Pergamos, the church in Thyatira, the church in Sadis, the church in Philadelphia, and the church of the Laodiceans, is the same as mentioning names of specific churches. Therefore, God can mention names of specific churches – it is Scriptural! And that your church's name was not mentioned does not guarantee that it is better than those that might have been mentioned: so, check yourself, and correct anything that is to be corrected.

Now that one person is controlling all the branches of the churches, ministries, or fellowships in a particular country (or even in the whole world), why wouldn't his name be mentioned by God? Apostle Paul rebuked Apostle Peter publicly (Gal. 2:11-14); did he judge or condemn him by that? Was he not trying to put him in the right order out of brotherly love?

If you hadn't known it, Apostle Peter had greater authority than Apostle Paul in the Church. "Do not rebuke an older man (an elder, the KJV), but exhort him as a father (1 Tim. 5:1)," must be interpreted well. Advising Timothy on the administration of the church, Paul said, "Those who are sinning rebuke in the presence of all, that the rest may also fear (1 Tim. 5:20)". What of where an elder is sinning and committing sin that is open to everybody and leading them astray?

Remember that the purpose of rebuking before all, according to the Bible, is for others to fear and avoid doing the same (or similar) things. And Jesus Christ, after saying, "Do not judge (Matt. 7:1)," also said, "Judge with righteous judgment (Jn 7:24)." So, learn to interpret the Word of God well in every situation.

That Apostle Paul wrote more books, and did extended Gospel work among the Gentiles, didn't make him rise above Peter. Think of it, even though Elisha got the double portion of Elijah's anointing (or the Holy Spirit upon him), he didn't rise above Elijah. And you know that Elijah was carried alive to Heaven, while Elisha died from sickness, and had his body decayed. Though John the Baptist didn't perform any recorded healing miracle, yet the miracle-working Moses didn't rise above him. And John the Baptist came in the spirit of Elijah, and not of Elisha!

For those who may say, "Never listen to any of those revelations," if revelations and visions (or listening to them) will be discouraged, because false revelations and visions exist, then reading Christian books and literatures, or listening to preachings and teachings must also be discouraged, since false preachings, teachings, and 'Christian' books and literatures also abound.

And you know that God Himself put preachers and teachers in His Church (even after having given us the Bible and Scriptures), just as He also put prophets too. No one man has all the inspirations, preachings, teachings, and ministries that God wants to pass across to His people. Yes, the devil and his demons can also give dreams, visions, revelations, audible voices, prophecies, and miracles; therefore, always study your Bible to know the Mind of God.

But do not let any person – preacher or what – stop you from hearing what God wants to tell you! And you can be sure that the devil doesn't promote the Cause of God and His Word, when analyzed, summarized, and weighed very well. And those from God don't and can't contradict the Word of God, when well interpreted and understood. In the last days, visions and revelations will abound – both good and bad, God-Sent and devil-sent.

And one of the signs of the last days is that people (even Believers) will harden their hearts from God's Voice and Messages, and try to disprove them with such misleading questions and comments as: (1) "In the Bible when the rich man asked Abraham to send Lazarus to his living brothers, Abraham said, 'If they don't hear Moses and the prophets, neither will they be persuaded though one rise from the dead' (Lk. 16:31)." Was it Abraham or Jesus Christ that made the statement? Certainly, it was Abraham, and not Jesus Christ.

Read the story very well, as told by Jesus Christ. Abraham didn't even have the ability to make Lazarus pass the gulf that was between the Paradise (where they were) and Hades (where the rich man was) to give the rich man a drop of water if Abraham had wanted to send Lazarus to the rich man. How then could that level of decision of sending Lazarus to the rich man's brothers be taken by an ordinary 'dead' (though living) Abraham? Abraham neither had the authority to send Lazarus to them, nor the power to raise Lazarus from the dead.

This was before Jesus Christ's Death and Resurrection, when both Paradise (for righteous men) and Hades (for sinners) were still beneath the earth and 'near' each other; now, only Hades is beneath the earth: Paradise is now Above. Jesus Christ took the righteous people who were in the underneath Paradise up to Above after His Resurrection.

The Bible says, "And Jesus said to him, 'Assuredly, I say to you, today, you will be with Me in Paradise'" (Lk. 23:43). The forgiven criminal was going to the underneath Paradise, from where he was taken to an Above Paradise – Heaven – after the Resurrection of Jesus Christ. And the Word says, "And Jesus cried out again with a loud Voice, and yielded up His Spirit.

"Then, behold, the veil of the temple was torn in two from top to bottom; and the earth quaked, and the rocks were split, and the graves were opened; and many bodies of the Saints who had fallen asleep were raised; and coming out of the graves after His Resurrection, they went into the holy city and appeared to many" (Matt. 27:50-53). Notice that they could only come out of their graves after Jesus Christ's Resurrection. And they were taken to an Above Paradise!

Of course, you can see the level of the rich man's torment in Hell. But I want you to notice that Abraham, based on the rich man's request, told him that his brothers have Moses and the Prophets, that they should hear them. Abraham was saying that the living should obey the Word of God, to avoid going to Hell. Therefore, those who do not obey the Word of God, but live to please the desires of their hearts and minds, will end in Hell.

Then again, when the rich man told Abraham that his brothers would hear if someone rises from the dead to preach to them, Abraham told him that if they did not hear Moses and the Prophets (the Word of God being preached and taught), neither would they be persuaded though someone rose from the dead. First, it was Abraham, and not God or Jesus Christ, who told the rich man that. God knows better than Abraham; and if He knows that people will listen to someone that rises from the dead, He can send the person.

Abraham couldn't even cross the gulf between Paradise and Hell; how then could he send Lazarus back to the earth? He did not have that level of authority or power to send a dead person to the living; but God has the power, ability, and authority to do that. Also, notice that Abraham did not say that nobody (none) could/would hear the dead that rises from the dead, but that the rich man's brothers would not hear. Why would they not hear? Because they had made up their minds on what they wanted; and they might have even scorned the fellow, saying that he did not actually die. (And, being hardened, they could have even said that it was a spirit posing as a human, who was dead, if Lazarus had appeared to them physically).

But many people will believe the story that would be told them by someone who rises from the dead; and many people will still not believe the story told them by someone who rises from the dead, no matter what, because the devil has hardened their hearts and they have made up their minds on what they want. The Bible says, "And behold, there was a great earthquake; for an angel of the Lord descended from Heaven, and came and rolled back the stone from the door, and sat on it.

"His countenance was like lightning, and his clothing as white as snow. And the guards shook for fear of him, and became like dead men. …Now while they were going, behold, some of the guards came into the city and reported to the chief priests all the things that had happened. When they had assembled with the elders and consulted together, they gave a large sum of money to the soldiers,

"Saying, 'Tell them, "His Disciples came at night and stole Him away while we slept." And if this comes to the governor's ears, we will appease him and make you secure.' So they took the money and did as they were instructed; and this saying is commonly reported among the Jews until this day" (Matt. 28:2-15). Can you imagine the hardness of men's (some men's) hearts and minds?

Instead of being grateful to God for saving them from death, and also giving them the opportunity to witness such a great sight, they decided to accept money and spread false story. Who will blame God when He judges and punishes sinners with Eternal Death in His Great Wrath? But His Hands are still open now for whoever will submit to His Word and Grace!

Notice also that it was some of the guards (not all of them) that went to report; some of them might have repented from that incident. Yet the religious chief priests and elders hardened their hearts. Abraham was right when he told the rich man that his brothers would not hear though someone rises from the dead, because whereas some people will accept the testimony of the person who rises from the dead, many will still never believe his testimony, because their minds are made up.

(2) "That person said that she didn't know of this particular church, how then did she say that she heard the church is a holiness church?" Even with common sense, when the person was called by a woman on Monday to enquire about the very church, having given the woman answers, what stops her from asking about the church between Monday and Wednesday before the Lord spoke to her (as she said) on that Wednesday when the statement she made applied?

(3) "This is not the Bible (or even Koran) Jesus." The person was saying that Jesus Christ can't be too harsh with people to punish them the way described by the testifier(s) {or, maybe, the person was speaking of the way one of the testifiers was punished by God}, without knowing that our God, Who is also a Consuming Fire, destroyed everybody with the Flood (except Noah and his family), rained down fire to destroy all the dwellers of Sodom and Gomorrah (except Lot and his family), and even judges Believers with death, because they eat at the Lord's Table unworthily.

(4) "That person said, 'I Am That I Am,' on coming out of the experience; therefore, it can't be from God." When the prophets prophesied in the Name of the Lord, didn't they speak on Behalf of God? (5) "That testifier said that the only woman in Heaven is Mary, the mother of Jesus." When on earth did the person say such a thing? The person actually said that only a small percentage of people that left the earth made Heaven; and out of the people that made Heaven, only a small percentage of them are women, partly due to their attachment to jewellery, indecent dressing, make-up, and weavons/attachments.

(6) "If God really wanted to speak to the world through that person, He would have made her death and coming back public." Do you see the sense of man, when he decides to allow the devil to deceive him? (7) "Those people just used that boy to organize previous testimonies

(reports) from others." Man, why do you want to be lost in Eternal Damnation in Hell Fire? (8) "The (those) testimonies are (were) made to make money." Make money from you by lying to get you ready for Heaven, and ending in Hell themselves?

(9) "Who has gone to Heaven and come back?" They wilfully forget that Apostle Paul and Apostle John went to Heaven and came back. (10) "No one can see God and live." Forgetting that Moses, Isaiah, Ezekiel, and John saw the Similitude of God (and hence saw God), and lived. (11) And one 'preacher' said, "If God wants to tell Believers or people something, He wouldn't use a dead or/and 'risen' person, but He will use pastors (or preachers)." Is that pride or deception?

These are few questions (or related statements) which people asked (or made) to disprove those Divine Revelations. And somebody (or some people) called them DEVELATIONS, trying to indicate that they came from the devil. People, why do you want satan, the devil, to take you to Hell Fire? And somebody may say that the Bible is our final authority (which is a very true statement).

But why do very many different persons, Believers, preachers, teachers, and ministers all say that the Bible is our final authority and standard, and also declare that they are preaching and teaching the raw and undiluted Word of God; and yet, in practice, they preach, teach, and practice different things? This is the more reason why you should maintain a tender heart, and allow the Holy Spirit speak to you.

Yes, the Bible is the final say and standard for all of us. Yet the things in the Bible were got by visions, revelations, dreams, audible voices, and inward inspirations/revelations. Can the Bible tell you which school to attend, which supermarket to shop in, or which vehicle to board? The Bible goes alongside with the Leading of the Holy Spirit.

However, we must disregard whatever contradicts the Bible. But true reports do not contradict the Bible; rather, their reports promote the Bible, except when you had allowed yourself to be loaded/filled with whatever false and misapplied teachings and doctrines you desire, because they suit your flesh; and you don't want to change.

The Bible tells us about Heaven and Hell: what we should do to gain Heaven, and what we must avoid to avoid Hell. But many Believers don't even regard and obey the Bible as they should. This is why God, seeing that many people have entered (and are heading towards) Hell, is giving more revelations and visions to spur us into taking the Bible serious (or more serious).

Someone may say, "How do you know that they have actually gone to Heaven?" Does asking that question not confirm and guarantee that God did not tell you that they didn't go to Heaven? And if you say that you were told that they didn't go to Heaven or/and Hell, who told you that − God or satan?

Many of those testimonies have been shared (or posted) in the Internet. Things shared in the Internet are read by many people. If one person who reads the post(s) gets and receives the Message being passed across, he may run with it, by spreading it to others; by that, the knowledge is more widely spread. There are millions of people who are following some preachers and ministers, even those outside their ministries and churches; and many of them think that because they prophesy and perform miracles, then all the things that they preach, teach, and practice are right.

But this is not true, in the ultimate sense. Therefore, instead of keeping quiet, and allowing them to follow anyone to Hell Fire, while Jesus Christ is crying for the abundance of lost souls, we are to stand up for God and warn the people. Much of the corruption in the church-world today is because people say that they want to mind their own business, even when the Lord wants them to mind His Own Business.

We are labourers together with God; and we have divisions and inter-mingleness of labour in the Kingdom of God. One may receive a Message from God; another may run with the Message to spread it; while another may be involved with fighting the devil, who may want to stop or hinder the spreading of the Message; another may be involved with taking care of those who were wounded by the devil in the course of doing their duty in the Kingdom; yet, we are working for the Same God.

Brother, if you had not known it, it is not an impossible thing that any of those testifiers can still backslide, if we don't give them any helping hand and support (but our God will hold them strong in Him!). Some of those testifiers are spiritual babies, who don't know the Bible well; and they need those who would prove, by the Bible, that their revelations are Biblical. I remember what Jesus Christ told one converted Muslim when he was taken to Heaven (or beyond the earth) and shown/told some things.

The Muslim (who turned to a preacher) had been a very rich Muslim, who was also involved in many secret societies (his conversion and testimony were not hidden and secret; he is from Northern Nigeria, Sokoto, and had Saudi Arabian citizenship: And Muslims fought hard to kill him after his conversion, because of the many things he exposed about Islam).

Now, after showing/telling him some things, and giving him a commission, Jesus Christ asked him, saying, "Will you be faithful to do what I have told you to do?" He answered Him with a Yes. The Lord Jesus Christ told him that He was asking him, because He had taken many people, both from his country (Nigeria) and from other countries of the world, and shown them extra-terrestrial things (like Heaven and Hell); yet, after they had gone back to the world, after some times, some (or many) of them started thinking that it was just a dream that they had.

And we will not sit back and watch those, who don't want to hear the Spirit of God, destroy these Heavenly Messages. So, we will not fold our hands and leave the testifiers stranded; but we will (by the Help of the Holy Spirit) use the Bible and inward inspirations to support and help them.

The Church is marching on; and gates of Hades shall not prevail against the Church of Jesus Christ, the Son of the Living God! The issue is: whether you yourself, as a preacher, was mentioned or not, or the church you attend was mentioned or not, let each and every one of us correct himself/herself of whatever is Biblically wrong — of whatever is wrong in the Sight of God. And for those who might have been mentioned, what have they done to correct themselves? God is calling, because He loves us!

Also, know that the churches and ministers that might have been mentioned are just samples, because there are thousands of needing-revival, requiring-purging, backslidden, half-bred, falsely indoctrinated, fake, satanic, demonic, and false ministers, apostles, prophets, evangelists, pastors, teachers, deacons, elders, musicians, church workers, church members, churches, ministries, and fellowships in our different countries and the whole world at large.

Let me include some things the Lord Jesus Christ told the seven churches in the second and third chapters of the Book of Revelation. The seven churches were in Asia Minor. They included the churches in Ephesus, in Smyrna, in Pergamos, in Thyatira, in Sardis, in Philadelphia, and in Laodicea. The churches were in different states of spirituality and carnality, just as the churches of today. The Lord had to encourage them, and warn them, by the hand of Apostle John.

The Lord was happy with those who did well (or, their good deeds); and He was unhappy with those who did not do well (or, their evil deeds/conditions). Even some who did well still had areas they had to correct. Because He desired that all of them do well, He had to send Messages to them according to their works and needs. The Messages sent to these churches are of benefit to us in this present age, if we open our hearts and minds to the Holy Spirit, and allow Him to purge, sanctify, consecrate, and edify us, so that we may become what the Lord wants us to be.

He was not happy with some of them; and He rebuked them. Some of them had left their first love. Some held to the doctrine of Balaam, who taught Balak to put a stumbling block before the children of Israel, to eat things sacrificed to idols, and to commit sexual immorality. They had also those who held the doctrine of the Nicolaitans, which thing He hates (hated). They allowed one Jezebel, who called herself a prophetess, to teach and seduce His Servants to commit sexual immorality and eat things sacrificed to idols.

Some had name that they were alive, but they were dead. He did not find the works of many of them perfect before God. Many of them were neither cold nor hot. The Lord wished that they were either cold or hot. And because they were lukewarm, and neither cold nor hot, He was going to vomit them out of His Mouth.

Some said that they were rich and had become wealthy, and had need of nothing. They did not know that they were wretched, miserable, poor, blind, and naked. No wonder the Bible says that we should neither be wise in our own eyes nor lean on our own understanding (Prov. 3:5-7). There is a way that seems good to a man, but the end of that road is death and destruction (Prov. 14:12). If we judge ourselves, we would not be judged (1 Cor. 11:31).

He warned them to remember where they had fallen from. He told them to repent and do the first works, else He would come to them quickly and remove their lampstand from its place – unless they repented. He told (and tells) anyone that had (and has) ear to hear to hear what the Spirit said (and is saying) to the churches. He advised them to not fear any of those things which they were about to suffer.

Indeed, the devil was about to throw some of them into prison, that they might be tested; and they were to have tribulation ten days. He commanded them to be faithful until death. The Lord told many of them to repent, or else He would come to them quickly and would fight against them with the sword of His Mouth. If Jesus Christ rebuked those churches, for them to repent and become faithful Believers, who are you to get annoyed when God decides to rebuke you? He rebukes and chastens those that He loves.

By the way, neither me nor anyone needs to approve or recognize the testimonies before they become true; for none of us is God! This race needs God's Grace and Mercy. Even as I write, I myself needs God's Grace and Mercy to make it to the end, because these last days are perilous. As an apostle who has evangelistic and teaching ministries, I need the grace to do what I teach.

When you teach or preach the Word of God sincerely, you teach and preach under the Anointing of the Holy Spirit. But when you finish, you have become that 'small' and 'ordinary' Christian, who must also discipline himself and bring his body under subjection to his spirit, to be able to obey God like every other Believer. To this end, Apostle Paul said, "But I discipline my body and bring it into subjection, lest, when I have preached to others, I myself should become disqualified" (1 Cor. 9:27).

Now, I say these things for the wellbeing of Christianity: If all these people who troop to crusades, ministries, and churches live to please God with perfect hearts, I tell you that Jesus Christ may be coming sooner! I would want to have a church of one hundred members, where about ninety of them are ready for the Coming of Jesus Christ, than to pastor ten thousand members, of which God may not even find five people who are ready for the Coming of His Son.

And it is better to have a mini crusade, where people sincerely repent and are faithful to God, than to organize a mega crusade, where thousands come out for altar call and go back to live however they want. Therefore, we evangelists, if we are troubled by the decadence in Christianity, knowing that many people trust us, should also use the opportunity we have to, at least, point out these things to, at least, the ministers and church-workers.

Some ministers say that they have special revelations on particular areas. Well, I myself have the revelation to help people understand the Truth of the Word of God and to follow the Leading of God's Holy Spirit. It is like I used to think a certain man of God was a 'holiness preacher/teacher' until listened to some of his messages I collected from one of his pastors. Then I understood that he is not a 'holiness preacher/teacher,' but a man of God who teaches the Word of God (of which holiness, which he emphasizes on, is included) and also demonstrates the Spirit and power.

The man demonstrates (has demonstrated) great miracles, signs, and wonders that many of the people we celebrate haven't done. But the thing is that he doesn't like proclaiming himself but God, Who does (did) those things; and he found out early enough that without holiness, no eye shall see the Lord. He found out that if one has all the miracles, healings, breakthroughs, deliverances, and anointing, and loses Heaven, the fellow lost everything and gained nothing.

Therefore, no matter the area you may say that you are called to 'specialize' on, preach, teach, and practice the Whole Counsel of God. And whatever we may have or achieve, we are nothing before God; and we must know that without holiness no one can see the Lord. Let us and those who follow us be aware of this real Truth.

Some people 'want' revelations, visions, and prophecies to be tested by the Word of God. Those people know whether they are sincere or whether they want to deceive others, having been deceived. I am a strong believer in this approach, because it is Biblical. The Bible says, "Prove all things; hold on to that which is good (1 Thes. 5:21). Beloved, do not believe every spirit, but test the spirits, whether they are of God... (1 Jn 4:1). Let two or three prophets speak, and let the others judge (1 Cor. 14:29)."

To explain some things, Jude speaks of sinners being reserved for the blackness of darkness forever (Jude 1:13). Jesus Christ Himself speaks of the sons of the Kingdom being cast into the Outer Darkness; and there will be weeping and gnashing of teeth (Matt. 8:12). Of course, you are already familiar with the heat of the fire of Hell. The Word says that their worm does not die, and the fire is not quenched (Mk 9:44).

Hell is a combination of fire, worms, darkness, etc. This does not mean, however, that you cannot see/notice/recognize someone in Hell, because you are more sensitive in Hell than you are on earth. This is why your spirit and soul can know things you didn't really perceive with your physical senses. Some people say that since they will be many in Hell Fire, they will put off the fire of Hell; but they don't know that the God, Who can mix fire and darkness, knows the frequency and magnitude of the fire which can comfortably absorb even trillions of entities! I hope you know that human beings have neither filled up the earth's surface nor used up all the oxygen, in spite of thousands of years of occupying the earth!

You have got to know that the time of the demons has not come; hence they spoke to Jesus Christ, saying, "Have You come to torment us before the time?" (Matt. 8:29). It is not the devil that formed Hell; it is God that formed it. It is not the devil that sends people to Hell; but God is the One Who sends people to Hell, as a way of punishing sinners and the disobedient. Even though a demon may carry or take you to Hell; but it is just because God has sent you there by releasing you to them. But on the case of men, it is appointed unto men to die once, and after that the judgment (Heb. 9:27).

Yes, the fire of Hell may not touch the demons now, because their time has not come; but when their time comes, God will either change their bodies to feel the effect of the fire, remove/neutralize the power that makes them not to feel the heat, or change the power and mode of the fire to burn them. Or, don't you know that even now someone can enter into physical fire and not feel the effect, because of demonic and satanic powers, after having performed some satanic rituals?

Even on the positive side, the fire of Nebuchadnezzar refused the bodies of Shadrach, Meshach, Abed-Nego, because God was there with them. And remember that the Bible says that Death and Hell will be cast into the Lake of Fire (Rev. 20:14). Therefore, if the demons don't feel the fire of Hell, they will certainly burn, cry, wail, and weep in the fire of the Lake of Fire. Understood?

Know that Hell or Hades is a temporary place of suffering for the dead sinner. The Lake of Fire, which the devils and sinners will be put into later, is actually the permanent place of extreme suffering for both the devils and human sinners. And the devil and his demons, for now, may be tormenting those who are presently suffering in Hell. But at the fulness of time, the devil and his fallen angels and demons will be cast into the Lake of Fire. And any person whose name is not found written in the Book of Life will also be cast into the Lake of Fire.

It is true that the time of fallen angels and demons has not come; but when their time comes, they will know that God has the kind of fire, that is available in the Lake of Fire and

Brimstone, which will burn and torment them to wail and cry. The Bible says, "The devil, who deceived them, was cast into the Lake of Fire and Brimstone where the beast and the false prophet are. And they will be tormented day and night forever and ever.

"Then I saw a Great White Throne and Him Who sat on it, from Whose Face the earth and the heaven fled away. And there was found no place for them. And I saw the dead, small and great, standing before God, and books were opened. And another Book was opened, which is the Book of Life. And the dead were judged according to their works, by things which were written in the books.

"The sea gave up the dead who were in it, and Death and Hades delivered up the dead who were in them. And they were judged, each one according to his works. Then Death and Hades were cast into the Lake of Fire. This is the Second Death. And anyone not found written in the Book of Life was cast into the Lake of Fire" (Rev. 20:10-15).

As for whether Jesus Christ can accompany someone to Hell to show the person something in Hell, as someone said: "How can Jesus, as holy as He is, enter Hell with the guy, as if they are going on excursion; and don't you know that people in Hell can't see God's Face, how come the woman had the opportunity to be asking Jesus for forgiveness while she was already in Hell?" Bible and spiritual knowledge will tell you that it is possible.

If satan could come to where the sons of God came to present themselves to God (Job 1:6), and even spoke to God, how can't someone in Hell see Jesus Christ when He goes there on a mission to show someone mysteries about Hell? Yes, sinners cannot see God's Face; but you have to know that even though Jesus Christ is God, yet He is the Son of God and Mediator between God and men; and many sinners who couldn't see God saw Jesus Christ while He was on earth.

God created Hell, and He can enter there if He wants to; and the fire and heat of Hell cannot touch Him, even as the Fourth Person (Who had the Form of the Son of God) (Dan. 3:25) entered the fire of Nebuchadnezzar. And remember that God is everywhere (though His Manifest Presence is not everywhere). The Word says, "Where can I go from Your Spirit? Or where can I flee from Your Presence? If I ascend into Heaven, You are there; if I make my bed in Hell, behold, You are there" (Psa. 139:7-8).

The magnitude of the pain, either from the heat of the fire of Hell or the torments of the demons of Hell, is irrelevant for now; because Hell is a place of great suffering and torment; and no one will want to suffer, either from the heat or from the torments.

No one church is the only bearer of the Truth of the Word of God. And it is not only the churches that might have been mentioned for disobedience or rebellion that are taking their members to Hell by their teachings and practices.

Evil people do not have Eternal Life but eternal death. Men's souls are eternal; and demons and devils are eternal beings also: Therefore, they will suffer forever in the Lake of Fire. We see that Jesus Christ states in the Book of Mark that their worm does not die and the fire is not quenched (Mk 9:44). Did (Does) our Lord lie when He said (says) that the fire is not quenched? Hell Fire is forever!

To clear doubts, the Bible itself says that Hell Fire is eternal (and not just forever). Let me say this, because of those who say that Hell Fire is forever but not eternal. Yes, everlasting or forever can stand for a period of time or for eternity. Everlasting or forever actually means till the stated time expires, and eternity means that there is no time limit.

But the Bible tells us specifically that the everlasting and forever of Hell Fire (the Lake of Fire) is eternity. The Word says, "...are set forth as an example, suffering the vengeance of eternal fire" (Jude 1:7). Therefore, Hell Fire is everlasting, forever, and eternal.

Yes, evil people go to Hell or Hades immediately after death, even though there is a corridor between death and either Heaven or Hell. And some people have actually come back from that corridor without either entering Heaven or Hell, but having seen them; though God actually takes some people (either in vision or in death) to Heaven or/and Hell to show them things they will report to the children of men when they come back.

He does these things, because He loves men and does not want any person to enter Hell. But many people are so hardened like the brothers of the rich man, of whom Abraham said, "If they do not hear Moses and the Prophets, neither will they be persuaded though one rise from the dead" (Lk. 16:31).

On the case of the possibility of increasing the heat or fire of Hell, God has different functions for His creatures, including angels. But have you ever seen it in the Bible where King Nebuchadnezzar told his men to increase his own fire seven times? (Dan. 3:19). Even in physics, though water boils at 100 degrees Celsius (which temperature human beings cannot withstand), yet it takes higher degrees of Celsius temperature to melt aluminum or iron into liquid form, not talk of vapuorizing any of them.

For one particular testifier, at the point of her death, she was not born again, and so was left to the power of the demons; and demons torture people who are dead in Hell, which God formed for the torment of the disobedient. Yes, there are torture places in the kingdom of darkness for those who disobey their rules; but these are not (necessarily) the same place where those who are dead are tortured.

And after the devil and his fallen angels have tortured those that go contrary to their commands, when they actually die physically, they go to be punished and tortured in God's Own torture place, which is Hell (though devils increase people's torments there). The fact that there are prisons and death sentences and executions by men for criminals and murderers does not negate God's Own 'prison' and Hell.

Yes, the final Judgment has not come; but dying without Jesus Christ, or in sin, is as good as having been judged. God sees differently, and says, "...but he who does not believe is condemned already..." (Jn 3:16). Now and the final Judgment are the same, as long as the fellow is dead and appointed for judgment. Therefore, a sinner who dies now goes to Hell (and even if you hang for some time, you will still go to Hell after some time).

And even when you are still alive and have made up your mind that nothing can make you change your evil ways, then you are as good as having been judged, in a way, because the Bible says that it is the Word of God that will judge people on the Last Day; though with God, nothing shall be impossible.

Are there not many agents of the kingdom of darkness, who, though will experience what should show them that God's Power is superior to the power of devil, yet they do not change or embrace Jesus Christ, because their hearts (minds) have been hardened by satan? And satan can also harden the heart (mind) of someone, who may be carrying Bible in pretence (or, might have even known Christ).

When one particular testifier spoke of a force pulling her out of Hell, that was God's Power that pulled her out of that torment, because of His Mercy, so that she could come back to the earth, repent, accept Jesus Christ, and testify. Remember that God will have mercy on whom He chooses to have mercy on.

As for cleansing, you have got to know that our God is high and highly lifted up! He doesn't do everything by Himself: He has assigned different functions to different beings, including men and angels. When the devil rebelled against Him, He didn't fight the devil; that would have been giving much credit to satan. What God just did was to empower Michael the archangel and His warring angels; and they expelled the former Lucifer from Heaven.

God used one of the seraphim to touch Isaiah's tongue or mouth with the coal of fire (live coal) so that his iniquity was taken away and his sin purged (Isa. 6:6-7). When satan withstood Joshua, the high priest, because he was wearing filthy garments, the Angel of the Lord (God Himself) spoke and said to those who stood before Him, saying, "Take away the filthy garments from him" (Zech. 3).

I tell you that if she had not come back to life, she couldn't have been saved, because God cannot contradict His Word. However, God sees the end from the beginning. This is why, speaking to Abraham, He said, "I have made you father of many nations," when as yet he didn't have Isaac. He didn't say, "I will make you father of many nations." God had (has) a special mission for her, out His Love and Mercy, not because she is better than others.

This is why God can overshadow His chosen vessels with His Spirit, even before they actually submit to Jesus Christ; but if they refuse to submit, He will destroy them. Did God not call and speak to Adam even after he had sinned? God created and formed all things; therefore, He can relate with sinners (in some ways), just as He spoke to satan himself on the case of Job. Angels of God protect even the unbelievers to an extent; if not, the devil would have wiped them out.

Our 'headache' shouldn't be whether we will be in Heaven or in the New Earth. Our concern should be to please God and make His Kingdom at last. Angels come to earth from Heaven; and they also go to Heaven from the earth. And Jesus Christ says that we shall be like the angels, if we are counted worthy for the Resurrection from the dead (Lk. 20:35-36). Do you think that it is not possible for us to live both in Heaven and the New Earth?

In Hell Fire, worms, which do not die, eat (pass through) people's bodies. I have already stated that Hell Fire is eternal, as the Book of Jude tells us. God told Adam that he will die in the day that he eats of the forbidden fruit. Did Adam cease to exist on the day he ate the forbidden fruit? But he died spiritually, being separated from the Life of God. There are spiritual death (separation from God), physical death (ceasing to live physically), and the Second Death (Eternal Torment in Hell Fire or the Lake of Fire).

Sin separates you from God (spiritual death); and at death, spiritual death leads to eternal suffering of God's Punishment (Second Death) in Hell Fire. The Bible says, "...are set forth as an example, suffering the vengeance of Eternal Fire" (Jude 1:7). If you had been thinking that when people are cast into the Lake of Fire, then they are annihilated forever by way of being cut off from existence, then you had been making a great mistake.

And I tell you, if it all ends with the Judgment, then sinners somehow may assume they didn't 'lose.' If you 'enjoy' your life on earth, living in disobedience to God, and after the Judgment you cease to exist, do you think you 'really lost' anything, though losing Heaven is losing a very great thing? Then many more people can start living however they want; after all, when they are judged, they cease to exist! Then why didn't God wipe out the entire human race and create another set of good human beings?

The Bible says, "And they shall go forth and look upon the corpses of the men who have transgressed against Me. For their worm does not die, and their fire is not quenched. They shall be an abhorrence to all flesh" (Isaiah 66:24). So, God is going to leave a reminder for the good and faithful resurrected humans and the angels, in order to discourage any future disobedience or rebellion!

If you thought that when satan and his cohorts are cast into the Lake of Fire, then they will cease to exist, then what did they 'really lose'? And why did God allow them to continue to exist in the world, deceiving people and causing problems for human beings, and trying to destroy God's Plans? When then will they taste their torment? Don't misinterpret the Bible. The Bible didn't say that Hell and death have an end, but that they will be cast into the Lake of Fire; and the Lake of Fire is forever and eternal, according to the Book of Jude.

God does not tell us to follow man-made denomination; anyone whose preaching or teaching is not focused on the Kingdom of God, but on denomination, belongs to the group which will not make Heaven, but Hell. The fellow is not working for God, but for satan. However, be careful that you are not misinterpreting the preaching, teaching, action, or practice of some of those testifiers.

When you are lying down and sleeping, you don't know what is happening around you; yet you see yourself doing or saying things in your dream: God has used dreams to tell you that you are not all about that sleeping body, but you have got a soul and a spirit; why not be wise and learn from your dream experiences? Or you think your dreams are meaningless and non-existent?

When Adam lost the Life of God by disobedience, it was enough death; when somebody is tormented in the Lake of Fire, along with the devil and his fallen angels, that is great death in operation! When you die without Jesus Christ, or in sin, you are as good as having been judged (Jn 3:18). God, being the God of order, has given time to all humans (who die after some period of time), and when that time expires, He will call all of them (living and dead) for the Final Judgment.

You are actually judged at your death, and counted as holy, righteous, and justified, or sinful, evil, and condemned; the Final Judgment is actually for formality (Heb. 9:27; Jn 3:18).

The things that we need to know have been given and revealed to us. Even God taking people (through visions and death) to show them Heaven or/and Hell is just because we don't take His Word serious, because those things are found in the Bible, and can be known if we are open to the Spirit of God.

Concerning the resurrection from the dead at the Last Day, you need to ask yourself: "Is it resurrection from what/where to what/where?" Your soul does not die; so also is your spirit. Those people that they said they saw in Hell are not there with their physical bodies, but with their souls (which do not die). And just as you feel the effect of your enjoyment or suffering in your dreams, that is how you will feel the joy of Heaven (Paradise) or the suffering of Hell, when you die, as you wait for the resurrection.

Now, that resurrection is the resurrection of your soul putting on physical body again to be judged physically by God, because you existed as a physical being. But that is not now. Of course, before the Final Judgment and expiration of man's time, there would have been the Rapture of the Saints and the Millennium Reign of Jesus Christ with His faithful Saints.

But, whereas the Saints will resurrect with glorified bodies, the sinners will resurrect with the ordinary fallen bodies. Prophet Daniel said: "And many of those who sleep in the dust of the earth shall awake, some to Everlasting Life, some to shame and everlasting contempt" (Dan. 12:2). Here the Bible says that the state of both the righteous and the unrighteous (after resurrection) will be everlasting, but opposite to each other (just as light and darkness, or good and evil, are opposite to each other).

Jesus Christ Himself tells us that in Hell Fire, you do not cease to exist, but you will be going through on-going suffering, torment, and pain; and you will have your full sensitivity (even greater) there. Refer to the Book of Luke, chapter sixteen, and verses nineteen to thirty-one.

If you gain the whole world, and lose your soul in the end, you gained nothing. To tell you the truth, if you have all the miracles and prophecies you want from God, and in the end, hear, "Get behind Me, you worker of iniquity," you lost everything. If you live contrary to the Word of God, you better get ready for the Coming of Jesus Christ, because that your prophet or pastor, who tells you what the devil inspired him to say, will not save you from the Wrath of God.

God is no respecter of persons, whether you carry Bible or call Jesus. "But why do you call Me, 'Lord, Lord,' and do not do what I say?" (Lk. 6:46). And for those who put their trust of being saved on church attendance, baptism, communion, full membership, payment of big tithes and big donations to church projects, and friendship with the pastor, somebody should tell you that you are on your way to Hell Fire without a living relationship with Jesus Christ as your Lord and personal Saviour, and living to please Him.

Those of you who spread pornographic images in the internet, Hell Fire does not respect film actors, actresses, producers, and directors: get ready, because you will come to realize that worldly fame is satanic deception! God loves you and does not take delight in your perishing in Hell Fire; but if God turned His Face away from Jesus Christ Himself when He was carrying the sins of the world at the Cross of Calvary, who are you that God will allow you into His Kingdom with sin?

If you want to know the terror of Hell Fire, look at the Suffering of Jesus Christ (God Himself). And for those of you who don't believe in Hell Fire, no matter what you chose to believe, you will come to terms with the reality in the end. Let no one deceive you; and don't deceive anyone!

Many are called, but few are chosen; and it is not all those who are chosen that will be glorified, because the Bible says that it is the faithful that will be glorified. Therefore, among the few that are chosen, it is the fewer, who will be faithful and obedient, that will be glorified. The Word says, "Enter by the narrow gate, for wide is the gate and broad is the way that leads to destruction, and there are many who go in by it.

"Because narrow is the gate and difficult is the way which leads to life, and there are few who find it. Beware of false prophets, who come to you in sheep's clothing, but inwardly they are ravenous wolves. You will know them by their fruits..." (Matt. 7:13-16). It is not by their miracles or prophecies, because many false prophets will rise up and deceive many. False christs and false prophets will rise and show great signs and wonders to deceive, if possible, even the Elect (Matt. 24:11,24).

And because lawlessness (iniquity) will abound in the last days, the love of many will grow cold. But he who endures to the end shall be saved (verses 12 & 13). The Bible states: "For such are false apostles, deceitful workers, transforming themselves into apostles of Christ. And no wonder! For satan himself transforms himself into an angel of light. Therefore it is no great thing if his ministers transform themselves into ministers of righteousness, whose end will be according to their works (2 Cor. 11:13-15).

"Now the Spirit expressly says that in latter times some will depart from the Faith, giving heed to deceiving spirits and doctrines of demons, speaking lies in hypocrisy, having their own conscience seared with a hot iron (1 Tim. 4:1-2). For the time will come when they will not endure Sound Doctrine, but according to their own desires, because they have itching ears, they will heap up for themselves teachers; and they will turn their ears away from the Truth, and be turned aside to fables (2 Tim. 4:4).

"Take heed to yourself and to the Doctrine. Continue in them, for in doing this you will save both yourself and those who hear you (1 Tim. 4:16). But there were also false prophets among the people, even as there will be false teachers among you, who will secretly bring in destructive heresies, even denying the Lord Who bought them, and bring on themselves swift destruction. And many will follow their destructive ways, because of whom the way of Truth will be blasphemed" (2 Pet. 2:1-2).

I maintain that, by my understanding of the Scriptures and the inward conviction by the Holy Spirit of the Living God, that perming, jerry curling, or frying your hair (male or female) and the use of weavons and wigs are sinful, satanic, demonic, of mermaid, against God, anti-Christ, worldly, and Hell-attracting. Why? Because, when you perm your hair or use weavon, you are accusing God (consciously or unconsciously) that He is an imperfect Creator.

And it is inferiority complex, which says that the hair of the whites is superior to the hair of the blacks, that makes people insult our Awesome God. There is no difference between frying your hair and bleaching your skin (which some people do, to tell God that He is stupid for giving them the skin complexion that they have), whether or not you agree with the Truth.

Of course, you can still repent and correct your ways before death or the Coming of our Lord Jesus Christ; because, except you repent, you cannot enter Heaven but Hell, because no sin can enter Heaven. That is iniquity and living in sin. Many people say that they don't believe in Hell Fire: whatever you choose to believe, you will come to terms with the reality of Hell Fire in the end; then, you will have no second chance, but to suffer everlasting suffering in Hell Fire.

But if you will listen to the Voice of the Holy Spirit, you will escape the punishment of Hell Fire and eternal separation from the Almighty God. Many people like the thought that Hell Fire doesn't exist in order to comfort themselves in their sins. Who is satan, the devil? Was he not the Lucifer who was very close to God and well-honoured? Who was Adam? Was he not the one that was made in God's Image and represented God on earth? How come two of them became God's enemies?

Two of them, who were holy and perfect before God, made themselves sinners and God's enemies by pride and disobedience. Whoever makes himself a friend of the world makes himself an enemy of God (Jas 4:4). It doesn't matter how long you have been a Believer, how much of the Bible you know, how big your church or ministry is in people's eyes (because all those multitude of people may be going to Hell Fire with you), or how much anointing you have.

Perhaps you may need to be reminded that God made an ass to speak to Balaam in a human voice; and He used a heathen King Cyrus to build His Temple in Jerusalem. What is very different if God uses you to perform miracles? Maybe, you need to be told that Jesus Christ Himself said that, because of iniquity, He will reject many people who had prophesied, cast out demons, and done many wonders in His Name (Matt. 7:21-23).

And the Lord says, "STRIVE to enter through the NARROW GATE, for many, I say to you, will SEEK to ENTER and WILL NOT BE ABLE" (Lk. 13:24). Brothers and sisters, don't be deceived by all these miracles, falling down, breakthroughs, and deliverances. Healings, deliverances, signs, wonders, miracles, breakthroughs, and prosperity are small things to God. The One Who made the whole universe, what can He not do? His Concern is your soul, because He has determined, by an everlasting decision, that no sin, unrighteousness, or iniquity will cross the gate of Heaven.

The Business of God is drawing people to Jesus Christ, and getting them prepared for the Rapture and Heaven. Every other thing is extra and secondary. Think of it! God loved man so much that He sent His Son to die for men. Why didn't He wipe out all sins, since His Son has died? Why does He still require that you MUST believe in His Son?

If you have not understood the horror and penalty of Hell Fire, consider the terrible nature of Hell Fire by considering that Jesus Christ allowed Himself to be insulted and crucified by ordinary men, so that men will not enter Hell Fire. Just as God values a soul more than all the gold and silver of this world, He did not consider His Life dear to Him; but He gave His Life up for you, so that you will not end in Hell Fire.

But if you chose to spend everlasting torment and punishment in Hell Fire, God will execute it for you. Of all the multitude of people in the world in Noah's time, only Noah and his family were saved from the Flood that destroyed the whole world. It was only Lot and his family that escaped the fire from Heaven, of all the multitude of people in Sodom and Gomorrah.

Though God delivered all the Israelites with a Mighty Hand, and they experienced Divine and supernatural manifestations, yet, God destroyed all of them (who had come to age) that sinned against Him, except Joshua and Caleb. And even in this dispensation, He has told us that it is only few people that will be saved. Why? Is it because He does not love them? No!

Rather, it is because men (even when they call themselves Believers and preachers) are stubborn and obstinate; they choose what they want to obey, and despise God's Word and Spirit. But the Word of God has this for the Believers: "You believe that there is One God. You do well. Even the demons believe – and tremble!" (Jas 2:19). God will wait for everybody at His Judgment.

And those of you women that design your blouses to show us your breasts and armpits, get ready to face the Judgment Seat of God. Those of you that cut and divide your skirts to show us your laps, to help and encourage the devil to spread his lust-wave, prepare for your eternity.

Those who paint their faces and wear artificial nails, encouraging the activities of satan, who invented those lipsticks and cortexes, what will you do if when you appear before God's Judgment, He tells you, "You said these things didn't matter, but they matter to Me; depart to Hell Fire, which is prepared for satan and those that obey him"? And any design of dressing (male or female) that glorifies the devil and encourages his desires and works are from him.

The spirit of the antichrist tells people to combine Christianity with worldliness; they decide what they want, and use Bible quotations to deaden their consciences (as satan quoted the

Scriptures to Jesus Christ). And, inasmuch as many people dress and appear like Godly ladies and women, while keeping hatred, bitterness, unforgiveness, etc in their hearts (which will still send you to Hell Fire if you don't repent), how much more will the inside of many of those who don't care about their outward appearance be worse!

When you hear some preachers say that they preach and teach the Word of God, you need to pity them; because they have been blinded by the devil to put materials things before the souls of men. In the last chapter of the Bible, the Word says, "He who is unjust, let him be unjust still; he who is filthy, let him be filthy still; he who is righteous, let him be righteous still; he who is holy, let him be holy still.

"'And behold, I am coming quickly, and My Reward is with Me, to give to every one according to his work'" (Rev. 22:11-12). THE WISE WILL LISTEN TO THE SPIRIT OF GOD, BUT THE STUBBORN WILL LAUGH OVER THESE THINGS AND RIDICULE THE LORD; BUT WAIT TILL THE COMING OF JESUS CHRIST!

To be sincere with you, if you have all the blessing, anointing and falling down, deliverance, healing, breakthrough, and miracles that God can give to any person, if you lose Heaven, you lost everything and gained nothing. Let no one deceive you: Many agents of the kingdom of darkness pretend to be ministers of Jesus Christ; and the devil uses them to keep people's focus out of Heaven, but on earthly and material things.

Even, many ministers who were called by God have been led astray by the devil, so that they are used to deceive other Believers by making them to set their minds on the things of the earth. Study the Bible by yourself to find out what God wants from you: what you should do and avoid. Be open to the Spirit of God, and don't harden your heart to what you want, so that He can lead and direct you to please God. Jesus Christ died for us; what have we done for Him?

The highest achievement you can have in life is that you are in Christ, and when Jesus Christ looks at you, He doesn't see any impediment which can withhold you from being raptured if He were to come now! Therefore, let us cleanse ourselves from all filthiness (sin) of the flesh and spirit, perfecting holiness in the Fear of God (2 Cor. 7:1).

The highest thing that separates God from satan is holiness; and this is why the angels sing, "Holy, Holy, Holy, Lord God Almighty..." and not, "Power, Power, Power, Holy Lord God...." God will allow you into His Heaven if you are poor, sick, and suffering without sin; but if you have all the miracles, deliverance, breakthrough, success, prosperity, healing, health, and prophecies with sin or disobedience, He will tell you: "Without holiness, no eye shall see the Lord."

If you love the Lord, then keep His Commandments (Jn 14:15). And why will you, after you have spoken in tongues, prophesied, cast out demons, and done mighty works in His Name, hear, "I never knew you; depart from Me, you who practice lawlessness"? A word is enough for the wise!

Satan, the devil, has blinded and gripped the Roman Catholics with idolatry, and taken captive many Pentecostals and charismatics with worldliness and it-doesn't-matter. Some people are concerned with, "Do not judge." But if you knew the millions of people who are going to Hell Fire, because of false, fake, half-bred, unbiblical, selfish, hardened, satanic, and demonic apostles, prophets, evangelists, pastors, teachers, and ministers, you would have long gone to seek God's Face in Bible study and prayer with fasting.

Others are of, "Let the wheat and the tares grow together till the Last Day," without knowing that the wheat and the tares will always grow together till the Last Day. But God Himself has sent many people to emphasize strongly that not all the plants are wheat; but there are tares among the wheat and in the church-world, so that people can decide beforehand whether to be a wheat (and plan for Heaven) or a tare (and wait for Hell)!

However, still know that it is not all supernatural revelations that come from God and His Spirit. In these days when God is revealing mysteries and hidden things to many people, to warn us of eternal realities (though the Bible contains eternal realities in it), know that the devil will also be giving his own revelations and visions to people.

The purpose of the devil in doing this is to lead men to sin and stubbornness, to put confusion among Christians, and to make Believers to not believe God-given revelations and visions. Originals are imitated; but we do not have to do away with the original because of the imitation!

Also, if you are listening to a testimony of someone telling you what Jesus Christ told him (or what he believes that Jesus Christ told him), you should be sensitive enough to separate (detect) what the Lord Jesus Christ told him and what he himself might add, in attempt to explain something to clarify issues.

However, many times, visions may be symbolic with the actual interpretation being given to the person in his heart/spirit. This is one danger of dreams' interpretations; some people have even made books of interpretations of different kinds of dreams.

Whereas they may be right (or nearly right) in many cases, yet some things are symbolic; and they can mean different things to different people. But even at that, the person who had the dream, vision, or even heard the audible voice, can add or subtract something(s) in attempt to tell us what he received, consciously or unconsciously.

A Biblical example may be seen in the about three places in the Book of Acts of the Apostles, where the encounter of Saul (Paul) with Jesus Christ is narrated by Paul himself (with Luke or and Luke). If you are very sensitive, you will perceive that the three accounts are not exactly the same, even though it was the same Paul or/and Luke who gave the report/testimony.

The spirit of man works with the mind and brain of man while he is giving a testimony; and there are things which you may not remember in some occasions. Similar examples are seen in the four Gospels Books.

Mathew and John were among the apostles of Jesus Christ; but Mark and Luke were not among the twelve apostles of the Lord. You may realize, if you are careful and sensitive, that there are times when more than one of them reported the same incidents, but the accounts were not exactly the same.

It is not that any of them lied, but whereas Mathew and John might have heard directly from the Mouth of Jesus Christ, Mark and Luke might have heard from a report of what Jesus Christ said.

And even the ones, who heard directly from His Mouth and saw the miracles, healings, and encounters, with their own eyes, had different levels of mental understanding and spiritual development, not to talk of the possibility (as humans) of forgetting some things at some times.

And John himself said, "And Thomas answered and said to Him, 'My Lord and my God!' Jesus said to him, 'Thomas, because you have seen Me, you have believed. Blessed are those who have not seen and yet have believed.'

"And truly Jesus did many other signs in the presence of His Disciples, which are not written in this Book; but these are written that you may believe that Jesus is the Christ, the Son of God, and that believing you may have life in His Name (Jn 20:28-31).

"Then Peter, turning around, saw the Disciple whom Jesus loved following, who also had leaned on His Breast at the supper, and said, 'Lord, who is the one who betrays You?' Peter, seeing him, said to Jesus, 'But Lord, what about this man?'

"Jesus said to him, 'If I will that he remain till I come, what is that to you? You follow Me.' Then this saying went out among the brethren that this Disciple would not die. Yet Jesus did not say to him that he would not die, but, 'If I will that he remain till I come, what is that to you?'

"This is the Disciple who testifies of these things, and wrote these things; and we know that his testimony is true. And there are also many other things that Jesus did, which if they were written one by one, I suppose that even the world itself could not contain the books that would be written. Amen" (Jn 21:20-25).

Notice that in the issue concerning Jesus Christ, Peter, and John (who was writing), the Lord's Statement was misunderstood. And this can also happen in giving of testimonies of revelations, visions, and mysteries.

But unconsciously, unknowing, and unwillingly misinterpreting, misunderstanding, mispresenting, adding to, or subtracting from the vision or revelation given to you is different from when you consciously, carefully, and knowingly misinterpret, mispresent, add to, or subtract from the revelation or vision given to you or to somebody else.

To this end, the Bible says, "For I testify to everyone who hears the Words of the prophecy of this Book: If anyone adds to these things, God will add to him the plagues that are written in this Book;

"And if anyone takes away from the Words of the Book of this prophecy, God shall take away his part from the Book of Life, from the Holy City, and from the things which are written in this Book" (Rev. 22:18-19).

However, this is not an excuse for you to say, interpret, or present what you do not understand, unconsciously or unknowingly, because the Bible also says, "My brethren, let not many of you become teachers, knowing that we shall receive a stricter judgment.

"For we all stumble in many things. If anyone does not stumble in word, he is a perfect man, able also to bridle the whole body" (Jas 3:1-2).

INDECENT DRESSING AND WORLDLY APPEARANCE

Writing to Timothy, Apostle Paul said, "Take heed to yourself and to the Doctrine. Continue in them, for in doing this you will save both yourself and those who hear you" (1 Tim. 4:16). This means that it is possible for both you and those who believe (look up to) you to not be saved, because of wrong doctrine and practice. And you know that he was writing to a preacher and minister of the Gospel who had some (many) Believers (people of God) under him.

A New Testament apostle, writing to New Testament Believers, wrote: "Therefore, having these promises, beloved, let us cleanse ourselves from all filthiness of the flesh and spirit, perfecting holiness in the Fear of God" (2 Cor. 7:1). Notice that Apostle Paul spoke of the filthiness of the flesh and spirit. Surprisingly, he put the filthiness of the flesh before the filthiness of spirit. But many will forget (or wilfully ignore) the filthiness of the flesh, while many will still not make their followers to be conscious of the filthiness of spirit.

And the Word of God, which cannot be broken, but endures forever, says, "...present your bodies a living sacrifice, holy, acceptable to God, which is your reasonable service. And do not be conformed to this world..." (Rom. 12:1-2). God looks at your heart, as well as your body, which is to be presented holy and acceptable to Him as a living sacrifice.

If the devil doesn't get you with lying, he will try to get you with pride; if he doesn't get you with fornication, he will try to get you with bitterness, hatred, unforgiveness, cheating, or stealing. If he doesn't get you with murder, he will try to get you with examination malpractice or falsification of result or age. If you say that you will not do this or that, because God told you not to do it, he will tell you to do it just once, confess, and God will mercifully, lovingly, and faithfully forgive you.

The devil tries as much as possible to take you to Hell Fire, because he knows that God can neither compromise His Standard nor condole sin. The devil, satan, was created as the holy Lucifer; but he became the wicked and evil satan, because of pride and rebellion.

Adam was formed as the pure and holy Adam; but due to disobedience to the Commandment of God, he became the sinful Adam. Do you know that the Father even removed His Face from Jesus Christ, as He carried the sins of the world on the Cross of Calvary, so that Jesus Christ cried out, saying, "My God, My God, why have You forsaken Me?"

The same blindness that holds many Roman Catholics, so that no matter how you tell them that worshipping images and praying to (or through) Mary (or, do they call it honouring her?) is unbiblical and anti-God, they do not seem to understand, is also holding many Pentecostals, orthodoxes, evangelicals, and charismatics, so that no matter how you tell them that indecent dressing and worldly appearance is unbiblical and anti-Christ, they hope and say that it doesn't matter.

But the devil will try as much as he can to hold you blind, captive, and disobedient until you find yourself in Hell Fire with no second chance. And many people don't even know that many people who carry Bible and call Jesus are actually agents of satan in disguise.

To this end, the Bible says, "For such are false apostles, deceitful workers, transforming themselves into apostles of Christ. And no wonder! For satan himself transforms himself into an angel of light. Therefore it is no great thing if his ministers also transform themselves into ministers of righteousness, whose end will be according to their works" (2 Cor. 11:13-15).

Apostle Peter, writing in the New Testament, to those who were born again, said, "Now if the righteous one is scarcely saved, where will the ungodly and the sinner appear?" (1 Pet. 4:18). When our Lord Jesus Christ says that He will tell many people on the Day of Judgment that He never knew them because they were workers of iniquity, He was speaking of those who had been born again, filled with the Holy Spirit, spoken in tongues, prophesied, cast out demons, and done mighty signs and wonders in His Name (Matt. 7:21-23).

I was passing a church when I saw somebody who was leading a prayer session speaking in tongues. She was seriously speaking in tongues, walking to and fro; but, behold, though I was inside a bus along the road (there was a kind of traffic slowdown, or rather, the bus was moving slowly), I saw part of her breasts all the way from the road due to the 'open-breast' blouse she was wearing; how much more the people with her there inside the church! Hell Fire has enlarged itself to accommodate very many people (Isa. 5:14).

The devil will tell you that there is no God; if you overcome him, he will say, "Okay, there is God, but there is no Jesus Christ." If you say that there is Jesus Christ Who died for you, he will say, "Okay, there is Jesus Christ, but wait till tomorrow before you give your life to Him." If you win him by giving your life to Jesus Christ, he will tell you: "You have the Righteousness of Jesus Christ; it is not by your righteousness that you were saved; therefore, don't worry how you live your life because you are the Righteousness of God; and as for outward appearance, what God looks at is the heart."

If you can't sacrifice small things like your dressing and appearance for Jesus Christ, can you lay down your life for His Sake? And He tells us that anyone who loves his life more than Him is not worthy of Him. Jesus Christ is coming very soon; get ready to receive Him.

If it is contrary to the Word of God, then it is from satan – the devil and God's archenemy – who deceived Eve (from the beginning) with: "Did God really say…." That which is against God and His Word cannot be from God, the Maker of all things Who holds the whole world in His Hands, because God's Word and His Spirit agree. Whatever glorifies the devil, and does not glorify God, is not of God.

The Lord Jesus Christ, Who defeated satan on the Cross of Calvary about two thousand years ago, is the Same – yesterday, today, and forever. He is coming very soon; get ready to meet Him: Heaven and Hell are real; let no one deceive you!

Many of those girls, ladies, and women, that expose their breasts (or breast cleavages), laps, and armpits in churches, in streets, at schools, in your compounds, in buses and cars, in markets, on Facebook, etc, are not just people who dressed seductively; make no mistakes about it! Many of them are agents of the kingdom of darkness, who have sold their souls to the queen of the coast and satan, the devil (who is their chief coordinator), to destroy the souls of men through lust, fornication, and adultery, because they want to entice, persuade, force, and drag people to Hell at any cost.

They may pretend to be Christians, harmless, good people, and ignorant of what they are doing; but they are out to serve the intent, plan, and purpose of the devil. This is one reason why many of them will not adhere to any preaching, teaching, instruction, or advice to get them dress like girls, ladies, and women who appreciate God's Work in them and value their bodies.

Many of them are blind agents of satan (because they do not know that satan is directly using them), while many of them are conscious agents of the kingdom of darkness and witches (who are doing and carrying out what they were told to do in the kingdom of satan, the fallen Lucifer). For many of them, only deliverance can change their mentality and mindset.

The Bible says, "For you were bought at a price; therefore glorify God in your body and in your spirit, which are God's" (1 Cor. 6:20). The Bible says that you should glorify God with both your body and your spirit, the two of which belong to God. When you are washing your plate, do you wash only the inside? No; but you wash both the inside and the outside, to be happy and satisfied. Why will you think otherwise with God?

The Bible says that if your eye causes you to sin, you should pluck it out (Matt. 5:29). If you can't leave lipstick, cortex, earrings, and weavon, can you pluck out your eye for the salvation of your soul if necessary? Your eye and lipstick, cortex, earring, or weavon, which one do you esteem above the other?

The Bible says, "Do not love the world or anything in the world. If any man loves the world, the Love of the Father is not in him; for all that is in the world: the lust of the eyes, the lust of the flesh, and the pride of life come not from the Father, but from the world. And the world passes away with its lusts, but he who does the Will of God abides forever" (1 Jn 2:15-17).

Adulteries, fornications, murders, and thefts are outward acts; yet the Lord says that they come from the heart and defile a man (Matt. 15:17-20). Eating with unwashed hand will not defile you, because you did not have evil thoughts to eat the food. But you can also eat with evil thoughts, like: gluttony and drunkenness.

Therefore using of lipsticks, weavons (wigs), artificial nails, etc defiles you, because it comes from evil thoughts of accusing God of imperfect creation and loving worldliness. And wearing seductive dresses and attire of the harlot come from the evil thoughts of wanting to expose your sensitive parts to command ungodly attention.

God calls hatred murder, calls lust fornication, calls changing your nature worldliness, calls dressing seductively causing your brother to fall, and calls painting yourself works of the flesh and of the devil. Lust is desire to fornicate; and God calls both the desire and the act the same thing – fornication. Using weavons and applying lipsticks and cortexes is to change God's Image which He made.

The Bible says, "A good tree cannot bear bad fruit, nor can a bad tree bear good fruit. Every tree that does not bear good fruit is cut down and thrown into the Fire. Therefore by their fruits you will know them. Not everyone who says to Me, 'Lord, Lord,' shall enter the Kingdom of Heaven, but he who does the Will of My Father in Heaven.

"Many will say to Me in that Day, 'Lord, Lord, have we not prophesied in Your Name, cast out demons in Your Name, and done many wonders in Your Name?' And then I will declare to them, 'I never knew you; depart from Me, you who practice lawlessness!'" (Matt. 7:18-23).

In some churches, people collect up to two, three, or more different kinds of offerings on Sundays; but they fail to tell their members to dress well. Is this hypocrisy or compromise? People put time, energy, and other kinds of efforts to convince (or will I say, pressurize?) people to give tithes/offerings and sow seed-faith; but when it comes to dressing, they will hypocritically say that the Holy Spirit will teach the Believers in Christ how to dress well.

Being born again is of the spirit (heart) of man by the acceptance of the Lord Jesus Christ (Jn 3:6). So someone can receive Jesus Christ while she is indecently dressed. Jn 3:3 says that unless one is born again, he cannot see the Kingdom of God. Jn 3:5 says that unless one is born of water and the Spirit, he cannot enter the Kingdom of God. The water there refers to the Word of God, according to Eph. 5:26. Being born again gives you the ability to become a child of God (Jn 1:12), so that you can live the way that God wants.

So whoever wants to enter (and not just to see) the Kingdom of God must be born again (led and directed) of the water (the Word of God) and the Spirit of God (Jn 3:5). To this end, Paul wrote to born again Believers to present their bodies a living sacrifice, holy and acceptable to God, and to renew their minds (Rom. 12:1-2). They themselves were to do the presenting and the renewing (God was not going to do it for them). This is why Paul himself said that he beat his body and brought it under subjection to his spirit, so that after he had preached to others, he himself will not be a castaway (1 Cor. 9:27).

So the one who knows the good he or she is to do, and does not do it, is sinning (Jas 4:17). And sinners spend eternity in Hell Fire. He who refuses to present his body a living sacrifice, holy and acceptable to God, is disobedient; and disobedient people go to Hell Fire. Remember that Adam was pure before God until he disobeyed God; and Lucifer was holy before God until iniquity was found in him.

Yes, if you receive Jesus Christ now with all your heart, while you are indecently dressed, God will wash away your sins and make you His child, and can even fill you with the Holy Spirit. But when you go to your house, the Spirit of God will speak to your heart to dress decently; if you refuse to obey, you will become a disobedient person (a fallen Adam). If you don't repent before you die or Jesus Christ comes, disobedient people go to.... Paul did not only preach faith towards Jesus Christ; rather, he preached faith towards Jesus Christ and repentance from dead works (Acts 20:21).

And the Word says, "Beware of false prophets, who come to you in sheep's clothing, but inwardly they are ravenous wolves. You will know them by their fruits. Do men gather grapes from thornbushes or figs from thistles? Even so, every good tree bears good fruit, but a bad tree bears bad fruit. A good tree cannot bear bad fruit, nor can a bad tree bear good fruit. Every tree that does not bear good fruit is cut down and thrown into the Fire. Therefore by their fruits you will know them.

"Not everyone who says to Me, 'Lord, Lord,' shall enter the Kingdom of Heaven, but he who does the Will of My Father in Heaven. Many will say to Me in that Day, 'Lord, Lord, have we not prophesied in Your Name, cast out demons in Your Name, and done many wonders in Your Name?' And then I will declare to them, 'I never knew you; depart from Me, you who practice lawlessness!'" (Matt. 7:15-23).

Apostle Paul, writing under the Unction, Anointing, and Inspiration of the Holy Spirit, said, "In like manner also, that the women adorn themselves in modest apparel (New International Version says, "Dress modestly, with decency and propriety"), with propriety and moderation, not with braided hair or gold or pearls or costly clothing, but which is proper for women professing Godliness, with good works" (1 Tim. 2:9-10, the New King James Version).

And Apostle Peter, being another witness, said, "Whose adorning, let it not be that outward *adorning* of plaiting the hair, and wearing of gold, or of putting on of apparel; but let it be the hidden man of the heart, in that which is not corruptible, even the *ornament* of a meek and quiet spirit, which is in the Sight of God of great price" (1 Pet. 3:3-4, the King James Version).

May you be changed by the Word of God! And may you learn to listen to the inner voice and witness in your spirit by the Holy Spirit, instead of following the multitude. May the Almighty Lord God give you wisdom and understanding in all things! Amen!

And instead of putting these things aside, criticizing them, or even getting annoyed over them, open your heart to the Holy Spirit and let Him speak to you further in your inner man: don't follow the multitude of disobedient and hardened people!

For the benefit of doubt, the things I have written down, as inspired by the Holy Spirit, are applicable to any tribe, people, nation, or country of the world, whether they are civilized or uncivilized, advanced or not advanced, developed or underdeveloped. To clarify you further, these things are applicable to Americans, Europeans, Asians, Africans, and others.

Let me state, categorically and without mincing words, that any preacher (no matter how anointed you may be, no matter your Knowledge of God, and no matter the years of service in the Kingdom of God), who encourages the use of cortex, lipstick, wigs or weavons, jewellery (jewelry), artificial nails, etc is encouraging the activities of the mermaid.

Much of the current wave of sexual immorality came from these things, even as they also use their demonic ladies and women to pull men into lust, fornication, and adultery. The only woman in the Bible who painted herself was Jezebel; and do you like the Jezebelic lifestyle and spirit? Beware of the attire of the harlot and prostitute! (Prov. 7).

If you do, you are encouraging, knowingly or unknowingly, the purposes and plans of the marine (water) kingdom of darkness, and the activities of the devil (satan), who is their chief-coordinator. You can fight against God without your knowledge; and you can encourage the devil without your knowledge.

And I will add that we preachers are responsible for most of the things happening in the world today, both on the positive side and on the negative side. All these people who misbehave and live their lives however they want, don't they go to churches?

When someone comes to church with his sin-partner (what many people call girl-friend), and leaves the church with the same sin-partner, without fear or shame, is it not enough to prove to you that the preachers are responsible for much of the evil in the society?

There is a way that seems right to a man, but its end is the way of death (Prov. 14:12; Prov. 16:25). God is warning us, because He loves us and does not want anyone to perish. But just as they never listened to Noah, many will not listen to the Truth; and just as Sodom and

Gomorrah perished without Lot, those that will listen to God and do His Word and Will, will be saved!

Concerning the Bible passages we read before, I want you to see that there is the ornament or beauty of the spirit (heart). The word – fine – is not in the original text; and that is why it is italicized in the New King James Version. Apparel (according to the King James Version) or fine apparel (according to the New King James Version) refers to fashion and worldly ways of designing clothing. God wants you to look 'good'; but He detests worldly fashions.

Putting your mind on costly clothing makes clothing your idol. But how costly is the costly? Costly and expensive clothes encourage pride and idolization. For instance, if they make this clothing material as a material for the 'reigning' or 'current' people, then you have to remove yourself from it, because you are a different person – God's son or daughter.

People dress indecently and seductively these days, especially girls, ladies, and women. Of course, some men dress indecently also. But whereas even unbelieving men dress decently, many ladies who claim they are Christians, who go to different churches and call on the Name of the Lord, dress indecently to work, school, shopping, and even church.

The dressing and outward appearance of Christians must be different from those of unbelievers. If a Muslim will value covering herself well, how much more should you value it? The problem is that many people will find it easier to manage bondage than liberty. But do not use your liberty as an opportunity for sin and disobedience (Gal. 5:13).

Concerning jewellery (jewellery is British English, while jewelry is American English), Apostle Paul stated, "…that the women adorn themselves…not with…gold or pearls…" (1 Tim. 2:9, the New King James Version). The King James Version also says, "…women adorn themselves…not with…gold, or pearls…." Apostle Peter stated: "Do not let your adornment be *merely* outward…wearing gold…" (1 Pet. 3:3, the New King James Version). Now, take up your own New King James Version of the Bible, and read this portion of the Scripture. There you will see that the word 'merely' is italicized, which is to say that it is not in the original Greek text of the Bible.

Italicized words in the King James Version (which is the authorized version) or the New King James Version of the Bible are added for clearer understanding, and are not in the original Greek text; but I believe that this 'merely' added in the New King James Version, which, I thank God, is not added in the only authorized version of the Bible – the King James Version – was added because of human acceptance over time based on demonic deception.

This is why you may see some versions of the Bible which will add 'merely' or 'only' without even italicizing it, which will make someone who doesn't have a certain level of understanding of versions and editions of the Bible to think that the words 'merely' or 'only' are in the original Greek text (and it is not there). Versions of the Bible (like KJV, NKJV, NIV, ASV, etc) are 'straight' translations of the Bible from the original Greek text, while editions of the Bible (like the Living Bible, Good News, etc) are 'interpreted' translations/descriptions of the Bible, either from the original Greek text or from a version of the Bible.

For your confirmation, the King James Version says, "Whose adorning let it not be that outward…wearing of gold…." There is no 'only' or 'merely' there. Apostle Peter said, "Let it not be outward wearing of gold (which is jewellery)." And Apostle Paul said, "Women are not to adorn themselves with gold or pearls (which, also, is jewellery). For the benefit of doubt, first, Apostle Peter didn't say anything about modesty. Secondly, hear Apostle Paul himself: "…women adorn themselves in modest apparel…" (1 Tim. 2:9).

Read it again from your own Bible, and you will see that he spoke of modest apparel, and not modest braiding of the hair or of wearing of gold or pearls (There is no such thing as modest braiding of the hair or modest wearing of jewels for Christians and Believers who want to make Heaven). We will see apparel and modest apparel, in dressing or clothing, later.

Some translations used 'modest appearance' instead of 'modest apparel', saying that the women should adorn themselves in modest appearance; but any translation, edition, or version of the Bible that uses 'appearance' either made mistake or purposely put it there to deceive people. Don't you know that some translations, editions, or versions of the Bible were done by some people to represent what they believe and accept? And you have got to know that the devil has agents (conscious or no conscious) in this regard. The Greek word used there is *katastole*, which means: apparel, dress, or clothing; it does not mean appearance.

Concerning plaiting or braiding of the hair (plaiting is British English, while braiding is American English), Apostle Paul clearly stated: "…that the women adorn themselves…not with braided hair…" (1 Tim. 2:9). Apostle Peter stated: "Whose adorning let it not be that outward adorning of plaiting the hair…" (1 Pet. 3:3, the King James Version). Apostle Peter said, "Don't adorn yourself by plaiting your hair." Apostle Paul said, "Don't adorn yourself with braided hair."

Neither Peter nor Paul spoke of modest plaiting or braiding of the hair, though Paul spoke of modest apparel. There is no modest braided or plaited hair. Your hair is to be natural as God made it. If it grows to the extent you find it difficult to comb it, then you can reduce it, but not as low as men's hair. Braiding or plaiting of the hair didn't come from God, but from the devil.

American, European, African, Asian, and Australian demons can give (or has given) American, European, African, Asian, and Australian methods and systems of braiding or plaiting of the hair. No matter how long the custom or culture has existed, the Bible says, "No braiding or plaiting of your hair, as a Christian woman." To dress the hair is to arrange someone's hair into a special style; and the devil has given braiding, plaiting, and weaving of the hair as ways in which many women and ladies dress or arrange their hair.

Concerning apparel or clothing, Apostle Paul clearly stated: "…that the women adorn themselves…not with…costly clothing" (1 Tim. 2:9, the New King James Version). The King James Version says, "…not with…costly array." Apostle Peter stated: "Whose adorning let it not be that outward adorning of…putting on apparel" (1 Pet. 3:3, the King James Version). The New King James Version says, "Do not let your adornment be…putting on *fine* apparel." If you read the New King James Version, you will see that the word 'fine' is italicized, which means that it is not in the original Greek text. Therefore, Apostle Peter says, "Don't adorn yourself with apparel."

Apostle Paul said, "Don't adorn yourself with costly clothing or array." He said, "Adorn yourself in modest apparel." According to the Longman Dictionary of Contemporary English, 1995 edition, apparel is a formal word used for clothes, especially those worn for special occasions. So, apparel refers to special clothes. This not talking of normal clothes, but special clothes: this is talking of fashion and/or costly clothing. They are to use inexpensive or moderately priced clothes or clothing.

The Bible commands women to use modest apparel (1 Tim. 2:9). This particular, "In like manner also, that the women adorn themselves in modest apparel…" is not even talking of its price, but its style. According to the Longman Dictionary of Contemporary English, 1995 edition, modest clothing covers the body in a way that does not attract sexual interest. How many of our women, ladies, and girls dress modestly – in ways that do not attract sexual interest?

God hates dressing like the people of the world. He said: "And it shall be, in the day of the Lord's Sacrifice, that I will punish…all such as are clothed with foreign apparel" (Zeph. 1:8). Foreign apparel speaks of the kind of dressing that is not for God's people.

The Bible says, "Now when Jehu had come to Jezreel, Jezebel heard of it, and she put paint on her eyes…and looked through the window" (2 Kgs 9:30, the New King James Version). The King James Version says, "…she painted her face…." Painting your eyes, lips, and face is demonic and Jezebelic.

The Word says, "Now when Jehu had come to Jezreel, Jezebel heard of it, and she…adorned her head, and looked through the window" (2 Kgs 9:30, the New King James Version). The King James Version says, "…she…tired her head…." The New International Version says, "…she…arranged her hair…." Arranging, adorning, plaiting, braiding, or weaving the hair is demonic and Jezebelic.

Why didn't the Bible say, "Now when Jehu had come to Jezreel, Jezebel heard of it, and she looked through the window," but, "Now when Jehu had come to Jezreel, Jezebel heard of it, and she painted her face and adorned her head, and looked through the window." It was because she painted her face and adorned her head (or, arranged her hair) to look seductive and unnaturally attractive to seduce Jehu.

The Bible tells us that man looks at outward appearance (1 Sam. 16:7). Even in the secular world, appearance can decide your acceptability in many areas of life. Escape for your dear life; run before it is too late. The five foolish virgins lost their target. Remember that they were virgins, but they lacked something they didn't remember or deem necessary.

Please, open your eyes well, well; the devil has intruded into the Church: his ministers now parade themselves as ministers of Jesus Christ, to deceive and destroy the souls of the children of men.

Be careful of any church where people are allowed to dress anyhow to, no matter how anointed you may think the preacher is or how knowledgeable he is concerning the Bible. It is a different case when unbelievers dress anyhow to crusades, maybe, for the first time.

The Bible says that out of the abundance of the heart, the mouth speaks. Your actions and your words show what is on the inside of you. Your physical appearance reveals your inner man. If you don't care about what people think about your indecent dressing, then your spirit has a serious problem, and your mind has been corrupted. I don't care what you may think about it.

Even unbelievers will find it difficult to believe you are a Christian when you dress indecently as they do. There must be a difference between the dressing of a Christian and a non-Christian.

Many ladies think that they attract marriage partners by dressing seductively. Well, you can only attract a carnal man when you dress that way. How can a reasonable spiritual man decide to marry someone that is worldly in appearance? Will you paint your face with lipstick, eye-pencil, and decorative powder as the wicked and ungodly women, Jezebel, painted hers (2 Kgs 9:30)?

Concerning the dressing or arranging of the hair, using of weavons (or wigs) and attachments is devilish and worldly. Many of those weavons are actual human hairs that were cut and sold. Many of the weavons and attachments are manufactured with demonic materials to enslave the children of men.

I don't care whether you call it wool or what; it is still an attachment. You can't confuse God; He knows more than you do! Even, the using of thread to wind your hair (as many Believers do) is still attachment and unnatural hair. If you don't know, it is not a Christian style of hair-style but traditional style.

If you doubt this, check it out and see that traditional unbelievers use thread for their hair too. As a woman, wash your hair and comb it; there are suitable combs made for long hairs. Allow your hair to be natural; and you can pack it or allow it fly. And I am not telling you to cut your hair low like the general size of that of men of the same race as you, except you are going to cover it or wear cap on it, even outside the church.

Also, when you use weavons and attachments, when you perm and jerry curl your hair, you are saying that God is stupid (or, is an imperfect Creator) to have made your hair the way He made it. Relaxing your hair artificially (whether you call it science or technology) is of the devil. When people refuse to cover their hairs, they resort to worldly means of weavons for a covering. Of course, your must have a sign of authority on your head in church meetings or gatherings, as a woman. What do you lose by veiling your hair?

Much of those things women use for beauty and for their hair, in perming and jerry-curling, is manufactured from alantoin extracted from aborted babies. The worst is that some men even fry their hair.

I read a story of a woman who when she was still a young sister was warned by God to desist from using attachments on her hair. And anytime she disobeyed that Instruction, God will chastise her. She told God that there were other good Christians that were using attachments, and referred to one particular woman who was a spiritual mother to them, whom she saw as a model.

The story had it that then (as at the time of the reporting) the sister is married to a pastor for many years then, and she is a strong pillar in the ministry doing exploits for the Lord. On the other hand, she then makes her hair with attachment, weavons, and other materials without any further warning from the Lord. And she said that her relationship with the Lord is still intact.

This story, though 'funny', is painful. Can you see how someone who believes in Jesus Christ can so much love the things of this world to the extent that her conscience will get hardened to do what God told her not to do, and even make God to give her over to a reprobate mind, and also refuse to speak to her again, because she loves doing her own thing instead of God's Thing? And she still 'believes' that God is happy with her!

Start appreciating your hair the natural way God made it. If you find it difficult to comb it, then reduce it to manageable or easily-combable size, but not as low as the general size of that of men from the same race as you (the men who have the kind of hair that you have). This will solve all these problems of perming the hair, relaxing the hair, 'jerry-curling' the hair, wearing of weavons or wigs, braiding or plaiting your hair with natural hair, attachments, wool, and thread.

If your hair is very long, as a woman, it is good; but the Bible says, "If a woman has a long hair," and not, "When a woman has a long hair." If you have the kind of strong hair that will not be long (or very long) in its natural state without relaxing it artificially, then reduce it to manageable or easily-combable size, but not as low as the general size of that of men from the same race as you (the men who have the kind of hair that you have). Also, the use of veil, hair scarf, and caps can help you remove unnecessary worries.

Satan has entered the Church and has deceived many. Many are sincerely deceived. Those cortexes, lipsticks, make-ups, and many other painting materials and cosmetics, apart from being worldly, are manufactured from demonic materials, aborted babies' placentas, and human fat and blood. This is a mystery that many have not realized. When people use those things, they get demonic problems they don't know where they came from.

Blouses that show too much of your back; tight-fitting and revealing dresses; mini-skirts; spaghetti or line-sleeve and transparent dresses; blouses showing your breast; cobweb and body-hug dresses; blouses revealing your belly; and any such dresses are devilish, satanic, demonic, and worldly.

For men, sagging your trousers and dread-locking your hair are satanic also. Women shouldn't put on trousers, because they look more decent in skirts and gowns. In biology, when women mature, their buttocks get enlarged; this is why when they wear trousers, they reveal their body contours and look seductive.

Any attire or dress that glorifies the devil, and does not glorify God, is worldly and devilish. There are no two ways about this matter. If you doubt this, wait till the Day of Reckoning when you will cry and wail in Hell Fire! Then you will repent one thousand times in a short while without any second chance.

We now come to the issue of earrings, necklaces, and bangles. These things are worldly also. God made you look fine; what advantage is it in decorating your body, which is the Temple of the Holy Spirit, with those things?

We wear cloths and dresses to cover our nakedness. Before Adam sinned, we didn't even need dresses, for God's Glory covered us. Earrings were classified among foreign and ungodly things which Jacob purified his household from; and he buried them, after he had collected them from all the members of his household and those that were with him (Gen. 35:1-5). The Knowledge of God advanced from Abraham, to Isaac, and to Jacob.

God hates jewellery (jewelry) and ornamenting your body. Get rid of rings, chains, bangles, necklaces, and such things. Jewellery is designing your body with jewels. To God, it is idolatry; and the devil uses it to make women look worldly and seductive. By this, he seduces our men into lust, fornication, and adultery more easily.

Even though you may argue, can you prove to me why you need them when God made you beautiful? The problem is that many of these things have continued for so long that many don't even know why they do what they do. Personally, I don't see those things as beauty; and God does not like them.

Some argue that God told the Israelites to collect those things from the Egyptians as they departed from Egypt. Well, if you had not known it, God did not tell them to collect them from them because He wanted them to be given to jewellery. Those things were Egyptian and foreign, even though the Israelites might have been influenced by them after having stayed there for four hundred years.

He told them to collect them from them because they were made from gold, silver, and other materials; and they were to plunder Egypt. Those materials were needed for construction and other works by them and for the Work of God. Where do you think that they would have got the gold for the construction of the sanctuary and tabernacle?

See the Bible speak: "And when the people heard this bad news, they mourned, and no one put on his ornaments. For the Lord had said to Moses, 'Say to the children of Israel, "you are a stiff-necked people. I could come into your midst in one moment and consume you. Now therefore, take off your ornaments, that I may know what to do with you."' So the children of Israel stripped themselves of their ornaments by Mount Horeb" (Exo. 33:4-6).

God spoke to His people, after they had used their ornaments to make a calf and worshipped it as the god that brought them out of Egypt, and said, "...take off your ornaments...." Is it not clear enough? The Israelites removed their jewellery and stripped themselves of their ornaments, because God commanded them to do so; will you yourself obey God's Voice today and save your soul from Hell?

Also, notice that verse 5 didn't say, "The Lord said to Moses..." but, "For the Lord had said to Moses...." In order words, they didn't just remove the ornaments on their own in verse 4. Verse 4 happened because the Lord had instructed it. And verse 6 affirms that they stripped themselves of their ornaments.

Also, notice that because they still needed the materials from which the ornaments were made – gold, silver, etc – for construction purposes, God didn't tell them to throw away those ornaments; they kept them, not for future wearing of them, but for the preservation of the materials of gold, silver, etc, for which purpose He told them to collect them from the Egyptians in the first place – to be used for construction works.

To this end, the Bible says, "'Take from among you an offering to the Lord. Whoever is of a willing heart, let him bring it as an offering to the Lord: gold, silver, and bronze....' They came, both men and women, as many as had a willing heart, and brought earrings and nose rings, rings and necklaces, all jewellery of gold, that is, every man who made an offering of gold to the Lord.

"Everyone who offered an offering of silver or bronze brought the Lord's Offering. And everyone with whom was found acacia wood for any work of the service, brought it" (Exo. 35:5,22,24). I didn't say this for you to keep your jewels, because you must not.

Someone may ask, "But why did God tell the Israelites to put the jewellery on their wives, sons, and daughters?" The answer is not hard, if you are sincere and God opens your eyes. Many times, we don't see the Truth of the Word of God when we read the Bible, because we already have what we want it to say in our minds, and we force it to say the very thing!

Hear God: "And I will give the people favour in the sight of the Egyptians; and it shall be, when you go, that you shall not go empty-handed. But every woman shall ask of her neighbour, namely, of her who dwells near her house, articles of silver, articles gold, and clothing; and you shall put them on your sons and your daughters. So you shall plunder the Egyptians" (Exo. 3:21-22, the New King James Version).

The King James Version (which is the only authorized version of the Bible) says, "But every woman shall borrow of her neighbour, and of her that sojourneth in her house, jewels of silver, and jewels of gold, and raiment: and ye shall put them upon your sons, and upon your daughters; and ye shall spoil the Egyptians" (Exo. 3:22).

Notice that the purpose of the borrowing and the putting on was to plunder the Egyptians. The Hebrew word used there is 'shaal'. It means 'borrow', and in some instances, may be rendered/translated as 'ask' or 'request'. It is true that the NKJV used 'ask' instead of 'borrow'; but what God told them was to borrow them from them. Why?

Hear the Bible: "Afterwards Moses and Aaron went in and told Pharaoh, 'Thus says the Lord God of Israel: "Let My people go, that they may hold a feast to Me in the wilderness."' And Pharaoh said, 'Who is the Lord that I should obey His Voice to let Israel go? I do not know the Lord, nor will I let Israel go.'

"So they said, 'The God of the Hebrews has met with us. Please, let us go three days' journey into the desert and sacrifice to the Lord our God, lest He fall upon us with pestilence or with the sword'" (Exo. 5:1-3). Look at what Pharaoh said, "You are idle! Idle! Therefore you say, 'Let us go and sacrifice to the Lord'" (Exo. 5:17).

After some plagues, Pharaoh said, "Go, sacrifice to your God in the land." And Moses said, "It is not right to do so, for we would be sacrificing the abomination of the Egyptians to the Lord our God. If we sacrifice the abomination of the Egyptians before their eyes, then will they not stone us?

"We will go three days' journey into the wilderness and sacrifice to the Lord our God as He will command us." So Pharaoh said, "I will let you go, that you may sacrifice to the Lord your God in the wilderness; only you shall not go very far away. Intercede for me" (Exo. 8:25-28).

After other plagues, Pharaoh said, "Go, serve the Lord; only let your flocks and your herds be kept back. Let your little ones also go with you." But Moses said, "You must also give us sacrifices and burnt offerings, that we may sacrifice to the Lord our God. Our livestock also shall go with us; not a hoof shall be left behind. For we must take some of them to serve the Lord our God, and even we do not know with what we must serve the Lord until we arrive there" (Exo. 10:24-26).

I put those portions of the Scripture to help you understand why they were to borrow the jewels. In what they told Pharaoh, they were going on a three-day journey into the wilderness to sacrifice to the Lord their God. And it seems that what Pharaoh understood from their statement(s), was that they were going on a three-day journey into the wilderness to sacrifice to the Lord their God, and after the sacrifice, they would come back to Egypt.

Was God deceiving the Egyptians then? No, He is God; and that was His Method of plundering the Egyptians, as He had told Abraham that his descendants, after serving a foreign land, would come out with great possessions (Gen. 15:14). And notice that neither God nor Moses told any of them that they would come back after the sacrifice!

In God's Sight, the Egyptians were paying for having held His people for hundreds of years in their land. He was punishing them for punishing His people. The same kind of thing happened when Jesus Christ was crucified. The devil, in his desperation, killed Jesus Christ; but it was after He was killed that satan realized that Jesus Christ had to shed His Blood in order to redeem mankind.

Then satan, wanting Jesus Christ to come down from the Cross, entered some people, and they said, "If You are the Son of God, come down from the Cross, and we will believe You (Matt. 27:41-43)"; but it was too late! The Bible says, "Which none of the rulers of this age knew; for had they known, they would not have crucified the Lord of Glory" (1 Cor. 2:8).

What I want you to know is that it was after the Israelites had left Egypt that the Egyptians actually realized that Israel was gone! And this added to their punishments, because there were drown in the Red Sea when they pursued Israel. The Bible says, "Now it was told the king of Egypt that the people had fled, and the heart of Pharaoh and his servants were turned against the people; and they said, 'Why have we done this, that we have let Israel go from serving us?'" (Exo. 14:5).

So, you can see, if you want to, why God said, "Borrow those articles and put them on your wives, sons, and daughters." They were not going to ask for it and keep it in their purses; you borrow things for urgent need. And that was why they had to put the articles on them: It was borrowed articles, which their wives and children were in urgent need for use in the special sacrifice they were going to make for their God in the wilderness after a three-day journey.

For those who want to wear wrist watch, it must not be with chains, for it would be the same as wearing chains. If you want to wear wrist watch (not for beauty, but for keeping time), use the one that is made of plastic, rubber, or leather belt; and let it be of simple and inexpensive type, because it is for checking time and not for fashion. For this same reason, your waist belt must not be the chain type; and it is to be the simple type. And don't even wear the rubber or plastic wrist bangles which carry different kinds of advertisement/write-ups, whether of church, ministry, Bible, Christianity, or whatever.

The Bible says that God looks at the heart (I Sam 16:7). The Word of the Lord says that the Almighty does not look as man looks. How does man look? He looks at the outward appearance. This means that outward appearance is very important in our relationship with men, because they would look at our appearance. Could it be that God does not see in the physical? How can He, Who created the physical out of the spiritual, not see the physical, while we that were created see it?

The Bible says that out of the abundance of the heart, the mouth speaks. This means that what we say has something to do with what is in our heart (which we don't see). The appearance of men could be deceitful. An armed robber could dress like a banker or a pastor. Why will he do that? Because he knows that the appearance of the banker or the pastor is appreciated by responsible people.

However, the banker or the pastor will never want to dress like the armed robber (if there is how they dress). Why would he not want to dress like that? Because he knows that armed robbery is one of the ills of the society.

My brethren, how you dress and how you appear matter before people (responsible people) even when they don't confront you. From this day, make up your mind to glorify God in your dressing no matter the cost. Make up your mind not to offend God through your dressing.

I tell you, many of the girls, ladies, women, boys, young men, and grown up men you see in the towns are agents of the kingdom of darkness. Even many children are witches, and they have direct and conscious relationships with the dark kingdom. Of course, there are blind witches, who don't have conscious relationship with demons and fallen angels, but are demonically remote-controlled.

Will it surprise you to be told that there are many agents of the kingdom of darkness in many churches? Many operate as preachers; some operate as deacons, deaconesses, and elders; others operate as group leaders; still, many are in the choir and in other departments.

It is not that God wants it to be so, or that it is so in every church. It is because many churches, fellowships, and ministries are not at the place God wants them to be, that agents of the kingdom of darkness come into their midst and relax. This is not just saying that we are the Pentecostals or the charismatics, and we speak in tongues always.

Brother, have you ever asked yourself where all those people that flood into your church are going to? People will come to church with their girl-friends, and leave the church with their girl-friends, without fear and shame. If they had tried it in the Early Church, they would have seen what would have happened to them!

The increase of evil in these last days is not only because of the desperation of the devil. As a matter of fact, the devil has always been desperate since the time of Adam. Preachers are responsible for much of it. Apart from preachers who are direct agents of satan, many preachers who were called by God have compromised the Word of God and Christian standards, because of ignorance, fame, and love of money.

Many want to be known as the most popular preacher, the richest preacher, or the most influential preacher. Others want to have the largest congregation, the fastest growing church, or the biggest cathedral. Many ministers have lost the vision of the souls of men, and they are interested in money and other material things.

Why do Christians dress and appear like the people of the world? It is because there are many Jezebels and agents of the kingdom of darkness (especially the mermaid water kingdom) in many churches. This is why many preachers and churches have accepted what they used to call sin before, as being good and harmless now.

Many of them get committed in church activities, that the pastors wouldn't even know that they are agents of the kingdom of darkness; and the pastors begin to promote them, thereby helping them in their seductive and destructive works. When they dress that way and speak their demonic tongues, giving their demonic prophecies, the pastor and others will welcome them.

They will say, "Since this sister dresses like this, wears this, and paints this way, and yet is too spiritual, then nothing is really wrong with these things." And the devil will ask the other Believers and Christians, "Did God really say that it is sinful to dress this way, wear weavons, and paint this way?"

Then the other Believers and Christians will become 'sincerely' deceived (if sincerity is applicable at all, because many of them want it; and if you stop or forbid them, they will criticize and hate you). And when the pastor sees that many or majority of his members are like that, it will be as if water was poured on his spiritual energy to speak against those things.

I have observed that girls, ladies, and women like what appeals to the eyes. I am talking of believing girls, ladies, and women. In fact, the Christianity of many of them doesn't reach that side. If you speak against their worldly appearance, you will become their enemy. They will try as much as possible to find what they will use to justify themselves, because they want to look attractive and 'sharp.'

This is the same thing that put the world into the mess it is in today. In the beginning: "The woman saw (and they still see) that the tree was good for food, that it was pleasant to the eyes (Have you seen and confirmed what I am saying?), and a tree desirable to make one wise, she took of its fruit and ate" (Gen. 3:6).

My sister, whether or not you like it, the way to Heaven is a narrow way. And the Bible says, "Enter by the narrow gate; for wide is the gate and broad is the way that leads to destruction, and there are many who go in by it. Because narrow is the gate and difficult is the way which leads to life, and there are few who find it" (Matt. 7:13-14).

Luke added something when he said, "Strive to enter through the narrow gate, for many, I say to you, will seek to enter and will not be able" (Lk. 13:24). How many people are willing and ready to strive to enter through the narrow gate?

Yet, don't be deceived by appearance, because many agents of the kingdom of darkness dress like Christian ladies, to deceive people into thinking that they are Christians. To this end, know that some of them wear long skirts, tie headties, and wouldn't paint their lips. Be careful, so that the devil will not trap you down!

These days are last days, and the devil is fighting tooth and nail to draw as many people as he can to Hell Fire, to suffer eternal torment and punishment with him. The devil hates the human race with great passion; the human agents he uses are deceived into thinking that he loves them.

We are talking of indecent dressing and outward appearance. And what we have said so far concerns other areas of the life of a Christian. There are many things that people (Believers) do today, and say that they do not matter. It may strike your mind to know that even many unbelievers know that Christians should not live or be those ways.

You have to decide what you want. Do you want to please God or yourself? Do you want to obey the Truth or false teaching? Do you want to make it to Heaven or Hell? Do you want to receive abundant reward from the Lord or suffer loss? Make your decision now before it becomes too late!

Worldliness has crept into the lives of many Believers, especially in these last days. But one thing is that God's Word and Standard cannot change for any person or group of persons. God's Word is forever settled in Heaven: God hates worldliness. Worldliness is living like the people of the world. And concerning what we are discussing, it is appearing like the people of the world.

One of the major problems in many churches today is what somebody called 'churchiality without Christianity.' It is going to church, without being born again. It is being born again, without being committed to the Lord Jesus Christ. It is to be led and directed by the flesh, instead of being led and directed by the Word of God and His Holy Spirit.

Because many are in the churches, without being born again and committed to the Lordship of Jesus Christ, they live and appear like the people of the world; and before you know it, many Believers start joining or following them to live and appear like the people of the world, because they assume that those people, since they are members of our churches, are fellow Believers.

James put this matter in a strong form: "Adulterers and adulteresses! Do you not know that friendship with the world is enmity with God? Whoever therefore wants to be a friend of the world makes himself an enemy of God. Or do you think that the Scripture says in vain, 'The Spirit Who dwells in us yearns jealously (or, lusteth to envy, KJV)?'" (Jas 4:4-5).

What are you thinking, as you are reading this material? That you will change tomorrow? Tomorrow may be too late. Furthermore, if you don't make up your mind and take the right decision, accompanied by prayer, the devil can come and remove the Word from you. You may find out that the same Word that is burning in your heart now will not be felt much by you tomorrow.

How did people who rejected worldliness before accept it latter? By carelessness, lust of the flesh and the eyes, and by false teachings. A woman told me that she can never use weavon (or, is it attachment?) again, not just because I said it, but because she has known the truth about it. Brother, before you know what happened, she had started using it again. God told me the woman loved the world.

When preachings go forth, the women and ladies repent, cry, weep, and sob more than the men. Yet they are the ones that are easily deceived and led astray more than the men. Why is this the case? Apostle Paul said that it was not the man that was deceived, but the woman (1 Tim. 2:14).

If you see the kinds and appearances of dresses that parents put on their children, you will weep, if your understanding has been sharpened along this line. And those parents will expect those children to stop wearing those kinds of dresses when they grow up. They have been deceived, and they think they are wiser than God, Who said, "Train up the child in the way he should go, and when he/she is old he/she will not depart from it" (Prov. 22:6).

Any skirt or gown that is at the knee level as you are standing, which when you sit down, people can see your laps (even if it is a small part of your laps) is from the devil. Any skirt or gown that will require your covering yourself with handkerchief when you sit down is of demons (demon-inspired design). Any skirt or gown which when you sit down in a car, either as the driver or as a passenger, somebody can see your laps, originated from the wisdom of satan.

Read Exodus 20:26. Read also Exodus 28:42. If God was so much interested in the nakedness of His priests (which were even men) not being seen by people, how much more in this New Testament does He not want the nakedness of His daughters to be seen by men! And you say that you are a New Testament priest: why then are you not happy with making your gowns and skirts to be long enough to prevent people from seeing your laps (even when you are sitting down)?

Many women and ladies live in hypocrisy: when there is cold, the women cover themselves well to avoid it; but they will not care if their dressing is instigating lust and causing men to go Hell. Do they love Jesus Christ in reality?

In clearer words, the gown or skirt of a Christian and Godly woman, lady, or girl should not be shorter than halfway between her knee and her ankle, as she is standing up. This will guard against people seeing her laps when she sits down. These modern-day short (knee-level) gowns and skirts came from the wisdom and plans of the devil and his devils, whether or not you believe this Truth! The devil is very subtle and crafty.

If God is not interested in your body (or how you appear), why do you ask for (or claim) bodily healing or Divine health on your body? Many Believers allow the devil to deceive and mislead them with foolishness. How can you do try-and-luck (bet) with your eternal destiny in Heaven or Hell, when there wouldn't be any second chance?

What many people bind the devil of, are nothing but the works of the flesh. If you refuse to take up your responsibility, by obeying the Word of God, you will open a way for the devil; because he, who breaks the hedge, will be bitten by the serpent. Obey God, and those devils will leave by themselves! This will make it possible for you to have fewer things to pray and fast about.

The problem of many churches today is the presence of mixed multitude and great multitude. Yes, great multitude is good; but are you directing their hearts to the Lord and His Word? Today, you see unbelieving chorus leaders and musicians in the church. Many of them sing under the influence of drugs and alcohol. Some of them smoke. What a pity!

This is why you see worldly tones of music being played in many churches today. When you hear worldly tones of reggae, disco, awilo, makosa, etc, you should know that the end time is here with us. They will call God, Jesus, and speak Biblical things in the music; but the tone and beat is demonically programmed and attracts demons.

Choreographic dance is of the devil, for at least two reasons. First, it sends lustful impulses and thoughts to male watchers, which is one of the reasons why the devil introduced it into churches. Also, it makes people to put and focus their attention on the dancers and their body movements instead of focusing on worshipping God. Also, traditional dances are not to be used in the church, because they originated from demons who inspired those heathen traditions.

Concerning music and dancing, the Bible says, "Now the works of the flesh are evident, which are…revelries…of which I tell you beforehand, just as I also told you in time past, that those who practice such things will not inherit the Kingdom of God (Gal. 5:19-21).

"For we have spent enough of our past time in doing the will of the Gentiles – when we walked in…revelries…" (1 Pet. 4:3). According to the Longman Dictionary of Contemporary English, revelry means wild noisy dancing. God is against worldly, satanic, and demonic dancing, music, and tones, even in the church!

The Word of God tells us to prove or test all things, and to hold fast what is good (1 Thes. 5:21). Apostle John put it this way: "Beloved, do not believe every spirit, but test the spirits whether they are of God; because many false prophets have gone out into the world (1 Jn 4:1). Apostle Paul gave us another striking Word when he said, "Let two or three prophets speak, and let others judge" (1 Cor. 14:29).

Have you seen that even prophecies are to be judged and tested with the Word of God and the intuition or witness in your spirit by the Holy Spirit? When we talk of false prophets, many people seem to detect or suspect possible false prophets from their states or countries, and they count the foreign preachers as true ministers. My brother, they exist – locally, nationally, and internationally.

If they were preaching and teaching the Truth, without bringing people into satanic and demonic bondages, I wouldn't have been so much concerned. Why? Because Jesus Christ spoke to His Disciples, saying, "The scribes and the Pharisees sit in Moses' seat. Therefore whatever they tell you to observe, that observe and do, but do not do according to their works; for they say, and do not do" (Matt. 23:2-3).

They also use the Bible, quoting it to you, as the devil quoted it to Jesus Christ in the wilderness, to deceive people. They mix the Bible with the doctrines and teachings of demons and seducing spirits, and they deceive many. People hear them and say, "That is a great man of God!" People clap hands for them, and say, "Ride on, pastor!"

How do you know a false minister? By his words and practices. If his teachings and practices are against Sound Doctrine, run away from him. If he is interested in your money and not your soul, run away from him.

I am not just talking about somebody who may be making a minor mistake, because somebody may make a mistake (though God doesn't want it). But many of them know what they are doing. They know that they are working for the devil. They know they are working for money and fame.

I will tell you that many (or most) of all these beauty salons in town are owned by agents of the kingdom of darkness. Even those who are not direct or conscious agents have been demonized, in that their minds have been influenced or obsessed by the devil into doing that business, because the business glorifies the devil a lot.

When your business expands the works of the kingdom of darkness, are you not their agent? Whether or not you attend their night meetings, you are working for them. I know that, just as many Believers use those materials ignorantly, there are people who do the business, though they are not conscious or direct agents of the kingdom of darkness.

Yet, it doesn't change the fact that they are standing or working for the devil. Am I saying that women shouldn't take care of their hair? No, but they should do it in a Godly manner. Every sincere Christian lady or woman, who seeks to know, will be directed by the Holy Spirit on how to take care of her hair.

Therefore, if you take care of people's hair, as a Believer, you have to do it in a Godly manner. Any business that glorifies the devil and expands the kingdom of darkness, cannot be from God.

The beauty salons, the beauty stores, and the fashion centres, what do they stand for? The person that sales bleaching creams, and helps people to call God stupid for giving them the skin complexion they have, is he or she working for God or for satan? I will rather tell you the Truth and you hate me, than thwart the Word of God, and your blood will be on my head; after all, I am not interested in your sinful money!

If you are a tailor or a clothing designer/maker, what type of dresses and wears do you make for your customers/clients? We have demonic fashion designers also. They tell our good Christian ladies and women, "This style will not make you look 'sharp' and attractive." They will not use the word – seductive, because they are bent to deceive.

And before you know what is happening, you will see a Christian girl, lady, or woman wearing what will show us her armpits, her breasts, and her laps. Some demonic ladies will even carry those types of wears, and sit in front of the church congregation, so as to attempt to lead the man of God on the altar into lust and fornication, so that he will be reduced to an ordinary man, like the Philistines, with their Delilah, did to the 'powerful' Samson.

So, when you sell those marine weavons, demonic attachments, satanic nails, devilish cortex, bloody make-ups, and many other things in the group, are you a Christian, a Believer, or a Disciple? If you are a disciple, are you a disciple of satan or a Disciple of the Lord Jesus Christ? Who are you working for? What do you stand for?

Even those of you, who will make a long skirt, and divide (or, will I say, 'tear') that long skirt at the back, side, or front so that it reveals what a miniskirt or a short-skirt reveals, are you saying that you don't know what you are doing? If you say you did it to be able to walk freely, then why did you make a tight-fitting skirt in the first place? Others will cut their blouses or gowns to show us their back.

Get ready, for judgment is coming. I am not a prophet of doom, but a prophet of the Word of God; and I know that the Great Judge is ready to judge all unrighteousness! Therefore, count your soul more precious than your appearance now!

Those worldly and fashionable wedding gowns should be abolished for Believers and churches. Those wedding gowns are made to be glamorous, flamboyant, gorgeous, and for show and fashion. You may say that it is your day; but the Bible says, "Let your moderation be known unto all men. The Lord is at hand" (Phil. 4:5). Many people even go to the extent of making or using wedding gowns that reveal their sensitive parts.

Men wear (or make) normal wears or suits that they still wear even after the wedding ceremony. Therefore, the bride's wear or dress should be made to be normal and in such a way as to be something she can still wear at any other time after the wedding ceremony. It can be a gown or a skirt and blouse. Yes, make it to look good, but not something for fashion, show, or glamour.

Saying things like this may seem somehow, because my wife used wedding gown during our wedding. Even though the one she used covered her, yet, if I were to wed now, I cannot allow my wife to wear the conventional wedding gowns (even though now, weddings are done in many churches with those wedding gowns), because it does not reflect moderation, humility, Christ-likeness, and the Bible: it shows excesses for show.

But just because I didn't know the Truth at that time will not make me not to say the Truth when I know it. For instance, 'naturally', I myself hated (and I still hate) rings; but when I married, I loved (I think it was not just a liking) wearing wedding ring (maybe for the love of a husband for the wife). But I cannot wear a wedding ring again, because it is still a ring. Will I encourage wearing wedding rings because I loved or worn it?

Formerly, when people had good sense and judgment, the blouses of women were made in such a way that they didn't have buttons at the front, from their chest to their waist. But now, satanic fashion designers have designed what they call blouses for women which have spaced buttons from their chests downwards. And when they wear them, their breasts will push the material, so that someone can see their breasts from the spaces between the buttons.

The devil knew what he did in that demonic design. If their blouses are to be made that way, then they must have very well sealed zips, and not spaced buttons. When people listened to their consciences, men's shirts were made with spaced buttons, because men don't have breasts that will push open their chests. And don't wear those hanging blouses, which when you sit down or lift up your hands, your underwear will be exposed. Say "Amen!"

Men must button up their shirts (that is, they are not to leave their chests open). If you, as a woman, must wear a blouse with buttons, make sure it is not the kind that will reveal your breast or brassiere in-between the buttons. Zips are preferable to buttons for women's blouses; complete undivided blouses with neither zips nor buttons are best for women. Those short hanging jackets worldly women wear are satanic.

If many of our ladies and women will devote the energy they use to beautify themselves, to work on their spirit and soul, brother, many husbands will be running to their homes immediately they are through with their work and business. However, even in the homes of many Believers, the husbands prefer to stay away from home as much as possible.

When you talk to your husband as if he doesn't have authority over you, do you think that he will want to stay with you? This is one of the reasons why many unbelieving husbands go after strange women, because when they see the lady that will honour and respect them, the devil tells them, "Have you seen?"

And the Bible says, "Wives, likewise, be submissive to your own husbands, that even if some do not obey the Word, they, without a word, may be won by the conduct of their wives, when they observe your chaste conduct accompanied by fear" (1 Pet. 3:1-2).

On this issue of the dressing of the women, women should make their dresses – blouses, skirts, gowns, and wrappers – in such a way that they will cover their sensitive parts. When you dress, people shouldn't see your laps, breasts, and armpits. Make your skirts in such a way that even when you sit down, people shouldn't see your laps. If you use handkerchief to cover it when you sit down, are you hypocritical?

Your sensitive parts are for your husband; therefore reserve them for him, and not for us. When you keep on straightening your skirts or you use handkerchief to cover your laps as you are sitting down, why didn't you tell them to make it longer than it is, when they were making it? Or, are you deceiving yourself?

Use the blouses that were made with well-sealed zips. Condemn those blouses which, when you put them on, people, other than your husband, see your breasts in-between buttons; you understand? You are a Christian, and not an unbeliever! The neck of your blouse is to be in such a way that even when you bend down, no one will see your breast.

Don't wear body-hug dresses, because they reveal your body contours. Don't wear see-through dresses. What do I mean by see-through dresses? In physics, the scientists talk of transparent, translucent, and opaque materials. The translucent materials are semi-opaque and semi-transparent. The see-through dresses are the semi-covering and semi-uncovering dresses.

Many Believers wear short-skirts, and they 'think' that because the skirts are not miniskirts, then nothing is wrong with the skirts. A sincere, serious, and dedicated Christian whose mind is in Heaven (and whose eye has not been blinded by the devil) will not be comfortable wearing a short-skirt. A short skirt or gown is the one which when you sit down, somebody can see any part of your laps; while a miniskirt or mini-gown is the one which even when you are standing up, somebody can see your laps.

If, as a man, I open the back or front of my shirt the way some women open the back or front of their blouses and gowns, will you be happy? And if a man will not open his front or back, how much more the women!

Your armpits are not to be seen when you lift up your hands; therefore, the sleeves of your blouses and gowns must be made, both in length and in design, in such a way as to guard against this.

In your church, ministry, or fellowship, be mindful of the dressing and appearance of those who minister, speak, or appear before the crowd, especially those that appear before them often; because they, consciously or unconsciously, tell the rest of the people how they should dress and appear.

To this end, the pastor and minister should be mindful of how his wife dresses and appears, because many women, ladies, and girls in the church, ministry, or fellowship will likely learn from her. Many churches, ministries, and fellowships that dress and appear like the people of the world became that way because of the ministers' wives and other women leaders and ministers.

And don't even wear shorts or trousers inside your skirt or gown; use your appropriate underwears. Somebody may say that she will wear shorts to avoid being raped; but it is God Who keeps and protects you. By the way, even trousers will not stop being raped; but God will stop it. The person who can forcefully rape you can also pull the trousers; and at gunpoint, if you fear weapons instead of believing and trusting God, you yourself will pull the trousers out. But if you do the right thing, angels of God are there to intervene on your behalf. Also, don't use trousers for night-wears: don't allow the devil to deceive you.

Be careful of the pictures and signs that are drawn or imposed on your blouses, shirts, wears, and dresses. The devil puts satanic, demonic, devilish, and occult pictures and signs on some wears and dresses to entangle and enslave people. Those pictures and signs can attract and permit the presence of demons and their works.

Do not use Lycra material to make your dresses and clothes. Lycra material is a material that stretches, which is used for making tight-fitting clothes. This is because it tights your body and shows your body contours, thereby sending lustful messages and impulses to the opposite sex. God hates the use of it for dresses and clothes.

Do not send your children to any school where they are forced to wear sleeveless dresses and clothes as their school uniform: they will end up corrupting them. And the schools which use such school uniforms either have demonic targets from the leadership, have been deceived by the devil and his demons, or they have satanic workers/teachers (conscious or unconscious). Of course, this is not to say that all schools where they wear sleeved dresses and clothes are free from demonic works.

Men dress up to cover their chest and back; who then designed (or planned the design of) the open chest blouses or gowns that show women's breasts' cleavage and breasts, or the open back blouses or gowns that show their back? It could be no other beings/people than satan and his associates; they are the beings/people that stand against the Will of God and promote lust among men.

For those who say that they use pairs of trousers to guard against cold, the human race has been in existence for about six thousand years on the surface of this earth: Did people not keep themselves safe from cold from the beginning of the human race till about some decades ago when women started wearing trousers, which many of them hypocritically call slacks?

You, as a Christian lady, should appear natural. What do we men lose by appearing natural? You may say you want to attract people, but you are attracting men (whether or not they are Believers) who have not known the Truth, because those things get me annoyed, when I see them on the bodies of believing ladies and women. Therefore, all those lipsticks, cortexes, demonic/artificial nails, and paint or pencil will not be required.

Somebody asked me, saying, "Can I use brown powder since I use white powder?" One needs to wonder why some women want to look horrible the way they look. Why do people really want to paint themselves as if they are buildings that need to be painted and repainted? Many of those women seem not to know that their minds have been obsessed by demons, and they 'do not even know' what they are doing to themselves. I wonder why many husbands allow their wives to dress and appear the way they appear! Some men even tell their wives to look that horrible.

Well, as for the question of, "Can I use brown powder since I use white powder?" Why do you want to use the brown powder? The Bible says, "Moreover, when you fast, do not be like the hypocrites, with a sad countenance. For they disfigure their faces that they may appear to men to be fasting. Assuredly, I say to you, they have their reward. But you, when you fast, anoint your head and wash your face, so that you do not appear to men to be fasting, but to your Father Who is in the Secret Place; and your Father Who sees in secret will reward you openly" (Matt. 6:16-18).

Here Jesus Christ tells you to use ointment on your head and wash your face instead of disorganizing your head (hair), wearing sackcloth, and sitting on ashes, to appear to men to be fasting. But notice that the purpose for anointing your head (rubbing oil/ointment on your hair) and washing your face is for you to look normal, so that people will not know that you are fasting.

Of course, it is not compulsory that you anoint your head and wash your face whenever you fasting, because if you were to be in the desert, on the mountain, or in the room alone, where people will not see you, you may decide to neither anoint your head nor wash your face, at least for some time. However, the purpose of the anointing (rubbing) and washing is to appear normal.

So, whereas somebody may use white powder to remove or neutralize oil on his or her face, another person may just wipe his or her face with a handkerchief to remove the oil that might have been accumulated on his or her face, maybe due to heat. But why will you even paint/parch your face with white powder or brown powder? Do you want white or brown colour for your face and 'building'?

Therefore, apart from the brown powder issue, there is certainly a difference between using white powder to neutralize oil on your face and using white powder to paint your face. So, apart from using white powder to neutralize oil on your face, using white powder (maybe the medicated one) to stop or treat heat rashes on your body, or for any other good special case(s), do not even paint your face with white powder for beauty. Of course, this concerns both males and females.

Don't put your mind on costly or expensive things. Never be obsessed by them. Moderately priced and inexpensive clothing is good for the women. It helps to prevent pride. Don't pressurize your husband to buy expensive things for you; for it will not be to your advantage. If the man starts misbehaving and disobeying the Word of God in order to satisfy you, you will suffer it more.

Why? Because when someone starts stealing, lying, or cheating, the fellow can also start following strange women, since they are all from the same heart. Any person, who can be committing evil and hiding it from men, without fearing God Who sees all things, can do what you may not believe.

God said to Jacob, "Arise go up to Bethel and dwell there; and make an altar there to God, Who appeared to you when you fled from the face of Esau your brother." And Jacob said to his household and all who were with him, "Put away the foreign gods that are among you, purify yourselves, and change your garments. Then let us go up to Bethel...."

So they gave Jacob all the foreign gods which were in their hands, and the earrings which were in their ears; and Jacob hid (buried) them under the terebinth tree which was by Shechem. And they journeyed, and the Terror of God was upon the cities that were all around them, and they did not pursue the sons of Jacob (Gen. 35:1-5).

Earrings were among the things they purified themselves from to be clean before God. The Egyptians, Babylonians, Assyrians, Mesopotamians, and the other foreign and heathen nations were given to these things, just as the people of the world today. When you leave the world, you will also leave these things.

And piercing your ear to wear earrings is of the devil. Why do you pierce your ear? Are you a slave? If your ears were pierced by your parents, having repented from it, how can you wear earrings in it again? Where then is your repentance?

When God told Moses to tell the children of Israel to collect those things from the Egyptians, God wanted to plunder the Egyptians, because they made those things from gold and silver. And the Israelites, instead of keeping those things for the construction of the Ark of the Testimony and other things, they started with using them to construct a calf which they worshipped, and said that it was the calf that brought them out of Egypt (Exo. 32). God was very angry with them for that act; and had it not been that Moses interceded for them, He would have wiped them out!

People wear and use things that bring them into the bondage of the devil, even unknowingly. And God says that His people are destroyed for lack of knowledge (Hos. 4:6); and His people have gone into captivity, because they have no knowledge (Isa. 5:13). When you use the things that God has condemned, you are selling yourself to the devil, and he will oppress you. The devil, satan, is a master-strategist: he wants to have your spirit, soul, and body; and if he doesn't get this one, he will go for the other.

Earrings, bangles, rings, necklaces, and such things are not needed on your body by God. They promote the desire of the devil, which is ornamenting your body. Even wedding rings won't be necessary. Of course, you would have seen some who would even put an extra ring on top of the wedding ring to make it look more beautiful. Who even invented the wedding ring as a means of distinguishing the married from the unmarried? Get rid of wedding rings and engagement rings from your fingers, brothers and sisters! Your soul is much more precious than wedding rings and engagement rings.

Some people try to use Abraham (or his servant) to defend themselves in this issue; but they fail to know that Abraham didn't know everything at the same time. Before Jacob grew up and matured, having come from Isaac of Abraham (many years after Abraham), they would have known how God reacts to those things.

Remember that Abraham was a heathen and idol worshipper (from Ur of the Chaldeans – Babylonians) before he was called by God; and he had learned their ways. It still took some time to refine him. Abraham lied on two different occasions, because of fear (and Isaac also lied over his wife, because of fear). Does that make lying good, because Abraham lied?

If your dresses are worldly in appearance, condemn them, because of Jesus Christ and your soul. Don't be afraid, for God is able to provide you with new good dresses. Don't put your trust in man, no matter what he owns: put your trust in God, and His angels will bring all you need to you in due time.

The same things that were happening when God destroyed the whole earth with the Flood are happening now. The same things that the Israelites (God's people) did, for which God destroyed them in the wilderness, are happening today in many churches.

When God destroyed the world, they didn't carry arms for Him; they didn't shoot at Him with guns: they were disobedient to His Commands, and they lived to gratify the lusts of their eyes and the desires of their flesh.

And the same things that happened to the people of old, will happen to many (even Believers) in the Last Day, but in a different dimension – Hell Fire. The Church is giving the Lord Jesus Christ more 'headache' and trouble than the world! But just as the Jews didn't believe Prophet Jeremiah until they were engulfed in the disaster that God brought upon them, many will not believe this Message and Word until they will end in Hell Fire.

God is not from any nation, and He owns all nations. Though we know, from the Bible, that God has a special link with the nation of Israel, yet, He is not from Israel. Israel cannot dictate for Him; and He will not change His Standard because of Israel. God cannot change His Standard for anyone and for any church. No matter how anointed you are, no matter what you may have, all came from God.

Many people do the things they do, because they think that since people from this or that nation do the same things, they must be right; but this is not true in the ultimate sense. The thing that many people seem to fail to understand is that the devil is working in every nation of the earth.

No matter the nation you may come from, the devil had been working in your nation before you were born, and he will continue to work there. The devil has succeeded to work in many nations without being recognized.

There are many things that are being done in some nations of the world, which people don't see as having come from the devil. For instance, when a country legalizes abortion, whether or not they know it, the work of the devil is being fulfilled in their midst.

God hates abortion; for no one has right to take any other person's life. No matter the theory or proposition medical science may make to make abortion look good, they are just dancing to the tone of the devil's deception. Once the zygote has been formed, a human being has come.

Let us consider the issue of women liberation movements. Have you noticed the rate of divorce and juvenile delinquencies these days? These are the long-term effects of women liberation movements.

When women decide to abandon their basic responsibilities in pursuit of secondary issues, the devil is at work, whether they recognize it or not. Women have the responsibility to be helpers suitable to their husbands.

We will now consider the issue of whether it is good for women to put on trousers. One thing about dresses is that they are meant to cover the person putting them on, whether they are men or women.

Gowns, wrappers, skirts, blouses, trousers, shirts, etc, are to cover the person wearing them. I want you to know that over the years, in every continent (America, Europe, Africa, Asia, etc), there have been changes in the modes of their dressing.

However, any dressing or change in dressing that does not glorify God is satanic and demonic, no matter what any person may think or say, even though you may not have it in mind as you put them on. That is the Truth. The devil prefers to work under cover and without being noticed.

When women put on sleeveless blouses, mini-skirts, tight-fitting and partly transparent (revealing) dresses, they are glorifying satan, and helping him to fulfil his purpose, whether or not they know it.

As I said before, considering the biological features of women, women should not use pairs of trousers. Why? When a woman is matured sexually, one of the features that biologists tell us will be noticed in her is enlarged buttocks. Have you never noticed that trousers show their body contours for everybody to see? Trousers reveal their buttocks and laps seductively.

Now, don't say that you are going to allow your children wear pairs of trousers, and when they mature they will stop using them. If you train them up that way, when they are old, they will not depart from it (Prov. 22:6).

But seductive dresses or dressing seductively helps the devil spread his lust wave, and people get into the sins of lust, fornication, adultery, etc. Some will say that whoever wants to fall will fall; but you and I know that some things can make someone fall, when he wouldn't have fallen without them.

Let the Spirit of God lead you, and do not be led by your mind and thought. Trousers are neither an American culture nor a British culture. It started at a time, and got so much opposition there then; but over so many years later, the opposition has waned so much that some think it is their culture.

After all, was there anything like America until Amerigo sailed past the Atlantic Ocean and found the land which was later developed to be America? And it is Britain that developed and colonized America before they got their independence. And all countries and continents of the world will appear before God for judgment.

Know this once again: any dressing that helps the devil fulfil his will, plan, and purpose is from him. If you can't stop dressing this or that way because of Jesus Christ, can you lay down your life for Him? (Matt. 10:39). Don't you want to be worthy of Him?

Christians (both males and females) should avoid wearing jeans materials for some reasons. Jeans tight your body to show your body-contours. Jeans seem to have been made/designed by the devil to provoke rough, wild, and worldly feeling and lifestyle, as evident in the fact that you may see some of them as stone-wash jeans, jeans which look like they have been decolourized (or partly decolourized), perforated jeans with different kinds of openings, patched jeans with pieces of the material sewn on it, torn jeans proudly worn as style (whereas other clothing materials that are torn would make the same person feel ashamed), jeans trousers or shorts with rough cutting or design at the edges, etc.

If the physical appearance of many Believers are worldly, how much more the sins of spirit and soul (inward sins) that are hidden from us! If many Believers don't care about their worldly appearance, how much more do they care less concerning the hidden sins (inward sins) which we do not see!

God hates tribal marks and tattooing your body, as He said, "You shall not make any cuttings in your flesh for the dead, nor tattoo any marks on you: I am the Lord" (Lev. 19:28). No matter the kind of design or picture you tattoo yourself with, it is evil.

Funky (modern and fashionable) style of hair cut like what is called 'punk', 'afro-cut', etc must not find its place in you. Also, leave your hair the natural shape it has in haircut; and avoid carving it, for it gives it an unnatural or/and fashionable shape.

There are many reasons why Christians should not use weavons. Using weavons is like telling God that He is stupid and imperfect for giving you the kind of hair you have. It is like bleaching, which many do; they feel that God should have made them fair in complexion instead of dark. But on the Day of Judgment, you will find out that you tried to degrade God. Using relaxer and hair extensions for your hair or another person's hair is demonic and satanic in origin, and leads to Hell Fire.

The Word says, "For this reason God gave them up to vile passions. For even their women exchanged the natural use for what is against nature. Likewise also the men, leaving the natural use of the woman, burned in their lust for one another, men with men committing what is shameful, and receiving in themselves the penalty of their error which was due" (Rom. 1:26-27).

This place implies turning the nature to artificial/perversion in women/men. Turning the nature to artificial/perversion in women/men does not only apply to lesbianism and homosexualism. Of course, the Bible emphasized on homosexualism here; but on the side of the women, it says, "…women exchanged the natural use for what is against nature."

And you see the exchanging of the natural for what is against nature and God's Plan, Wisdom, and Ability in bleaching the skin, perfuming the body, painting the nails with cortex, fixing of artificial nails, frying and perming the hair, artificially relaxing and extending the hair, painting the face with lipstick and eye-pencil, dyeing the hair, fixing of eyelashes, using and wearing of weavons and attachments, tattooing the body, etc.

And, "The Wrath of God is revealed from Heaven against all ungodliness and unrighteousness of men, who suppress the Truth in unrighteousness, because what may be known of God is manifest in them, for God has shown it to them" (Rom. 1:18). You can see that God has given and shown you the reason why you shouldn't change His Handiwork; therefore, if you do, then you decided to corrupt yourself, turn yourself against God, suffer unnecessary things in this earth, and finally deprive yourself of Heaven!

God asked whether a leopard can change its spot, because He has made it that way (Jer. 13:23); and many human beings say, "God, we are wiser than You and leopards, and we know how to change our skin." The Ethiopians would have refused to change their skin in the old times; now many of them may do it because of science and technology.

It is like those who use high-heel shoes to increase their height, because they feel that they should be taller than they are. When Jesus Christ tells you not to worry about your height, because you can't add a cubit to it (Matt. 6:27), you say, "God, I know how to increase my not-good size in height."

Some use perfume to say, "Why must people not identify my scent? This natural neutral 'scent' is too boring!" Why do people try to bring themselves into different bondages? Others use breast-pads to make their breasts look big and seductive. When you see some others paint themselves with powder, you wonder why they want to look that way in the first place!

Many others say, "God, it is not now that I should have grey (gray) hair; I am still young." (Grey is British English, while gray is American English). And they end up dyeing their hair. Many spend hours designing themselves – time they should have used for Godly and spiritual things. The silver-haired head is a crown of glory, if it is found in the way of righteousness (Prov. 16:31). The glory of young men is their strength, and the splendour of old men is their grey head (Prov. 20:29). Silver-haired or grey head is the Handiwork of God!

Also, many of those weavons are real human hair which were cut and sold. How can you be wearing another person's hair as a Christian lady or woman? This is worldliness; this is satanic and demonic; sister, the ground you are treading on is dangerous.

Then, even though some of those weavons may be synthetic or artificial (which the first point still condemns), many of those weavons ladies use are manufactured in the water-kingdom of darkness and brought to this earth for sales to contaminate the people of the world.

The thing that some people don't know is that some companies which exist physically on this earth came from the dark kingdom of satan, especially the water-world of the devil. In fact, many things we see physically came from the dark kingdom. Even many legal and morally good things (like pre-fabricated food) we see are manufactured in the dark kingdom, some of which I wouldn't mention here.

This is why you need to pray over and sanctify the things that you use, especially edible things. But how will you want to sanctify the things that the Lord has rejected and condemned (like weavons, artificial nails, wet-lips, lipsticks, eyelashes, etc)? You are already offending God!

Everything is not demonic, don't misunderstand me; don't live in fear either, because greater is He that is in us than he that is in the world. The anointing breaks every yoke of the enemy. But many Christians create loopholes for the devil through sin, disobedience, and worldliness.

You need to be watchful and sober, because if you are not, the devil can lead you into sin and worldliness; and if the Lord Jesus Christ meets you in that state at His Coming, or you die in that state, you will miss Heaven and go to Hell.

But that is not God's Plan for you; and He did not bring you out of the world to condemn you later. Therefore, don't condemn yourself. You condemn yourself by despising His Word and the Promptings of His Spirit.

Many are busy 'binding and loosing' the devil while they are the ones that are inviting the devil. Preachers and ministers, many of you are busy saying you are destroying the works of the devil, while the devil is binding people comfortably through worldliness among Believers. May their blood not be on your hands because you refused to tell them the Truth!

Some say that it is not written in the Bible that you must not smoke. Okay, continue to destroy your body, which is the Temple of God (1 Cor. 3:16), until you hear, "Get behind Me, you who practice iniquity!" Cigarette is a destructive tool of satan, the devil. It is suicide in disguise.

Others say that it is alright to drink alcohol as far as you don't get drunk (or in small quantity). Firstly, assuming that the wine which Apostle Paul told Timothy to drink was not a totally non-alcoholic wine, little sense should have told you that if the Believers of the New Testament were drinking it in small quantity, Apostle Paul wouldn't have needed to tell Timothy to take small of it as medicine.

Even if you have stomach problem, do you now envy that archaic and unrefined medical practice when you have always wanted development and civilization, just because you want to satisfy your flesh? Will you have the boldness to defend yourself before God on the Judgment Day? Can you forsake alcohol for God and for your soul?

Secondly, according to the Dake's Annotated Reference Bible's explanation of 1 Tim. 5:23, "With two kinds of wine mentioned in the Scripture – one, unfermented new wine found in the cluster (Isa. 65:8), we can be assured that Timothy was not urged to take the intoxicating kind to strengthen him." Someone may ask, "If this is true, then why did he tell him to drink little of it?" First, you don't even have to drink non-alcoholic drink to excess.

Second, who knows whether they (Timothy was his disciple and associate) had altogether stopped drinking even non-alcoholic wine as a kind of self-denial, continuous partial fasting, or living the fasted life, even as John the Baptist did not eat and drink all kinds of even morally good food and drinks? Even now, many Believers and ministers decide to (or, are commanded by God) to stop or minimize the intake of certain kinds of food or/and drinks as a way of self-denial and living the fasted life.

The Bible says, "Who has woe? Who has sorrow? Who has contentions? Who has complaints? Who has wounds without cause? Who has redness of eyes? Those who linger long at the wine; those who go in search of mixed wine. Do not look on the wine when it is red, when it sparkles in the cup, when it swirls around smoothly; at the last it bites like a serpent, and stings like a viper. Your eyes will see strange things, and your heart will utter perverse things" (Prov. 23:29-33).

Here, the Bible says, "Do not look on the wine...." Can you take a small amount of what you are not supposed to look on to? That is to say, "Don't even desire any amount of wine or alcohol." Whether the wine contains 1% or 5% of alcohol, it is still alcohol and sinful. Can you allow small amount of alcohol to take you to Hell?

When a company that manufactures wine puts '5% alcohol' on the label of the wine, it shows that they know the difference between wine that is free from alcohol and the one with alcohol. And there was no alcoholic content in the wine that Jesus Christ made. No wonder the master of the feast said, "…You have kept the good wine until now!" (Jn 2:10). Jesus Christ made a good quality wine with a difference!

People used to abort unborn human beings in secret before; now satanic and demonic laws have empowered them. And subtly and craftily, the enemy (satan, the devil) has 'moralized' abortion in certain birth-control measures.

People used to smoke secretly before; now they are bold to smoke anyhow outside. Homosexuals and lesbians used to practice their wickedness in secret and darkness, being ashamed of it; now they even boast that they are homosexuals and lesbians. Boasting and waiting for damnation in Hell Fire!

The devil has penetrated and destroyed many people through films. Most of those films from Hollywood, Nollywood, and others promote the works of the devil. Even, many (or most) of the so-called Christian films still advertize and promote the works of the devil.

When films are promoting immorality, indecent dressing, vices, violence, hatred, and other demonic activities, do they promote God? Be careful with the type of film that you and your family watch! Many of those films are dedicated to the devil to serve his interest and increase sales; and so, playing them attracts the presence of demons into your house (and to the watchers). Watching of wrestling, karate, horror films, and many others are inspired by the devil.

So, you film director, producer, actor, or actress, whose interest are you serving? Who is inspiring you, and who are you working for? Sometimes, the devil will wittingly package some of the films in such a way that they look harmless; but ultimately, his interest is being promoted.

Just as many Believers and ministers preach and teach heresies and anti-Christ, anti-God, and unbiblical doctrines and practices, when half-baked and non-Biblically sound Believers direct and produce their so-called Christian films, they end up expanding false teachings and doctrines.

The Internet is a major way that the devil uses to enslave the children of men. Through the Internet, the devil has made many people to go into indecent dressing, lust, and sexual immorality. In Twitter, Facebook, Google, etc, you will see things that can lead you away from the Word of God, if you are not careful, disciplined, and determined.

There are many satanic, demonic, and occult websites in the Internet. Even many of those sites, blogs, and websites which were not opened by conscious agents of satan have things that can still make you to be corrupted and polluted if you are not careful. Many times, even when you are doing something else in the Internet, they will start flashing you with seductive pictures and worldly things.

You might have observed that many of the programmes, movies (films), music, and activities that are spread by televisions, digital satellite stations, cables networks, and radio stations are satanic and demonic in origin. Therefore, be careful of what you watch and ponder on, and what you allow your children and family to watch, listen to, and be exposed to.

Beware of the cartoons that you allow your children to watch, because many of those cartoons are demonic, and they are capturing souls for the devil. Evil spirits possess people when they watch some cartoons. Also, many of the video games that people play are demonic and satanic; and they get people who play them demonized. Horror films are from the devil, and they promote his plans and works.

These are apart from the time that people spend on these things and more, and the passion with which they pursue and get attached to them, thereby making them their gods. When you use the time you should use for God and His Things for activities that do not glory His Name, the Jealous God gets jealous and angry!

Change your name if it is satanic and demonic. Dissociate yourself from any satanic, demonic, and ungodly name. Don't you say that what you confess is what you possess? Why then do you want satanic, demonic, or negative confession on what you are called by? Do you think that God will like to call you by satanic or demonic names?

Concerning the covering of the hair, the Bible says, "Every man praying or prophesying, having his head covered dishonours his head. But every woman who prays or prophesies with her head uncovered dishonours her head, for that is one and the same as if her head were shaved. For if a woman is not covered, let her also be shorn. But if it is shameful for a woman to be shorn or shaved, let her be covered.

"For a man indeed ought not to cover his head, since he is the Image and Glory of God; but woman is the glory of man. For man is not from woman, but woman from man. Nor was man created for the woman, but woman for the man. For this reason the woman ought to have a symbol of authority on her head, because of the angels.

"…Judge among yourselves. Is it proper for a woman to pray to God with her head uncovered? Does not even nature itself teach you that if a man has long hair, it is a dishonour to him? But if a woman has long hair, it is a glory to her; for her hair is given to her for a covering. But if anyone seems to be contentious, we have no such custom, nor do the churches of God" (1 Cor. 11:4-16, New King James Version).

I want you to notice that it did not say that her 'long hair' is given to her for a covering, but her hair. I also want you to notice that this place is talking about covering the hair, and not about long or short hair. To convince you that it is speaking of covering or veiling your hair, the Bible says, "Every man praying or prophesying, having his head covered dishonours his head" (verse 4).

Covering the hair indicates using something (not your hair) to veil your hair. Forget about the distortion of the Bible: according to the Longman Dictionary of Contemporary English, 'veil' is a thin piece of material worn by women to cover their faces at formal occasions such as weddings or for religious reasons.

You can see that this portion of the Scripture is dealing with veiling yourself, as a woman, and not about long or short hair. Speaking of long or short hair, it says, "Does not even nature itself teach you that if a man has long hair, it is dishonour to him?" (verse 14). This is to say that, naturally, long hair doesn't befit a man.

Speaking on the being good if a woman has a natural long hair, it says, "But if a woman has long hair, it is a glory to her; for her hair is given to her for a covering" (verse 15). This is why I ponder on it when I see Christian women cut their hair as low as a man's hair (and I am talking of even outside the church building).

If a woman has to cut her hair as low as men's hair in any given society or nature of hair (because the nature or natural texture of the hair will affect the length), then she should also be ready to wear cap on it, because, naturally, it doesn't befit a woman, except that 'human civilization' and disregard for God-ordained procedures has gripped many. This is what these women liberation movements, which are inspired by satan, have caused over time: disregard for God-ordained authority and natural tendencies.

And know that it didn't say that the long attachment or weavon of the woman is given to her for a covering, because God didn't give any woman any attachment or weavon. Therefore the attachment or weavon on the head of the woman is no glory, but satanic and demonic bondage, whether or not she knows of it.

It says, "But if a woman has long hair…" and not, "When a woman has long hair…." So your hair may not be 'long' or very long, but should not be as short as men's hair in the race/nation you are from (I am not talking of mixed society: where the society is mixed, consisting of people from different nations and races, then use the shortness of men's hair from the same nation or race as you to ascertain the minimum length of your hair); but it is best long, as far as the being 'long' or very long is not achieved by perming or artificially relaxing your hair or with the use of attachments or weavon!

If you find it difficult to comb it or keep it neat, then shorten, reduce, or cut it, to the length that you can comb it well and keep it neat; but do not let it be as low as the general length of the hair of the men from the same race or nation as you, except you are going to wear cap or hair scarf on it as you go around.

Look at what verses 4 and 7 say: "Every man praying or prophesying, having his head covered dishonours his head. For a man indeed ought not to cover his head, since he is the Image and Glory of God; but woman is the glory of man." This is telling a man, who already has a short hair (or may decide to be shorn) to not cover his hair in the church. To be shorn is to shave someone's hair clean, as you would shear the skin of the sheep. Is this not clear enough that what the Bible is talking about here is covering the hair and not short or long hair?

And verses 5 and 6 say: "But every woman who prays or prophesies with her head uncovered dishonours her head, for that is one and the same as if her head were shaved. For if a woman is not covered, let her also be shorn. But if it is shameful for a woman to be shorn or shaved, let her be covered." And this place is saying that the woman whose hair is not covered (veiled) in the church is the same as being shorn (shaving her hair clean).

And verse 10 says that a woman should have a symbol of authority on her head because of the angels. That is either to teach the angels submission to God, or in order not to grieve the angels of God, who, normally, are present in any Believers' meeting; because angels don't like disorder and unrighteousness. Lucifer and his cohorts rebelled against God; they were angels, just like the present obedient angels. Genesis 24:65 says: "...So she took a veil and covered herself." Rebekah, whose hair was already long, took a veil to cover herself to show respect for Isaac.

The Greek word used in verses 6 and 7 of First Corinthians, chapter eleven, for covered and cover is 'katakalupto'. Katakalupto means veiled. It had been a custom for ages for women to be veiled. Only public prostitutes in the East went without veils. But those who want all they can do to avoid covering their hair use: "But if a woman has long hair, it is a glory to her; for her hair is given to her for a covering" (verse 15). They misapply this verse to do what they want to do.

For whoever may be contentious about these things, Apostle Paul wrote: "We have no such custom, nor do the churches of God" (verse 16). Could he be saying that there is no custom of covering hair when he took many verses to persuade the women to cover their hair? I don't believe so; rather, I believe that he is talking of the custom of the contentious person saying that it makes no difference if women cover their hair {or even try to convince people that covering of hair is not for Believers (those in the church, or their church)}.

Many people do not take time to consider some things about the design of many women dresses – gowns, blouses, and skirts. Consider how the design and making of even average unbelieving men are – how they do not expose their armpits, laps, and chests. Just take time to consider the length of the sleeves of their shirts (even their short-sleeved shirts) and that of their trousers; and I know that the men also want fresh air.

Compare it with how many women move around with gowns, blouses, and skirts that show people their armpits, laps, breasts, and shapes. Can you not detect that satan and mermaid spirits are at work in the lives of many women (even Believers) whether or not they are aware of it, as far as dressing is concerned? The devil wants to corrupt men and the human race; and one great weapon he uses is women and their dressing.

Please, if you are a Believer, when you go to buy an already-made dress, check the design and method of their making before buying them. And when you meet a dress designer and maker for your dresses, tell them how they should make your dresses. No wonder the world (which is ruled by satan) has decided to call them fashion designers, because many of them design what satan and demons inspire and tell them to design!

Just take time to consider how those satan-inspired fashion designers design and make women dresses! Some of them will make a long gown, but they will make its sleeves to be so short (and even sleeveless) so that the armpits will be the point of attraction and seduction.

Some other demons-prompted designers will make the blouse that has a good length of sleeve, but they will 'cut' the back or the front in such a way as to show their back, breasts, and breast cleavages; because what satan wants to seduce men through the blouse is her breasts and exposed body.

Others will make long skirts, but they will cut and divide the skirt at the back, by the side, or at the front, because the point of seduction is their laps. Then others will design and make short skirts and gowns which when the women wearing them sit down people will see their laps and even underwears, because that is the heart and desire of the devil.

And others will not care and make mini-skirts, so that even if they are standing, people will be seeing their laps and what they call long legs. Do you know that many women (even Believers) are serving the devil, even without their knowledge? And surely, serving the devil has rewards (or do I say punishments?).

I wonder why many women spend hours in making and dressing their hair with attachments, wool, and thread! This is the love of the world and idolatry in operation. Notice that the modern frying of hair and the use of attachment were not even in existence among the unbelieving Israelites and Jews of the days of the Early Church, and also among the Gentiles of the places where Paul ministered! Therefore they had no business writing about frying of hair and the use of attachments (they did not even know the possibility or the reality of people trying such abominations).

You can use map to check the places where Apostle Paul ministered in his first, second, and third missionary journeys to see whether the inhabitants of those places (except possible immigrants) have the kind of hair which those that fry their hair and use attachments to make their hair long use nowadays.

Yes, they wrote about braiding or plaiting, and also of jewellery, which existed in their days among the unbelievers and possibly among some Believers who had carried their worldly lifestyle of hair dressing into their Christian faith. And you can see what they wrote about braiding/plaiting the hair, use of jewels, and wearing of fashions and costly clothing and apparel (and women relationship with their husbands) in First Timothy 2:9-10 and First Peter 3:1-6.

When God created everything, He saw that all the things He created were good, that the Bible says, "Then God saw everything that He had made, and indeed it was very good" (Gen. 1:31). Who are you to challenge the Handiwork of God? Bleaching your skin, painting your face, perming your hair, wearing weavons, dyeing your hair, painting your nails, etc are ways of challenging God's Creative Ability.

Someone may say, "But Jesus Christ said that it is not what enters a man that defiles the man, but what comes out of the man" (Matt. 15:11). You have to understand well what He was saying. But if what goes into a man doesn't defile a man, why did Jesus Christ rebuke the church in Thyatira for allowing Jezebel to teach His Servants to eat things sacrificed to idols? (Rev. 2:20). And when there was a debate/argument on what the Gentile Christians should keep, why did the counsel at Jerusalem tell them to abstain from things polluted by idols, from strangled meat/animals, and from blood? (Acts 15:20).

Somebody may say that Apostle Paul said that idol is nothing, but fail to see that he said that if your brother will be offended, because you ate the meat sacrificed to idol, you are to avoid it (1 Cor. 8; Rom. 14). When somebody says that Jesus Christ said that not what enters a man defiles a man, but what comes out of the man, he doesn't even know that they were discussing about washing of the hands before eating.

By the way, does vomiting defile you before God, since it came out of you? And those who want to destroy themselves have used that excuse to drink alcohol and smoke cigarettes, destroying their bodies, which is for God and should be kept holy for our God. Think of it! If the Believers were already drinking alcohol by little measure, why will Apostle Paul tell Timothy to use little wine for his stomach's sake (as a kind of soothing medicine, in that their ancient and unrefined medical practice)?

A WORD IS ENOUGH FOR THE WISE! Shall we continue to sin that grace may increase? (Rom. 6:1) Is faith without works not dead? (Jas 2:17). What will make Jesus Christ to tell those that had prophesied, cast out demons, and done mighty works in His Name, that He never knew them? (Matt. 7:21-23). Surely, they had known Christ before. I am not reducing righteousness and holiness to physical things, physical appearance, and dress code alone? Why did the Word of God put the sin of the flesh first before sin of spirit in Second Corinthians 7:1?

Some people say that we are laying unnecessary burdens on people. Which burden (if it were even to be a burden, as you think) is greater than sacrificing small things for Jesus Christ and Heaven? If you can't deny yourself of small things, because of Heaven, can you lay down your life for Jesus Christ? He who loves his life more than Christ Jesus is not worthy of Him.

By the way, have you ever seen it in the Bible that Apostle Paul gave ordinances to New Testament Believers? He wrote, saying, "Now I praise you, brethren, that you remember me in all things and keep the traditions (ordinances, the King James Version) just as I delivered them to you" (1 Cor. 11:2). Was he putting burdens on them? Certainly the Corinthian church was a 'Gentile' church.

Apostle Paul wrote: "But beware lest somehow this liberty of yours become a stumbling block to those who are weak. And because of your knowledge shall the weak brother perish, for whom Christ died? But when you thus sin against the brethren, and wound their weak conscience, you sin against Christ. Therefore, if food makes my brother stumble, I will never again eat meat, lest I make my brother stumble" (1 Cor. 8:9-13).

Writing to the Galatians, he said, "For you, brethren, have been called to liberty; only do not use liberty as an opportunity for the flesh, but through love serve one another. And those that are Christ's have crucified the flesh with its passions and desires. If we live in the Spirit, let us also walk in the Spirit" (Gal. 5:13,24,25).

Jesus Christ rebuked the scribes and the Pharisees, not because they paid tithes (because God commanded them to pay tithes), but because they neglected justice, mercy, and faith, while paying tithes (Matt. 23:23). Will you cancel tithe (for example), because they neglected justice, mercy, and faith? Certainly, no! Or you will still be disobeying God.

In other words, because somebody can dress virtuously and Godly like a Christian and still be evil, immoral, and wicked on the inside, will not cancel the fact and Truth that a Christian is to dress and appear like a Christian. By that, I mean that Christians and Believers are to dress decently, Godly, and Biblically. Inside and outside, you are to be like Christ – Christian.

As a woman, it is either you decide to worship and serve God in Spirit and Truth, or you join the rest of the women and ladies who follow their minds instead of the Mind of God. Writing to the Corinthians, Apostle Paul said, "But I fear, lest somehow, as the serpent deceived Eve by his craftiness, so your minds may be corrupted..." (2 Cor. 11:3).

The devil deceived Eve at the Garden of Eden by craftiness, just as he has been deceiving many women and ladies today, especially in the areas of indecent dressing and worldliness. When God told Adam and Eve to avoid the fruit of the tree of knowledge of good and bad, telling them that they will die any day they eat from the fruit, satan came afterwards to tell Eve: "You will not surely die..." (Gen. 3:4).

But what happened when they ate the fruit? They died spiritually, being separated from the Life of God. Apart from the spiritual death, God had intended that they live forever; however, when they disobeyed God, they could now die physically after some years. Though you may not see the punishment for your disobedience now, if you don't repent and change, know that you can't enter into the Kingdom of Heaven. Do you want to end in Hell after speaking in tongues and carrying Bible?

The Bible says, "For you were bought at a price; therefore glorify God in your body and in your spirit, which are God's (1 Cor. 6:20). But if you are led by the Spirit, you are not under the Law (Gal. 5:18). Both your body and your spirit are God's – belong to God – and you have to glorify God in both of them.

Furthermore, it is those who are led by the Spirit of God who are not under the Law. The essence of God making us to not be under the Law is because He expects us to be led by His Spirit. But if your flesh and desires still lead you, then you are not led by the Holy Spirit; and there is danger.

The Book of Romans says that those who are led by the Spirit of God are those who are the sons of God. You wash both the outside and the inside of your plates. Why do you think of the opposite concerning God and His people? Certainly, God wants both the inside and the outside of His people to be clean, purified, and holy.

Many people talk against many things in the name of Old Testament; but they will readily teach about blessings from the twenty-eighth chapter of the Book of Deuteronomy, and expound tithes and offerings from the third chapter of the Book of Malachi – both in the New Testament.

Let us know that we have not arrived in Heaven yet; therefore, we are to be careful of how we live our lives and of the utterances we make, including how we think and reason. Let us always be open to the Holy Spirit to direct and lead us all the days of our lives till we see the Face of Jesus Christ in Heaven.

(For an in-depth Scriptural study on this subject, refer to the book: *Indecent Dressing and Outward Appearance* by *GODSWORD GODSWILL ONU*)

ABOUT THE BOOK

The ministers and church-workers should be trained well so that they can perform well, and do God's Assignments for them faithfully and satisfactorily. Many are in the ministry today without adequate training, and they have either messed things up or performed, by far, below God's Expectation from them. A minister is not supposed to be a novice, and he is to hold the mystery of the faith with a pure conscience. The Word says, "If you instruct the brethren in these things, you will be a good minister of Jesus Christ, nourished in the Words of Faith and of the Good Doctrine which you have carefully followed" (1 Tim. 4:6).

ABOUT THE AUTHOR

Apostle Godsword is the *President and Overseer* of WHOLE LIFE SPIRIT-WORD MINISTRIES (a.k.a. HOLY GHOST AND GODSWORD CHRISTIAN NETWORK). Godsword, *a Teaching Prophet* and *Evangelist,* is a *Minister* of the Lord Jesus Christ who *believes* in the *Demonstration* of the Spirit and Power and *takes delight* in the *Declaration* and *Teaching* of the Word and Will of God.

Godsword Godswill Onu studied Building Construction in his First Degree, and later had Master of Urban and Regional Planning (MURP) from Abia State University, Uturu.

BOOKS BY APOSTLE GODSWORD

1. *75 Great Biblical and Spiritual Truths (As Inspired by the Holy Ghost)*
2. *Preparing for Our Maker (The Cry of the Spirit and the Lord's Witness)*
3. *Lessons from the Seven Churches*
4. *Vessels and Instruments of Honour and Dishonour*
5. *Divine Protection*
6. *The Power-filled Life*
7. *From Glory to Glory*
8. *Always and Without Ceasing*
9. *The Whole Life from God to Men*
10. *Right and Wrong Thinking, Belief, and Confession*
11. *He Came to Set You Free*
12. *A Better Covenant Based on Better Promises*
13. *Apostles, Prophets, Evangelists, Pastors, and Teachers*
14. *Being Strong in the Lord*
15. *Real Freedom and Gain*
16. *Faithfulness and Diligence in Stewardship*
17. *Heirs of God and Joint-heirs with Christ*
18. *Open and Closed Heavens and Doors*
19. *A Heaven to Gain, and a Hell to Avoid*
20. *The Anointing and Power of the Holy Spirit*
21. *The Glory, Presence, and Power of God*
22. *The Fulness of the Blessing of the Gospel*
23. *Prosperity and Success*
24. *Seducing Spirits and Doctrines of Demons*
25. *My God and Father*
26. *The Works of the Flesh and Youthful Lusts*
27. *The Spiritual Christian*
28. *The Commandments of the Lord and Master*
29. *The Total Man*
30. *The Virtuous Woman*
31. *Contending with the Forces of Darkness*
32. *Developing a Strong Relationship with God*
33. *Secrets to God's Miracle-working Power*
34. *Concerning the Roman Catholics*
35. *Ministers-Workers Training Manual*
36. *The Christian Virtues*
37. *The God-approved Minister*
38. *Taking It by Force*
39. *God's Generals*
40. *Blessings, Curses, and Spiritual Attacks*
41. *Pressing Towards the Mark*
42. *My Father's Business*
43. *Walking in the Anointing*
44. *The Weapons and Armour of Our Warfare*
45. *Tithes and Offerings*
46. *Greater Levels and Glory (An Annual Reading)*
47. *God is Not from Any Nation*
48. *The Power and Authority of the Believer*
49. *Sin, Disobedience, and Rebellion*
50. *Wisdom, Knowledge, and Understanding*
51. *The Christian Marriage and Home*
52. *Patience, Endurance, and Longsuffering*
53. *Indecent Dressing and Outward Appearance*

Any of the titles (ebooks) can be bought/downloaded immediately from Lulu Publishers, Amazon Inc., the Apple Ibookstore, Barnes & Noble Nook, Sony, Smashwords, and others. And the printed books, if it is not available at your local bookstore, can be ordered from Lulu, Amazon, and others.

NEVER PIRATE ANY OF THE EBOOKS/BOOKS!

For enquiry, you may contact Apostle Godsword Godswill Onu, by calling or texting him on +2348030917546.

Made in the USA
Columbia, SC
25 July 2024

39358353R00187